Turkish Islam and Europe
Türkischer Islam und Europa

Europe and Christianity as reflected in
Turkish Muslim discourse
&
Turkish Muslim life in the diaspora

BEIRUTER TEXTE UND STUDIEN

HERAUSGEGEBEN VOM
ORIENT-INSTITUT
DER DEUTSCHEN MORGENLÄNDISCHEN GESELLSCHAFT

BAND 82

TÜRKISCHE WELTEN

BAND 6

Turkish Islam and Europe
Türkischer Islam und Europa

Europe and Christianity as reflected in
Turkish Muslim discourse
&
Turkish Muslim life in the diaspora

Papers of the Istanbul Workshop
October 1996

edited by
Günter Seufert
and
Jacques Waardenburg

ISTANBUL 1999
IN KOMMISSION BEI FRANZ-STEINER-VERLAG STUTTGART

Umschlaggestaltung: Wolf-Dieter Lemke
unter Verwendung von Pressephotos

Die Deutsche Bibliothek —CIP-Einheitsaufnahme

Turkish Islam and Europe : Europe and Christianity as reflected in Turkish Muslim discourse & Turkish Muslim life in the diaspora ; papers of the Istanbul Workshop October 1996 = Türkischer Islam und Europa / ed. by Günter Seufert and Jacques Waardenburg. - Stuttgart : Steiner, 1999

(Türkische Welten ; Bd. 6) (Beiruter Texte und Studien ; Bd. 82)

Beitr. teilw. dt., teilw. engl., teilw. franz.

ISBN 3-515-07645-X

Gedruckt mit Unterstützung des Schweizerischen Nationalfonds zur Förderung der wissenschaftlichen Forschung.

Gedruckt auf alterungsbeständigem Papier.
Druck: Kıyı Yayınları - FastPrınt
Printed in Turkey

Contents

Preface

This book is the fruit of a workshop which we organized in Istanbul in October 1996. We wished to examine Turkish Muslim views of Europe since 1980 and the situation of Turkish Muslim migrants in Germany. So we decided to invite some Turkish researchers and scholars on a private basis and ask them to present their work and experience as far as it touched on the subject and to engage in discussion on their papers. Fundamentally, it should be and was a Turkish meeting, attended by only three non-Turks, two of whom were able to follow the discussions held in Turkish.

The idea found a warm welcome. Some papers treated theological, others historical subjects. Participants who had spent some time in Western Europe for study or research reported on their experiences, which had not always been pleasant. Two Europeans also presented papers in Turkish. All of this led to animated questions, observations, discussions and also debates during both the working sessions and the breaks and meals following them. After the official part the ice was broken and Turkish, German, French and Dutch jokes were exchanged. It is safe to say that the workshop left all the participants with excellent memories.

It seemed to us that the results of this workshop were important enough to be published. So we made a selection from the papers that had been presented and we asked their authors to prepare them for publication. Moreover, in order to round the book off we added four papers -- three by Turkish authors: one from Turkey, one from Germany and one from Holland, and one paper by a German author -- who all not been present at the workshop but who have innovating ideas on Turkish-European and Christian-Muslim relations. All had practical experience with the Turkish diaspora in Europe. It took some time before the final texts went to the printer, but the reader now has the result in his or her hands.

The book has three prominent themes. The first is the emergence of new orientations on all sides towards Muslims and Europeans living together at the present time, and possibly coming to practical cooperation and dialogue. The second is Turkish Muslim self-understanding and views of Europe, as far as they are expressed in intellectual terms. The third is the ways in which Turkish Muslim life in the European diaspora is organized. It will be clear that these three themes are interrelated and consequently the three parts of the book are not independent of each other. The papers are in the three current European languages and although we could not publish papers in Turkish, we are confident that Turkish readers will find their way in the book in its present form. The introduction contains extended summaries of the contributions in German and French.

It is our hope that this book is a step towards intellectual cooperation. May it enhance further Turkish-European dialogue on a scholarly basis, in the framework of increasing Euro-Turkish relations in the cultural and other fields.

In conclusion, our thanks go first to the authors who took much trouble in preparing their papers. We are grateful to the Swiss National Foundation for Scholarly Research whose subsidy made the workshop and this publication possible. Nothing would have been realized, however, without the positive interest of Professor Angelika Neuwirth. As the director of the Orient-Institut der Deutschen Morgenländischen Gesellschaft she made it possible to organize our workshop in the Istanbul Branch of this scholarly body. And she was willing to consider publication of these papers as a volume in the reputed series Beiruter Texte und Studien. For her continuing encouragement we owe her great thanks.

Istanbul, November 1999

Jacques Waardenburg
Günter Seufert

Introduction

Historical relations

The history of European-Turkish relations has never been simple. And if we also take into account the relations of Mongol and Turkic rulers with Eastern Europe, and of the Czars with Transcaucasia and Central Asia, we can safely speak of "great" history, at least as far as Europe is concerned. Indeed, had it not been for oil, Euro-Arab relations would only have been a shadow of Euro-Turkic relations.

Even the history of Ottoman-European relations has been tremendously important for both parties. Three centuries of Ottoman wars of conquest were followed by two centuries of wars of reconquest from the European side. It was not only a matter of political relations and wars between the Ottoman Empire and Austria and Russia. There was also the complication of the rise of first local and then national independence movements throughout the Balkans. And just as the demise of the Ottoman Empire in World War I had very serious consequences for the Near East because it created a power vacuum provisionally filled by Britain and France, the Ottoman defeats after the Greek war of independence left the Balkans a prey to their own divisive tendencies, with tensions and conflicts which have arisen again during the last decade.

After World War I, however, the Turkish Republic followed its own course. Turkish-European relations changed during World War II and took a new form during the Cold War. Turkey has maintained a certain stability in its relations with Western Europe through its participation in NATO, the Council of Europe and the OECD. Trade relations have increased and Turkey has taken Europe as a model in its modernization process, although since World War II it has also looked to the USA as an example. European scholars study the past and present of Turkey and Turkish students, researchers and scholars study and work at European universities.

Besides this external history, however, the Empire and later the Republic had their internal history with its own complexities. Secularism started in the 19th century if not earlier and became the official doctrine under Atatürk. Modernization jumped ahead between the two World Wars. The State was defined, organized and sometimes reorganized in unforeseeable ways. The country lost most of its Christian inhabitants and projected itself towards its minorities as a homogeneous Turkish Sunni Muslim state. The Westernized elite cherished high hopes of developing ever closer links with Europe. At the same time European economic interests in Turkey increased.

A new element in Euro-Turkish relations arose in the early 1960s when large numbers of Turkish workers were engaged for work in Germany and other European countries. They gradually obtained an immigrant status when their families followed them. Another new element has been the revitalization of Islam since the 1970s, causing Europeans to wonder which long term course Turkey will choose to take.

All of this makes good information about Turkey and Turkish views of Europe increasingly necessary. Likewise, good information is needed in Turkey about Europe and what Europeans think of the Turkish political structure and internal and foreign policies, and of the treatment of Kurds, Alevis, and other minorities in the country and its human rights record. It may be a long way to Europe but there are positive signs. Intellectuals at least, used to confront problems, have less difficulty in understanding each other than the guardians of power, tradition or other 'vested interests'.

Such facts constitute the context of this book. Present-day relations between Turkey and Europe have a historical dimension which I wanted to mention here, since the papers hardly deal with the past. The weight of history, however, is palpable in so many meetings between Turks and other Europeans. One day this common history should be written by Turkish and non-Turkish historians together. It has provided common memories and affinities but it has also inflicted wounds and emotional hang-ups -- rightly or wrongly connected with Islam and Christendom - which present an intellectual challenge in the first place.

I shall now give a brief survey of the contributions to the three

Parts of this book, paying special attention to the texts in French and German which will be summarized here.

Part One: New Muslim and Christian orientations towards Living Together and Dialogue

Our first speaker in the workshop, Professor *Hayreddin Karaman*, summarizes the legal perspective on relations between Muslims and non-Muslims as it was elaborated in classical Islamic *fiqh (fıkıh)*, Islamic legal thought, based on Qur'an, Sunna and subsidiary sources. These rules were developed during the first centuries of Islam when great numbers of non-Muslims lived under Muslim political authority. Christians and Jews -- and also Zoroastrians -- whose religions possess a Scripture and are considered to be of "heavenly" origin, obtained the status of *dhimmi-s (zimmî)*. This was a lower social status than the Muslims had and it meant for instance that they had to pay the *jizya (ciziye),* the poll-tax. They were allowed, however, to organize their own religious community life. This old distinction between Muslims and non-Muslims with recognized religions who lived in Muslim territory developed in the Ottoman Empire into the well-known *millet*-system. Though formally abolished in the mid-19th century, it came to a definite end only with the establishment of the Republic in 1923.

The rules of the *fiqh* pertaining to Muslim minorities living outside Muslim territory and subjected to non-Muslim political authority differed slightly according to the different *madhhab*-s (mezheb), the Muslim schools of law. All schools of *fiqh* agreed, however, that this situation should be avoided if possible. The Hanafi *madhhab* which was the official one in the Ottoman Empire, was lenient in stating that, if the case presented itself, the Muslims concerned had to recognize the authority of the non-Muslim ruler for the sake of peace and order, on condition that the ruler allowed them to practice the religious precepts of Islam. "Dialogue" in terms of *fiqh* implies the correct relationships between members of different religions, both as individuals and as communities. In terms of *kalâm (kelâm),* Islamic theological thought, "dialogue" implies the correct evaluation of other religions from an Islamic point of view. Jews and Christians -- also Zoroastrians -- as "People of Scripture" are considered to have real or true i.e. *haqq (hakk)* religions; other religious communities are held to have false i.e. *bâtil (batıl)* religions. Once Islam has been preached, those who refuse to recognize Muhammad's prophethood are to be considered as unbelievers according to current Islamic doctrine.

The second paper, by *Kadir Canatan*, presents what may be called a new Muslim view on multi-cultural societies in which Muslims participate. Looking at the Turkish Republic he is satisfied neither with the secular modernization project which has led to the struggle between "Islamists" and adapts of secularism, nor with the project of one homogeneous Turkish nation which has not provided for the case of a clash between the Turkish state and Kurdish activists. Realistically speaking, the present-day Republic is neither a modern secular society nor a homogeneous nation, whatever the norms that have been imposed. He adds that the Turkish case is but one illustration of the broader rule that in a globalizing world all differences between varieties of cultural life and between identities tend to be suppressed.

This leads him to present an alternative Islamic project of pluralistic society, drawing on Muhammad's "Covenant of Medina" (*Medine Vesikası*) and the later Ottoman *millet*-system. Quoting the contemporary Turkish thinker Ali Bulaç, Kadir Canatan criticizes the very concept of a nation state, including that of an Islamic state. He contends that instead of the principle of domination which is proper to the state, that of participation should be adopted as the only way in which group relations can be articulated satisfactorily. In the present-day world, unlike the medieval one, Muslims can no longer see themselves as those who should dominate the others; they are just one of a number of existing social groups or political blocs. The principle of inequality between communities which characterized the *millet*-system should be replaced bythat of equality, leading to participation instead of domination. Canatan argues that such a view is based on the Qur'an, which recognizes the diversity of peoples and man's own reponsibility for the religion or way of life which he chooses to follow. Besides the Qur'an, Sufism with its formulas of "unity in diversity" and "diversity in unity" is another source from which solutions for the problem of how to live together can be derived.

The author contends that the concept of multi-culturalism does not describe a situation that exists at present. In Europe the concept serves largely to conceal much factual discrimination of the Muslim diaspora and as a means for Europeans to create a positive image of themselves. A multicultural society, however, with equal rights and mutual acceptance of the groups that compose it is not yet a fact but a norm to be striven for and realized. As a norm it implies that the various participating groups, besides their own specific group identities, accept one common broader "societal" identity. This identity, however, should not be imposed by the receiving society - be it by its "pluralists" or its "universalists" - but it should be constructed, defined and realized by the local population and the immigrants together. Constructing this common identity of the groups composing the society will be crucial if one wants to avoid a war of cultures in Europe, Turkey or elsewhere.

Georg Stoll's contribution presupposes a certain familiarity among the readers with European philosophy and Roman Catholic theological thought. It presents what may be called a new kind of Christian, and specifically Catholic, reflection on the three categories of the "foreign", the "secular" and the "universal". It exemplifies advanced Christian thinking on the problem of dialogue, philosophical erudition and refers to statements made at the Second Vatican Council (1962-65).

The author first compares two official German Catholic Church publications about the presence of Muslims and Islam in Germany. They date from 1982 and 1993 and reflect different approaches. The first concentrates on Muslims as foreign guest workers (*Gastarbeiter*) in Germany whereas the second focuses on the question how Christians and Muslims should live together in Germany. The latter admonishes Christians to adhere to Christian principles as formulated by the Catholic Church and to respond to what is called the challenge of the Muslim presence in Germany. It expects the Muslims to take a serious approach to German society and it stresses the need for mutual understanding of Muslims and Christians and respect in living together. In the present situation it invites Muslims and Christians to a continuing discussion about secular society; the two groups by and large take different positions on this issue. It recognizes that Muslims in Europe face Christianity as well as secular society.

In the next part the author moves toward a more theological perspective. He discusses what is understood by "foreigners" in contemporary European philosophy and he analyzes carefully what is said -- in a mostly positive sense -- about "foreigners" in the Bible, both the Old and the New Testament. He then examines church history, observing that in the course of time the attitude towards foreigners changed. At the time when the Catholic Church, for instance, elaborated strategies of expansion, all non-Catholics were seen as "foreigners". They were doomed in the hereafter but could be saved through intense missionary work. The author characterizes Catholic church history from the end of the 15th until the mid-20th century as the history of a "colonial Christianity".

In the third part the author signals the new turn taken at the Second Vatican Council. When it recognizes secular society as it exists and when it takes pluralism seriously, the Church opens up to dialogue. Stoll discusses at length the nature of this dialogue engaged in by the Church. He discerns a new approach in Catholic philosophical and theological thought, treating subjects like dialogue, secularity, spiritual experience and also the claims to truth of the Roman Catholic Church. He presents new views concerning reconciliation and healing, which the Church has the task of bringing about. Finally he suggests that the art of "telling one's life story" can have an important place in what is called the "dialogue of life".

This paper, especially from the second part on, presents a theological discourse which addresses a Christian, and specifically Catholic, readership. Along the lines of German fundamental thinking it represents a search for openness and dialogue quite distinct from Catholic thought in former times.

The last paper in Part One, "Europe and its Muslim neighbors. Some recent meetings of intercultural dialogue" by *Jacques Waardenburg*, starts from the fact that Europe, a peninsula of Asia, is surrounded by Muslim countries and now also includes its own Muslim societies and groups. The magic formula according to which the present-day political and cultural leadership in Europe views these countries and societies, is that of "dialogue". What does this in fact mean and imply?

The author discusses four conferences of Euro-Arab and Euro-Turkish dialogue which took place between 1991 and 1998 and which he had the privilege to attend. All four of them aimed to further intercultural cooperation and dialogue. Two of them, held in Europe, were organized by international organizations, the Council of Europe and the European Union. The other two were organized by the Municipality of Istanbul (March 1998) and the University of Jordan (April 1998) respectively. The paper presents the historical context, the organization, the official discourses and some particular features of these four meetings. At the end the author compares and offers a first evaluation of them.

He concludes that there is an urgent need for meetings of this kind on different levels, in different places and with different kinds of speakers and participants. Most people of a younger generation, from both sides of the Mediterranean, would like to meet, get to know and discuss with people from the other side. And the media should bring the subjects discussed at these intercultural meetings to the attention of a much wider public, which needs to be informed about them.

Part Two: Political and cultural influences upon Turkish Muslim self-understanding

The first author in Part Two, *Deniz Vardar*, treats the orientation of the Refah Partisi (Welfare-Party) which came to power after the general elections of December 24th 1995. Its leader Necmettin Erbakan was Turkish Prime Minister from June 1996 until June 1997. The party was then forbidden because of its "anti-secularist" activity. Since the 1960s, when it existed under another name, this party has moved to a less radical rightist postion and enjoyed broadening popular support.

In 1998 it was succeeded by a similar party with the name of Fazilet Partisi (Virture Party). Over against the state's secular orientation the Refah Party advocated that Turkey should be purified by returning to its Islamic sources. Foreign elements should be eliminated and a new "war of independence" should be fought against the West.

The political program of the Refah Party was the opposite of the politics of the Republic. Instead of secularism Islam should be the basis of the state, rather than integrating itself in Europe Turkey should distance itself from it, not universal values but the unique charakter of Turkey should be stressed, and instead of allying itself with the West

Turkey should align itself with the Muslim world and promote its unity.

The author analyzes the Refah Party's political discourse about Europe on the basis of its journal *Yörünge* (the Orbit) from June 1995 until September 1996. She concentrates on its coverage of the Customs Union of 1996 and Turkey's application for membership of the European Union. She follows up its emphasis on Turkeye's national sovereignity, its rejection of what is called signs of "westernization", including Turkey's recognition of the autonomy of the Oecumenical Patriarchate in Istanbul, and its insistance that the Aya Sophia should be reconverted from a museum into a mosque. The party and its journal have a radically anti-Western stance, "the West" -- presented as an enemy -- comprising here Europe, the USA and Israel. It strongly rejects the Turkish-Israeli treaties.

In her contribution *Deniz Vardar* reveals what she calls the party's "neo-racism" with anti-Zionist propaganda. The author elaborates on the party's radical rightist position clad in a populist vocabulary which does not, however, recognize the equality of all citizens The constant anti-European mobilization is carried out with reference to Islam, that is to say by presenting Islam with a view to the party's strategies to win votes from the people, its final aim simply being to obtain power. By reversing 180 degrees the values defended by the current political system and continuosly pointing to its negative sides, the Refah Party takes the sysem as a reference and in a way accepts and legitimizes its politcal game. This subversion of the system together with its Euroscepticism serves to strengthen the party's own exclusivist political project. It uses the formulas of human rights and democracy to promote its own search for power. In a country where the distance between the rich and poor is constantly widening, where fundamental decisions are taken beyond the reach of parliament, and where many young people are longing for a "Muslim democracy" the Refah Party enjoyed broad popularity until it was forbidden.

The Turkish debate about Europe has a long history but came to a climax in the 1980s when Turkey asked to be admitted to the European Economic Community at the time. This debate has not only been politically relevant for the decision on priorities in foreign policy. It is also revealing for the ways in which Europe has a symbolic value with regard to how the different political, social and religious orientations in present-day Turkey articulate themselves.

The second author in this Part is *Etienne Copeaux* who treats what he calls the blurred image of Christianity which prevails in present-day Turkey. After World War I Turkish identity was presented as a Muslim identity. The annihilation of the Armenians in 1915 and the departure of the Greeks from Anatolia in exchange for Turks from Greece in 1922 strengthened this identification. The Christian "otherness" was perceived in terms of confrontation and as a source of conflict which should be removed. This tendency has become stronger as Islam has occupied an increasing place in public life since the 1950s -- and especially since 1980. Events such as the Turkish invasion of Cyprus in 1974, and the rule of the Refah Party from June 1996 until June 1997 have reinforced it. A considerable number of Turks still sees Christianity as a dangerous alien presence.

Copeaux then discusses what ordinary people in Turkey know of Christianity. He distinguishes two types of knowledge which go back to two different sources. On the one hand Turkish Muslims draw on the information about Jesus contained in the Qur'anic texts mentioning 'Isâ (İsa). On the other hand they refer to critical Western scholarship on the Bible, in particular the Gospels, and to present-day critical voices in the West on the subject of Christianity. Neither of these are the Christianity of present-day Christians or of the churches.

The author has made a study of the ways in which Christianity is described in Turkish schoolbooks. Secondary school books on religion praise Christian moral values as of universal importance but they practically leave out the story of Jesus' passion and do not mention belief in his resurrection. The message of the Gospels and their character of truth is scarcely taken into consideration. Secondary schoolbooks on history give little positive information about the birth of Christianity and its expansion in the Mediterranean world; the Roman and Byzantine empires are hardly treated. The history of Christianity in Anatolia -- now Turkey -- with its more than thousand years of Byzantine and Armenian culture is hardly referred to. The Crusades obviously are depicted largely in black-and-white terms and later military European ventures against the Ottoman Empire are mostly stamped as ever repeated Christian Crusade efforts. From these history schoolbooks children must conclude that Christians have been enemies either from outside, such as the Crusaders and Europe or the West in general, or from inside, such as the Greeks and the Armenians in the Ottoman Empire. The sole exception in this sombre picture of Christianity is the Reformation, which is treated and praised as an important event in the history of Europe, over the obscurantism and tradition-based authoritarianism of the Roman Catholic Church. So much for the schoolbooks.

The author also looks at the role Christianity plays in the present-day national-religious discourse. This role is not negligeable. The theme of the Crusades is recurrent and the Turkish-Greek dispute is depicted as an equally religious confrontation. Some journalists "unmask" orientalists, teachers and people affiliated to Western institutions in Turkey as covert missionaries. Some authors see forms of Christian propaganda to undermine Islam behind Western social and cultural features that have entered Turkey in the course of time. They also express criticism of the way in which Christians celebrate Christmas, not only as a purely religious matter but also because of the cultural and social influence which these celebrations have on fashions, sales and business at large in Istanbul which is now a world city.

Whereas Christianity is labelled as fundamentally intolerant, Islam - and specifically Turkish Islam - is depicted as having been and being the religion of true tolerance. Turks tend to perceive Christianity as the antagonist of Islam, as a fundamental alien being or "otherness". Copeaux distinguishes two aspects of this. What he calls the Turkish Muslim view of the "minor otherness" of Christianity has its source in the Qur'an; here discussion and tolerance are admitted. The Turkish Muslim view of the "major otherness" of Christianity, on the other hand, has very different sources. It goes back to certain historical events which had a traumatic impact such as the rebellions against the Ottoman empire, humiliations by the European powers or acts of violence that directed at what was sacred for Muslim Turks. This "major" religious otherness often then stands as a symbol for the national otherness of European nations confronting the Ottoman empire or the Turkish state. When nation and religion become mixed, nationhood tends to become sacralized, and religious and national sensitivities then reinforce each other.

In conclusion, the Turkish vision of Christianity seems to be distorted less by ignorance than by painful memories from history: the Ottoman-Balkan (including Austrian and Russian) wars, the Turkish-Greek national confrontation (strengthened through the Cyprus conflict), and the fact that Turkey has not been admitted to the European Union (something for which many Turks give a religious explanation: there being no place for Muslims in Europe). What in scholarly analysis appear as human reasons is explained in many Turkish perceptions in terms of an eternal antagonism between Islam and Chritianity.

The next two contributions are in English, so they will be presented more briefly here.

Ali Köse, in his "East is East and West is West. Remarks on Muslim perspectives on Europe and Christianity", draws attention to the other, moral side of the medal. If there is a need for dialogue, both sides have to search for their deeper motivations in order to be honest to each other and themselves. Four areas in particular are relevant.

First, the history of the relations between the Western and the Islamic worlds needs to be studied. This includes the study of views held in the West about Islam and of events that are at the root of current tensions, such as the Crusades and the period of European imperialism. The author observes that the Turks as well as other Muslims today view the West more positively than the Western world views them. One hang-up of the colonial era is a kind of Western superiority complex due to what Erich Fromm has called "national or racial narcissism" which needs to be overcome in order for relations to be normalized.

A second area of attention is the portrayal of the Islamic world and of Muslims in the West and in particular in the Western media. Current presentations lead to Muslims being viewed with suspicion and Islam being seen as a threat. Muslims consider the Western media's portrayal of them as deeply insulting.

The third area where dialogue is needed is that of the double standard or discourse which the West applies to itself and to Muslims, and of the way it treats Muslims notwithstanding the elevated principles it proclaims.

The fourth, and perhaps most important subject of further and deeper dialogue is the present marginalization of religion in the West and the consequences which this has for Muslims primarily in the West but also in the Muslim world. The phenomenon of secularization in the West, in particular in Europe, causes anxiety in the East. Muslims who do not want their religion to be eroded by secularism tend to blame the West and Christianity for the weakening of religious observance among younger generations of Muslims. Muslim immigrants living in the West who cannot distinguish between Christianity and secularism, tend to blame Christianity for the secularization of the West and for the present situation of Muslims both in the West and in the Muslim world. Köse also draws attention to Muslim suspicions about the real intentions of Christians who seek dialogue with Muslims. The Muslim concern is not so much that these people are Christians but that they are Westerners with potential imperialistic tendencies. A Muslim-Christian dialogue should be carried out by people of the same country or region. Muslims are also suspicious of that Westerners who themselves have lost their faith tend to hope that the same will happen to Muslims and they may work for it.

In these four major areas there needs to be intense dialogue between the Western and the Islamic worlds.

In his paper "Conflictual Images of Turkey and Europe" *Ali Murat Yel* delves into the mass of wrong perceptions and judgments which have been and are still current in Europe and Turkey about the other's - and also one's own - culture. This situation should not lead to defeatism but to a committed dialogue. As an anthropologist Yel is more aware than others of the hidden loopholes that present themselves suddenly and painfully when people from cultures that have been at war ideologically or really have to live together.

Yel's reporting of his own experiences as a student and researcher in England and Portugal gives a particular liveliness to his paper. Having been educated at a Turkish school in the belief that Turkey is part of Europe, his discovery that Europeans did not consider him a European at all was disconcerting, to say the least. This discovery became the starting-point of his further questioning exactly why Islam, and the Turks in particular, are represented in the West as being so bad. While looking for answers he not only discusses the universal claims of Western liberal thought and the schemes by which the West categorizes the rest of the world with the desire to dominate it, or the West's double standard especially in political matters. He also has an awareness and feeling for the socio-psychological "underground" sources of, for instance, the West's fears of Islam, the West's united front against Islam, and the European states' unanimous non-admittance of the Turks to the Union. And yet, as Hichem Djaït has put it, it is easy to see that more than ever before, "the West" is a heterogeneous composite and a unified power called "Islam" has ceased to exist. Prevailing images are blinding us to obvious realities, and it is these realities that we should face.

Speaking about the Turkish immigrants, Yel contrasts the sad treatment which they undergo in Europe and specifically in Germany with the open reception which European tourists enjoy in Turkey. This treatment is logically conducive to increasing Turkish ethnic solidarity. It crystallizes around religious communities which maintain Turkish common values and uphold human dignity, where one feels respected and not discriminated against, as in the foreign society.

The author puts his finger on the deeper dimension of domination, fear and illusion that play a role in European-Turkish relations, a dimension which most social scientific studies hardly mention. Yel's recommendations for a viable future deserve to be summarized: (1) to stop creating each other as the "other" (but rather accept others as human beings with different cultures, religions and worldviews); (2) to stop treating Islam as if it were trying to sweep Christianity away (at least in Europe there is no chance of that); (3) to stop creating false images of "the others" (but instead to engage in dialogue with them in order to discuss realities). Intellectuals on both sides should do their utmost "...to improve their relationships with each other through organizing formal dialogues like symposia, panels, discussion groups, or teaching other religions in their respective schools".

In his essay "A government agency between religion and state" *İsmail Kara* discusses the history and status of the Diyanet İşleri Başkanlığı (in short: Diyanet). The author contends that the radical measures taken with regard to religion by the Republic in the fifteen years since 1923 go back to the westernization policies of the Ottoman Empire since the late 19th century. However, whereas in Ottoman times a modern reinterpretation of Islam was still considered to be a necessary condition to arrive at the modernization of society, the policy regarding religion in the Republic went much further. Here religion was used to legitimate the political aims of the state and served as a means to influence the people in this sense.

To explain the rise of this new policy around 1923 the author hints at the probability that it originated during the negotiations for the Treaty of Lausanne and that it was meant primarily to strengthen the position of Turkey in its relations with the European powers at the time. The very idea, as launched in 1923, that Islam could be an obstacle to progress was relatively new in Turkey. In order to marginalise this "reactionary" Islam, the goverment policy was to rob the religious leaders (ulama and dervish sheikhs) of both their power and authority.

To this end three decisive laws were enacted by the National Assembly on 3 March 1924. The first abolished the Caliphate. The second unified all educational institutions under the Ministry of Education. Consequently the medreses, the Imam Hatip schools (until 1930) and the Faculty of Theology at the Darulfünun in Istanbul (until 1933) came under the National Ministry of Education (Millî Eğitim Bakanlığı) as well as later the Faculty of Theology in Ankara (1949), the reopened Imam Hatip schools and the Higher Islam Institutes (Yüksek İslâm Enstitüleri).

The third law established the Diyanet İşleri Başkanlığı in Ankara as a government agency subordinated to the Prime Minister. It replaced the Ministry of Religious Law and Pious Foundations (Şeriye ve Evkaf Vekaleti) which had existed in Ankara from 1920 until 1924. It did not inherit its competences, however. The administration of the prescriptions of religion (din) for daily life (muamelât) which once fell to the kadis of the Sharia Courts subordinated now to the National Assembly which enacted laws in this field. And the administration of the Pious Foundations (evkaf) now came under a Directorate also subordinated to the Prime Minister.

The author shows that the new Diyanet is only competent in matters which did not fall under the old Sharia Courts: worship, religious truth and religious rules settled by fetwas. It is a government agency in a secular state and its officials are civil servants. As a consequence, the Diyanet is fundamentally different from the office of the Şeyh ul-

İslâm in the Ottoman Empire which was a state that was legitimated by religion. Its titular Sultan Caliph was represented by the Grand Vezir in all political matters and by the Şeyh ul-İslâm in religious and in some other matters like the administration of justice and education.

According to Law Nr. 633 of 1965 (Art. 1), the Diyanet has the following three tasks:

1) to deal with questions of faith, cult and morality (ahlâk) in Islam;

2) to enlighten society in matters of religion;

3) to administer mosques.

Ad 1) There is reason to assume that the political center of the Republic did not want faith, worship and morality follow their own development, be it on the level of convictions, be it on the level of social behaviour. The task of upholding morality was already discussed in 1947 and was assigned by law to the Diyanet in 1965. Through its directives for readings and sermons in the mosque and through its many publicaitions the Diyanet has an indirect influence on the formulation of the truth of Faith and of the rules of worship.

Ad 2) The task of enlightening society in matters of religion limits itself in practice to giving directives for readings and sermons in the mosque, providing fetwas concerning questions connected with religion, and publishing religious books, journals, calendars and cassettes. Such publications are meant to purify religion from superstitious beliefs and practices and reconcile it with the revolutions and ideology of the Republic.

Ad 3) According to the law of 1924 which established the Diyanet, its main task was that of administering the mosques. The law of 1965 extended this task considerably. In 1998 the Diyanet was declared responsible for establishing and administering the mosques in Turkey; all mosques were now considered to be public property under the Diyanets authority.

The Diyanet is financially dependent on the state, its budget is part of the state budget.

The author's conclusions on the place and role of the Diyanet in the relations between state and religion in Turkey are worth mentioning. The Republic did not envisage a separation of religion and politics (state) according to the Western model. It could even see the

Western kind of separation as dangerous in the Turkish context. As a consequence, the policy makers decided that the competences of the Diyanet should be kept modest, that they would narrow down the field of religion and that they should also control ordinary religious life. As a consequence, the relation between state and religion in Turkey is to be understood as a subjection of religion to the state and a narrow definition of the field of religion. Religion thus becomes an object of politics and it is either seen as a threat to the peace in society or as a means of political legitimation.

The Constitutional Court formulated this clearly in 1970. The Diyanet is not a religious organization but an agency of the state administration; its officials are civil servants. This is the result of historical constellations, specific conditions of the religion and specific needs of the country. The aim of this state control is "to prevent religious fanaticism, to keep religion as a means of upholding morality in society and in this way to ennoble the Turkish nation and bring it to modern civilization" (1970). And "...given the conditions of Turkey, secularism cannot be understood here in the same way as in a Western country, even if this country has a fundamentally open attitude toward Western civilization" (1983). These measures of the state, therefore, cannot be understood as a way of furthering religion, but only as a political response to specific conditions and needs.

Throughout its history the Diyanet has indeed moved within the limits indicated above. It has served the religion of the state rather than the religion of the Muslims. It has adapted its interpretations of religion to state polities. It seeks to change the way in which people are accustomed to understand religion. During its first decades the Diyanet was clearly meant to fight the tendency of religion to fall into the hands of a special class, and then, reduced to a series of dogmas and prescriptions, to try to take worldly matters under its authority. The Diyanet challenged the status of the established traditional religious authorities, such as the ulema and dervish sheikhs, so that the Republic would become a modern state and society.

The Diyanet is thoroughly dependent on the state. Not only are its funds allocated from the state budget. In addition the appointment and dismissal of its president are decided by the Prime Minister in agreement with the President of the Republic. Dismissals have taken place in cases of tension between the president of the Diyanet and the political authorities who want to have the final say. This testifies to the Diyanet's relatively weak position on the Turkish political scene. The relatively short terms that presidents of the Diyanet have been in office (often no more than four years) have made any large scale vision and politics practically impossible.

Part Three: Organizing Turkish Muslim Life in the Diaspora

This Part, more sociologically oriented, presents four different Turkish Islamic organizations in Europe.

Fulya Atacan's paper, The "Union of Mosques and Mosque-Communities" (İslamî Camiler ve Cemaatler Birliği, İCCB) founded by Cemaleddin Kaplan in Western Germany offers a description and analysis of the "Union of Mosques and Mosque-Communities", which was established by Kaplan in Cologne in 1985 and has continued to exist even after the latter's death in 1995. It is not generally known that Kaplan worked within the Turkish Directorate for Religious Affairs (*Diyanet İşleri Başkanlığı,* in short: *Diyanet*) from 1966 until 1981 as a mufti in Adana. In 1981 he retired from the Directorate and migrated to Germany. Inspired by the Iranian revolution, he took increasingly radical positions first inside and after 1983 outside the Millî Görüş organization. As the leader of the community he had to cope with the many problems confronting Turkish migrants in Germany.

The paper enhances our knowledge about what is known as the "Kaplan Group" in Germany, first of its history and its modern organizational structure, then of its particular ideology which rejects both democracy and communism and exhibits an animosity toward the state of Israel and Jews in general, and finally of the social base of the movement, which consists of poor if not wretched Turkish immigrants who, experiencing continuous open or covert discrimination in German cities have responded to it with a radical interpretation of their religion. The author stresses the ghetto existence which the group has to lead, with external problems compounded by internal ones. Contrary to certain opinions held in Europe, the radical Islamic discourse which the group developed was aimed not so much at European institutions than at changes to be brought about in Turkey, where they hoped that an Islamic state could be established. In the last analysis this discourse instills patience and endurance and gives the members a sacred meaning to the immigrants' experience of suffering. It covers in fact a fatalistic worldview.

The second contribution, by *Günter Seufert*, concerns the Turkish state's Directorate of Religious Affairs (in short: Diyanet) and its representation among Turkish migrants in Europe. This institution can now be compared with a state secretariat; it is subordinated to the Prime Minister. Only in 1980 did the Diyanet become active in taking care of the religious organization and needs of Turkish migrant workers in Europe. This seems to have been largely in response to the success which other Turkish religious organizations which were forbidden in Turkey had in the diaspora. The Diyanet accused them of taking the wrong path.

One important task of the organizations and institutions which represent the Diyanet in Europe is to exercise a certain control over the Turks living abroad. In Germany the relevant organization is the DİTİB, founded in 1984, which has no legal status independent of the Diyanet. It is in fact the organization through which the Turkish state can control the mosque communities of Turkish migrants abroad. This also includes appropriating their property (land and buildings). There are no exact data about the number of mosque organizations in Germany which actually belong to the DİTİB, nor about the number that have made over their property to the Diyanet.

For some time opinion in Europe considered that the Diyanet organizations in Europe represented a moderate, liberal and open-minded version of Islam oriented toward dialogue. Was the state behind them not a secular state which would not want religion to be involved in political activities? As a consequence of this wide-spread view, official circles in Germany recommended cooperation with the DİTİB. It may, however, legitimately be asked, first, which version of Islam is in fact presented by the DİTİB and, secondly, which interests the Diyanet may have in caring so much for the Turkish migrants in Germany and elsewhere in Europe. Behind this is the broader question how the Diyanet perceives Europe and what its intentions are. This is the subject of an inquiry about the publications of the Diyanet, which the author divides into two groups.

The first group consists of what may be called theological and legal publications including fatwas which are based on the Qur'an, Sunna and authoritative Islamic writings of the first centuries. All of them go back to the Scriptural sources of Islam. They treat issues concerning Muslim behavior toward non-Muslims in non-Muslim societies, and Muslim attitudes toward the non-Muslim countries where they happen to live. They make clear that there are rules for individual behavior and rules which apply to the Muslim community as such but not to individual Muslims. They stipulate that the Shari'a can only be applied in a country which finds itself under Muslim rule. As a general rule in Hanafi law, Muslims in non-Muslim societies should respect the authority of the state where they live and cooperate with non-Muslims for the sake of justice and social order. The author observes that in this perspective the Muslim is held to be a-political; he has to submit to the state authority of the country where he lives and should not act without specific instructions from the Muslim state to which he belongs.

The second group of Diyanet publications consists of what may be called practical and ideological considerations concerning the present-day situation. They are not deduced from the sources of Islam. One example is the description of Christianity which is given in a textbook for pupils of (*imam-hatip*) schools for future preachers. It presents 19th century European expansion and colonization, for instance, as an effect of the Christian missions and of the wider Christian inclination to subvert and finally destroy other cultures and to uproot other peoples from their own values. Christian churches are depicted as enemies of the Turkish Republic and Nation. Seufert characterizes this historiography as a "religious" reading of the history of Europe and the Third World, a religious reading which one might expect from Islamists but not in a history book produced by a secular state. Christianity is not studied and judged here as a religion or a religious doctrine in its own right, but as a weapon of ideological warfare used by European politicians. It is the political role of Christianity which is examined and it is the political danger of Christianity which determines the judgment.

Seufert contends that such a political vision of Christianity precludes distinguishing the religious from the secular components of

Europe. A Europe which is not really understood cannot but give rise to feelings of being threatened. Consequently, the Turkish Muslims living in the European diaspora are bound to have the greatest difficulty in understanding the religious and the secular dimensions of Europe, and the unavoidable tension which exists between them. And their lack of understanding will lead them to respond with emotions of fear.

The author then discusses the ways in which the Diyanet itself views this tension between Europe's religious and secular dimensions, again basing his analyses on Diyanet publications. He elaborates to what extent the Diyanet sees Christianity as the unmistakable nature and character of Europe, and to what extent it perceives the Christian mission as an ongoing European endeavor. These Diyanet publications show no understanding of European history and society. They advise Turkish migrants in Europe simply to isolate themselves as Turkish Muslims and to erect walls between themselves and the society in which they are living.

One may legitimately ask why the Diyanet is so afraid of Christian influences on Turkish Muslims in Europe? The author's answer is that this is not so much because they might forfeit their eternal destiny but fundamentally because such influences would weaken the Turkish nation-state. The explanation for this lies in the formula of the so-called Turkish-Islamic synthesis according to which national and religious values are interwoven. It was explicitly formulated in 1980 when the Turkish state assumed the right to give its culture direction within the framework of one homogeneous nation which is both Turkish and Sunni. This view excludes the recognition of ethnic groups in Turkey other than the Turkish one, or of religious groups other than the Sunni Muslim one. In the official view, based on the formula of the Turkish-Islamic synthesis as the "golden rule" of Turkish policies, these groups simply should not exist.

The implications of the Diyanet's views of Christianity, Europe and the Turkish state for its view of Turkish Muslim migrants in Europe are clear. It is a political, rather than a religious danger, which the Diyanet perceives in any weakening of Islamic faith and practice among Turkish migrants. For these then risk becoming alienated from the Turkish nation and possibly engaging in political opposition. For the same reason the Diyanet sees any weakening of the patriarchal family structure among Turkish migrants as a weakening of morality which may lead to a weakening of the Turkish family and consequently of the nation. If Islamic faith and practice in Europe are held to be threatened by Christianity and its missionary impulse, Islamic morality is held to be threatened by Europe's secular dimension of Europe. Both religion and secularism in Europe are seen as threats. And the Diyanet fights against these threats not so much because of religious or moral concerns, but because its final task is to protect the Turkish state and nation against any weakening of the Turkish-Islamic synthesis.

Whereas the first kind of Diyanet publications presents a classical Islam based on the religious sources, the second kind reveals a practical and ideological Islam with little content of its own, mainly serving the state. And whereas the first group of publications allows for dialogue and understanding between Muslims and Christians within the framework given in the Qur'an, the second group on the contrary favors Turkish Muslims' isolation from European society for the sake of the Turkish nation-state. In the final analysis, the Diyanet's task is to ensure that Turkish Muslims in the diaspora keep their national and religious identities. And the Turkish state uses the Diyanet to impose a particular national-religious identity on Turks living abroad, to maintain them as a distinct group in the diaspora, and so to establish in European countries a lobby which will remain loyal to Turkey.

Besides this specific role toward Turkish citizens abroad, the Diyanet also entertains extensive relations with Turkic peoples in Asia, with Muslim peoples who remained in the Balkans after the demise of the Ottoman Empire, and with the Muslim world in general. But it does not show any awareness of religious differences which exist among Muslims. It simply functions in the service of a state that incorporates what the author calls "state nationalism", that is, an ideology in which the state creates the nation by which it wants to legitimate itself, and that nation should be completely homogeneous. In the author's view, the Diyanet's perception of European societies and their institutions is marked not only by a lack of insight but also by deep mistrust.

The Islamic migrant organization called Millî Görüş is the subject of *Günter Seufert*'s second study which uses especially materials of the years 1995 and 1996. Millî Görüş had close links with the Welfare Party in Turkey whose leader was Necmettin Erbakan. Although it claims to be a religious organization, there is no doubt about its political character, not only because it has links with personalities of the Welfare Party but also because of its own discourse and activities in Europe and Turkey. Millî Görüş is strongly interested in Turkey and Turkish politics and entertains many exchanges and other links with the country. It often adopts specific Turkish views of Europe and of problems related to it as they are formulated in Turkey. The general orientation of its journals is that of taking sides with Muslims resisting oppression in many countries, fighting for the right to organize themselves in accordance with the law and spirit of Islam. The journals refer repeatedly to the sufferings which Muslims undergo at the hands of all who consider Islam as an enemy.

One important issue is that of the relationship which Millî Görüş seeks with society in Germany, where the organization has its headquarters. Its discourses stress incompatibility between Islam and the West, and also its own specific character, which marks it off clearly from its non-Muslim context. It continually calls for Islam to be here. Millî Görüş attaches importance to founding Islamic institutions parallel to German ones, from childcare crèches and schools to hospitals and homes for the aged. These institutions are founded on the initiative of and according to the financial possibilities of Millî Görüş. Notwithstanding its ideology of antagonism, in practice Millî Görüş branches interact increasingly with German society and are far further on the way of integration than the branches of the Diyanet for instance. An interesting feature in this respect is that some Millî Görüş intellectuals consider subjects like the Turkish language or Turkish nationalism no longer a taboo. The synthesis of Islam and national feeling, as has been proclaimed by the Turkish government especially since 1980, is not always accepted by the younger generation of this group. They tend to distance themselves from official Turkish nationalist ideology.

The author contends that the Millî Görüş's strict return to Qur'an and Sunna as the sources of Islam has encouraged the beginnings of a critical attitude to existing *volk*-religious traditions and a more general reflection about religion. In this way "religion" is developing from a tradition-bound way of life to an object of conscious reflection, and the community is evolving from an ethnic or national "minority" to a community of faith. Such a development can bring about new interpretations of Islam, so as to face the problems of modern society and the intellectual challenges of modernity.

Through its political concerns Millî Görüş also addresses social problems in German society itself, in the form of a social commitment not only to its own community and organization but also to the well-being of society at large. Some spokesmen, for instance, have affirmed that Muslims can give moral support to European societies to promote a multicultural climate and strengthen the civic sense and moral fibre of society. Regarding the first point they refer to Muhammad's covenant of Medina and the *millet*-system of the Ottoman empire. As to the second, Millî Görüş accepts certain general values of European societies like democracy and human rights, not least to support the Muslims' own moral claims. According to Seufert this represents a step toward participating in the development of social thinking and acting in Germany and other European countries. It should be seen as a form of integration on the basis of general (European) values and specific (Islamic) moral attitudes.

As a result, Millî Görüş maintains a clear ideological distance from European societies, from its own political perspective. On the other hand it has developed religious argumentations which are based on Scriptural data and on a wider reflection on religion, that may in fact open possibilities for integration through interaction. The religious discourse of the Millî Görüş is now developing more and more in Europe itself, legitimizing action and participation in European societies. According to the author, this could lead in the end to the members adopting more secular attitudes concerning values and to their political participation for the wellbeing of society.

In the last part of the book, dealing with the ways in which Turkish Muslim life has been organized in the European diaspora, the final chapter by Yasemin Karakaşoğlu-Aydın presents a recently founded Islamic academy near Cologne. For a long time Protestant and Catholic academies have existed in Germany, with the aim of furthering instruction in Christianity and offering courses on social and cultural issues in the light of the Christian faith. These academies are centers of exchange and dialogue and they have devoted numerous weekend meetings to promoting better knowledge about Christianity, Judaism and Islam, and their mutual relations. Turkish immigrants in the Cologne area, after consulting local authorities, have now taken the initiative to establish a similar academy with an Islamic outlook in Cologne Mühlheim. The official name *Islamische Akademie Villa Hahnenburg* is shortened to ISLAH, an Arabic word denoting reform and improvement. The academy is financed by the Association of Islamic Cultural Centers (*Verband der Islamischen Kulturzentren*, VIKZ) in Germany. In her contribution the author describes the academy, its activities and its relationships to the VIKZ.

The academy is housed in a stately mansion of four stories, with a prestigious outfit of furniture reminding the visitor of 19th century Ottoman as well as German higher culture. It opened its doors at the end of 1998 and has developed a number of programs directed by two ladies, Nigar Yardım and Ceviye Güler. In these programs the academy addresses various groups of people.

First of all, courses for Muslims of Turkish descent in the area offer practical instruction in matters of social work, job preparation, health care, Arabic language etc., with special emphasis being laid on the instruction of women. Second, the academy provides training courses for professional and voluntary personnel in and around the mosques. The program pays attention for example to Christianity, child psychology and the way in which the German school system is organized. One underlying idea is that the instruction in and practice of religion should be adapted to the needs of future generations of Muslims of Turkish descent in Germany. The German language and elements of German cultural style (for instance in the manner of preaching) should be taken into account. The broader cultural elite is encouraged to follow courses of continued education and it is hoped that in the future the academy will be able to provide for the schooling of imams and teachers of religion. And thirdly, the academy addresses the German public by offering lectures and courses, for instance on the history of Islam, and focusing on intercultural themes and Muslim-Christian dialogue. In all of its activities the academy strives for the integration of Muslims in German society and their participation in its development. A particular effort is made to train a Muslim intellectual elite who can take part in Muslim-Christian dialogue.

The author then focuses on two problems with which the work of the Islamic academy finds itself confronted.

1. The question is raised of a specifically Islamic approach to life and thought. This approach is based on the idea of *tevhid* (Unity: of God, and of human faith, thought and action). On one hand religious knowledge should be transmitted; on the other hand problems of rational thought are to be taken seriously. This leads to the question to what extent it is permissible according to Islam to study religious themes using a secular scholarly approach. The Protestant culture of continuous critical learning (*Lernkultur*), even with regard to one's own religion, earns a certain admiration in Muslim intellectual circles.

2. The other question raised is that of the relationship of the ISLAH to the VIKZ, formally established in Germany in 1973 and better known as Süleymanlı. The Cultural Centers in Germany are clearly related to the Süleymanlı movement of the Naqshbandi sheikh Süleyman Hilmi Tunahan (1888-1959); both groups concentrate on intensive Koran courses. In the 1980s the Süleymanlı in Germany moved from a rather closed to a more open attitude towards German society and Christianity. The strictly centralist hierarchical organization was retained, however, and the Süleymanlı did not publish a specific journal or develop a separate women's department as other Muslim organizations in German had done. They also retain their strong common community awareness.

When discussing the relationship between ISLAH and VIKZ the author mentions five features distinguishing the former from the latter. ISLAH has an open door policy and gives free access to all interested persons regardless of religion or nationality. Non-Muslim speakers from different sections of German society participate in the lectures and courses. There is an open, non-hierarchical communication between all those who work at the academy, men and women. In the leading positions women play a prominent role. Various German non-Muslim institutions and persons participate in the academy's scholarly Council (*Wissenschaftlicher Beirat*).

The new orientation of the Islamic Academy Villa Hahnenburg clearly differs from the dominant attitude of the German Süleymanlı organization on which it is however financially dependent. But more important in the long run is the fact that the very foundation and activities of the Islamic academy imply an emancipation of Muslims of Turkish descent in Germany. From having been a community cared for by German welfare organizations, Christian or otherwise, the Muslim community in Germany is increasingly establishing its autonomy and taking proper responsibility for the course it should follow. And if this holds true for Germany now, it may, or will, become the case elsewhere in Europe too.

Summarizing the summary

The three themes to which the different parts of the book are devoted constitute in fact three lines of scholarly research.

The first concerns keeping track impartially of current developments of Muslim and European -- including Christian -- thinking on the practice of Muslims and Christians living together and cooperating in Europe. For centuries the two groups' thinking about each other took place separately and within the confines of two religious structures which were held to be antagonistic. This framework was justified and strengthened through political and military confrontations. Standing aside, we can now ask what the nature of these two religious structures was, and which new orientations have arisen transcending the earlier separation of Europeans and Muslims and the domination of one by the other. It is especially important to pursue these questions with regard to those Muslim and European groups present in Europe who express their thoughts about each other. Since so many of the Muslims living nowadays in Europe have come originally from Turkey and are associated with that country, Turkish thinking about Europe and European thinking about Turkey merits special attention.

The second theme concerns the various orientations of current self-understanding among Turkish Muslims and their perceptions of Europe as an entity to be aspired to, to be refused, or to be communicated with. There is a rich gamut of ideological orientations in Turkey and among Turks nowadays, both on an official and an unofficial level, and they deserve to be better known in Europe. This holds especially true for those orientations which lead to particular views of Europe.

The third part of the book concerns the conditions of Muslims within the European diaspora. This holds particularly true for Turkish migrants some of whom have organized themselves but the majority of whom do not belong to any organization. Existing studies tend to stress the distinctive features of these organizations, the ways in which they differ from each other. It is also legitimate, however, to look for the common cultural and social features of migrants from the same country of origin and to interpret differences as different options they follow to orient themselves in Europe.

Conclusion

The workshop that was at the origin of this book was a meeting of Turkish and European intellectuals who entered into dialogue. The meeting was a happy combination of rigorous and vigorous interaction. We had a more or less realistic view of the others who were present and we made a more or less conscious effort to distance ourselves from established positions. We simply wanted to be honest with ourselves. We had the advantage of being few enough to sit around one table. Those who wanted to say something were listened to. And at one moment or another, we all discovered that speaking of the images which others have also implies exposing the images we have of ourselves.

If I remember well, those present at the workshop shared an underlying desire to arrive at a Euro-Turkish dialogue. In fact, the workshop of October 1996 is only one of a number of Euro-Turkish meetings held in Istanbul lately. The Turkish Historical Association and the European Science Foundation organized together a scholarly conference on "Individual and Society in the Muslim Mediterranean" in July 1998. The Oecumenical Patriarchate organized a Muslim-Christian dialogue meeting in June 1997. An Intercultural Dialogue meeting was organized by the Municipality of Istanbul in March 1998. And no doubt Istanbul will continue to fulfill its vocation as a Euro-Turkish meeting-place.

Both Turkish and other European intellectuals share a persisting interest in further research, practical cooperation and dialogue. The subjects treated in this book could be expanded to include, for instance, more emphasis on European perceptions of Turkey and Turks and Euro-Turkish interactions not only in the past but also at the present time. We hope this small Istanbul workshop has not only provided an example of cooperation between scholars in Turkey and elsewhere in Europe but also pointed the way to new investigations on fruitful relations. It will then have borne fruits for the future.

Istanbul, 29 November 1999

Jacques Waardenburg

Klassisches sunnitisches Fiqh (fıkıh) für Muslime in der europäischen Diaspora

Hayreddin Karaman
Marmara Üniversitesi, Istanbul

Grundlegende Begriffe[*]

Fıkıh, die islamische Rechtswissenschaft

Die *islamische Theologie* (İslâmî ilimler) entstand aus der systematischen Auslegung der Verse (ayet) des geoffenbarten Korans und der *Prophetentradition*[1] (sünnet) in eigens dafür verfaßten Werken, die sich mit Themen wie den *Glaubenswahrheiten* (inanç), den *Regeln der Anbetung* (ibadet), dem *Gemeindeleben* (cemiyet hayatı) und der *Ethik* und Sittlichkeit (ahlâk) befassen. Die *islamische Rechtswissenschaft* (fıkıh) ist einer der Zweige der islamischen Theologie, und ihre Gegenstände sind der Kult, das Gemeindeleben, die Wirtschaft, die Politik sowie das islamische Recht im engeren Sinne.

Religionen

Bei ihrer Behandlung von Fragen zur Ehe, zu Speisevorschriften, zu Krieg und Frieden, zur Bestattung und Trauer, bei ihren Entscheidungen über Erbschaftsfragen und selbst bei ihrer Bewertung von öffentlichen Arbeits- und Beschäftigungsverhältnissen bezieht die islamische Rechtswissenschaft auch zu den anderen Religionen und zu ihren Anhängern Stellung. Grundlegend ist hierbei, daß der Islam die anderen

[*] Alle Fußnoten sind Anmerkungen des Übersetzers aus dem Türkischen, Günter Seufert. Islamische Termini wurden in der heutigen türkischen Schreibweise wiedergegeben, auch wenn sie arabischen Ursprungs sind. Namen und Werke der arabischen Autoren hingegen wurden nach der Umschrift der Deutschen Morgenländischen Gesellschaft transliteriert.

[1] Verstanden als die *Überlieferung des mustergültigen Handeln des Propheten Mohammed und seine als autoritativ anerkannten Äußerungen* (hadis).

Religionen in zwei Gruppen unterteilt, in *Buchreligionen* und *Nicht-Buchreligionen*[2] (kitablı ve kitabsız dinler), und daß er Buchreligionen wie dem Christen- und Judentum eine Reihe von Privilegien[3] gewährt.

Interreligiöser Dialog

Die islamische Rechtswissenschaft versteht den interreligiösen Dialog als eine Form der Beziehung und des Verhältnisses von Einzelpersonen und Gruppen unterschiedlicher Religion zueinander. Eine solche Beziehung kann sich in unterschiedlichen Rahmen konkretisieren: Muslime und Nichtmuslime können Staatsbürger ein und desselben Staates sein, die Muslime können sich vorübergehend in einem nichtislamischen Lande aufhalten, die beiden Gruppen können die unterschiedlichsten Beziehungen zueinander aufnehmen und sich gegenseitig die Grundrechte und Grundfreiheiten, also die Menschenrechte, zugestehen.

Thematik und Quellen

Themen, wie die[4] Bewertung einer anderen Religion und ihrer Gläubigen, Streitschriften wider andere Religionen, *Apologetik* (reddiye) und Heilslehre gehören der *islamischen Dogmatik*[5] (kelâm) zu. Dahingegen ist das konkrete Verhältnis von Einzelnen, von Gruppen und von Gesellschaften verschiedener Religionen zueinander ein Thema des Fıkıh, der *islamischen Rechtswissenschaft.*

Das Verhältnis von Muslimen zu Nichtmuslimen ist eines der ältesten Themen sowohl der islamischen Rechtswissenschaft als auch der islamischen Dogmatik und beschäftigte schon die Muslime des ersten Jahrhunderts, denn das Verhältnis von Muslimen zu Nichtmuslimen und die Frage, wie es zu gestalten sei, kommt bereits in den Versen des Korans und in den Hadis zur Sprache. Das Thema findet sich in den grundlegenden Werken zur allgemeinen islamischen Rechtswissenschaft aus dem zweiten Jahrhundert[6] und in den mehr spezifischen

[2] Auch *transzendente* (semavî) und *menschliche* (beşerî) Religionen genannt.
[3] (vor den Nicht-Buchreligionen und deren Anhängern)
[4] (theologische)
[5] (ein weiterer Zweig der islamischen Theologie)
[6] (= 8. Jahrhundert nach Christus)

Werken (siyer) zum *Öffentlichen und zum Privatrecht der*[7] *Staaten.* Zu nennen sind in diesem Zusammenhang die uns noch heute zur Verfügung stehenden Werke von Šaybānī[8] (gest 182/789)[9], ein Schüler von Abū Ḥanīfa, dem Gründer der hanefitischen Rechtsschule[10]; von Awzā'ī[11] (gest. 157/773) und von Šāfi'ī (gest. 204/819). Das Buch Aḥkām ahl aḏ-ḏimma[12] von Ibn Qayyim (gest. 751/1350), das 1961 in Damaskus erneut herausgegeben wurde, beschäftigt sich vor allem mit den Regelungen zum Privatrecht für die Nichtmuslime[13].

Das islamische Recht und die islamische Dogmatik unterscheiden die Religionen grob in zwei Gruppen, in die *wahre, gerechte* (hak) Religion und die *falschen, eitlen* (batıl) Religionen.[14] Die wahre Religion ist diejenige, welche den Menschen über seine Propheten von Allah mitgeteilt worden ist. Die Offenbarung der wahren Religion begann mit Adam, dem ersten Menschen, und endete mit Mohammed, dem Propheten des Islams. So wie schon zu den Zeiten Abrahams[15] *Islam* die Bezeichnung für die wahre Religion (Koran, Vers 22/78)[16] gewesen ist, so ist auch heute *Islam* die Bezeichnung für die wahre Religion.

Was die *Angehörigen der Buchreligionen* (ehlü'l-kitab) betrifft, finden sich im Fıkıh zwei Definitionen: Der Lehre der hanefitischen Rechtsschule nach sind Ehlü'l-kitab die nichtmuslimischen Gläubigen all der Religionen und ihrer Bücher, die von Allah geoffenbart worden sind, unabhängig davon, ob die Bücher dieser Religionen später verfälscht und sie selbst degeneriert sind. Danach gehören zu den Ehlü'l-kitab neben den Christen und den Juden auch alle, die an die Bü-

---

[7] (islamischen)

[8] Šaybānī = Al-Šaybānī, Abū 'Abd Allāh Muḥammad b. Al-Ḥasan b. Farqad.

[9] (islamischer/christlicher Zeitrechnung)

[10] (der die Mehrzahl der türkischsprachigen Muslime in der Türkei angehört)

[11] Awzā'ī = Al-Awzā'ī, Abū 'Amr 'Abd Al-Raḥmān b. 'Amr.

[12] (=Regelungen zu [dem Umgange mit] den Schutzbefohlenen) Ibn Qayyim Al-Ǧawziyya, Šams Al-Dīn Abū Bakr Muḥammad b. Abī Bakr Al-Zar'ī: Aḥkām ahl aḏ-ḏimma, Damaskus 1961.

[13] Im islamischen Sprachgebrauch *zimmî* = Schutzbefohlene (arab. ḏimmī).

[14] Dabei gelten die bereits genannten Buchreligionen als wahre und die Nicht-Buchreligionen als falsche Religionen.

[15] Der biblische Abraham wird als Prophet anerkannt.

[16] Sure 22 al-Ḥaǧǧ = *die Wallfahrt*, Vers 78: "... Die Religion eures Vater Abraham! Er (d.h.) Gott hat euch Muslime genannt, (schon) früher und (nunmehr) in diesem (Koran), damit der Gesandte Zeuge über euch sei, und ihr über die (anderen) Menschen Zeugen seiet. ..." Deutsch nach Rudi Paret: *Der Koran*, Kohlhammer, Stuttgart u.a. 1979.

cher Abrahams und Davids glauben. Hingegen lehrt die Rechtswissenschaft der anderen islamischen Rechtsschulen[17], die gegenüber den Hanefiten die Mehrheit bilden, daß *Angehörige der Buchreligionen* nur diejenigen sind, die an die Thora (tevrat) und an das *Neue Testament* (incil) glauben, also die Juden und die Christen (Zainaddīn b. Ġazzāl b. Zainaddīn 'Abd b. Abū Al-Malībārī: Al-Fatāwī 'l-hindīya, Band S. 282[18]; Al-Ǧaṣṣāṣ, Aḥmad b. 'Alī Abū Bakr Al-Rāzī: Aḥkām al-qur'ān, Istanbul 1335, Band 2, S. 327).
Der Islam lehrt, daß der Inhalt der Bücher, die vor dem Koran geoffenbart worden sind, auf zweierlei Weise eine Änderung erfahren hat. Einige der dort formulierten *konkreten Verhaltensregeln* (amelî hükümler) wurden durch den Koran aufgehoben, ein anderer Teil wurde von den Menschen willkürlich *verändert, entstellt und umformuliert* (tahrif). Aus diesem Grunde sagt der Prophet[19] (s.a.): "So die Angehörigen der Buchreligionen euch etwas lehren wollen, so bestätigt es nicht, noch trachtet, es zu widerlegen, sagt vielmehr zu ihnen: 'Glaubet das, was Allah offenbart hat'" (Aḥmad b. Ḥanbal: Musnad, Band 4, S. 136)[20]. In diesem Sinne beschäftigt sich die Methodolgie des Fıkıh unter anderem mit der *Verläßlichkeit und Rechtsgültigkeit* (Şer'u-men kablenâ) der vorkoranischen Bücher. Obwohl zu diesem Komplex unterschiedliche *Lehrmeinungen* (içtihad) vorgetragen worden sind, wurde doch bereits in der Zeit von Imam Šāfi'ī[21] (gest. 204/820) vertreten, daß *die* Vorschriften dieser Bücher, die vom Koran nicht aufgehoben worden sind, nach wie vor Gültigkeit haben. Imam Ġazālī[22] (gest. 505/1111) überliefert folgende Haltung des Rechtsschulengründers Imam Šāfi'ī: "Finden wir in den islamischen Quellen keine Angaben zu der Frage ob diese oder jene Nahrung *erlaubt* (helal) oder *verboten* (haram) ist, ziehen wir *das religiöse Recht der früheren Religionen* (önceki şeriatlar)[23] zu Rate. Solange islamische Quellen nichts Gegensätzliches sagen, gilt uns das als erlaubt, was

[17] Zu nennen sind die sunnitischen Hanbaliten, Schafiiten und Malikiten sowie die schiitischen Dschaferiten.
[18] Auch Fatāwī 'ālamgīrī, zusammengestellt von: Şeyh Nizām Burhānpurlu, hrsgg. von İsmail Karakaya, Gaye Matbacılık, Ankara 1983.
[19] (in einer Hadis)
[20] Aḥmad b. Ḥanbal: Musnad, Beirut 1389 <1969>
[21] Šāfi'ī = al İmām Abū 'Abd Allāh Muḥammad b. İdrīs.
[22] Ġazālī = Al-Ġazālī, Abū Ḥamīd Muḥammad b. Muḥammad Al-Ṭūsī
[23] Der Begriff *Scheriat* steht also für das *religiöse Recht* allgemein, auch für das Kirchenrecht und nicht ausschließlich für das *islamische religiöse Recht*.

dort als erlaubt bezeichnet wird und das als verboten, was dort verboten ist." Hierbei wird ausdrücklich auf die Scheriate von Adam, Noah, Abraham, Moses und Jesus[24] (Friede sei mit ihnen) verwiesen (Ġazālī: Kitāb al-manḫūl fi 'l-uṣūl, Damaskus 1980, S. 231-234).

Es wurde bereits darauf hingewiesen, daß die Angehörigen der Buchreligionen[25] einige Privilegien (imtiyaz) genießen, eines davon ist, daß die "Nahrung der Angehörigen der Buchreligionen auch den Muslimen koscher ist" (Koran, Vers 5/5).[26] Der Islam hat den Genuß von Schweinefleisch verboten, aber den Verzehr des Fleisches anderer Tiere erlaubt. Obwohl nun einige *Koranexegeten* (müçtehid) gefordert haben, daß der Muslim nur das Fleisch von Tieren, wie Schafen und Hühnern, verzehren darf, die nach islamischen Vorschriften geschlachtet wurden, wird doch auch die Meinung vertreten, daß den Muslimen auch das Fleisch der Tiere erlaubt sei, die nach den Vorschriften der Buchreligionen geschlachtet worden sind, und daß die Muslime dazu gegebenenfalls Auskunft bei den jüdischen Rabbinern und den christlichen Priestern einzuholen hätten (Ibn Al-'Arabī: Aḥkām al-qur'ān, Kairo 1974, Band 2, S. 556). Diese Haltung fordert geradezu einen Dialog zwischen Muslimen, Christen und Juden, muß doch der muslimische *Schriftgelehrte* (alim) sich - bevor er seine Empfehlung, seine Fetwa abgibt - Auskunft beim Religionsgelehrten der Ehlü'l-kitab einholen.

Im Hinblick auf das Vermögen der anderen Religionen, den Menschen zu gottgefälligem Handel und Wandel zu führen und ihn der Glückseligkeit[27] teilhaftig werden zu lassen, hat die *islamische Dogmatik* (Kelâm) eine originäre Bewertung der anderen Religionen entwikkelt. Imam Ġazālī, der sowohl auf dem Gebiet des Fıkıh als auch auf dem der Kelâm eine Autorität darstellt, hat die Frage danach, wo die Grenzen zwischen Glauben (iman) und Unglauben (küfür) verlaufen, und die Beurteilung verschiedener Religionen und Konfessionen hinsichtlich ihrer Fähigkeit, den Menschen zum Heil zu führen, in seinem Werke Faiṣal at-tafriqa bain al-islām waz-zandaqa behandelt (Kairo 1901). Unglaube, Nichtmuslim-Sein, bedeutet ihm zufolge die gänzli-

[24] Jesus gilt als einer in der Reihe der Propheten, die die wahre Religion und ihr religiöses Recht verkündet haben.

[25] (gegenüber den Gläubigen anderer Religionen bei den Muslimen)

[26] Sure 5 = Mā'ida = *der Tisch*, Vers 5: "... Und was diejenigen essen, die (vor euch) die Schrift erhalten haben, ist für euch erlaubt, und (ebenso) was ihr eßt, für sie ..." (Paret)

[27] (und dem Heil im Jenseits)

che oder teilweise Zurückweisung, Ablehnung und Leugnung der Botschaft des letzten Propheten Allahs, der Botschaft des Propheten Mohammed; Glaube hingegen verlange die vollständige Anerkennung und Übernahme dieser Botschaft. In dieser Perspektive sind die Juden und Christen, die Mohammed nicht als Propheten anerkennen, Ungläubige, ganz genauso wie die Brahmanen[28], die überhaupt keinen Propheten anerkennen, wie die Angehörigen der Dehriye-Sekte[29], die weder von den Propheten noch von Gott und vom Jenseits etwas wissen wollen, sowie die Polytheisten (müşrik), die andere Götter neben Allah haben (S. 19-33).

Nach Ġazālī und seinen Schülern werden die Ungläubigen dann in der Hölle schmoren und unablässig Pein erleiden, wenn sie durch die unmittelbare Nähe mit den Muslimen Gelegenheit hatten, den wahren Islam kennenzulernen und trotzdem an ihrer alten Religion festhalten und somit den Islam offenkundig bestreiten. Hingegen können Ungläubige, die aufgrund räumlicher Entfernung, vollkommener Unwissenheit oder entstellter Informationen über den Islam nicht konvertierten, trotzdem der Gnade Allahs teilhaftig werden und von der Hölle verschont bleiben (S. 72-79, s. für gegensätzliche Stellungnahmen Abū'l-Mu'īn Maimūn b. Muḥammad Al-Nasafī Al-Makḥūlī: Tabṣirat al-adilla, Damaskus 1993, Band 2, S. 766-791; Abū Bakr Muḥammad b. Al-Ṭayyib Al-Baṣrī Al-Bāqillānī: Tamhīd ad-dalā'il watalḫīṣ al-awā'il, Beirut 1987, S. 403).

Verschiedene Religionsgruppen, verschiedene Beziehungsformen

Beziehung mit Nichtmuslimen in nichtislamischen Ländern

Es ist viel darüber gesprochen und geschrieben worden, ob der Krieg oder der Frieden die grundlegende Beziehung der islamischen Gemeinschaft, der Gemeinschaft der Muslime (ümmet), mit den anderen Völkern und Nationen sei. Eine gewichtige Mehrzahl der Exegeten argumentiert, daß diese Beziehungen grundsätzlich solche des Friedens seien. Es ist nicht das Ziel des Islams, alle Menschen dieser Welt mit kriegerischen Mitteln zu Muslimen zu machen oder sie an einen

[28] Meint hier die Hindus allgemein.

[29] Dehriye = Dahrīya, nimmt Bezug auf Koran XLV 23, eine gottverleugnende naturalistische Haltung, die nur die Materie und die Zeit (al-dahr) als ewig anerkennt.

islamischen Staat zu binden. Mit diesem Ziele kann kein Krieg geführt werden, sondern der religiös gerechtfertigte Krieg, der Dschihad, ist nur dann führbar, wenn den Muslimen keine andere Wahl bleibt und wenn die gegnerische Seite eine freiheitliche und gerechte Weltordnung verhindert, und trachtet, die Menschen zu bedrücken, zu unterdrücken und ihr Länder zu besetzen (vgl. Koran 4/75-76, 22/39-41, 2/193, 28/4-5 und 38, 16/34)[30]. Wenn hingegen ein Staat, eine Nation oder eine soziale Gruppe von der Unterdrückung und Bedrückung abläßt und aufhört, Rechte zu brechen, ist der islamische Staat verpflichtet, das anzuerkennen[31] (Koran 8/61)[32]. Der Islam will eine Welt ohne Bedrückung, Unterdrückung und Ausbeutung (sömürü)[33], eine Weltordnung, in der die Menschen ihren Glauben wählen und ihm gemäß leben können. In diesem Sinne leben die Muslime – je nach den Verhältnissen – mit den Nichtmuslimen entweder im Krieg oder in Frieden.

Mit denen, gegen die man kämpft, die eines Feind sind, kann natürlich von Dialog nicht die Rede sein. Doch den Ländern gegenüber, mit denen man Frieden schloß, denen man durch Verträge über Zusammenarbeit verbunden ist, hegt man nur Gutes, wahrt man den Frieden und hält man sich genauestens an alle Abmachungen.

---

[30] Sure 4 = Nisā' = *die Frauen*, Vers 75-76: "Warum wollt ihr (denn) nicht um Gottes willen und (um) der Unterdrückten (willen) kämpfen, ... Kämpft nun gegen die Freunde des Satans! ..." , Sure 22 = al-Ḥağğ = *die Wallfahrt*, Vers 39-41: "Denjenigen, die (gegen die Ungläubigen) kämpfen (so nach einer abweichenden Lesart; im Text: die bekämpft werden), ist die Erlaubnis (zum Kämpfen) erteilt worden, weil ihnen (vorher) Unrecht geschehen ist. ... (Ihnen) die unberechtigterweise aus ihren Wohnungen vertrieben worden sind, nur weil sie sagten: Unser Herr ist Gott ... (Ihnen) die, wenn wir ihnen auf der Erde Macht geben, das Gebet verrichten, die Almosensteuer geben, gebieten, was recht ist, und verbieten, was verwerflich ist. ..." , Sure 2 = Baqara = *die Kuh*, Vers 193: "Und kämpft gegen sie, bis niemand (mehr) versucht, (Gläubige zum Abfall vom Islam) zu verführen, und bis nur noch Gott verehrt wird! Wenn sie jedoch (mit ihrem gottlosen Treiben) aufhören (und sich bekehren), darf es keine Übertretung geben (d.h. dann sind alle weiteren Übergriffe versagt), es sei denn, gegen die Frevler." Sure 28 = Qiṣṣa = *die Geschichte*, Sure 16 = Naḥl = *die Biene* (Verweisen auf die israelitische Geschichte, dt. nach Paret)

[31] (und Frieden zu schließen)

[32] Sure 8 = Anfāl = *die Beute*, Vers 61: "Und wenn sie (d.h. die Feinde) sich dem Frieden zuneigen, dann neige (auch du) dich ihm zu (und laß vom Kampfe ab)! ..." (Paret).

[33] Der Begriff hat denselben Stamm wie Kolonie (sömürge) und Kolonialismus (sömürgecilik).

Beziehungen zur Nichtmuslimen in islamischen Ländern

Nichtmuslime, die als Staatsbürger (vatandaş)[34] dauerhaft in den islamischen Ländern wohnen, haben – bis auf wenige Ausnahmen – die gleichen Rechte und Pflichten wie die Muslime; und diejenigen Nichtmuslime, die sich nur vorübergehend in islamischen Ländern aufhalten (müstemin)[35] , haben – mit der Ausnahme, daß sie kein Recht auf dauerhaften Aufenthalt haben – die gleichen Rechte und Pflichten wie die *zimmî*.

Dahingehend, daß ein Nichtmuslim und Angehöriger der Buchreligionen nur über seinen freien Willen nichtmuslimischer Staatsbürger eines islamischen Staates (zimmî) werden, kann herrscht[36] Einigkeit. Unterschiedliche Meinungen bestehen jedoch in der Frage, ob dieser Status (zimmilik)[37] auch Angehörigen anderer Religionsgemeinschaften zugesprochen werden kann. Die hanefitischen Rechtsschule erlaubt es, alle Nichtmuslime – jeweils per Vertrag – zu Schutzbefohlenen zu machen, alle, außer heidnischen Arabern. Die Rechtsschulen der Awzā'iyya, Mālikiyya und Zaidiyya machen selbst diese Ausnahmen nicht, und erlauben es, mit allen Nichtmuslimen Zimmî-Verträge abzuschließen (Ibn Qayyim: Zād al-ma'ād, Kairo 1950, Band 3, S. 224; ders.: Aḥkām ahl aḏ-ḏimma, Band 1, S. 6; Karaman: Mukayesili İslam Hukuku, İstanbul 1987, Band 3, S. 236).

Ein weiteres Privileg der Angehörigen der Buchreligionen[38] liegt darin, daß es muslimischen Männern erlaubt ist, christliche und jüdische Frauen zu ehelichen. Eine solche Ehe ist in jeder Hinsicht gültig, sie sichert[39] alle Rechte eines Ehevertrags; die Frau darf nicht zur Konversion gezwungen werden und ihr müssen alle Möglichkeiten eingeräumt werden, den Ritus ihrer Religion zu pflegen.

Die nichtmuslimischen Staatsbürger[40] genießen alle die Rechte und Freiheiten, denen auch die Muslime teilhaftig sind, die einzige Aus-

[34] Dieser Begriff wird benutzt, obgleich in Zeiten islamischer Rechtsprechung von *Staatsbürgern* keine Rede sein konnte. In Klammern findet sich jedoch die korrekten osmanischen Begriffe *Ehlü'z-zimme, Zimmî*, die mit *Schutzbefohlene* übersetzt werden können.
[35] (= müsete'min, müste'mine = *Zufluchtsucher*)
[36] (unter den Exegeten)
[37] (Schutzbehfohlener-Sein)
[38] (gegenüberden Nichtmuslimen anderer Religion)
[39] (der Frau)
[40] (eines islamischen Staates)

nahme davon sind einige Rechte, deren Inhabe den Muslimen vorbehalten ist, so kann etwa ein Nichtmuslim nicht Staatspräsident eines islamischen Landes werden.

Die Nichtmuslime eines islamischen Landes können wählen, ob sie ihre Rechtsstreitigkeiten vor dem staatlichen (islamischen) Gericht oder vor dem Gericht ihrer eigenen Gemeinschaft austragen, und sie besitzen in diesem Sinne juristische Autonomie. In dem Falle, daß sie sich für das islamische Gericht entscheiden, wird in privatrechtlichen Streitigkeiten ihrer eigenen Religion gemäß verhandelt. Das in der Geschichte letzte Beispiel für eine solche Rechtspraxis ist das 1917 vom Osmanischen Reiche erlassene Familiengesetz (Hukuk-ı Aile Kararnamesi), das in jedem Abschnitt erst die Paragraphen für die Muslime und dann die für die Juden und für die Christen festlegte.

Generell genossen die Nichtmuslime weitestgehende Religions- und Gewissensfreiheit, ihre Kultstätten waren tabu, sie hatten das Recht, ihre Zeremonien, solange diese die öffentliche Ordnung nicht beeinträchtigten, frei auszuüben, ihren Kindern religiöse Unterweisung und Erziehung zukommen zu lassen und die ihnen von ihrer Religion vorgeschriebene Kleidung zu tragen. Im Alltag gute Nachbarschaft und Freundschaft mit Nichtmuslimen, im Geschäftsleben Partner- und Teilhaberschaft mit ihnen, gemeinsame Anstrengungen zur Verwirklichung der sittlichen Aufgaben, die uns die von Gott geoffenbarten Religionen stellen und in all dem Beachtung der Rechtsgrundlagen; all das befürwortet der Islam.

Ergebnis

Eine Prüfung der Beurteilungen anderer Religionen durch den Islam und seiner Regeln[41] zeigt, daß der Islam insofern nicht "pluralistisch" ist, als er alle anderen Religionen als gerechtfertigte anerkennte, die ihre Gläubigen zum ewigen Heil zu führen in der Lage wären. Im Gegenteil, der Islam gesteht den anderen Religionen nicht zu, daß sie und ihre Gläubigen wirklich vor den Augen Allahs Gnade finden, und letzter Erlösung teilhaftig würden; er gesteht den Gläubigen dieser Religionen jedoch das Recht zu, in dieser Welt ihrer Religion gemäß zu leben, und übt keinerlei Druck zur Konversion aus. Er erkennt das Existenzrecht der Nichtmuslime, die innerhalb der Gemeinschaft der

[41] (die er hinsichtlich des Umgangs mit Nichtmuslimen aufstellt)

Muslime leben, und ihrer Gemeinden an und fordert seine Gläubigen dazu auf, um gutnachbarliche Beziehungen bemüht zu sein. Er erkennt auch die auf Offenbarung beruhenden Vorschriften der anderen Religionen an, soweit diese nicht durch den Koran aufgehoben worden sind, und erachtet diese Vorschriften[42] als verpflichtende. Dies ist der Rahmen, in dem die Muslime interreligiösen Dialog führen können.

[42] (auch für seine eigenen Gläubigen)

Einheit und Vielfalt

Ein muslimisches Modell für multikulturelle Gesellschaften

Kadir Canatan
Universiteit Utrecht

Einleitung *

Der sozialen Praxis islamischer Gesellschaften in Vergangenheit und Gegenwart sind Themen wie *Multikulturalismus* oder *kulturelle Pluralität* nicht fremd, dennoch ist die breit angelegte Diskussion, die in den 90er Jahren in der Türkei von islamischen Intellektuellen über diese Begriffe initiiert wurde, ein Meilenstein in der gesellschaftspolitischen Entwicklung der modernen Republik. Die Triebkräfte für und das Bedürfnis nach einer solchen Diskussion lassen sich sowohl mit den inneren Prozessen der Türkei als auch mit den gravierenden Veränderungen in der Welt in einen sinnvollen Zusammenhang bringen.

Im Hinblick auf Fragen nach kultureller Identität und gesellschaftlichem Pluralismus ist die Türkei in den letzten zehn Jahren einer ernsthaften Prüfung ausgesetzt. Obwohl große Teile der Intelligenz und auch der einfachen Bevölkerung darin übereinstimmen, daß die Gesellschaft der Türkei einem kulturellen Mosaik gleicht, zeigt die politische Praxis seit den Gründertagen der Republik, besonders hinsichtlich der kurdischen und der muslimischen Identität in der Bevölkerung, daß dieser Tatsache keine allzu große Bedeutung zugemessen wurde. Auch heute halten die Privilegierten des Landes, die über das politische, ökonomische, kulturelle und bürokratische Leben der Türkei bestimmen, mit Nachdruck an dem Projekt eines modernen Nationalstaates und der dazugehörigen Schaffung einer Nation (nationbuilding) fest.

Das Modernisierungsabenteuer der Türkei, ist das Bemühen, ein

* Aus dem Türkischen von Nurcan Yılmaz und Günter Seufert.

Land, dessen Geschichte und Kultur mit der des Mittleren Ostens verbunden sind, in eine moderne, westlich orientierte Gesellschaft zu transformieren. Die Realisierung dieses Projekts verlief -- und verläuft noch immer -- zweifellos in zentralstaatlich-autoritären und damit undemokratischen Formen. Denn unter den Bedingungen der Türkei bedeutet Modernisierung eine vollständige kulturelle Umwälzung. Bis zu einem gewissen Teil ist diese heute jedoch abgeschlossen. Die politische und bürokratische Elite hat sich der Mission verschrieben, alles Islamische und Östliche zu bekämpfen. Symptomatisches Beispiel hierfür ist, daß in einem muslimischen Land der Disput um das Kopftuch unbeendbar und die damit zusammenhängende Frage unlösbar scheinen.

Im Streit der Gegensätze wurde das Kopftuch zum Symbol, und generell wird die Auseinandersetzung primär auf der symbolischen Ebene geführt. Für die Elite der Verwestlicher ist das Kopftuch eine anti-moderne Kleidung und repräsentiert den politischen Islam. Diesem Verständnis zu Folge steht das Kopftuch im Dienst der *religiösen Reaktion* (irtica), d.h. es steht stellvertretend für den Wunsch nach einer Rückkehr zu längst überwundenen Zeiten und Verhältnissen, ein Wunsch, der von rückwärtsgewandten Kräften und Bewegungen gehegt wird. Religiöse Reaktion, dieser Begriff aus den Gründungszeiten der Republik wird heute immer noch benutzt, und oft steht er stellvertretend für *Fundamentalismus.* Die Zahl der modernistischen türkischen Intellektuellen jedoch, die um die Herkunft des Wortes Fundamentalismus aus dem Protestantismus weiß und Kenntnis von den Bewegungen hat, die heute im Westen unter diesem Begriff zusammengefaßt werden, ist jämmerlich gering. Dies jedoch scheint generell das größte Problem in der Türkei zu sein: Der Inhalt und die Bedeutung vieler weitverbreiteter Begriffe sind nicht eindeutig, man verwendet sie, wie es einem gerade paßt, und die Begriffe verkommen zu Klischees.

Der Streit zwischen Islamisten und Anhängern des Laizismus bestimmt mehr und mehr den politischen Alltag der Türkei. Aufgrund der verdeckten Intervention der Militärs haben heute letztere die Oberhand. Ungeachtet dessen haben sich die gesellschaftlichen und politischen Gewichte in der Türkei innerhalb des letzten Jahrzehnts gravierend verändert, und in naher Zukunft wird der Islam die Geschicke der Türkei verstärkt prägen. Dabei hängt die Rolle, die der Islam zukünftig in der Türkei spielen wird, nicht nur von den einheimischen Eliten und Interessengruppen ab, sondern auch von der Anziehungskraft der Projekte, die im Namen des Islams vorgestellt werden.

Das pluralistische islamische Gesellschaftsprojekt, auf das wir wenig später in groben Zügen eingehen werden, hat selbst bei Teilen der sozialistischen Intellektuellen Interesse gefunden, weniger jedoch bei der mittlerweile verbotenen Refah Partisi, RP (Wohlfahrtspartei), die den politischen Flügel der islamischen Bewegung vertritt. Denn die RP hält nachdrücklich an dem Projekt einer vom Staat zu errichtenden *Gerechten Ordnung* (adil düzen) fest, das freilich noch genauerer inhaltlicher Ausgestaltung harrt. Welche Politik und welche Projekte die neu gegründete Fazilet Partisi, FP (Tugendpartei), entwickeln wird, ist momentan noch nicht absehbar.[2]

Islamisten und offizielle Staatsideologie (Kemalismus) stehen zueinander im Widerspruch, doch die Türkei hat auch mit einer Kurdenproblematik zu kämpfen, einem weiteren Ergebnis ihrer Bemühungen zum Nationenbau. Diese beiden grundlegenden Probleme zeigen überdeutlich, daß der offizielle Diskurs von einer homogenen Gesellschaft ein Klischee ist, das nur der Verschleierung der Realität dient.

Die Türkei hat es in Wirklichkeit weder geschafft, ein im westlichen Sinne modernes und laizistisches Land zu werden, noch hat sie auf dem ihr verbliebenen geographischen Erbe des Osmanischen Reiches eine Nation im eigentlichen Sinne des Wortes schaffen können. Deshalb befindet sich das türkische Modernisierungsprojekt in einer ernsten Krise. Das von muslimischen Intellektuellen thematisierte islamische Pluralismus-Paradigma ist eine der Antworten auf diese Krisensituation.

Doch nicht nur die Türkei steht vor der Aufgabe, ein friedliches Zusammenleben unterschiedlicher Nationalitäten zu sichern. In über 80 Ländern gibt es heute ethnische und religiöse Auseinandersetzungen, so die UNO. In 25 dieser Länder haben diese Spannungen zu leichteren oder schwereren gewalttätigen Auseinandersetzungen geführt. Sollte es im Verlauf dieser Auseinandersetzungen zu einer Zellteilung aller dieser Länder kommen, erhöhte sich die Zahl der beste-

2 [Unter dem Druck der oben genannten politischen Entwicklung hat sich die *Tugendpartei* (Fazilet Partisi) offiziell mittlerweile vom Projekt einer *Gerechten Ordnung* verabschiedet., Alle Anmerkungen in eckigen Klammern von Günter Seufert]

henden circa 200 Nationalstaaten nochmals um etwa 100 nationale Kleinstaaten.

Die Welt durchlebt gleichzeitig eine Ära der Globalisierung und der Regionalisierung, und die politische Zersplitterung nimmt zu. Dies zeigt, daß sich die Moderne im allgemeinen und der Nationalstaat im besonderen in einer ernsten Krise befinden. In der sich globalisierenden Welt tritt deutlich hervor, daß kulturelles Anderssein und abweichende Identitäten unterdrückt werden. Dies gilt aber nicht nur für die südliche, sondern auch für die nördliche Hemisphäre. Auch dort stellt sich die Frage nach der Möglichkeit friedlichen Zusammenlebens. Tatsache ist, daß auch Westeuropa mit seinen ethnischen Minderheiten und Zuwanderern Probleme hat. Auch wenn diese Länder ein hohes Wohlstands- und Demokratieniveau erreicht haben, ist die Frage, wie man aller Unterschiedlichkeit und Gegensätzlichkeit zum Trotze zusammenleben kann, noch immer offen.

Islamische Intellektuelle der Türkei diskutieren diese Fragen heute im Rahmen der Auseinandersetzung um das osmanische millet-System[3] und um die *Gemeindeordnung von Medina* (Medine Vesikası).

Auf den theoretischen Hintergrund und auf die geschichtlichen Umsetzungsversuche dieser Modelle können wir hier nur kurz eingehen. Uns interessiert mehr, in welcher Weise sie unsere sozio-politischen Perspektiven auf die Pluralismusdiskussion bereichern.

Desweiteren sollen in diesem Artikel die philosophischen und epistemologischen Grundlagen des islamischen Pluralismus-Paradigmas hinsichtlich ihrer Originalität mit den anderen heute diskutierten Ansätzen verglichen werden.

Zum Abschuß möchten wir diese Denkansätze und Modelle dahingehend betrachten, was sie zur Etablierung eines besseren Verhältnisses der islamischen Zuwanderer zur einheimischen Bevölkerung in Westeuropa beitragen können und sie dahingehend bewerten.

Ein Gesellschaftsprojekt auf der Grundlage eines Sozialvertrags

Die Diskussion über eine pluralistische Gesellschaft auf der Grundlage der *Gemeindeordnung* wurde in der Türkei Anfang der 90er Jahre von dem pro-islamischen Wissenschaftler Ali Bulaç begonnen. Seine

3 [Osmanlı-millet-sistemi = die Organisation der Bevölkerung nach Religions- und Konfessionsgruppen.]

Gedanken wurden von führenden islamistischen Köpfen und von sozialistischen Intellektuellen aufgenommen und in mancher Hinsicht weiter entwickelt.[4] Sehen wir uns zunächst Bulaçs Annäherung an diesen Themenkomplex an:

Bulaç, der sich von den sechziger bis in die siebziger Jahre hinein allgemein mit Themen wie Modernisierung und Modernität auseinandersetzte, hat sich in seinen späteren Arbeiten auf die Kritik des Nationalstaates konzentriert.[5] Seine Gedanken in Bezug auf den modernen Nationalstaat bilden den Ausgangspunkt seiner Auseinandersetzung mit kultureller Pluralität. Daher müssen wir uns diesem Thema auch von hier aus zuwenden.

In der Menschheitsgeschichte stellt der moderne Nationalstaat ein vollkommen neues Gebilde dar. Er ist ein quasi mechanischer Apparat, im Zuge der Aufklärung entwickelt, um eine neue Gesellschaft zu errichten, deren primäres Merkmal ihre nahezu beliebige Gestaltbarkeit ist. In dieser Perspektive kann die Gesellschaft vollständig neu gebaut werden und es ist nur legitim, daß der Staat für diesen Zweck alle Autorität für sich beansprucht. Um ein 'Paradies auf Erden' zu schaffen, monopolisiert der Staat das Bildungswesen, die Bürokratie und die Gerichtsbarkeit und vernichtet alle religiösen, rechtlichen und lokalen Besonderheiten der Gesellschaft. Er verleiht ihr damit eine vollkommen homogene Struktur und macht sich selbst zum Zentrum der Gesellschaft.

Den modernen Staat kennzeichnen drei Charakteristika: Er ist zentralistisch organisiert, territorial begrenzt und auf eine wesenhaft verstandene Nation bezogen. Im Grunde ist die Schaffung dieser Nation sein vornehmlichstes Ziel, einer Nation, die auf einer Trennung des

---

[4] Die Diskussion wurde von Bulaçs Aufsatz İslam ve Çoğulculuk (Islam und Pluralismus) ausgelöst, der in der islamistischen Monats-Zeitschrift *Kitap Dergisi* erschien. Nach einer gründlichen aber konstruktiven Kritik Taner Akçams in der sozialistischen Monatszeitschrift *Birikim* 43 (11/1992), wurde das Thema ausführlichst in verschiedenen Magazinen und sogar in Tageszeitungen diskutiert. Die islamistische Drei-Monats-Schrift *Bilgi ve Hikmet* widmete der Thematik eine ganze Ausgabe (1994-95).

[5] Seine Ansichten zum Modernismus faßte Bulaç 1990 in seinem Buch *Din ve Modernizm* (Religion und Modernismus), 2. Auflage, Endulüs Yay. Istanbul 1992, zusammen. Bulaç betrachtet dieses Buch als sein "Manifest". Seine Überlegungen zum Thema Nationalstaat veröffentlichte er in dem Buch *Modern ulus devlet* (Der moderne Nationalstaat), İz Yay. Istanbul 1995. Diese Werk ist gleichzeitig der Schlüssel zu einem pluralistischen Gesellschaftsvertrag (çoğulcu toplum sözleşmesi).

Wir von *den Anderen* basiert. Die Nation ist hierbei ein homogenes Gebilde, das von einer zentralen Autorität auf deren Territorium hervorgebracht wurde. Gleichzeitig schließt sich die Nation durch die Grenzen ihres Landes deutlich von anderen Nationen ab. Daher beinhaltet der Nationalismus einer Nation unweigerlich die Schaffung eines Bildes von den Anderen, den Feinden. Die nationalen Interessen stehen über allen regionalen und globalen Interessen. Der Nationalismus legitimiert selbst Imperialismus, Ausländerfeindlichkeit und Kriege.

In der Moderne steigt die Spannung zwischen dem Nationalstaat und dem tatsächlich vorhandenen kulturellen Puralismus seiner Gesellschaft, ihren verschiedenen kulturellen Identitäten an. Denn jede Positionierung einer zentralen Kultur auf den Fundamenten einer bestimmten Ethnizität trägt die Tendenz in sich, diese zur bestimmenden und offiziellen, zu einer Nationalkultur werden zu lassen und die verschiedenen religiösen, kulturellen und ethnischen Minderheiten des Landes dieser offiziellen Kultur zu assimilieren. Der Versuch, die gesamte Gesellschaft zu homogenisieren produziert einen Konflikt zwischen der tatsächlich multikulturellen Gesellschaft und dem auf ihre Homogenisierung bedachten Staate. Aus dieser Perspektive betrachtet, stellt der Nationalstaat in seinem Kern eine totalitäre und gewalttätige politische Kraft dar.

Auch die Demokratie hat für diesen Streit zwischen dem modernen Nationalstaat und kultureller Pluralität keine Lösung. Denn der dominante Maßstab der Demokratie ist zahlenmäßige Überlegenheit, sie rechtfertigt politische Herrschaft, die Herrschaft der 51 über die restlichen 49 Prozent. Daher können die Minderheiten (seien es religiöse, kulturelle oder ethnische) auch in einem demokratischen Rechtsstaat nicht sicher sein, ob die Mehrheit die Rechte der Minderheit(en) wirklich anerkennt.

Hinzukommt, daß die partizipatorische Dimension vieler nominell demokratischer Staaten nur schwach entwickelt ist und sich nur in wenigen von ihnen eine entwickelte Bürgergesellschaft findet, welche die nationalistisch-reaktionäre Politik des Staates ausgleichen könnte.

Bulaç ist ein vehementer Kritiker des Nationalstaats. Er kommt zu dem Ergebnis, daß dieser letzen Endes überwunden werden muß, und er entwickelt sein pluralistisches Gesellschaftsprojekt aus den Leitlinien der *Gemeindeordnung* als Alternative zum Nationalstaat. Bulaç erkennt, daß der *Islamische Staat*, der gestern und heute von islamischen Vordenkern entwickelt und von islamischen Strömungen propagiert worden ist und wird, im Grunde ein vom Nationalstaat abgeleitetes Modell ist und nur in dessen Begrifflichkeit verständlich wird. So ist der Islamische Staat seinem Äußeren und seinem Namen nach islamisch, in seinem Wesen nach aber ist er ein moderner Nationalstaat. Bulaç lehnt jedoch jede ideologische und [damit tendenziell] totalitäre Staatsidee ab. Seiner Ansicht nach sollte sich der Staat auf die Wahrnehmung seiner klassischen Staatsaufgaben beschränken und allmählich verschlankt werden. Die durch die Verschlankung des Staates entstehende Lücke sollte durch die bürgerliche Gesellschaft und durch ihre zivilen Institutionen geschlossen werden.

Interessant ist ferner, daß Bulaç auch dem historischen Modell des Kalifats nichts abgewinnen kann. Seiner Ansicht nach schreibt der Islam dieses Modell keineswegs vor, sondern es stelle lediglich die Form der politischen Vereinigung dar, die sich die Muslime der ersten Stunde gegeben haben und das Kalifat ist deshalb nur Teil ihres geschichtlichen Erbes.

Die *Gemeindeordnung von Medina*, die Verfassung des vom Propheten Mohammed gegründeten Staates in der gleichnamigen arabischen Stadt, liefert für Bulaç das ideale Modell für einen Staat. Natürlich kann die *Gemeindeordnung* angesichts der Voraussetzungen, die wie heute vorfinden, nicht ohne weiteres als Verfassung Gültigkeit erlangen. Wichtig sind dagegen ihre wesenhaften Besonderheiten und die Tatsache, daß sie auf den Prinzipien *Partizipation* und *Ausgleich verschiedener gesellschaftlicher Gruppen* fußt. Bulaç faßt die Prinzipien und Kernaussagen einer nach der *Gemeindeordnung* gestalteten Verfassung in folgenden zehn Punkten zusammen:

1. Das Individuum hat das Recht, frei über seine religiöse, politische oder philosophische Haltung zu entscheiden.

2. Die Individuen, die den gleichen Glauben, die gleiche Einstellung teilen, haben das Recht, eine Gemeinschaft zu gründen und diese durch die Aufnahme neuer Mitglieder zu vergrößern.

3. Jede Gemeinschaft entscheidet selbst darüber, welche Normen und Werte sie anerkennt, diese deklariert sie gegenüber der Gesellschaft. Auf diese Weise gewinnt jede der einzelnen [religiösen und

weltanschaulichen] [Gruppen-]Identitäten Legalität.

4. Religiöse, kulturelle und rechtliche Autonomie stellen unveräußerliche und unübertragbare Rechte dar. Jede dieser autonomen Gemeinschaften gestaltet ihre Bildungs-, ihre Kultur-, Wirtschafts-, Kunst- und Sportpolitik et cetera nach ihren eigenen Richtlinien und Gesetzen.

Die [so entstehenden] unterschiedlichen Rechtsgemeinschaften oder Sozialen Blöcke bestimmen im Rahmen eines gemeinsamen Vertrages über den öffentlichen Raum, über seine Verwaltung, sowie über [ihre] Rechte und Pflichten. Der Vertrag ist eine Art Verfassung und wie jede Verfassung legt er fest, wie die politische Organisationsform gestaltet wird, wie gemeinsame und nicht trennbare Dienste geleistet werden, wie innere und äußere Sicherheit gewährleistet werden sollen und wie diese Dienste und Einrichtungen zu finanzieren sind.

Der Vertrag kommt durch einvernehmliche Beschlüsse der natürlichen und der gewählten Führer der einzelnen Rechtsgemeinschaften zustande. Erreicht man einen Kompromiß, so wird dieser in den Vertrag aufgenommen, Themen, über die Meinungsverschiedenheiten bestehen, werden dem Binnenrecht der einzelnen Rechtsgemeinschaften überlassen. Keine dieser Gemeinschaften hat das Recht, den anderen ihre Prinzipien und Regelungen zu oktroyieren.

Jede Gruppe hat das Recht, entsprechend ihrer Mitgliederzahl Abgeordnete in die kommunalen und regionalen Vertretungen und ins Parlament zu entsenden. Die Vertreter werden durch Wahl bestimmt.

Zwecks Erfüllung von Diensten für die eigene Gemeinde, aber auch für gemeinsam zu organisierende Aufgaben erhebt jeder der sozialen Blöcke Steuern und teilt diese Einkünfte nach billigem Ermessen zu.

Streitigkeiten und Gerichtsverfahren zwischen den einzelnen Rechtsgemeinschaften werden von einem Sondergericht oder einem Obersten Gericht entschieden, das aus Vertretern der einzelnen rechtlichen Gemeinden besteht. Im Falle einer Einigung über diese Frage, können die streitenden Parteien bestimmen, nach welchem Recht der Prozeß geführt wird. Können sich die Beteiligten nicht einigen, so entscheidet ein 'Oberste Gericht' auch diese Frage.

Solange der Gesellschaftsertrag nicht verletzt oder gegen die Interessen einer anderen Gruppe verstoßen wird, kann jeder soziale Block mit jeder anderen Gruppe zusätzliche Verträge abschließen.

Eine gesellschaftliche und eine staatliche Struktur, die sich unter diesen Vorzeichen bilden, bieten nach Bulaç die Gewähr dafür, daß *Partizipation* und nicht *Herrschaft* ihr grundlegendes Prinzip ist und Gesellschaft und Staat damit aller totalitären und unterdrückerischen Tendenzen ledig sind. Dieses gesellschaftspolitische Projekt sichert die Rechte der verschiedenen kulturellen Gruppierungen und schafft die Grundlagen für ein einträchtiges Zusammenleben.

Man beachte, daß Bulaç und so wie er denkende Intellektuelle den Islam hier nicht als eine übergeordnete Identität präsentieren und ihn der Gesellschaft auch nicht als die offizielle Ideologie zur Stützung einer bestimmten Ordnung vorgeben. In ihrem Konzept sind die Muslime nur einer unter mehreren sozialen Blöcken und nicht berechtigt, über diese zu herrschen.

An diesem Punkt verliert der im traditionellen islamischen Recht zentrale Begriff zimmî (= nicht-muslimischer Untertan) seine Bedeutung. Der traditionelle zimmî-Status hat den Nichtmuslimen [in der Geschichte] zwar weitgehende Rechte und eine gewisse Autonomie verschafft, im Endeffekt jedoch sah er die Herrschaft der Muslime vor. Im Rahmen des zimmî-Ansatzes sind die Muslime oder ihr Staat berechtigt, den Rechten der Nichtmuslime mehr oder weniger enge Grenzen zu ziehen.

Der zimmî-Status war konstitutiv für das im Osmanischen Reich gültige millet-System. In diesem System waren die Muslime die herrschende Schicht bzw. Gruppierung und ihre Religion den anderen Religionen übergeordnet. Das heißt, auch wenn die nach dem millet-System des Osmanischen Reiches organisierte Gesellschaft eine multikulturelle war, ruhte sie doch nicht auf dem Prinzip der *Gleichheit*, sondern auf dem der *Ungleichheit* und auf hierarchischen Beziehungen. Außerdem hatte keine ihrer einzelnen Gruppierungen ein Recht auf politische Mitbestimmung und Partizipation.

Der grundlegende Unterschied zwischen dem Gesellschaftsmodell, daß sich rechtlich an der *Gemeindeordung* orientiert und dem millet-System im Osmanischen Reich, liegt demgemäß in der Ausgestaltung der Beziehungen zu den jeweils anderen.

In den Ländern, die die Muslime friedlich betraten, haben sie im allgemeinen ein auf Verständigung und auf Verträgen basierendes Beziehungsnetz aufgebaut, und sich nicht in das gesellschaftliche und kulturelle Leben der Nichtmuslime eingemischt. Doch die Muslime haben neue Ländereien normalerweise durch die *Erschließung für den Islam* [= Eroberung] gewonnen, weshalb die *Gemeindeordnung,* dieses erste historische Gesellschaftsmodell des Islams, in der Praxis nur selten angewandt wurde und in der sozialhistorischen Praxis der Muslime keine größeren Spuren hinterlassen hat. In der Regel kam deshalb das auf das Kriegsrecht zurückgehende zimmî-Recht zur Anwendung. Geprägt von der schweren Last des geschichtlichen Erbes, vermochten es die muslimischen Politiker und Intellektuellen in moderner Zeit deshalb nicht, ein originäres politisches Regierungs- und Staatsmodell zu entwickeln. Dies ist der Grund dafür, daß sie sich noch heute gezwungen sehen, sich zwischen geschichtlichen und traditionellen Modellen einerseits und westlichen Modellen andererseits zu entscheiden.

Dabei bietet das pluralistische Gesellschaftsmodell den Muslimen eine neue Lösung an. In den heterogenen muslimischen Gesellschaften gewinnt dieses Modell heute, da sich der Nationalstaat in einer schweren Krise befindet, stark an Attraktivität.

Der Sufismus als philosophischer Hintergrund des islamischen Pluralismus

Die islamischen Intellektuellen, die in der Türkei das pluralistische Gesellschaftsprojekt befürworten, legitimieren ihre Vorstellungen nicht nur mit den sozio-historischen Erfahrungen des Islams, sondern führen auch den Koran als Beleg an. In diesem Sinne verstehen sie die Akzeptierung von Unterschiedlichkeit und den Respekt vor ihr als notwendige Anerkennung des göttlichen Willens.

Der Koran lehrt, daß die Menschen als Mann und Frau geschaffen wurden und daß alle Menschen von diesem Paare abstammen. Nach Koran (49:13)[6] entstanden neue Völkerschaften und ihre Religionen dadurch, daß sich die ersten Generationen gespalten und sich an-

[6] [Sure 49: Die Gemächer, Vers 13: "Ihr Menschen, wir haben euch geschaffen (indem wir euch) von einem männlichen und einem weiblichen Wesen (abstammen ließen), und wir haben euch zu Verbänden und Stämmen gemacht, damit ihr euch (auf Grund der genealogischen Verhältnisse) untereinander kennt. Als der Vornehmste gilt bei Gott derjenige von euch, der am frömmsten ist." Deutsche Übersetzung nach Rudi Paret, *Der Koran*, Kohlhammer, Stuttgart u.a. 1979]

schließend unterschiedlich entwickelt haben. Daß sich Menschen in Sprache und Hautfarbe unterscheiden, ist demnach gleichfalls *Ausdruck* des göttlichen Willens, *Zeichen* des göttlichen Willens (Koran 30:22)[7].

Der in diesem Koran-Vers verwendete Begriff ayet [Gottes-Zeichen, mit dem im Türkischen die einzelnen Verse des Korans bezeichnet werden], steht im Arabischen für *Anzeichen, Hinweis, Beweis, Indikator.* Sowohl die *Zeichen* im Koran selbst [d.h. seine einzelnen Verse] als auch die *Zeichen* der Außenwelt [= die Schöpfung] symbolisieren die Existenz Gottes. Das heißt, wir können mit Ihm auf zweifache Weise in Verbindung treten: indem wir die uns gesandte heilige Schrift lesen oder indem wir den Kosmos studieren, die Schöpfung, die uns quasi ein zweites Buch für die Erkenntnis Gottes ist.

Der Grund, weshalb Gott die Gesellschaft in verschiedene Völker und Gruppen gesondert hat, ist, daß sie nur so einander kennenlernen können (Koran 49:13). Das heißt, nur wo Unterschiedlichkeit besteht, ist gegenseitiges Kennenlernen möglich.

Ist die Vielfältigkeit Ausdruck des göttlichen Willens, ist es natürlich unumgänglich, diese auch anzuerkennen. Auch der Koran geht ganz natürlich von der Tatsache aus, daß Menschen unterschiedlicher Religion, Hautfarbe, Sprache und Kultur sind. Demgemäß akzeptiert der Koran keinen Zwang im Wege zum Heil und duldet keine religiöse Unterdrückung (2:256)[8].

Nach dem Koran steht *Religion* für eine bestimmte *Art zu leben*, für eine bestimmte *Lebensweise*. In diesem Sinne sind auch Ideologien, kulturelle- und andere Glaubensrichtungen *Religion*, sind Kategorien, die an ihre Stelle treten können. Die Menschen wählen ihre Religion bzw. ihre Überzeugung und sind verantwortlich für ihre Wahl (Koran 18:29)[9] .

Darüber hinaus hat Vielfältigkeit für den Koran noch eine weitere

---

7 [Sure 30: Die Byzantiner, Vers 20: "Und zu Seinen Zeichen gehört es, daß Er euch aus Erde geschaffen hat. Hierauf waret ihr auf einmal Menschen, die sich (...auf der Erde) ausbreiteten.)]

8 [Sure 2: Die Kuh, Vers 256: "In der Religion gibt es keinen Zwang (d.h. man kann niemanden zum (rechten) Glauben zwingen.) Der rechte Weg ist (durch die Verkündigung des Islam) klar geworden (so daß er sich) vor der Verirrung (des heidnischen Unglaubens deutlich abhebt.]

9 [Sure 18: Die Höhle, Vers 29: Und sag: (Es ist) die Wahrheit (die) von eurem Herrn (kommt). Wer nun will, möge glauben, und wer will möge nicht glauben! ...]

positive Seite. Sie ermöglicht den Wettstreit der Menschen im *Tun von Gutem*; in diesem Wettstreit müssen die Menschen sich bewähren (Koran 5:48)[10]. Dieser Wettstreit ist darüberhinaus die Quelle für die intra- und intergesellschaftliche Entwicklung.

Innerhalb der islamischen Tradition kommt das sich auf den Koran beziehende Pluralismus-Verständnis am bestem im Sufismus zum Ausdruck. Zahlreiche Fragen, die in der islamischen Geistesgeschichte und in der Philosophie keine Lösung gefunden haben, werden im Sufismus auf einer höheren und abstrakteren Ebene beantwortet. Selbst heute ist der Sufismus eine nicht versiegende Quelle, eine Anschauung, die Licht auf zahlreiche Angelegenheiten zu werfen vermag.

Für die Art und Weise der Auseinandersetzung des Sufismus' mit der Realität steht die Wendung *Einheit in Pluralität* (kesrette vahdet), die besagt: Die Erscheinungen der Außenwelt sind vielfältig, ihr Wesen jedoch ist eins.

Das Realitätsverständnis des Sufismus hat einen paradoxen Zug. Diesem Verständnis nach hat die Realität zwei Ebenen: Die eine ist *offenbar* (zahir), die andere ist *verborgen* (batın). Besonders seit der Positivismus der Wissenschaft seinen Stempel aufgedrückt hat, leugnet die moderne Welt die Existenz der zweiten (batınî) Ebene und beschränkt Wirklichkeit auf die wahrnehmbare Ebene. Der modernen Welt sind nur materielle, wahrnehmbare und messende Kriterien von Bedeutung, der Rest ist ihr Metaphysik und Spekulation.

Dabei besteht ein großes Paradox zwischen der Manifestation von Wirklichkeit und ihrem Ursprung. In der materiellen Welt erscheint alles als vielfältig und voneinander losgelöst, doch auf der verborgenen Ebene stellt sich die Wirklichkeit vollkommen anders dar. Die scheinbare Beziehungslosigkeit und Vielfalt ist in Wirklichkeit Zeichen für eine Einheit, die eine gemeinsame Wurzel hat. Beispiel für diesen Sachverhalt ist das Bild vom Baum. Seine Äste und Blätter vermitteln aufs Erste einen Eindruck von Vielfältigkeit und Verschiedenheit, ein Eindruck, der jedoch nur oberflächlich und äußerlich ist. Denn Zweige und Äste vereinigen sich im Stamm, aus dem sie her-

10 [Sure 5:Der Tisch: Vers 48: "... Und wenn Gott gewollt hätte, hätte er euch zu einer einzigen Gemeinschaft gemacht. Aber er (teilte euch in verschiedene [Glaubens] Gemeinschaften auf und) wolle euch (so) in dem, was er euch (d.h. jeder Gruppe von euch) (von der Offenbarung) gegeben hat auf die Probe stellen. Wetteifert nun nach den guten Dingen! ...]

vorgehen.

So ist es auch mit dem *Baum des Lebens*. Die Vielfalt, die sich in der Welt zeigt, wird in Gott, der sie geschaffen hat, zur Einheit. Im Sufismus ist die Welt nichts von Gott Losgelöstes. Die Beziehung der Welt zu Gott gleicht der der Sonne zum Licht. Wie das Licht aus der Sonne so entspringt die materielle Welt aus Gott. Licht und Sonne sind weder dasselbe, noch sind sie losgelöst voneinander. Genauso ist die Welt weder eins mit Gott, noch ist sie von ihm getrennt. Auf diese Weise löst der Sufismus zahlreiche Fragen, auf die die islamische Geistesgeschichte und andere philosophischen Traditionen keine Antwort gaben. Einige Philosophien und Religionen betrachteten die Welt und Gott als Einheit und gelangten zum Pantheismus, andere lösten Gott vollkommen von der Welt, beraubten sie damit göttlichen Lichts, göttlicher Erleuchtung und gelangten zum Deismus. Diese Haltung fand ihren Ausdruck in der Newtonschen Kosmologie und der Betrachtungsweise der modernen Welt. Sie vergleicht die Welt mit einer Uhr, die von einem Uhrmacher zusammengesetzt und danach sich selbst überlassen wurde: das Universum stammt von der Hand Gottes, aber seine Bewegungen sind unabhängig von Ihm.

Auch wenn der Sufismus seinen Ausdruck vorwiegend auf ontologischem und theologischem Gebiet fand, können seine Einsichten auch auf die Bereiche der Epistemologie und der Soziologie übertragen werden. Sie eröffnen uns eine vollkommen neue Perspektive, die es uns erlaubt, Fragen zuzulassen und zu lösen, die in den Paradigmen von Pluralismus und Monismus innerhalb der westlichen Philosophie unbeantwortet geblieben sind. Darauf kommen wir später zurück. An dieser Stelle ist nur anzumerken, daß der Sufismus weder schlicht von einer *Einheit* noch einfach von einer *Vielfalt* ausgeht. Die Lehre des Sufismus kann auf die Formel *Vielfalt in Einheit* oder *Einheit in Vielfalt* gebracht werden.

Diese Sichtweise gestattet es beispielsweise weder, den Begriff *Familie* soziologisch auf eine soziale Einheit von Mutter und Vater zu reduzieren; noch erlaubt sie es, die Familie als bloße Vielheit von Individuen zu betrachten. Die Familie ist sowohl Einheit als auch Vielheit. Also *Einheit in Vielheit*. Begeben wir uns von diesem Punkt aus auf die Reise, so ist die gesamte Menschheitsfamilie (ethnisch, religiös, sprachlich etc.) trotz aller Vielfältigkeit eine Einheit. Denn verfolgt man sie bis zu ihrem Ursprung, so erkennt man, daß sie sich in der einer Mutter und dem einen Vaters vereinen.

Pluralismus und Islam in Westeuropa

In der Auseinandersetzung mit den in Westeuropa diskutierten Fragen zur Multikulturalität wird die Originalität der Formel *Vielfalt in Einheit* oder *Einheit in Vielfalt*, die allgemein im Islam und speziell im Sufismus ihre Wurzel hat, deutlich. Der Begriff *Multikulturalität* wird in der westlichen Literatur unterschiedlich verwendet, doch läßt sich, was er faßt, unter zwei Überschriften zusammenzufassen:

Die deskriptive Verwendung des Begriffs:

Bei der deskriptiven Verwendung des Begriffs steht er für die Zuwanderung [von Arbeitsmigranten] in die westlichen Länder und für die sich daraus entwickelnde gesellschaftliche Situation faktischer Multikulturalität. Der Begriff *multikulturell* soll in diesem Zusammenhang Ausdruck dafür sein, daß ein auf gegenseitigem Respekt basierendes Zusammenleben existiere und daß verschiedene kulturelle und religiöse Systeme nebeneinander beständen.

Die gesellschaftliche Wirklichkeit sieht allerdings vollkommen anders aus, und von einem gleichberechtigten Austausch der verschiedenen Gruppen, insbesondere der Einheimischen und der Zugewanderten, kann ebensowenig die Rede sein, wie von einer generellen Toleranz der Einheimischen den Einwanderern gegenüber.

Stattdessen versucht die einheimische Bevölkerung, das große Gefälle, das hinsichtlich Einfluß und Status zwischen ihr und den Neuhinzukommenden besteht, zu verdecken und verwendet dazu und zwecks Schaffung eines positives Selbstbildes sehr häufig den Begriff *Multikulturalismus*. Das heißt, wichtiger als der tatsächliche Sinngehalt des Begriffes ist in diesem Zusammenhang seine Funktionalität. Der Begriff *Multikulturalität* verkommt hier zum Klischee. Diese Verwendung des Begriffs verdeckt die Realität und begrenzt unseren Horizont.

Die normative Verwendung des Begriffs:

Bei der normativen Verwendung des Begriffs geht es eher darum, was sein sollte, als darum, was tatsächlich ist. In diesem Sinne wird festgestellt, daß es momentan so etwas wie Multikulturalität nicht gibt, daß sie jedoch nicht nur realisierbar, sondern auch notwendig ist. In einer multikulturellen Gesellschaft herrscht zwischen den unterschiedlichen Gruppierungen Gleichberechtigung und gegenseitige Akzeptanz. Um diese zu erreichen, um ein neues Verhältnis zwischen Einheimischen und Zuwanderern zu konstituieren, ist bewußtes politisches Handeln notwendig. Dieses politische Handeln sollte die Aufhebung der Benachteiligung von Migranten zum Ziel haben und die rassistischen und [fremden-]feindlichen Tendenzen unter der einheimischen Bevölkerung bekämpfen.

Die Verfechter einer so verstandenen multikulturellen Gesellschaft erklären die ungünstige gesellschaftliche Lage von Minderheiten mit ihrer Ausgrenzung durch die einheimische Bevölkerung und sind insofern Antirassisten. Sie glauben, daß die Probleme der Minderheiten nicht durch deren Verhalten und deren Einstellungen entstehen, sondern durch das Handeln der gesellschaftlichen Institutionen und durch die nur schwer änderbaren Vorurteile der Mehrheit. Minderheitenpolitik müsse von der Bekämpfung dieser Vorurteile ihren Ausgang nehmen. Solange ein ungleiches Kräfteverhältnis zwischen Zuwanderern und Einheimischen existiert, solange sei eine multikulturelle Gesellschaft nicht zu etablieren.

Bei einer normativen Verwendung des Begriffs Multikulturalität ist nicht davon auszugehen, daß diese große Zustimmung findet. Das genaue Gegenteil ist momentan der Fall, und die Auseinandersetzung zwischen den Verfechtern von Multikulturalität und ihren Widersachern hält an.

Die Pluralisten, die der Multikulturalität positiv gegenüberstehen, sehen Vielfalt als Bereicherung für die Gesellschaft und betonen, daß Unterschiede akzeptiert werden müssen. Auch wenn es innerhalb der Vertreter einer Politik der gegenseitigen Akzeptanz unterschiedliche Standpunkte gibt, lehnen sie es im allgemeinen ab, eine Kultur über eine andere zu stellen und ihre Ausgangsposition ist die Gleichwertigkeit der Kulturen.

An diesem Punkt werden die Pluralisten jedoch mit einer ernsten Frage konfrontiert: Wenn die Gleichwertigkeit der verschiedenen Kulturen [die bisweilen einander entgegengesetze Wertvorstellungen verteidigen], anerkannt wird, wie [in Bezug auf welche Werte] sollen dann [zwischen-]kulturelle Auseinandersetzungen gelöst werden? Die Universalisten [die glauben, daß die Werte einer bestimmten Kultur -- meist die der Mehrheit -- universelle Werte darstellen], plädieren für ein Über- und Unterordnungsverhältnis zwischen den Kulturen, und dafür, daß kulturelle Auseinandersetzungen in diesem Rahmen zu behandeln seien. Sie nutzen den Zwiespalt der Pluralisten aus und behaupten, daß gesellschaftlicher Pluralismus nur Chaos, Bindungslosigkeit und [moderne] Stammes-Auseinandersetzungen produziere.

Sie vertreten die Meinung, daß in einer Gesellschaft, in der unterschiedliche Kulturen und Religionen existieren, nicht die Akzeptanz der Unterschiede erforderlich sei, sondern Einigkeit und Geschlossenheit. Statt einer Politik gegenseitiger Akzeptanz verfechten sie die altbekannte Integrationspolitik. In ihren Augen bedeutet die Existenz verschiedener kultureller Gruppen primär Bedrohung. Sie glauben, es sei unmöglich, daß Kulturen unterschiedlicher Entwicklung miteinander harmonieren und sehen die Lösung darin, "niedere Kulturen" "höheren Kulturen" unterzuordnen. Mit anderen Worten, um eine stabile Gesellschaft zu schaffen, sei die Assimilierung der Neuankömmlinge unausweichlich.

Daß sich Pluralisten und Universalisten in dieser theoretischen und politischen Auseinandersetzung einigen, ist mehr als unwahrscheinlich. Auffällig ist, daß Pluralisten mit Begriffen wie Vielfalt oder Variantenreichtum (kesret) hantieren, während Universalisten mit völlig gegensätzlichen Begriffen wie Einheit oder Geschlossenheit (vahdet) argumentieren. Während die ersteren Unterschiedlichkeit preisen, unterschätzen sie — bewußt oder unbewußt — das Bedürfnis der Gesellschaft nach Ausgleich und Kompromiß. Die zweite Gruppe hingegen ruft ihre eigene Kultur als Hochkultur und damit als universell gültig aus, schlägt so eine ethnozentrische Richtung ein und grenzt die Anderen aus.

An diesem Punkte scheint es notwendig, sowohl die Einheits- als auch die Pluralismus-Ideologie durch eine solche zu ersetzen, die ein Gleichgewicht zwischen Einheit und Vielheit schafft; durch eine Ideologie der *Einheit in der Vielheit*. Die Funktion einer solchen Orientierung kann durch folgende Begriffspaare ausgedrückt werden: *Allgemeine* und *spezifische Identität* oder *gesellschaftliche* und *individuelle* bzw. *gruppenspezifische Identität*.

Die allgemeine bzw. gesellschaftliche Identität [des Individuums] ist das Ergebnis eines gesellschaftlichen Kompromisses, sie ist die Identität, die von den verschiedenen Gruppen innerhalb einer Gesellschaft geteilt wird. Einfach ausgedrückt, sie ist das Dach der Gesellschaft und steht für den gemeinsam geteilten öffentlichen Raum. In demokratischen Gesellschaften findet diese allgemeine bzw. gesellschaftliche Identität ihren Ausdruck in der Verfassung. Um eine Basis für die Verständigung mit anderen zu schaffen und ihre [jeweils spezifische] Gruppenidentität zu schützen, müssen alle Individuen einer Gesellschaft einen gemeinsamen Nenner finden. Die individuelle bzw gruppenspezifische Identität hingegen gehört in das Reich der Unterschiedlichkeiten, wo Vielfalt existiert.

Die multikulturelle Gesellschaft ist eine Gesellschaft, in der die verschiedenen Gruppen sich zwar organisieren aber ihre eigene Identität dadurch wahren, daß sie sich auf einen gemeinsamen Nenner einigen. In einer solchen Gesellschaft entsteht das Modell von der Einheit in der Vielheit. Als das System, das die größtmögliche Chance zur Vertretung und Teilnahme bietet, ist die Demokratie für den Prozeß der Bestimmung des gemeinsamen Nenners unverzichtbare Voraussetzung. In einer Gesellschaft in der die [politischen] Beziehungen nicht durch Partizipation, sondern durch Herrschaft gekennzeichnet sind, ist kulturelle Pluralität im normativen Sinne nicht möglich. Wir können dies auch andersherum formulieren: In Ländern, in denen zwischen Einheimischen und Zuwanderern keine gleichberechtigte Beziehungen bestehen, kann von wahrer Demokratie nicht die Rede sein.

Konsequenzen für die Lage der muslimischen Migranten in der westeuropäischen Diaspora

Betrachten wir die nun die Lage der Migranten in Westeuropa vor diesem Hintergrund:

Nachdem die Gastarbeiter in Europa ihren Gästestatus überwanden, ergaben sich zwischen der einheimischen Bevölkerung und den Zuwanderern ernste Fragen hinsichtlich des Zusammenlebens. Mit dem Verlassen ihrer Heimatländer erlebten die Zuwanderer eine Erosion ihrer allgemeinen oder gesellschaftlichen Identität. So war *Türkischsprechen* z.B. für die Türken in ihrer Heimat eine allen gemeinsame, spontane Handlung, während der Gebrauch des Türkischen in Europa diese Eigenschaft verlor und jetzt dem Bereich der individuellen oder gruppenspezifischen Identität zugehörte. An dieser Stelle wurden die Migranten mit einer doppelten Fragestellung konfrontiert: Wie sollten sie ihre eigene Identität bewahren, und welchen gemeinsamen Nenner würden sie mit der Gesellschaft der Einheimischen finden.

Sollte es nicht gelingen, zwischen diesen beiden Identitäten eine tragfähige Beziehung zu schaffen, werden schnell neue Probleme entstehen. Weder die Nivellierung der gruppenspezifischen Identität der Zuwanderer, sprich ihre Assimilation, noch der Versuch auf Seiten der Einwanderer, z.B. der Türken, ihre gruppenspezifische Identität als ihre allgemeine bzw. gesellschaftliche Identität zu verstehen, trägt zur Lösung der Probleme bei. Assimilation steht den Interessen der Einwanderer entgegen und entsprechende Versuche sind gegen alle Menschenrechte. Die türkische Identität als quasi *allgemeine Identität der türkischen Migranten* der Identität der Mehrheitsgesellschaft gegenüberzustellen, bringt nicht nur unlösbare Probleme mit dieser Gesellschaft mit sich, sondern verletzt auch deren Rechte. Kurz gesagt, politischer Druck oder gar Zwang sollten weder von *oben nach unten* noch von *unten nach oben* ausgeübt werden. Was tun?

Die europäischen Länder sollten als erstes die gruppenspezifische Identität der Türken und der anderen Ausländer und Minderheiten akzeptieren. Im Gegenzug haben sie das Recht zu verlangen, daß diese sich auf eine [davon unterschiedliche] allgemeine oder gesellschaftliche Identität einlassen. Dies ist eine Last, die den Minderheiten im Rahmen der sogenannten Integrationspolitik zufällt. Das heißt, die Erlangung von Rechten impliziert auch die Übernahme von Pflichten. In diesem Falle verliert Integrationspolitik ihre assimilatorischen Züge, die für die Migranten zum Albtraum geworden ist.

Allerdings ergibt sich im Hinblick auf die von allen geteilte gemeinsame Identität ein ernsthaftes Problem: Sie darf sich zu keiner Zeit zu einer *herrschenden Identität* entwickeln. Anders ausgedrückt, die von allen geteilte *gemeinsame Identität* ist nicht etwas was einfach da ist und übernommen werden muß, sondern etwas, das von Einheimischen und Zuwanderern erst hervorgebracht und errichtet wird. In einer demokratischen Gesellschaft bedeutet dies, daß den Minderheiten vollkommene Partizipation ermöglicht und gesellschaftlicher Konsens neu definiert wird. Dies ist ein Prozeß, und innerhalb dieses Prozesses müssen die Einheimischen den Migranten gewissen Vorteile gewähren und gewisse Zugeständnisse machen. Aber diese Vorteile und Zugeständnisse sollten [von der Mehrheitsgesellschaft] nicht als Verlust empfunden werden. Denn nur im Gegenzug auf diese Gewährungen werden die Zuwanderer sich auf eine von allen geteilte gemeinsame Identität einlassen und nur so wird es möglich sein, in Frieden miteinander zu leben. Andernfalls wird das Ergebnis nicht eine multikulturelle Gesellschaft sein, sondern ein Krieg der Kulturen und der Zivilisationen.

Es ist offensichtlich, daß wir heute neue Perspektiven und neue Modelle brauchen. Die herkömmliche Integrationspolitik ist einseitig auf gesellschaftliche Geschlossenheit und damit auf die Frage der allgemeinen bzw. gesellschaftlichen Identität fixiert. Um eine pluralistische Gesellschaft zu konstituieren, bedarf es jedoch einer Politik der gegenseitigen Akzeptanz. Nur so können die Belange der Zuwanderer geschützt und nur so kann die Schaffung einer multikulturellen Gesellschaft vorangetrieben werden, die sich auch die Erhaltung und den Ausbau der gruppenspezifischen Identitäten zum Ziele setzt.

Eine Herausforderung an christliche Theologie

Muslimische Migranten in Deutschland (das Beispiel der katholischen Kirche)

Georg Stoll
MISEREOR, Frankfurt

Die gesellschaftlich spürbare Präsenz von Muslimen in einem westeuropäischen Land wie Deutschland ist eine historische Begegnungssituation, für die es noch keine Modelle gibt und die alle Beteiligten vor neue Herausforderungen stellt. Zwar lassen sich in Deutschland einzelne muslimische Gruppen bis in die erste Hälfte des 18. Jahrhunderts zurückverfolgen,[1] doch blieben diese Gruppen und Gemeinden gesellschaftlich unauffällige Randerscheinungen. Von einer muslimischen Präsenz in relevanter Größenordnung läßt sich erst seit den sechziger Jahren dieses Jahrhunderts sprechen, als Arbeitsmigranten über bilaterale Anwerbeverträge auch aus islamisch geprägten Ländern und Regionen wie der Türkei, Marokko, Tunesien und den bosnischen Landesteilen des damaligen Jugoslawiens nach Deutschland kamen. Weiteren Zuwachs in beträchtlichem Ausmaß hat die muslimische Wohnbevölkerung in Deutschland zudem durch Flüchtlinge aus Ländern wie Afghanistan, dem Iran, Algerien, der Türkei oder Bosnien erhalten.

Die Migration und die migrationsbedingte Präsenz des Islams in Deutschland stellt an Christentum und Kirchen zwar keine gänzlich neuen Fragen und Anforderungen. Sie verschärft jedoch die Dringlichkeit der Auseinandersetzung mit einigen grundlegenden Fragestellungen im Zusammenhang mit dem eigenen religiösen Selbstverständ-

[1] Hier folge ich Abdullah, der 1981 die erste zusammenfassende Geschichte des Islams in Deutschland vorgelegt hat: M. S. Abdullah, *Geschichte des Islams in Deutschland*, Graz 1981.

nis. Es sind dies, so die Grundhypothese der folgenden Ausführungen:

- die Fragestellung des Fremden,
- die Fragestellung der Säkularität,
- die Fragestellung von Universalität und Partikularität.

Diese drei Fragestellungen sollen im folgenden näher umrissen werden. Dabei geht es nicht um die spezifischen Inhalte und Voraussetzungen eines christlich-islamischen Dialogs auf der Ebene der zentralen Glaubensaussagen dieser beiden Religionen oder vor dem Hintergrund ihrer gemeinsamen Geschichte. Es geht nicht um die Herausforderungen an die christliche Theologie durch den Islam allgemein, sondern um die Herausforderungen, die sich konkret durch die migrationsbedingte Präsenz des Islams in Deutschland seit einigen Jahren stellen.

Katholische Stellungnahmen zum Islam in Deutschland

Bevor die drei genannten Fragestellungen im einzelnen behandelt werden, zunächst ein kurzer Überblick über einschlägige offizielle Dokumente der Katholischen Kirche (auf die ich mich in diesem Beitrag beschränke). Die hier interessierenden Texte der Katholischen Kirche lassen sich in zwei Gruppen einteilen: Texte, die explizit auf die oben genannten Fragestellungen eingehen, sowie Texte, die explizit die migrationsbedingte Präsenz des Islams in Deutschland thematisieren. Texte der ersten Gruppe werde ich in ihrem jeweiligen Zusammenhang behandeln. Die wichtigsten Texte der zweiten Gruppe sollen im folgenden kurz vorgestellt werden. Es handelt sich dabei um zwei Veröffentlichungen in der Reihe der "Arbeitshilfen", die vom Sekretariat der Deutschen Bischofskonferenz herausgegeben wird. Die spätere der beiden Broschüren aus dem Jahr 1993 stellt dabei eine vollständig überarbeitete Aktualisierung der früheren aus dem Jahr 1982 dar. Beide Texte wenden sich ausdrücklich in erster Linie an die pastoralen Mitarbeiter und Mitarbeiterinnen der katholischen Kirche in Deutschland.

Die Arbeitshilfe von 1982

Als im Juni 1982 die Broschüre "Muslime in Deutschland" erschien, war es das erste Mal, daß sich ein längerer Text unter Mitverantwortung der Kirchenleitung ausdrücklich und ausschließlich dieses Themas annahm.[2] Zuvor hatte es nur einzelne sporadische Äußerungen, etwa im Zusammenhang mit der Frage religionsverschiedener Ehen oder dem Thema "Fremdenangst", gegeben. Sogar die Gemeinsame Synode der Bistümer in der Bundesrepublik Deutschland, die Anfang der siebziger Jahre im Anschluß an das Zweite Vatikanische Konzil in Würzburg tagte, erwähnte den Islam nur mit einem einzigen Satz. Das ist umso erstaunlicher, als der Synodenbeschluß "Der ausländische Arbeitnehmer — eine Frage an die Kirche und die Gesellschaft", in dessen Zusammenhang dieses Motto auftaucht, Ende 1973 verabschiedet wurde, genau in dem Jahr also, in dem die Bundesregierung den sogenannten Anwerbestopp verfügte. Allein die Zahl der türkischen Staatsbürger, die in Deutschland lebten, belief sich damals bereits auf 910 500 (1961: 6 500; 1969: 322 400).

Das kurze Vorwort der Arbeitshilfe benennt die Zielgruppen und die Absicht der Publikation. Das von einer bischöflichen Kommission erstellte Dokument hatte von Anfang an "Pfarrer und Gemeinden" als Adressaten im Blick. Von daher bestimmen sich auch seine Ziele: "Die Arbeitshilfe 'Muslime in Deutschland' soll einmal informieren und Verständnis wecken, zum anderen aber auch auf einige Probleme aufmerksam machen." (S. 5) Als Beispiel für mögliche Problemfelder werden Mischehen und katholische Kindergärten erwähnt. Im letzten Abschnitt weist das Vorwort schließlich darauf hin, daß sich die Arbeitshilfe "bewußt auf theologische Fragen" beschränkt habe. Sie signalisiert jedoch, daß sie sich trotz dieser Einschränkung der Vielfalt des islamischen Lebens bewußt ist.

Auf das editorische Vorwort folgen sieben Kapitel, in denen sich drei inhaltliche Schwerpunkte ausmachen lassen:

- eine kleine Islamkunde unter besonderer Berücksichtigung des Islams in Deutschland (v.a. in Kapitel 2, aber auch in den Kapiteln 1, 3 und 4);

2 Die evangelische Kirche hatte bereits acht Jahre früher mit einer Handreichung unter dem Titel *Moslems in der Bundesrepublik* auf die Situation reagiert.

- historische, theologische und pragmatische Überlegungen zum Verhältnis von Christentum und Islam (v.a. in Kapitel 3, aber auch in den Kapiteln 4 und 5);

- konkrete Probleme und mögliche Lösungsansätze, (v.a. in den Kapiteln 4 und 5, aber auch in den Kapiteln 1, 2 und 3).

"Fremde" in der Arbeitshilfe von 1982

Die Verknüpfung von islamischer Präsenz in Deutschland und Arbeitsmigration ist für den Text von 1982 ein bestimmender Zusammenhang. Die Arbeitsmigration hat den Islam in seiner jetzigen Größe und Gestalt nach Deutschland gebracht. Die Arbeitshilfe hält deshalb die Präsenz des Islams in Deutschland für ein ebenso unumkehrbares Faktum wie die Migration. Die Verknüpfung von Islam und Arbeitsmigration aber bringe es mit sich, daß gegenwärtig ein Muslim in Deutschland in aller Regel zugleich als Fremder und als "Gastarbeiter" wahrgenommen werde (S. 32). Dieser Zusammenhang von Zugehörigkeit zur islamischen Gemeinschaft und von Fremdheit könne sogar einen Teil der islamischen Identität in Deutschland selbst ausmachen. Jedenfalls beobachtet die Arbeitshilfe in ihrem Abschnitt "Gegenwärtige Aufbrüche" eine Selbststilisierung des Islams als Religion "der Fremden und Unterdrückten" in bewußtem Kontrast zum Christentum, das "als Religion der Weißen, der Sieger und der Unterdrücker" etikettiert werde (S. 23).

Die Koinzidenz in der Wahrnehmung von "Muslim" und "Fremder" wird, so die Arbeitshilfe, noch dadurch weiter verstärkt, daß eine Unterscheidung zwischen religiösen und kulturellen Aspekten gerade beim Volksislam kaum möglich sei. Die Broschüre führt das am Beispiel patriarchaler Familienvorstellungen aus (S. 12 und 19). Kulturelle Fremdheit kann somit unmittelbar auf die andersartige Religionszugehörigkeit übertragen werden, sowohl in der Wahrnehmung durch muslimische Migranten selbst als auch in der Wahrnehmung durch nichtmuslimische Deutsche. Entgegen ihrer Anfangsbemerkung, sich auf theologische Fragestellungen beschränken zu wollen, nimmt die Broschüre den Islam und die Präsenz von Muslimen in Deutschland in erster Linie als eine soziale und nicht als eine religiöse Herausforderung wahr. Die islamische Religionszugehörigkeit interessiert primär nicht als solche, sondern nur insofern, als sie einen weiteren und besonders schwierigen Aspekt der Fremdheit dieser Migranten darstellt. Klammert man die Frage der Mischehe einmal aus, so nehmen die diakonische Sorge für Migranten und die dabei auftauchenden Probleme deutlich mehr Raum ein als die religiösen Herausforderungen und Chancen der Begegnung von Christen und Muslimen.

"Säkularität" in der Arbeitshilfe von 1982

Hinsichtlich der säkularen Grundlage der deutschen Gesellschaft zeichnet die Arbeitshilfe von 1982 eine gewisse Unbestimmtheit aus. Einerseits setzt der Text eine klare Trennung von Religion und Politik für Deutschland voraus und scheint sie auch -- gegen die islamische Tradition -- zu bejahen; andererseits sucht er im Islam einen Verbündeten für das Christentum, um dem gemeinsamen Bekenntnis zu Gott auch im öffentlichen Leben Gehör und Wirksamkeit zu verschaffen. Gelegentlich erscheint die säkulare Gesellschaft als eine Art gemeinsamer Bedrohung für Christen und Muslime (S. 31 und 33). Wie das Verhältnis von Säkularität, öffentlich gelebtem religiösen Bekenntnis und Dialog zwischen verschiedenen Bekenntnissen aussehen soll, darüber schweigt das Papier.

"Universalität und Partikularität" in der Arbeitshilfe von 1982

Die zunehmend stärkere quantitative Präsenz einer Religion, die ebenso universale Geltungsansprüche erhebt wie das Christentum, konfrontiert die Kirchen in Deutschland auf neue Weise mit der Frage, wie sie die Universalität der Geltungsansprüche ihrer eigenen Glaubensaussagen mit der Partikularität der Kirchen vermitteln können. Dieses Problem wird in der Arbeitshilfe von 1982 zwar angedeutet, aber nicht ausgeführt. Das Kapitel "Christentum und Islam" geht zwar ausführlich auf den Begriff des "Dialogs" als zentraler Kategorie für eine theologische Neubewertung nichtchristlicher Religionen und damit auch des Islams ein, wie er vor allem im Gefolge des Zweiten Vatikanischen Konzils entwickelt wurde. Wo und wie eine Grenze zwischen ernsthaftem Dialog einerseits und den eigenen religiösen Geltungsansprüchen andererseits zu ziehen ist, wird jedoch nicht deutlich. Diese Unsicherheit teilt der Text freilich mit anderen kirchlichen Dokumenten zu diesem Thema, die er zitiert.

Bezeichnend für diesen Umstand ist beispielsweise, daß häufig von "Achtung" oder sogar "Hochachtung" die Rede ist, mit denen Christen den Muslimen begegnen sollen, solche Aussagen in Bezug auf den Islam selbst aber vermieden werden. In der pragmatischen Ausrichtung der Arbeitshilfe, die sich für das alltägliche Zusammenleben von Christen und Muslimen in Deutschland interessiert, mag diese verdeckte Unterscheidung zwischen Muslimen und Islam eine geringe Rolle spielen. Sie wird allerdings auch auf der lebenspraktischen Ebene spürbar. Denn während insgesamt die Rolle der katholischen Kirche gegenüber den muslimischen Arbeitsmigranten in der Arbeitshilfe als "Anwalt der Fremden" dargestellt wird, kann sie doch in eine Verteidigungshaltung umschlagen, wenn sensible Punkte berührt werden, bei denen die eigene religiöse Identität auf dem Spiele stehen könnte. Die wichtigsten Bereiche, bei denen das in der Arbeitshilfe deutlich wird, sind Mischehe und Schule bzw. Kindergarten. Ob ich Andersgläubige als schutzbedürftige Fremde oder als bedrohliche Konkurrenten oder in einer anderen Form wahrnehme, ist für einen "Dialog" von entscheidender Bedeutung. Die Wahrnehmung selbst aber hängt von der Antwort auf die Frage nach der Verhältnisbestimmung von Universalität und Partikularität meines eigenen Glaubens ab. Die Arbeitshilfe läßt diese Frage nicht nur unbeantwortet, sondern weicht ihr sogar aus.

Die "Arbeitshilfe" von 1993

Knapp elf Jahre nach der Arbeitshilfe von 1982 erschien unter dem Titel "Christen und Muslime in Deutschland. Eine pastorale Handreichung" eine vollständig überarbeitete Neufassung. Ziel und Zielgruppe der Broschüre werden bereits durch ihren Untertitel "Eine pastorale Handreichung" angedeutet. Das Vorwort benennt beides ausdrücklich: Die Schrift wende sich an alle "für den Umgang mit Muslimen Verantwortlichen" (S. 5). Im einzelnen werden Seelsorger, Erzieherinnen, Lehrerinnen und Lehrer aufgeführt. Als Ziel gibt das Vorwort neben der Vertiefung und Anpassung der alten Arbeitshilfe an, "die nötigen

Kenntnisse über den Islam zu vermitteln und Hinweise zu geben, wie in den verschiedenen Bereichen das Miteinander in Grundsatztreue und in Respekt voreinander gelebt werden kann." (S. 5)

Wenn damit Ziele und Adressaten insgesamt mit denen der Vorgängerbroschüre übereinstimmen, so ist doch eine Akzentverschiebung zu beobachten. Elf Jahre nach der ersten Arbeitshilfe ist nicht nur von Information und Verständnis die Rede, sondern auch von Grundsatztreue. Damit rückt nicht mehr nur die fremde Religion in den Mittelpunkt des Interesses, sondern zugleich und untrennbar davon auch die eigene, das Christentum. Von daher versteht sich der neue Titel, "Christen und Muslime in Deutschland" gegenüber dem alten, der nur die "Muslime in Deutschland" nannte, ebenso wie die beiden abschließenden Abschnitte des Vorwortes. Sie gehen ausdrücklich auf Christenverfolgungen "in manchen islamisch geprägten Ländern" ein und enden in einem Appell: "Bei allen notwendigen Informationen darf das Wichtigste nicht vergessen werden: daß die bei und mit uns lebenden Anhänger fremder Religionen unserem Gebet anvertraut sind und daß wir ihnen gegenüber 'immer mehr zu glaubhaften Zeugen der Güte Gottes werden'." (S. 6)

Im Unterschied zu ihrer Vorgängerin stellt die neue Arbeitshilfe mithin von Anfang an unmißverständlich klar, daß es ihr nicht nur um die Muslime in Deutschland geht, sondern um das Miteinander von Christen und Muslimen. Daß die Broschüre jetzt unter der Ägide der Pastoralkommission der Bischofskonferenz und nicht mehr wie ihre Vorgängerin unter Schriftleitung der Kommission für weltkirchliche Aufgaben herausgebracht wurde, fügt sich in diese Akzentverschiebung.

Die drei thematischen Schwerpunkte der Arbeitshilfe von 1982 finden sich auch im neuen Text wieder:

- eine kleine Islamkunde mit besonderer Berücksichtigung der Situation in Deutschland (Kapitel 1 und teilweise in Kapitel 2),
- Grundsätzliches und Praktisches zum Verhältnis von Christentum und Islam bzw. Christen und Muslimen (Kapitel 2 und 3),
- Probleme, die sich durch die "Islamische Präsenz" in Deutschland für die Muslime selbst (Kapitel 4, teilweise auch in Kapitel 1) und für die Kirche (Kapitel 4) ergeben, sowie Lösungsansätze.

Ein kurzes Kapitel ist dem “Verhältnis von Staat und Kirche” gewidmet (Kapitel 5). Es beschränkt sich auf Fragen der Anwendbarkeit der staatskirchenrechtlichen Vorgaben in Deutschland auf die hier lebenden Muslime. Auf die Frage nach dem unterschiedlichen theologischen Verständnis des Verhältnisses von Staat und Religion bzw. Religionsgemeinschaft in Islam und Christentum geht das Kapitel nicht ein. Der Anhang schließlich enthält eine Menge nützlicher Informationen wie Anschriften, Bibliographien, Glossar und anderes mehr.

Bei allen inhaltlichen Anknüpfungspunkten zu dem Dokument von 1982 wird doch bereits bei einem oberflächlichen Blick auf die Kapitelüberschriften ein Unterschied deutlich: In der Hälfte der Überschriften fällt das Stichwort “Herausforderung” auf, das man im Inhaltsverzeichnis des alten Textes vergeblich sucht.[3]

“Fremde” in der Arbeitshilfe von 1993

Die neue Arbeitshilfe ist sich bewußt, daß die Phase des “Gastarbeiter-Islam” in Deutschland der Vergangenheit angehört (S.7). Der Islam ist vielmehr auf dem Weg, sich auf Dauer in Europa einzurichten. Das Dokument zeichnet deshalb auch nicht mehr, wie 1982, das Bild einer schwachen und hilfsbedürftigen muslimischen Migrationsbevölkerung mit ihrem Pendant einer starken Kirche, die als “Anwalt” der Schwachen agiert. Mit dem Ernstnehmen der “Integrationsbemühungen der Muslime” (so der Titel eines Abschnitts) gesteht die Arbeitshilfe einerseits eine aktivere Rolle der Muslime ein, als das in dem Anwalt-Klienten-Modell ihrer Vorgängerin der Fall gewesen war. Andererseits erwartet sie aber auch mehr von der muslimischen Gemeinschaft in Deutschland.

Was sie erwartet, ist vor allem eine ernsthafte und aufrichtige Auseinandersetzung mit der deutschen Gesellschaft, wobei den Muslimen die Anerkennung der Grundlage und Gestalt dieser Gesellschaft zunächst einmal ebenso zuzumuten ist, wie sie selbst ihrerseits in und von ihr anerkannt werden wollen. Während die Arbeitshilfe aus dem Jahr 1982 in erster Linie Verständnis und Achtung der Christen gegenüber den Muslimen in Deutschland einforderte, wirbt ihre Nachfolgerin jetzt für gegenseitiges Verständnis und gegenseitigen Respekt.

3 Dort begegneten in den Untertiteln häufiger die Stichworte “Fragen” und “Aufgaben”.

Denn sie interessiert sich mehr für das Zusammenleben von Christen und Muslimen als für die fremde Lebensart einer kulturell und religiös fremden Migrationsbevölkerung.

Trotz dieser Akzentverschiebung bleibt der neue Text aber auch sensibel für die Diasporasituation der Muslime in Deutschland. Er versucht, die Auswirkungen dieser Situation für die Gestalt des Islams aufzuschlüsseln. Als einen Aspekt stellt er die Heterogenität der islamischen Gemeinde heraus, die zumindest für die Einwanderer unter ihnen in der europäischen Diaspora größer ist als in ihren islamisch geprägten Heimatländern. Dieses "vielschichtige Profil" (S. 9) habe jedoch als ebenso diaspora-typisches Phänomen seinen Gegenpart in der starken Betonung der islamischen "Einheit und Solidargemeinschaft gegenüber Nichtmuslimen" (S. 11), einer Einheit, die psychische Bedürfnisse erkennen läßt (S. 16), die aber auch unter Berufung auf den theologischen Grundbestand "der Einheit Gottes, des Islams, der Scharia und der Umma" (S. 12) eingefordert werde.

Die Verunsicherung durch die für viele Muslime neue, hautnahe Erfahrung der eigenen Pluralität wird in der Diaspora noch verschärft durch die Fremdheit des Lebensraumes, der den vertrauten Traditionen keine selbstverständliche Stütze mehr bietet. Diese Fremdheit erschwert nicht nur die alltägliche Praxis des Glaubens, sondern kann auch dessen Grundsätze in Frage stellen, so daß sie als Bedrohung der eigenen Identität erlebt werden kann. Auch von dieser Dimension der Diasporasituation sieht die Arbeitshilfe den deutschen Islam geprägt. War Fremdheit in der Arbeitshilfe von 1982 noch das konstitutive Element des "Gastarbeiter-Islam", so ist sie jetzt nur noch einer von mehreren wichtigen Faktoren für den Islam in Deutschland.

"Säkularität" in der Arbeitshilfe von 1993

In dem Dokument von 1982 war ein ambivalentes Verhältnis zur säkularen Verfassung der deutschen Gesellschaft sichtbar geworden. Nicht nur für Muslime, sondern auch für die Christen in Deutschland wurde sie einerseits als bejahte Grundlage eines friedlichen Zusammenlebens verschiedener Kulturen und Religionen gezeichnet, andererseits aber auch als Einfallstor religiöser Gleichgültigkeit und eines individualistischen Materialismus. In dem neuen Dokument ist diese Ambivalenz aufs Ganze gesehen deutlich abgeschwächt, das Bekenntnis zur säkularen Gesellschaft fällt weniger halbherzig aus. Damit wird die säkulare Gesellschaftsform zugleich in stärkerem Maße zu einem Diskussionspunkt zwischen Christentum und Islam.

Während die christlichen Kirchen die säkulare Verfassung des Staates grundsätzlich bejahen und als Institution einen stabilen Platz in ihr einnehmen, "findet sich der Islam auch heute kaum mit den Verhältnissen eines säkularisierten, religionsneutralen Staates ab", wie die Arbeitshilfe feststellt (S. 28). In der Perspektive der Arbeitshilfe beziehen westliches Christentum und Islam in ihrem Verhältnis zur modernen, säkularen Gesellschaft entgegengesetzte Positionen. Bestehe für die westliche Christenheit, vereinfachend gesprochen, die Gefahr in einem Zuviel an Säkularität, so liege sie für den Islam in einem Zuwenig. Auf diese Weise stellen die beiden Religionsgemeinschaften reziproke Herausforderungen füreinander dar, die positiv als Chance zu gegenseitiger Hilfestellung verstanden werden können. Der Islam kann westliche Christen zu einer Intensivierung ihres Glaubenslebens anspornen (S. 7), und Christen können ihrerseits Muslimen die Angst vor einer säkularen und pluralen Gesellschaft nehmen (S. 61, 69, 79). Theologische Argumente für eine positive Verhältnisbestimmung zur säkularen Gesellschaft sind allerdings auch in der neuen Arbeitshilfe nicht zu finden.

"Universalität und Partikularität" in der Arbeitshilfe von 1993

Wie bei der Arbeitshilfe von 1982 steht auch elf Jahre später der Begriff des "Dialogs" im Zentrum der Frage, wie sich das Christentum mit seinen universalen Geltungsansprüchen und dem daraus folgenden Verkündigungsauftrag gegenüber einer Religion verhalten soll, die aus ebensolchen Geltungsansprüchen ebenfalls einen Verkündigungsauftrag ableitet. Im Unterschied zu ihrer Vorgängerin spricht die neue Arbeitshilfe das Dilemma zwischen ernsthaftem Dialog und ernstgenommenem Verkündigungsauftrag jedoch nicht mehr nur zwischen den Zeilen, sondern ausdrücklich an: "Welchen Stellenwert hat die direkte Missionsarbeit noch, wenn es Heil auch außerhalb der Kirche in der Zugehörigkeit zu anderen Religionen geben kann?" (S. 35)

Eine Lösung des Dilemmas wird allerdings nicht vorgeschlagen. Ob sich der Kontrast zwischen Mission und Dialog dadurch entschärfen läßt, daß die Notwendigkeit des letztgenannten vor allem ethisch und nicht theologisch begründet wird, wie die Arbeitshilfe das versucht ("um die vielfältigen Bedrohungen der Menschenwürde abzuwehren" und "um das Leben und Überleben der Menschheit sicherzustellen"; S. 36), bleibt fragwürdig. Wenn das neue Dokument die Problematik einer Vermittlung zwischen Universalität und Partikularität, wie sie hinter dem Dilemma von Dialog und Verkündigung steht, im Unterschied zum Vorgängerdokument immerhin offen anspricht, bleibt es eine wirkliche Auseinandersetzung mit der gestellten Frage doch schuldig.

Theologische Reflexionsansätze

Die beiden Arbeitshilfen als die bislang einzigen ausführlicheren offiziellen Dokumente der katholischen Kirche in Deutschland zur Präsenz des Islams in diesem Land wenden sich in praktischer Ausrichtung an Mitarbeiterinnen und Mitarbeiter in der pastoralen Arbeit. Hier haben sie ihre Stärken. Sie liefern jedoch keine Ansätze für eine theologische Reflexion auf dieses relativ neue Phänomen und die mit ihm verbundenen Herausforderungen. Im folgenden sollen einige Anregungen in dieser Richtung versucht werden. Dabei werde ich den bereits eingangs erwähnten zentralen Fragestellungen des Fremden, der Säkularität sowie des Verhältnisses von Universalität und Partikularität folgen.

Fremde

Nach einem häufig zitierten Diktum des Soziologen Georg Simmel ist der Fremde derjenige, "der heute kommt und morgen bleibt". Darin unterscheidet er sich vom "Wandernde[n], der heute kommt und morgen geht".[4] Der Fremde ist "der potentiell Wandernde, der, obgleich er nicht weitergezogen ist, die Gelöstheit des Kommens und Gehens nicht ganz überwunden hat".[5] Er ist ein Wanderer, der ankommen

4 Georg Simmel, *Das individuelle Gesetz*, Frankfurt am Main 1968, S. 63.

5 Ebd.

will, auch wenn er zu Beginn seiner Wanderung noch nicht genau sagen kann, wo.

In dem Maße, wie in Deutschland aus "Gastarbeitern" "Arbeitsmigranten" und "Ausländer" wurden, oder auch, häufig in euphemistischer Verbrämung, "ausländische Mitbürger", und in dem Maße, in dem seit einigen Jahren die klassische Arbeitsmigration durch mehrere hunderttausend Flüchtlinge abgelöst wird, in diesem Maße gewinnt die Auseinandersetzung mit den Fremden und der Fremde an Bedeutung.

Der Gast kann die Ordnung der "Einheimischen" vielleicht stören, er kann sie nicht erschüttern. Solange die Einheimischen den Status von (guten oder schlechten) Gastgebern behalten, fühlen sie sich als Herren der Lage. Dem Gast mögen Sonderrechte eingeräumt werden; es sind die Gastgeber, die sie gewähren. Der Gast, der nicht geht, sondern bleibt, wird zum Fremden. Er oder sie begnügt sich auf Dauer nicht mit einem provisorischen Gaststatus, sondern begehrt Partizipation. Fremde wollen ankommen. Sie, die die Erschütterung der eigenen Ordnung in der Fremde erlebt haben und immer noch erleben, erschüttern jetzt die Ordnung der Einheimischen. Ihre Nähe als Fremde, ihr Beharren auf Partizipation und zugleich auf ihre vielfältigen Andersheiten, ihre Verweigerung von Assimilation, all das bedroht die etablierten Grenzen des Möglichen und Unmöglichen, des Guten und Schlechten, des Erlaubten und Unerlaubten, des Anständigen und des Unanständigen. Nicht diese oder jene Unverträglichkeit des Verhaltens des Fremden mit der einheimischen Ordnung verunsichert, sondern die Demaskierung der bestehenden Ordnung als konstruierte, als kontingente Ordnung, als eine Ordnung, die nicht das ist, was sie im Alltag ständig zu sein vorgibt: selbstverständlich. Der gesellschaftliche, kulturelle und juristische Rahmen, der bestimmt, was alles notwendig ist und was möglich und was unmöglich, wird durch die Fremden erfahrbar als ein Rahmen, der selbst nicht notwendig so ist, wie er ist.

Baumann hat beschrieben, wie die Festlegung der gegenseitigen Verantwortungsbereitschaft und die gemeinsame Verantwortungsverweigerung gegenüber Dritten in den Schemata von Freund und Feind konstitutiv ist für die Gruppen- und Gesellschaftsbildung.[6] Danach sind nicht die Feinde, sondern die Fremden die eigentliche Bedrohung für eine Gruppe, die die Kontingenz ihrer Identität verdrängt, um deren Leistungsfähigkeit bei der Herstellung sozialer Kohärenz und bei der Legitimierung sozialer Autorität nicht zu gefährden. Daher die bekannten Strategien zur Bändigung des Fremden: seine Exotisierung, seine Assimilierung, seine Verdrängung (im psychologischen wie auch im wörtlichen Sinn) bis hin zu seiner Eliminierung. Immer geht es darum, das Fremde "draußen" zu halten, um "innen" einen "reinen" Raum des Eigenen zu gewährleisten.[7] In der starren und um Reinheit bemühten Identität des Eigenen scheint das Fremde nur auf Distanz erträglich, an den Rändern und Grauzonen des Eigenen. Dorthin verbannt spielt es dann allerdings wieder eine, im wahrsten Sinne des Wortes "un-heimliche", sozial stabilisierende Rolle.[8] Da keine Ordnung ihre eigenen Voraussetzungen durchgängig zu begründen vermag, muß jede Ordnung mit ihrer eigenen Kontingenz und somit auch mit der Kontingenz ihrer Definitionen und Grenzziehungen leben. Jede Ordnung hat, eingestandenermaßen oder uneingestandenermaßen, nicht nur weiße Flecken des Noch-nicht-Bestimmten, sondern auch ihre Grauzonen des Unbestimmbaren.[9] Und genau diese Grau-

---

6 Zygmunt Bauman, Moderne und Ambivalenz, in: *Das Eigene und das Fremde*, Uli Bielefeld (Hrsg.), Hamburg 1992, S. 23-49, hier besonders S. 23-31; vgl. auch, mit anderer Terminologie aber ähnlichen Resultaten R. D. Laing, *Phänomenologie der Erfahrung*, Frankfurt am Main 1970, S. 69-90.

7 Zur Relation von Drinnen und Draußen als einer leiblich und nicht geometrisch bestimmten Dimension, vgl. die Ausführungen von Bernhard Waldenfels, *Der Stachel des Fremden,* Frankfurt am Main 1990, S. 28-40. Der Selbstschutz durch ein fiktives und symbolisches, "reines" Wir, das dann häufig seine Opfer fordert, findet sich übrigens nicht nur bei Einheimischen, sondern auch bei Fremden, vgl. Julia Kristeva, *Fremde sind wir uns selbst*, Frankfurt am Main 1990, S. 33f.

8 Vgl. die Analyse von Freud zur Herkunft des Unheimlichen vom verdrängten Heimischen: Sigmund Freud, *Psychologische Schriften*, Studienausgabe, Band IV, Frankfurt am Main 1970, S. 241-274. Manche Interpreten wenden die Analyse auf die Fremden-Thematik an, indem sie einen Projektionsmechanismus am Werke sehen, mit dem das verdrängte Eigene auf die Fremden übertragen und diese deshalb unheimlich werden, vgl. Bielefeld, Das Konzept des Fremden und die Wirklichkeit des Imaginären, in: *Das Eigene und das Fremde*, S. 97-128, hier: S. 104f.; F. Akashe-Böhme, *Frausein-Fremdsein*, Frankfurt am Main 1993, S. 19f.; Kristeva, S. 199-210). Die Anwendung durch Bielefeld und Akashe-Böhme scheint mir jedoch unzureichend, denn sie beschränken den Projektionsmechanismus auf das Verhalten der einheimischen Bevölkerung, ohne dafür Gründe zu nennen.

9 Vgl. Bauman, S. 25-31.

zonen sind im allgemeinen der Ort, den eine Ordnung dem Fremden zuweist.[10]

Dort, an den Grenzen des Eigenen oder jenseits dieser Grenzen, kann das Fremde sogar anziehend sein. Denn die Suspendierung der Notwendigkeit der eigenen Ordnung kennt neben ihrem bedrohlichen Charakter auch die Verlockung von Freiheit, sofern diese nur zeitweise gewährt wird und wieder zurückgenommen werden kann. Solange das Fremde und die Fremden an den Grenzen der eigenen Welt gehalten werden können, sind sie ungefährlich und "exo—tisch". Ganze Industriezweige, vor allem in der Medien- und Tourismusbranche, leben davon, das näherrückende Fremde mit technischen und psychologischen Mitteln auf der ungefährlichen Distanz von Objekten zu halten. Gelingt diese Distanzierung nicht mehr bzw. wird ihr illusionärer Charakter durchsichtig, bedeutet das die Herausforderung einer neuen Auseinandersetzung mit der Fremde.[11]

Ohnehin haftet in hochmobilen und plural organisierten Gesellschaften der Ortsbindung etwas Illusorisches an. "Drinnen" und "draußen" sind soziologisch und nicht topographisch zu verstehen. Gerade wenn gilt, daß Fremder ist, wer "seinen" Ort verläßt und in "unseren" Ort kommt, setzt das voraus, daß Orte nicht in geo-metrischer Abstraktion als Koordinaten, sondern in lebensweltlichem Verständnis als kulturell geprägte Räume aufgefaßt werden. Für Alfred Schütz, den Begründer einer lebensweltlich orientierten Soziologie, ist der Fremde der "newcomer", der seine "in-group" verläßt und sich einer anderen Gruppe annähert. Deren Andersheit besteht darin, daß in ihr andere Selbstverständlichkeiten, andere "Rezepte", andere "cultural patterns" des richtigen Verhaltens, gelten als in der Her-

---

[10] Für Beispiele aus dem sozialen Bereich, unter soziologischer Berücksichtigung religiöser Systeme, vgl. die Untersuchungen von Mary Douglas, *Reinheit und Gefährdung*, Frankfurt am Main 1988.

[11] Kristeva hat die Ambivalenz der Fremde zwischen Freiheit und Bedrohung, die auch für Migranten gilt, am Beispiel der Spannung zwischen sexueller Freizügigkeit und Krankheit skizziert, Kristeva, S. 39f. Sexualität und besonders das Motiv der fremden Frau spielen im Zusammenhang mit Fremde eine prominente und ambivalente Rolle, wie bereits ein Blick auf die genannten Bereiche Medien und Tourismus deutlich macht. Vgl. auch Akashe-Böhme, S. 33-58; die Autorin untersucht das Motiv der fremden Frau jedoch ausschließlich als Projektion des europäischen Mannes.

kunftsgruppe.[12] Das kulturelle Muster der Einheimischen macht den Neuankömmling zum Fremden, zu einem "Grenzfall außerhalb des Gebietes, das von dem innerhalb der Gruppe geläufigen Orientierungsschema abgedeckt wird."[13]

Wenn also der Ort der Ortsansässigen und die Ortlosigkeit der Fremden nicht so sehr geographisch, sondern sozial und kulturell bestimmt (und bestimmend) sind, dann ist die Ortsgebundenheit (im geographischen Sinn) kollektiver Identität in Frage gestellt. Nicht durch den Ort als solchen wird der Auswanderer zum Fremden, sondern durch das "cultural pattern" der dort lebenden Menschen, das nicht eindeutig in dasjenige der Bewohner seines Herkunftsortes übersetzbar ist. Sind solche kulturellen Muster aber notwendig ortsgebunden? "Innen" und "Außen", die zentralen räumlichen Kategorien, die bei der Bestimmung von "Eigenem" und "Fremdem" Verwendung finden, sind bereits kulturell überformt. Sie zeugen von einer leiblichen Aneignung von Raum, von einer Ordnung, mit der das vielfältige, neutrale Nebeneinander des geometrischen Raumes zur asymmetrischen Relation des Innen und Außen eines belebten Raumes organisiert wurde. Menschen beanspruchen Raum zum Leben, nicht nur als Individuen, sondern auch als Gruppen. Das bedeutet jedoch weder, daß dieser Raum als fester Ort mit starren, streng kontrollierten Grenzen organisiert sein muß, noch daß die individuelle und kollektive Identität ausschließlich oder auch nur notwendig an einen bestimmten Raum gebunden wäre.

Gerade die westlichen Gesellschaften mit ihren ständig wachsenden Möglichkeiten für -- und ihren Anforderungen an -- die Mobilität ihrer Bevölkerung, mit ihrer hochgradigen Segmentierung der Lebensbereiche und ihrer Funktionalisierung des öffentlichen Raumes, mit ihrer ununterbrochenen Steigerung von Geschwindigkeit und somit von realer Veränderung des erfahrenen Raumes, an die sich die virtuellen Räume der elektronischen Medien nahtlos anschließen, gerade

---

[12] Alfred Schütz, The stranger, in: *Race and ethnic relations*, G. Bowker & J. Carrier (Hrsg.), London 1976, S. 100-111. Für eine Anwendung des Begriffs newcomer auf die Situation der Muslime in Europa vgl. J. S. Nielsen, State, religion and laicité, in: *Muslims and Christians in Europe*, G. Speelman, J.v. Lin & D. Mulder (Hrsg.), Kampen 1993, S. 90-99.

[13] Schütz, S. 106: "a border case outside the territory covered by the scheme of orientation current within the group".

diese Gesellschaften also haben die Ortsbindung individueller und kollektiver Identität *de facto* zurückgedrängt. Die Nähe der Fremden stellt die moderne Gesellschaft deshalb nur vor die grundlegende Frage, die sie selbst geschaffen hat: Wie Pluralität und Einheit miteinander vermitteln?

Die in der bisherigen Geschichte einmalige migrationsbedingte Präsenz von Muslimen in Deutschland und in ganz Europa verleiht dieser Frage noch einen besonderen Akzent und eine besondere Schärfe, insofern sie Pluralität in zweifacher (und nicht widerspruchsfreier) Hinsicht herausfordert: gegenüber dem Christentum als Mehrheitsreligion, deren universale Geltungsansprüche sie streitig macht; und zugleich gegenüber dem Pluralismuskonzept einer säkularen Gesellschaft, deren Verzicht auf religiöse Grundlagen sie bestreitet.

Für den christlichen Glauben und für die christlichen Kirchen sind die Fragen des Fremden und der Fremde freilich nicht neu. Sie begleitet das Christentum von seinen Anfängen (und sogar schon in seiner "Vorgeschichte", wenn man die Geschichte des Volkes Israel bis zur Zeit Jesu ohne Vereinnahmung so nennen kann) bis in die Gegenwart.[14]

"Fremde" im Alten Testament[15]

Das Verhältnis zu Fremden in den Schriften des "Alten Testaments" ist geprägt einerseits von einer Ambivalenz zwischen Hinwendung und Ablehnung, andererseits von der bohrenden Frage nach dem Zusam-

---

14 Ähnliches gilt auch für den Islam. So ist auffällig, daß die islamische Zeitrechnung mit der Auswanderung des Propheten aus Mekka (arab. hidschra) und nicht etwa mit dem Beginn der koranischen Offenbarung ihren Anfang nimmt. Eine Evaluation der Ressourcen des Islams zum Thema Fremde fände zahlreiche Anknüpfungspunkte: neben der Hidschra und der Relation von Land des Islams = Land des Friedens (arab. dâr al-islâm) und Land des Kriegs (arab. dâr al-harb) wären das beispielsweise die *Schutzgewährung* und das Motiv der gottgewollten Verschiedenheit von Gemeinschaften und religiösen Wegen (vgl. Koran 5:48), die Reise in die Fremde als Motiv religiöser Erfahrung und als Übung religiöser Selbsterziehung im Sufismus, aber auch die problematische fremdbestimmte Festlegung anderer Religionen (v.a. Judentum und Christentum) mit höchster Offenbarungsautorität durch den Koran.

15 Vgl. Richard Friedli, *Fremdheit als Heimat*, Freiburg (Schweiz) 1974, S. 129-149; R. Hooker & C. Lamb, *Love the stranger*, London 1986; M. Görg, Fremdsein in und für Israel, in: *Die Fremden*, O. Fuchs (Hrsg.), Düsseldorf 1988, S. 194-214; R. Kampling, Fremde und Fremdsein in Aussagen des Neuen Testaments, in: *Die Fremden*, S. 215-239.

menhang zwischen dem eigenen partikularen Auserwähltsein Israels als "Volk Gottes" und dem immer wieder auch gegen die Grenzen dieses Partikularismus sich deutlich artikulierenden universalen Heilswillen Gottes.

Sowohl im ausdrücklichen Sprechen über Fremde als auch im Sprechen über Gott selbst läßt sich eine große Offenheit gegenüber dem Fremden entdecken. Die biblische theologische Sprache, so betont Berger[16], ist metaphorisch. Sie spricht nicht direkt von Gott, sondern bedient sich der vielfältigen Wirklichkeit als Zeichen. Daraus folgt eine Pluralität der Metaphern, in die auch religiöse Metaphern und religiöse Gottesbezeichnungen von Israels Nachbarvölkern Eingang finden können.

Für Israel ergibt sich darüberhinaus eine Identifikationsmöglichkeit mit den Fremden, weil Fremdling zu sein für das Volk Gottes selbst unauslöschlich in die eigene Entstehung und Geschichte eingeschrieben ist. Als Fremder kam Abraham nach Kanaan; als Fremdling mußte Jakob vor seinem Bruder Esau ins Exil fliehen; als Fremder kam Joseph nach Ägypten; als Fremde erhörte Gott sein Volk in der Bedrängung und führte sie aus dem "Sklavenhaus". Doch nicht nur Israel identifiziert sich deshalb immer wieder mit dem Fremden oder wird von seinen Propheten an sein eigenes Fremdlingsein erinnert, sondern auch Gott selbst kann im Alten Testament als Fremder und im Fremden erscheinen.[17]

Dieser Nähe und Offenheit gegenüber dem Fremden stehen jedoch andere Tendenzen schroff entgegen: die kompromißlose, gewaltsame Eliminierung von Fremden bei der "Landnahme" und eine rigoros geforderte Eindeutigkeit in Kult und Ethik. Hier darf es zu keiner Vermischung mit Fremdem kommen. Die Treue zu Gott hat neben der Forderung nach Gerechtigkeit in der Forderung nach Ablehnung aller Fremdkulte ihren vielleicht deutlichsten Ausdruck. Diese klare Trennlinie erlaubt es dann auch wieder, daß gegenüber den einzelnen Fremden, die in Israel leben, Gastfreundschaft, Schutz und solidarische Zuwendung möglich sind. Solange Solidarität und Gastfreundschaft

---

16 Klaus Berger, Fremdheit als Kategorie Biblischer Theologie, in: *Den Fremden wahrnehmen*, T. Sundermeier (Hrsg.), Gütersloh1992, S. 205-211.

17 Zur Unterscheidung der Fremdheit Gottes, der Fremdheit Israels und der Fremdheit der *in Israel wohnhaften Fremden* (ger) sowie der *Ausländer* (nokri) vgl. Görg, a.a.O.

nicht zur Einführung von kultischen Praktiken und ethischen Normen führen, die gegen das Gesetz Gottes an Israel stehen, sind sie göttliches Gebot der Gerechtigkeit. Denn Gott, so heißt es wiederholt in den alttestamentlichen Schriften, liebt den Fremdling.

Weit weniger explizit als die Frage nach dem Verhalten gegenüber den Fremden wird die Frage nach dem Verhältnis von eigenem Auserwähltsein und Gottes Willen für die gesamte Menschheit verhandelt. Das ist nicht verwunderlich, denn diese Frage ist weniger bedeutsam für den Alltag und seinen Bedarf an praktikablen Regelungen als die zuerst genannte Frage. Zugleich enthält sie aber erheblich mehr Sprengstoff für die eigene Identität. Und schließlich ist sie gerade als offene Frage einer der treibenden Motoren für die Entwicklung der biblischen Schriften selbst und deshalb mehr implizit als explizit wirksam.[18] Ständig aufs neue treibt sie das Volk Israel in seinem Bemühen um Verständnis des in seiner Geschichte sich offenbarenden Gottes zur Auseinandersetzung mit den empfangenen Verheißungen und Geboten und den damit oft widerstreitenden gegenwärtigen Erfahrungen und Prophetien. Wie ein versteckter Entzündungsherd sorgt diese Frage für ein latentes Fieber, das gelegentlich offen ausbrechen kann, sich aber einer eindeutigen Diagnose und Therapie zu entziehen scheint.[19]

"Fremde" im Neuen Testament

Die Texte des Neuen Testaments sprechen häufig von Fremden: die fremde Besatzungsmacht der Römer, die Samariter, die an den Rand gedrängten "Unreinen", die Städte der jüdischen Diaspora. Alte Grenzen fallen. Jesus wendet sich "abtrünnigen" Samaritern, römischen Soldaten und Aussätzigen zu. Petrus nimmt den römischen Hauptmann Kornelius in die Gemeinde auf. Paulus kämpft gegen die Dis-

---

18 Beauchamp hat diesen Gedanken im Rahmen seines bibeltheologischen Entwurfs entfaltet: Paul Beauchamp, *L'un et l'autre Testament*, Paris 1976; ders., *Le récit, la lettre et le corps*, Paris 1982, hier besonders S. 233-253; ders., *L'un et l'autre Testament*, t 2, Paris 1990, hier besonders: S. 411-427.

19 Für ein Beispiel vgl. Norbert Lohfink, Der neue Bund und die Völker, *Neukirchener Theologische Zeitschrift* 6 (1991), S. 115-133. Lohfink analysiert Textzeugnisse der Auseinandersetzung der Bundestheologie mit der Frage der (fremden) Völker und kommt dabei zu dem Schluß, daß eine Beteiligung der Völker am Bund Israels für die Endzeit der Geschichte offenbar angedacht wurde.

kriminierung und Assimilierung von "Heidenchristen" in der Gemeinde. Die Botschaft von der Nähe Gottes zu den Menschen und vom Reich Gottes, das alle Menschen umfassen soll, greift die alte Frage von der Erwählung und dem universalen Heil wieder auf und gibt ihr eine neue provozierende Wendung: Alle Menschen sind Gottes Barmherzigkeit anvertraut und alle sind auf sie angewiesen; alle Menschen sind zu Umkehr und neuem Leben gerufen. Unter den Christen soll es "weder Juden noch Griechen" geben.

Die Formel läßt es bereits ahnen: Alte Grenzen fallen, doch zugleich entstehen neue. Jesus, der sich den Fremden in seinem Volk zuwendet, wird selbst zu einem Fremden, angefangen von der Verfolgung durch Herodes und der Flucht nach Ägypten bis hin zur Verleugnung durch Petrus und der physischen Eliminierung am Kreuz. Der Satz des Johannesprologs "Er kam in sein Eigentum, aber die Seinen nahmen ihn nicht auf" zieht sich leitmotivisch durch die Evangelien. Auch in der jungen Gemeinde setzt sich das Muster fort. Die Jüngergemeinschaft überwindet alte Fremdheiten und errichtet zugleich neue Zugehörigkeiten und Ausschlüsse.[20]

"Fremde" in der Kirchengeschichte

Auch in der Geschichte der Kirche bleibt Fremdheit ein beherrschendes Thema. Die Grundmotive, die sich in immer neuen Variationen und Verschränkungen hinter den oft komplexen Ereignissen erkennen lassen, sind bereits in den biblischen Schriften angeklungen:

- die eigene Fremdheit gegenüber einer dominanten Umwelt, wie sie vor allem in den ersten Jahrhunderten, aber auch später noch außerhalb des "Christlichen Abendlandes" erfahren wird;

- die Fremdheit der anderen, der Nichtchristen, der "Heiden", der Juden, der Muslime, der Völker in der "Neuen Welt";

- die Fremdheit im Eigenen, die ablesbar ist in den Geschichten von Ketzern und Häretikern, in sozialen und spirituellen Randgruppen und Bewegungen, schließlich in Schismen und Kirchenspaltungen;

---

[20] Berger, S. 209f.; Kristeva stellt die Entwicklung der christlichen "Ekklesia" in den Rahmen der politischen Veränderungen im römischen Vielvölker-Reich, insbesondere der Herausforderungen durch die Migrationsströme aus dem Norden, Kristeva, S. 90-100.

- die Fremdheit des "Anderen", die immer wieder neu erfahrene Unberechenbarkeit und Unverfügbarkeit Gottes, wie sie sich beispielsweise im sprachlichen Niederschlag mystischer Erfahrungen und Reflexionen angedeutet findet.

Ein wichtiger Unterschied zu den biblischen Zeugnissen ist allerdings zu beobachten. Die im Alten Testament, aber auch im Neuen Testament (z. B. Röm 9-11) wirksame Dialektik von Partikularem und Universalem verliert zunehmend an Relief und weicht einer missionarischen Expansionsstrategie, die in Flächen und Orten denkt. Es gilt jetzt vor allem, das Gebiet sichtbarer christlicher (und das heißt unmittelbar: kirchlicher) Präsenz und Autorität nach Kräften auszudehnen, möglichst viele Orte diesem Gebiet einzuverleiben. Der universale Heilswille Gottes soll realisiert werden durch die Zugehörigkeit aller Menschen zur Kirche ("extra ecclesiam nulla salus"[21]). Diese Zugehörigkeit kann dabei eigenartig materialistische Züge annehmen, wie etwa vom Taufverständnis neuzeitlicher Missionare her bekannt ist.

Die Konsequenzen des in den Kategorien von Territorium und Expansion denkenden kirchlichen Selbstverständnisses für den Umgang mit Fremden waren oft ebenso verheerend wie die Folgen der Expansion des politischen Einflußbereiches "christlicher Länder" und gingen meist Hand in Hand mit ihr, wenn auch beide Expansionsbemühungen selten parallel geschahen. Hier wie dort lautete die Alternative in der Regel: Assimilierung oder Eliminierung des Fremden.[22] Das Fremde wurde in aller Regel, zumindest in den für zentral erachteten Bereichen, entweder dem Eigenen angeglichen oder als minderwertig degradiert beziehungsweise ausgeschieden. Auch wenn sich die Missionare ihre Arbeit im allgemeinen nicht leicht machten und hohe persönliche Opfer brachten, wurde das Ziel selbst nicht in Frage gestellt: die Expansion einer Kirche, die in ihrem Selbstverständnis und ihren

---

21 So beispielsweise in der Bulle "Cantate Domino" auf dem Konzil von Florenz (1442): "Die hochheilige römische Kirche ... glaubt fest, bekennt und verkündet, daß 'niemand, der sich außerhalb der katholischen Kirche befindet, nicht nur Heiden', sondern auch Juden oder Häretiker oder Schismatiker, des ewigen Lebens teilhaft werden können, sondern daß sie in das ewige Feuer wandern werden ...", lateinisches Original und deutsche Übersetzung in: H. Denzinger, *Kompendium der Glaubensbekenntnisse und kirchlichen Lehrentscheidungen*, Freiburg 1991, Nr. 1330. 1351.

22 Für eine anschauliche Analyse dieser Zusammenhänge und Mechanismen am Beispiel der "Eroberung" Amerikas vgl. T. Todorov, *La conquête de l'Amérique*, Paris 1982, hier besonders S. 48f.

europäischen Prägungen und Strukturen unangetastet blieb.[23]

Insofern scheint unter der Rücksicht des Verhältnisses zum Fremden die Qualifizierung der Kirchengeschichte vom ausgehenden 15. bis zur Mitte des 20. Jahrhunderts als "koloniales Christentum" durchaus gerechtfertigt. Nicht so sehr die Kollaboration der Kirchen mit den europäischen Kolonialherren, die es auch gab, ist mit dem Begriff des "kolonialen Christentums" gemeint, sondern die Parallele im Selbstverständnis: Weltkirche als über alle Grenzen expandierende westeuropäische Kirche. Friedli spricht deshalb in Abgrenzung von dieser Konzeption von einer "Entkolonisierung der Kirche und der Mentalität der Missionare" und meint damit das "Bewußtwerden, daß die Mission nicht als Selbstbestätigung und Selbstfortpflanzung der Kirche gesehen werden kann."[24]

Mit der politischen Unabhängigkeit der ehemaligen Kolonien und den ökonomischen, technologischen und demographischen Entwicklungen nach dem zweiten Weltkrieg haben sich die Parameter deutlich verschoben. Das Ende der politischen Entkolonisierung als Kampf gegen die Fremdherrschaft europäischer Nationen und gegen die mit dieser Fremdherrschaft verknüpfte Selbstentfremdung fällt zeitlich zusammen mit dem Beginn großer Migrationsbewegungen, die aus nichteuropäischen Ländern nach Europa führen und erneut die Erfahrung von Fremde und Entfremdung mit sich bringen. Kirchlicherseits hat in dieser Zeit eine kritische Auseinandersetzung sowohl mit der eigenen Vergangenheit als auch mit gegenwärtigen Positionen eingesetzt. Für manche Ortskirchen (lokale Kirchen) ergibt sich dabei die paradox anmutende Situation, daß sie ihre eigene Kultur erst jetzt wie etwas Fremdes neu zu entdecken beginnen, da eine kritische Distanz

23 Nicht nur Missionare, sondern später auch Ethnologen haben eine kritische Reflexion des Begriffs *kultureller Fremdheit* lange Zeit versäumt. Das geschah nicht trotz, sondern gerade aufgrund ihres wissenschaftlichen Selbstverständnisses, das ihnen "Objektivität" abverlangte. Vgl. T. Bargatzky, Die Ethnologie und das Problem der kulturellen Fremdheit, in: *Den Fremden wahrnehmen,* S. 13-29, hier: S. 15; für eine relativ frühe Auseinandersetzung mit dem Thema, die zudem die Verstrickung der Ethnologie in den Kolonialismus einbezieht, vgl. M. Leiris, L'Ethnographe devant le colonialisme, *Les Temps Modernes* 6 (1959), S. 357-374.

24 Friedli, S 48, Anm. 31. Auch Suess spricht von einem "nachkolonialen Christentum", dessen Grundlinien er bezeichnenderweise anhand des Verhältnisses zum Fremden entwickelt. Paulo Suess, Über die Unfähigkeit des Einen, sich des Anderen zu erinnern, *Orientierung* 58 (1994), S. 233-236 und S. 245-249.

zu den früher eingeführten Formen eines "kolonialen Christentums" gegeben ist.[25]

Zur gleichen Zeit stellt sich für katholische wie evangelische Ortskirchen in westlichen Ländern die Frage, ob sie in einem fortschreitenden Prozeß gesellschaftlicher Säkularisierung nicht selber zu Fremdkörpern im "christlichen Abendland" werden.[26] Nachdem für mehr als ein Jahrtausend in Europa gesellschaftliche und kirchliche Zugehörigkeit fast deckungsgleich waren, auch wenn Krisen immer wieder einen Abgleich erforderlich machten, so hat sich diese Situation in der Neuzeit zusehends geändert. Die Theologie sieht sich aus der Position einer übergeordneten Universalwissenschaft verdrängt und wird schließlich selbst zum Objekt von Humanwissenschaften wie Soziologie und Psychologie, nachdem sie bereits vorher das Monopol über die meisten ihrer Gegenstände an solche neuen Wissenschaften verloren hatte. Ebenso verliert die Kirche ihr gesellschaftliches Monopol als Instanz letztgültiger Sinn- und Normvorgabe. Ihre daraus abgeleitete Autorität und Funktion als Grundlage sozialer Kohärenz schwindet. Das Verhältnis zwischen Gesellschaft, Kultur, Staat, Religion und Kirche wird prekär. Dieser Prozeß, der mit zahlreichen Nachzugsgefechten bis in die Gegenwart andauert, hat dazu geführt, daß Kirche und christlicher Glaube in den westlichen Gesellschaften zunehmend mit der Distanz des Fremden wahrgenommen werden. Allenfalls als kulturelle Traditionen ohne normative Verbindlichkeit oder als Rohmaterial für säkulare Anleihen werden sie noch unhinterfragt zur Identität, zum Eigenen dieser Gesellschaften gerechnet. Ein beredtes Symptom dieser Situation sind die Medien und die Werbewirtschaft, wenn sie christliche und kirchliche Symbole als beliebige Versatzstücke für Botschaften verwenden, die von keiner religiösen Instanz mehr abgedeckt, geschweige denn kontrolliert oder autorisiert sind.

---

25 Vgl. A. A. Roest Crollius, Inkulturation als Herausforderung, in *Ignatianisch*, M. Sievernich & G. Switek (Hrsg.), Freiburg 1990, S. 613-623. Diese neue Suche nach dem fremd gewordenen Eigenen wird allgemein mit dem etwas unglücklichen Begriff "Inkulturation" bezeichnet. Versucht man, die möglichen Mißverständnisse dieses Begriffs zu umgehen --beispielsweise die Vorstellung einer kulturunabhängigen christlichen Botschaft --, so gelangt man schnell in die Nähe des Dialog-Begriffs, wie der zitierte Artikel zeigt. Ich werde mich deshalb im folgenden auf diesen Begriff beschränken.

26 Vgl. M. Kehl, Kirche in der Fremde, *Stimmen der Zeit* 118 (1993), S. 507-520.

Dialog

Die Migration ist und hat Teil an diesem Prozeß der Pluralisierung moderner Gesellschaften. Sie führt auch zu einem unleugbaren religiösen Pluralismus, und zwar nicht nur in Schulbüchern und Fernsehfilmen, sondern in Klassenzimmern und in der unmittelbaren Nachbarschaft. Allein schon diese Nähe des Pluralismus setzt das Thema Dialog auf die Tagesordnung und befragt die Universalitäts- und Autoritätsansprüche kirchlicher und christlicher Positionen. Bereitschaft zum Dialog bedeutet Bereitschaft zur Widerrede und damit Verzicht auf die Bequemlichkeiten und scheinbaren Sicherheiten des Monologs. Außerdem bedeutet die Migration eine faktische Umkehr der Bewegungsrichtung und damit auch der Initiative in der Begegnung zwischen europäischen Christen und Fremden anderer Religionszugehörigkeit. Auch wenn die Missionare, die aus den christlichen Ländern Europas "in die Missionen" zogen, nicht einfach vergleichbar sind mit den Millionen von Arbeitsmigranten und Flüchtlingen, die beispielsweise aus islamisch geprägten Ländern in ein inzwischen säkulares Europa kommen: Für die Begegnung mit Fremden macht es einen erheblichen Unterschied, ob sie in der Fremde oder im eigenen Land stattfindet. In der öffentlichen Rhetorik ist das deutlich abzulesen, wie bereits am Beispiel des Wandels vom "Gastarbeiter" zum "Ausländer" deutlich wurde. Im ersten Fall behalten die Einheimischen die Initiative und (zumindest vermeintlich) die Kontrolle, im zweiten Fall fühlen sie sich in die Defensive gedrängt und in ihrer Selbstbestimmung bedroht. Mit der gegenwärtigen Migration aber haben sich die Vorzeichen für eine expansionsgewohnte Gesellschaft und eine missionsgewohnte Kirche gründlich geändert.

Zwei einander entgegengesetzte Reaktionsmöglichkeiten scheinen sich anzubieten: ein mehr oder weniger kämpferischer Rückzug auf das Eigene oder eine Preisgabe des Eigenen, die je nachdem eher enthusiastische oder eher resignative Züge tragen kann. Hinter einem solchen bereitwilligen Verzicht auf ein kollektives Eigenes verbirgt sich allerdings unter den Bedingungen moderner, säkularer Gesellschaften häufig der Versuch, wenigstens ein individuelles Eigenes vor den Verunsicherungen zu retten, denen die kollektive Identität durch die Bestreitung ihres exklusiven Anspruchs auf bestimmte Orte ausgesetzt ist. Einzelne Elemente, deren Orte vormals in einem systematischen Ganzen von christlicher und kirchlicher Identität klar bestimmt waren, werden bereitwillig dem freien Markt übergeben, damit der einzelne sich anschließend aus diesem Markt wieder ohne die Kontrollmechanismen einer kollektiven Identität bedienen kann. Der Preis für diesen Verzicht auf klar umrissene Orte ist der Verlust von Grenzen und damit der Verlust eines gemeinsamen Profils und einer gemeinsamen Artikulation von Identität, die mit anderen leibhaft in Zeit und Raum geteilt werden könnte.

Genau in die andere Richtung zielt der Rückzug auf das Eigene. Die noch verbliebenen Machtpositionen der Kirche in der säkularen Gesellschaft müssen scheinbar unter allen Umständen verteidigt werden, Reservate werden zu Festungen ausgebaut, die Grenze zwischen dem Eigenen und den anderen (häufig: "der Welt") wird befestigt, die Gräben vertieft. Diese Art der Selbstbehauptung nach außen erfordert nach innen eine Maximierung der Kontrolle über die Reinheit des Eigenen und über die Kontakte zu anderen durch Zentralisierung, Verstärkung von Hierarchisierung und Betonung von Disziplin. Wo diese Form der Reaktion in die Offensive geht, tut sie es, um verlorenes Terrain zurückzugewinnen, verlorene Orte wieder zu besetzen; auch hier handelt es sich um einen Rückzug auf das vermeintlich Eigene.

Beide Reaktionsweisen weichen der eigentlichen Herausforderung durch das Fremde aus. Denn die Fremden im Eigenen demaskieren nicht nur die bequeme Selbstverständlichkeit des Eigenen, das sich in seinen Orten fest eingerichtet hat, sie stellen auch die Frage: Wer seid ihr wirklich? Die Fremden suchen in der Fremde ein Gegenüber. Allerdings sind sie nicht bereit, das Selbstbild ihres Gegenübers fraglos zu akzeptieren --allein deshalb, weil es für sie als Fremde im Unterschied zu den Einheimischen nicht fraglos ist. In der Frage "Wer seid ihr?" liegt die eigentliche Herausforderung, die sich durch die Präsenz von Fremden mit einem anderen Glauben auch an Kirche und Christen stellt. Sie verlangt gerade nicht den (unmöglichen) Verzicht auf Identität, wohl aber den Verzicht auf ihre starre Festschreibung. Sie verlangt die Bereitschaft, sich zu bewegen und bewegen zu lassen. Insofern ist diese Herausforderung durch den Fremden eine spirituelle, die über die Forderungen nach Gastfreundschaft, Solidarität und

Nächstenliebe, wie sie von kirchlichen Dokumenten wiederholt erhoben werden, hinausreicht.[27] Sowohl die Reaktion "Preisgabe des Eigenen" als auch die "Rückzug auf das Eigene" verweigern diese Bewegung, weil sie ihre Identität an anderen als den gewohnten Orten nicht riskieren wollen. Nicht in völliger Ortlosigkeit und nicht in völliger Bindung an die gewohnten Orte artikuliert sich die religiöse Identität von Christen und Kirche in einer Situation geschichtlichen Wandels, sondern in Bewegungen, die zwar keine definitiven Grenzen, wohl aber deutlich erkennbare Spuren hinterlassen.

Auch wenn in kirchlichen und christlichen Praktiken und Stellungnahmen die beiden Versuchungen eines Rückzugs auf sich selbst und einer diffusen Selbstaufgabe immer wieder durchscheinen, so sind doch auch die Ansätze nicht übersehbar, auf die spirituelle Herausforderung von Ortsverlust und Fremde auf spirituelle Weise zu reagieren: dadurch, daß Christen und die Kirche sich der geschichtlichen, d.h. pluralen und partikularen Wirklichkeit in dem Vertrauen darauf aussetzen, daß diese Wirklichkeit der Ort der Gottesbegegnung ist. Sucht man nach einem Oberbegriff für diese Öffnung, so drängt sich der Begriff des Dialogs auf, der seit der Zeit des Zweiten Vatikanischen Konzils in der katholischen Kirche Programm geworden ist.

Ohne hier im einzelnen auf die Entwicklung dieses Begriffs einzugehen, läßt sich festhalten, daß ein ernstgemeinter Dialog, d.h. einer, bei dem keine der beteiligten Parteien das Ergebnis schon vorwegnimmt, genau auf der Grenze zwischen dem Eigenen und dem Fremden zu verorten ist. Er setzt völlige Ortlosigkeit oder permanente Grenzüberschreitung weder voraus noch zielt er sie an. Was er voraussetzt, ist die Bereitschaft zur Grenzerfahrung in der Begegnung mit dem Fremden, die Bereitschaft, sich in Bewegung zu setzen und Raum zu gewähren; gegenseitiger Respekt lautet die Grundforderung, die in den einschlägigen kirchlichen Dokumenten immer wieder laut wird. Nicht den Verzicht auf eigene Verortung verlangt ein ernsthafter Dialog, wohl aber den Verzicht auf eine Identifizierung des Eigenen mit einem Ort, den Verzicht auf den Versuch, durch die ständige Beset-

27 Die Forderung der Nächstenliebe kann allerdings ebenfalls als Ausdruck dieser spirituellen Herausforderung verstanden werden, wenn jene Umkehrung der Fragestellung mitvollzogen wird, die Jesus im Gleichnis vom barmherzigen Samariter seinen Zuhörern zumutet: von der Frage "Wer ist mein Nächster?" zu der Frage "Wem erweise ich mich als Nächster?" (Lk 10, 25-37).

zung eines Ortes die Zeit beherrschen zu wollen. Räume zum Schutz eines vorgeblich reinen und unveränderlichen Innen gegen jede Möglichkeit der Veräußerung immunisieren zu wollen, bedeutet, sie zu mythologisieren und zu sakralisieren, sie der Geschichte und der Zeit entheben zu wollen. Dagegen hält beispielsweise die Enzyklika "Redemptoris missio" von Johannes Paul II. aus dem Jahr 1990 fest: "Der Dialog ist ein Weg zum Reich Gottes und wird sicherlich Frucht bringen, auch wenn Zeiten und Fristen dem Vater vorbehalten sind." (RM 57)[28] Die Bereitschaft zum Dialog beinhaltet somit auch die Anerkennung der Herrschaft Gottes über die Zeit. Damit wird jedem Versuch eine Absage erteilt, die Aporie zwischen Dialog und Verkündigung auf Kosten des Dialogs auflösen zu wollen.

Einschlägige lehramtliche Texte folgen bei der Verhältnisbestimmung zwischen Dialog und Verkündigung allerdings durchgängig einer Logik der Erfüllung. Dieser Logik zufolge habe zwar auch die Kirche wie andere Glaubensgemeinschaften den Dialog nötig, um zur Fülle der Wahrheit und zur Fülle des Reiches Gottes zu gelangen. Doch dieser historischen Komponente steht eine überzeitliche entgegen. Denn im Unterschied zu anderen Glaubensgemeinschaften sei die Kirche bereits grundsätzlich im Besitz dieser Fülle, auf die auch andere zustreben. Das "Wie" dieses Unterschieds hat mit Jesus Christus zu tun, doch wie es genau gedacht werden soll, wird nicht deutlich. So betont die gerade zitierte Enzyklika "Redemptoris missio" an anderer Stelle, "daß die Kirche der eigentliche Weg des Heiles ist und daß sie allein im Besitz der Fülle der Heilsmittel ist" (RM 55). Worin das "Eigentliche" des Weges besteht und wie diese Aussage mit der wenig später hervorgehobenen Rolle des interreligiösen Dialogs zu vereinbaren ist, bleibt offen.

Waldenfels hat darauf aufmerksam gemacht, daß der Dialog zum Etikettenschwindel werden kann, wenn er ganz darauf setzt, die Differenzen der Beteiligten im Prozeß des Dialogs in einem gemeinsamen Logos aufzuheben. Dieses Vertrauen auf die allen Differenzen übergeordnete Einheit des Logos, das als "Logozentrik" das neuzeitliche

[28] Der *Päpstliche Rat für den Interreligiösen Dialog* spricht in seinen Dokumenten zum Thema Dialog ähnlich von der "Zeit der Geduld Gottes" (in Päpstlicher Rat für den Interreligiösen Dialog, *Die Haltung der Kirche gegenüber den Anhängern anderer Religionen*, Rom 1984) und von der "Chronologie des Geistes" (in ders. & Kongregation für die Evangelisierung der Völker, *Dialog und Verkündigung*, Rom 1991).

Programm des Vernunftsubjekts kennzeichne, mache aus dem Dialog in Wirklichkeit einen Monolog mit verteilten Rollen. Die Fremdheit der Dialogpartner markiere in einem solchen Pseudo-Dialog nicht die Kontingenz von miteinander inkompatiblen Ordnungen, sondern lediglich das noch nicht Gewußte oder auch nur das noch nicht Gesagte der einen und einzigen universalen Vernunftordnung.[29]

Dieser kaschierte Monolog, in dem der andere als völlig identifizierbar erscheint, sei unproduktiv, da aller Sinn für ihn im Prinzip präfabriziert sei und nur noch in verschiedenen Situationen appliziert oder reproduziert werden müsse.[30] Waldenfels stellt diesem Scheindialog, der in der Begegnung mit dem Fremden versucht, ganz im Eigenen zu bleiben, ein "Grenzverhalten" gegenüber, "das sich auf Fremdes einläßt, ohne es dem Eigenen gleichzumachen oder es einem Allgemeinen zu unterwerfen."[31] An anderer Stelle spricht er von einem "Agieren und Denken auf der Grenze".[32] In diesem Grenzverhalten sei der Fremde nicht mehr eindeutig in eigenem Wissen oder eigener Erfahrung identifizierbar, ebensowenig wie das Eigene: "Eigenes und Fremdes entstehen zugleich und verändern sich zugleich."[33] Waldenfels greift ein Diktum von Kleist auf, wenn er von der "Verfertigung von Gedanken in der gemeinsamen Rede"[34] spricht, um auf die diskursive Produktivität des Grenzverhaltens aufmerksam zu machen. Die "Verflechtung" von Eigenem und Fremdem widersetze sich den Geltungsansprüchen eines präfabrizierten Sin-

---

29 Waldenfels, S. 43-56; vgl. auch die Kritik, die Suess in dieser Sache an dem diskursethischen Ansatz von Habermas übt, Suess, S. 236 und 245f.

30 Waldenfels, S. 52f. und 66. Den kritischen Anfragen an eine Logozentrik hat sich auch das Logos-Verständnis der Christologie zu stellen. Zu fragen wäre etwa, wie ernst die Theologie die Inkarnation des Logos nimmt und damit auch seinen Leib und seine Geschichte. Gerade bei der Frage der Universalität des Logos in der Geschichte kann ein rationalistisches Logos-Verständnis, zumal wenn es sich auf Gesagtes, Gedachtes und Gewolltes beschränkt und den Akten des Sagens, Denkens und Wollens keine Bedeutung beimißt, schnell in Sackgassen führen.

31 A.a.O., S. 39.

32 A.a.O., S. 64.

33 A.a.O., S. 65.

34 A.a.O., S. 66. Der Essay von Kleist trägt den Titel *Über die allmähliche Verfertigung der Gedanken beim Reden* und stammt aus dem Jahre 1805.

nes.[35] Ihre Produktivität vermag sie vor allem dann zu entfalten, wenn alle Beteiligten sich für die Begegnung auf die Grenze wagen. In einer Situation der Migration haben die Einheimischen dabei in aller Regel einen Nachholbedarf.

Ganz ähnliche Gedanken, wie Waldenfels sie aus der Sicht der philosophischen Phänomenologie entwickelt, finden sich auch bei dem französischen Theologen und Historiker Certeau. Er spricht von der "Arbeit an der Grenze"[36] und meint damit die Überschreitung des eigenen Ortes, der in den Grenzen seiner Partikularität erkannt ist. Da aber dieses Überschreiten ("dépassement") immer nur an einen anderen partikularen Ort und nicht zum Universalen führe, bleibe die Arbeit an der Grenze eine ständige Aufgabe, die sich aus einem ständigen Mangel ergebe. Der andere, der Fremde, dessen Fremdheit an der Grenze des Eigenen erfahrbar wird, fehle immer. Doch er lasse sich nicht durch die Ausdehnung der Grenzen des Eigenen einverleiben. Im Gegenteil, wenn ich den Fremden nicht ausgrenzen wolle, müsse ich ihm Platz machen im Eigenen.

Die Grenze ist hier nicht das Mittel zur Sicherung des Eigenen durch Ausgrenzung möglicher Eindringlinge oder Einverleibung von Außenstehenden. Sie ist die Markierung meiner Endlichkeit und Partikularität, die mir zeigt, wer und was mir fehlt.[37] Auch für Certeau gilt, daß Sinn nicht etwas Universelles, ein für alle Mal Präfabriziertes ist, sondern im geschichtlichen Plural partikularer Orte und ihrer Grenzen sich immer wieder angesichts eines Mangels am anderen neu

---

[35] Bei der Beschreibung dieser Verflechtung greift Waldenfels (unbemerkt?) fast wörtlich die christologische Formel von Chalkedon auf: "weder Verschmelzung im Sinne einer Nicht-Unterschiedenheit noch Trennung im Sinne einer Wohlunterschiedenheit", a.a.O., S. 65. Der in sich widersprüchliche Versuch, im Logos einer Sprache ein Verhältnis von zwei Fremden zu beschreiben, deren Fremdheit nicht in einem gemeinsamen Logos auflösbar ist, führt zwangsläufig zu widersprüchlichen Formulierungen, die nur noch aus der Negation heraus sich um präzise Bedeutung bemühen können ("un-vermischt, un-veränderlich, un-getrennt und un-teilbar" wie es in der chalkedonensischen Formel heißt). Solche Sprache ist poetisch in dem Sinne, daß sie sich selbst an die Grenze des Sagbaren begibt, um diese Grenze und damit ihr Jenseits, ihr Außen, von innen her zu bezeichnen. Das auf der Grenze zwischen Sagbarem und Unsagbarem Gesagte ist nach den Regeln der Sprachordnung, an deren Grenze es gesagt wird, notwendigerweise para—dox.

[36] Michel de Certeau, *La faiblesse de croire*, Paris 1987, S. 219 ("un travail sur la limite") und S. 225 ("un travail sur les limites").

[37] A.a.O., S. 216.

als Frage stellt und in Grenzüberschreitungen neu beantwortet wird.[38] Das, wie Michel de Certeau sich in Anlehnung an Heidegger ausdrückt, "Nicht ohne"[39] des Mangels verhindere, daß aus der Pluralität ein beziehungsloses Nebeneinander wird. Denn es gebe sich nicht damit zufrieden, den Mangel am anderen zu konstatieren, sondern versuche, dem anderen an der Grenze des Eigenen entgegenzugehen.

Werde dieses "Nicht ohne" im Auge behalten, so sei auch die Pluralität der Orte, von denen aus Menschen Bezug auf Jesus Christus nehmen, keine Bedrohung für deren Zusammenhang. Denn, und darin liegt eine christologische Zentralaussage von Certeau, Jesus Christus selbst habe diese Pluralität "autorisiert", d.h. ermöglicht und legitimiert, indem er in Tod und Himmelfahrt "Platz gemacht hat" für die Gemeinschaft der Glaubenden. Die Wahrheit seines Anfangs sei weder aus dem Willen oder dem Gesagten Jesu Christi vollständig rekonstruierbar, noch könne sie von irgendeinem partikularen Wissen oder irgendeiner partikularen Autorität vollständig repräsentiert werden: Vielmehr lasse sich der Anfang, für den Jesus Christus steht, nur im Plural geschichtlicher Erfahrung und christlichen Zeugnisses in Wort und Tat "verifizieren", wahr machen.[40] Bereits die vier Evangelien sind für Certeau Zeugnis dafür, daß sich der singuläre Anfang in Jesus Christus nicht von seiner pluralen Bezeugung trennen lasse.

Die streckenweise abstrakt anmutende Gedankenführung von Certeau hat weitreichende Konsequenzen für ein theologisches Verständnis der Bedeutung des anderen für Kirche und Christentum. Das "Nicht ohne", mit dem Jesus selbst der Gemeinschaft der Glaubenden Platz gemacht hat, bedeutet einen Verzicht darauf, Universalität anders an Partikulares zu binden als in der Form des Mangels. Nicht dieses oder jenes Wissen, diese oder jene Praxis, diese oder jene Institution ist der exklusive Raum der "Wahrheit" des in Christus gesetzten Anfangs, sondern allein der Plural geschichtlichen Handelns und Sprechens, der

38 A.a.O., S. 213, 215-218.

39 A.a.O., S. 111f.

40 A.a.O., S. 107f. und S. 214f.; zu Certeaus Begriff von Autorität als Autorschaft, die anderes als sich selbst ermöglicht und für dieses andere dann ebenso notwendig wie unzugänglich ist, vgl. a.a.O., S. 110-112. Die Nähe dieses Verständnisses von Autorität bzw. Autorschaft zu jenem Autortyp, den Foucault "diskursivitätsbegründend" nennt, ist unübersehbar; vgl. Michel Foucault, *Schriften zur Literatur*, Frankfurt am Main 1979, S. 24.

konkret an den Grenzen des Eigenen zu anderen erfahren werden kann und Ausgangspunkt für weiteres Handeln und Sprechen ist. Für den innerkirchlichen Dialog folgt daraus die plurale und gemeinschaftliche Form kirchlicher Autorität: "Allein ein *plurales Zeichen* ist der Autorität Gottes angemessen [...]".[41] Auch für das außerkirchliche Verhältnis zu anderen bedeutet das "Nicht ohne" eine grundsätzliche Bejahung der menschlichen Geschichte in ihrer Partikularität und Pluralität als dem einzigen Ort christlicher Erfahrung und christlichen Zeugnisses.

In der Entwicklung des christlichen und kirchlichen Selbstverständnisses, wie es sich um den Begriff des Dialogs zu artikulieren begonnen hat, nimmt der Fremde nicht mehr nur die Rolle des Nichtchristen (Nichtkatholiken) ein, dem die Kirche um seines Heiles willen die Glaubenswahrheit zu vermitteln hat, als deren einzig autorisierte Besitzerin und Hüterin sie sich selber sieht. Der Fremde rückt vielmehr als unverzichtbarer Partner der gemeinsamen Geschichte aller Menschen ins Gesichtsfeld, deren Pluralität an Lebensformen auch dann als Reichtum der Schöpfung Gottes und des Wirkens seines Geistes gewürdigt und gefeiert werden kann, wenn sie sich nicht den Grenzen einer Kirche einverleiben läßt, die ihre "Katholizität" auch immer nur in partikularen Formen zu realisieren vermag.

Im Rahmen dieser Entwicklung könnte die Migration vielleicht als ein "Zeichen der Zeit" verstanden werden: als Chance für die Kirche, die Wirklichkeit des Fremden, die neue Räume öffnen kann, nicht nur "draußen" in einer expansiv zu besetzenden Fremde zu entdecken, sondern "drinnen" im Eigenen, das auf diese Weise zwar als fest abgegrenzter und fixer Ort verloren gehen mag, dafür aber in Bewegung und Begegnung neues Leben gewinnen kann.

Säkularität

Der Dialog ist ein Stil des Handelns und Sprechens, der für die Kirche neu ist. Er ist ein Stil, der sich auf die Pluralität der Welt und ihrer Geschichte einläßt, ohne sich an die Stelle eines Gottes setzen zu wollen, der ihre Einheit und ihren Sinn bereits fest in den Blick nehmen könnte. Die Anerkennung dieser Pluralität nicht nur als ein Faktum,

---

[41] A.a.O., 107f.: "seul est proportionné à l'autorité de Dieu un *signe pluriel*" (Hervorhebung im Original).

das man nicht leugnen kann, sondern als eine legitime, d.h. von Gott in Christus "autorisierte" Pluralität, wird der westlichen Kirche im Laufe eines Prozesses abgerungen, der unter dem Etikett der "Säkularisierung" bekannt ist. Diese Umwertung der eigenen Position und der Positionen der anderen, die das gesamte System der theologischen und kirchlichen Verortungen in Bewegung gebracht hat, verdankt sich allerdings auch der Tatsache, daß die Säkularisierung ihrerseits an Entwicklungen und Konzepte anknüpfen kann, die Teil der christlichen Tradition sind. Die Anerkennung der Menschenrechte einschließlich des Rechtes auf Gewissens- und Religionsfreiheit sind ein Beispiel dafür.

Der Prozeß der Säkularisierung interessiert an dieser Stelle jedoch nur insofern, als er den gesellschaftlichen Raum geprägt hat, in dem die aktuelle Begegnung von Muslimen verschiedener "Konfessionen" mit Christen sowie mit anderen Menschen stattfindet, die sich keiner der beiden Religionen zurechnen. Weil es hier nicht um die historische Entwicklung, sondern um die Prägung der aktuellen Situation geht, verwende ich im folgenden auch nicht das geläufige Wort "Säkularisierung", sondern spreche von "Säkularität". Damit ist keine "Entzauberung der Welt" im Sinne von Weber gemeint, sondern ein spätneuzeitlicher Gesellschaftszustand, der sich durch hochgradige funktionale Differenzierung, Pluralität der Lebensformen und Wertorientierungen, Individualisierung der Biographien und Distanz zu institutionell verfaßter Religion auszeichnet. Säkularität bedeutet keine systematische Verbannung von Religion aus dem öffentlichen Leben, wohl aber eine entschiedene Absage an eine Legitimierung oder gar Kontrolle staatlichen Handelns durch Religion. Die Grundlage des Staates und die gesellschaftliche Kohärenz dürfen nicht einer bestimmten Religion verbindlich zugeordnet werden.

In einer so bestimmten säkularen Situation ist nicht nur die weitgehend fraglose Deckungsgleichheit von christlicher Religionsgemeinschaft und profaner Gesellschaft und Kultur verlorengegangen, sondern auch die Möglichkeit, ein geschlossenes Milieu des Katholizismus auszubilden, das als einheitlicher und alle Lebensbereiche umfassender, kirchlich kontrollierter Bezugsrahmen für alle Gläubigen funktioniert, wie es innerhalb der bürgerlich-industriellen Gesellschaft der sogenannten "halbierten Moderne" noch möglich war.[42] Dieses Milieu ist inzwischen so dysfunktional geworden, daß es sich als integrierender Gesamtrahmen aufgelöst hat und nur noch in engen Nischen überlebt.[43] Mit der Auflösung des geschlossenen Milieus verliert die vormals identitätsstiftende Dichotomie von Kirche und Welt ihre Plausibilität und Funktionalität.

Auch die kirchlichen Stellungnahmen zur Präsenz des Islams in Deutschland sind, wie die Analyse gezeigt hat, in ihren Positionen gegenüber der Säkularität der deutschen Gesellschaft nicht eindeutig. Diese mangelnde Eindeutigkeit verrät eine Unsicherheit in der Bewertung der Säkularität und in der Frage nach angemessenen christlichen und kirchlichen Reaktionen.

Gerade hinsichtlich der Gestaltung ihres jeweiligen Verhältnisses zur Säkularität westlicher Gesellschaften, hier konkret der deutschen, könnten christliche Kirchen und islamische Gemeinschaften wertvolle Partner füreinander sein. Allerdings kann sich dabei für die Kirche die paradoxe Situation ergeben, daß sie in dem Maße, in dem sie sich durch die grundsätzliche Bejahung der religiösen Pluralität einem wirklichen Dialog mit anderen Religionen öffnet, in die Gefahr gerät, von ihren potentiellen Dialogpartnern wegen der Bejahung dieses "säkularen" Prinzips nicht mehr als Religion ernst genommen zu werden. Umso dringlicher ist es, Dialog und Zeugnis so miteinander zu verknüpfen, daß die Bejahung von Säkularität nicht als Resignation oder Opportunismus, sondern als eine Bejahung aus genuin christlicher Motivation erkennbar wird.

Bei den kirchlichen Dokumenten hatte die Arbeitshilfe von 1993

---

42 Für eine knappe Skizze der Hauptmerkmale des Katholizismus s. K. Gabriel, *Christentum zwischen Tradition und Moderne*, Freiburg 1992, S. 80-82. Auch die begriffliche Unterscheidung von "Kultur" und "Religion", "profan" und "religiös" ist bereits ein Zeugnis des Auseinanderfallens einer vorher fraglosen Deckungsgleichheit und insofern erst in einer säkularen Situation möglich. Daraus folgt auch, daß eine Anwendung der genannten Begriffe außerhalb ihres europäischen Entstehungsraums nicht unproblematisch ist; vgl. Gabriel, S. 45f.; G. Evers, *Mission*, Münster 1974, S. 169-182. Pieris ist 1984 in einem Artikel auf die Konsequenzen eingegangen, die sich aus der Kontextbindung dieser Unterscheidungen für das Inkulturationsverständnis ergeben: Aloysius Pieris, *Theologie der Befreiung in Asien*, Freiburg 1986, S. 79-91.

43 Für die evangelischen Christen in Deutschland ist die Entwicklung insgesamt anders verlaufen. Ein dem Katholizismus entsprechendes, geschlossenes Großmilieu haben sie nicht entwickelt. Dennoch zeigen sich für die aktuelle Situation durchaus Parallelen, vgl. V. Drehsen, *Wie religionsfähig ist die Volkskirche?* Gütersloh 1994.

zum ersten Mal die Säkularität der deutschen Gesellschaft als ein Thema für Christen und Muslime erwähnt. Es ging dabei ausschließlich um die Hilfestellung, die das Christentum einer säkularen Gesellschaft dem Islam zu bieten habe. Diese Perspektive aber vernachlässigt den Argwohn, der christlichen Institutionen als Agenten des Säkularismus von islamischer Seite entgegengebracht wird,[44] sie verleugnet auch die Tatsache, daß die katholische Kirche ihr eigenes Verhältnis zur Säkularität noch keineswegs geklärt hat.

Nun ist eine solche Klärung keine Vorbedingung für gemeinsames Suchen Die Offenheit der Frage kann das Gespräch sogar fördern. Allerdings sollte diese Offenheit eingestanden werden. Nur so können Fragen geklärt werden, die sich im Verhältnis zum Islam ergeben, Fragen wie das Verständnis von Toleranz und Religionsfreiheit oder die Bewertung der Prägung des öffentlichen Lebens durch Religion sowie die rechtlichen Verankerung dieser Prägung.

Im Mittelpunkt eines solchen Gespräches zwischen Islam und Christentum zur Säkularität dürfte die Frage stehen, ob religiöse Pluralität ohne Säkularität auf einer Basis der Gleichberechtigung realisiert und abgesichert werden kann. Weder im Christentum noch im Islam kann diese Frage als beantwortet gelten. Muslimische Forderungen nach Gleichberechtigung für den Islam in Deutschland beispielsweise argumentieren explizit oder implizit in aller Regel mit der säkularen Verfassungsgrundlage, ohne jedoch ihre eigenen Prärogativen hinsichtlich einer rechtlichen Verankerung der islamischen Prägung des privaten und öffentlichen Lebens grundsätzlich in Frage zu stellen, obgleich diese in offenem Widerspruch zu der genannten säkularen Grundlage stehen. Umgekehrt mahnen kirchliche Dokumente immer wieder die Religionsfreiheit an, kritisieren und beklagen aber zugleich den Verlust an kirchlichem Einfluß in den westlichen säkularen Gesellschaften.[45]

---

44 Vgl. Ch. Troll, Mission und Dialog am Beispiel des Islams, Cibedo 4 (1990), S. 103.

45 Diese Ambivalenzen werden besonders in Texten sichtbar, die um die "christlichen Wurzeln Europas" und das Konzept einer "Neu-Evangelisierung" kreisen. Nicht immer kann hier der Eindruck vermieden werden, es gehe darum, die (katholische) Kirche wieder in eine gesellschaftliche Machtposition einzusetzen, die sie im Prozeß der Säkularisierung eingebüßt hat, vgl. G. Evers, Inculturation as New Evangelization, *Jahrbuch für kontextuelle Theologien* 2 (1994), S. 73-100, hier: S. 88-97.

Säkularität als spirituelle Herausforderung

Die Behauptung, die Säkularität stelle spirituelle Herausforderungen an die Kirche, enthält bereits eine Aussage über das Verhältnis von christlichem Glauben und säkularer Gesellschaft. Denn allein die Möglichkeit, daß Christen von ihrem säkularen gesellschaftlichen Lebenszusammenhang, nicht nur in ihrem Sozialstatus oder ihrer Standfestigkeit gegenüber profanen Versuchungen, sondern *in ihrem Glauben* herausgefordert werden können, widerspricht jeder Dichotomisierung von christlichem Glauben bzw. christlicher Glaubensgemeinschaft und säkularer, profaner Welt.[46]

Spirituelle Erfahrung ist nicht an spezifisch christlichen Inhalten festzumachen. Sie artikuliert vielmehr einen Riß im Lebenszusammenhang, den das kulturelle Kontinuum und seine von ihm nicht zu trennende religiöse Deutung bis dato gewährt haben. Die spirituelle Erfahrung eines solchen Bruches erlebt der Gläubige als eine fundamentale Enttäuschung. Hinter der Fassade des kulturellen und religiösen Kontinuums mit seinen universalen Geltungs- und Deutungsansprüchen und seinen transzendenten Verheißungen macht er eine Leere aus, die er dennoch nicht einfach mit der Abwesenheit Gottes zu identifizieren bereit ist. Die so verstandene spirituelle Erfahrung ist eine "Provokation": Sie ruft den Glaubenden aus seinen grundlegenden Zusammenhängen heraus. Sie fordert seine Bewegung, sein Exil, ohne ihm bereits mehr bieten zu können als diese Bewegung, jedenfalls kein neues Heim, das er nur zu beziehen hätte.

Der Riß geht sowohl durch das kulturell etablierte Verhältnis zur "Welt" als auch durch das religiös etablierte Verhältnis zu "Gott". Dieser Riß und die radikale Bereitschaft, sich ihm auszusetzen, sind charakteristisch für spirituelle Erfahrungen und Haltungen. In verschiedenen geschichtlichen Situationen prägen sie verschiedene Spiritualitäten aus. Ein unauflösbarer Zusammenhang zwischen Kultur, Religion und Spiritualität wird sichtbar: Jede Art von Spiritualität ist ein Versuch, Antworten auf die Fragen ihrer Zeit und ihrer Kultur zu finden, denen gegenüber sich die Instrumente dieser Kultur als ebenso stumpf erweisen wie die Instrumente der Religion, die in den Spra-

46 Kehl verwendet in seiner Ekklesiologie dafür den treffenden Begriff der "Schicksalsgemeinschaft mit der Moderne". Medard Kehl, Die Kirche, Würzburg 1992, S. 200f.

chen und Formen dieser Kultur artikuliert ist. Auch frühere Spiritualitäten können den Riß nicht überbrücken. In der Erfahrung des Risses im Kontinuum steht das Ganze in Frage. In dieser Situation wird es unabweislich, daß Fragen nach dem Verhältnis zur "Welt" und nach dem Verhältnis zu "Gott" nicht getrennt beantwortet werden können:

"Mit all dem, was sie [die spirituelle Enttäuschung; G. Stoll] an Schwäche, an verlorenem Gleichgewicht oder Illusion mit sich bringen mag [...], bezeugt sie einen Glauben, der weiß, daß er Gott dort finden muß, wo sich die Frage des Menschen stellt, und der es ablehnt, die Unzulänglichkeit der religiösen Zeichen für eine Abwesenheit Gottes zu halten."[47]

Eine so verstandene Spiritualität wendet sich gegen eine Auflösung des Spannungsverhältnisses von Kultur und Religion, sei es durch die Reduzierung eines der beiden Pole auf den anderen, sei es durch eine vollständige Trennung der beiden Pole. Damit stellt sie sich gegen

- eine Reduzierung von Religion auf einen begrenzten Sektor oder eine bestimmte Funktion innerhalb einer Kultur und Gesellschaft;
- eine totale religiöse Identifizierung und Bestimmung von Kultur;
- ein Heilsverständnis, das eine "Heilsgeschichte" von einer "Profangeschichte" abtrennt und in der Praxis sich um die Errichtung sakraler Enklaven in einer vorgeblich heillosen "Welt" bemüht.

Während der erste Punkt in der kirchlichen Tradition nie strittig war, haben der zweite und dritte Punkt ihre kirchliche Anerkennung erst in diesem Jahrhundert gefunden, vor allem in den Dokumenten des Zweiten Vatikanischen Konzils mit den beiden Zentralbegriffen des Dialogs und der Autonomie.[48]

Die erste und grundlegende Herausforderung der säkularen Gesellschaft an den christlichen Glauben und die christlichen Kirchen liegt also darin, die säkulare Gesellschaft und Kultur überhaupt erst als Ort spiritueller Herausforderung und damit der Präsenz des Geistes Gottes ernst zu nehmen und nicht nur als Gefährdung eines sakral verstandenen Glaubens und als Degenerationsform einer besseren, weil (scheinbar) durchgängig religiös bestimmten Kultur und Gesellschaft.

---

[47] Michel de Certeau, S. 42; meine Ausführungen verdanken seinen Gedanken viel.

[48] Für den Dialog wurden bereits Textnachweise gegeben. In Bezug auf die "richtige Autonomie der irdischen Wirklichkeit" vgl. die Konzilskonstitution *Gaudium et Spes*, Nr. 36, S. 41, 55f. und 76.

Dieses Ringen um die säkulare Dimension der christlichen Spiritualität, das einhergeht mit der Anerkennung der spirituellen Dimension der säkularen Realität, scheint mir auch für die Begegnung zwischen Christentum und Islam von hoher Bedeutung. Denn die Unbestimmtheit des Verhältnisses von "Religion" und "Kultur" zeigt sich im Zusammenleben von Menschen verschiedener Religionen und Kulturen immer wieder als Quelle von Mißverständnissen und von Gewalt. Die Klärung dieses Verhältnisses bedeutet aber die Annahme der spirituellen Herausforderung der Säkularität.

Das Zweite Vatikanische Konzil hat hier die wichtige Unterscheidung zwischen Kirche und Reich Gottes mehrfach in Erinnerung gerufen. Die Kirche ist nicht identisch mit dem nahenden Reich Gottes, und sie ist auch nicht für sich allein dessen vollständige Repräsentation. Geschichtliche Vermittlung bedeutet nicht mehr, wie es in früheren lehramtlichen Äußerungen häufig der Fall war, nur die Kommunikation und Umsetzung einer der Kirche anvertrauten Heilswahrheit, sondern eine spirituelle Suchbewegung, die durch die Erfahrung von Rissen sowohl in der gegenwärtigen Kultur als auch in deren religiöser Deutung wach gehalten wird. Die Fülle des Reiches Gottes aber kann auch die Kirche nur zusammen mit dem erwarten, was sie selbst nicht ist und nicht hat.

Indem die "Ordnung des Profanen", wie Benjamin schreibt, sich an der Idee des Glücks und nicht am Reich Gottes orientiert, erinnert sie durch ihre Autonomie gegenüber dem Reich Gottes daran, daß das Reich Gottes nicht als Ziel historischer Dynamik gesetzt, sondern nur vom Messias als Vollendung alles historisch Geschehenen eröffnet werden kann.[49] Auch die Christen und christlichen Kirchen, die sich auf Jesus Christus als den Messias berufen, können durch die ernst genommene Säkularität immer wieder an diese "messianische Intensi-

---

49 W. Benjamin, *Gesammelte Schriften*, Bd. II/1 hrsg. von Rolf Tiedemann & Hermann Schweppenhäuser, Frankfurt am Main 1977, 203f. Hier wird das grundsätzliche Defizit rationalistischer Geschichtstheologien deutlich, die versuchen, durch eine inhaltliche Auswertung von Offenbarung zu Grundaxiomen einer solchen historischen Dynamik zu gelangen. Der Messias aber wird nicht erhofft als ein Hermes, der göttliche Botschaften überbringt, sondern als Vollendung alles historisch Geschehenen, als Präsenz des Ganzen der Geschichte in der Geschichte, als deren Alpha und Omega. Für die Geschichte lassen sich daraus keine Gesetzmäßigkeiten ableiten, sondern nur ihr bleibender Status als Ort der Selbstmitteilung Gottes und seiner Begegnung mit den Menschen.

tät"[50] als den Motor der eigenen spirituellen Bewegung erinnert werden. Diese Bewegung geht dann nicht von einem zwar noch nicht verwirklichten, aber doch bereits faßbaren Ideal aus, sondern von den konkreten Erfahrungen von Mangel, in denen Fülle angezeigt, aber nie faßbar wird.

Das Erfüllungsmodell, dem die meisten lehramtlichen Texte bei der Bestimmung des Verhältnisses von Dialog und Verkündigung und damit auch von Geschichte und Wahrheit folgen, fordert zwar Aufmerksamkeit für die "Zeichen der Zeit" und die "Samenkörner des Wortes Gottes" außerhalb von Kirche und Christentum. Doch es bleiben zwei wichtige Fragen offen. Die erste ist die bereits angesprochene Frage, wie genau das Privileg der Kirche aussieht und zu begründen ist, nachdem diese trotz ihrer eigenen Angewiesenheit auf Umkehr und Erfüllung doch bereits als einzige die angestrebte Fülle irgendwie schon besitzt.

Eine zweite Frage meldet grundsätzlich Skepsis an, ob ein Erfüllungsmodell überhaupt in der Lage ist, das Spannungsverhältnis von menschlicher Geschichte und Reich Gottes angemessen zur Sprache zu bringen. Mag das noch angehen, solange man nur auf die "Reichtümer" der partikularen Religionen und Kulturen schaut und die Möglichkeiten gegenseitiger "Bereicherung", so drängt sich bei einem Blick auf die Opfer der Geschichte, auf die an den Rand Gedrängten und Ausgeschlossenen bald der Verdacht auf, daß das Erfüllungsschema seine theoretische Harmonisierungsleistung um den Preis eines erneuten Ausschlusses der bereits Ausgeschlossenen erkauft. Auf die Wunde dieses Mangels nicht nur an Fülle, sondern der Fülle selbst legen Vertreter von Befreiungstheologie und politischer Theologie immer wieder zu Recht den Finger.

Partikularität und Universalität — Der eine Gott und die Geschichte(n) der Menschen

Gerade die Migrationssituation bringt es, wie eingangs beschrieben, mit sich, daß viele, Migranten ebenso wie "Einheimische", sich als Opfer einer ungewollten und unkontrollierbaren Entfremdung erle-

50 Ebd.

ben. In den unheilvollen Erfahrungen innerer Zerrissenheit (etwa in zugespitzten Generationskonflikten in Migrantenfamilien) oder äußerer Konflikte zwischen "Fremden" schwingt mehr oder weniger latent der Faktor Gewalt mit. Das Zerbrechen der geschlossenen Einheit des "Eigenen" ist schmerzhaft und hinterläßt ein Gefühl der Ohnmacht. Um diese Risse zu heilen, bieten sich zwei Wege an: Selbstbehauptung und Versöhnung.

Die spontane Reaktion auf das "Ohne dich", das als Botschaft in der tatsächlichen oder vermeintlichen Mißachtung durch den anderen enthalten ist, ist meist ein Selbstbehauptungsreflex: "Nicht ohne mich". Von diesem "Nicht ohne mich" scheint jedoch der Weg zu einem "Ohne dich" mit verändertem Vorzeichen kürzer zu sein als zu einem gegenseitigen "Nicht ohne dich". Um nicht Opfer zu bleiben, versucht das Opfer Täter zu werden - dem ursprünglichen Täter gegenüber oder auch gegen unbeteiligte, vorzugsweise schwächere Dritte. Diese Ambivalenz der Opferrolle fördert einen Kreislauf der Gewalt, in dem erlittene Erniedrigung durch die Erniedrigung anderer vergessen gemacht werden soll. Die Unmöglichkeit, die Erinnerung an erlittene Gewalt durch Vergessen zu exorzieren, hält diesen Kreislauf in Bewegung. Rache statt Versöhnung. Doch das unversöhnte Opfer bleibt auch mit sich selber unversöhnt: Es kann sich durch die Gewaltbotschaft des "Ohne dich" anderen gegenüber seines eigenen "Nicht ohne mich" zu vergewissern suchen. Für seine Heilung, seine Einheit und Ganzheit, bleibt es dennoch auf das "Nicht ohne dich" der anderen angewiesen, das es jedoch nicht erzwingen kann.

Das verweist auf den zweiten Weg, den der Versöhnung. Versöhnung bedeutet nicht etwa Selbstaufgabe im Unterschied zur Selbstbehauptung, wohl aber das Eingeständnis bleibender Angewiesenheit auf die fremden anderen für die angestrebte Heilung des zerbrochenen "Eigenen". Wer Heilung des Zerrissenen in der Versöhnung sucht, erkennt an, daß er allein seine eigene Heilung nicht ins Werk setzen kann, sondern genau jene anderen dafür braucht, deren Fremdheit die Risse überhaupt erst ausgelöst hat. Der Selbstbehauptungsreflex klammert sich an die Illusion der Machbarkeit, um die verlorengegangene Selbstgewißheit wiederherzustellen. Damit bleibt er auf unfruchtbare Weise an die Vergangenheit gefesselt. Der Weg der Versöhnung ist dagegen nach vorne gerichtet, weil er um diese Illusion weiß. Dafür zahlt er freilich den Preis bleibender Ungewißheit über die Gestalt des Zieles. Wer Versöhnung sucht, verzichtet darauf, das Ziel, das nur gemeinsam mit den fremden Anderen erreicht werden kann, im Vorhinein festzulegen und den Weg dorthin zu kontrollieren.

Europe and its Muslim neighbors

Recent meetings of intercultural dialogue

Jacques Waardenburg
Université de Lausanne

With the establishment of Republican Turkey in 1923 and the independence of nearly all Arab countries before and after World War II, the relations between European and surrounding Muslim countries could enter a new phase, that of relations between politically independent partners. Moreover, in the course of the last quarter of this century some political changes have taken place which have had an important impact on these relations. Particular examples are the Euro-Arab dialogue which started with the oil crisis of 1973, Turkey's coming closer to the European Economic Community in the 1980s, and the initiative of the European Union to arrive at a wider Euro-Mediterranean cooperation and dialogue, as formulated at the Barcelona Conference of 27 and 28 November 1996. After the demise of the USSR and communism, Western Europe came into contact with Muslim regions and peoples which had been practically closed off at the time of the Iron Curtain. They include the Balkans (Bosnia, Albania, Kosovo, Bulgaria), present-day Russia (with the Tatar people spread over the country, and with Muslim regions like Tatarstan, Chechenia and other Caucassian republics) and Muslim countries beyond Russia (Azerbaidjan and the Central Asian republics and Kazakhstan).

Both, the European countries and their Muslim neighbors have been searching to define and develop new mutual relationships. This search has been most spectacular in the political and economic fields, but there have been considerable changes, too, in the field of cultural relations, which is our interest here. In the colonial era Muslim countries had more or less exclusive cultural relations with the particular country to which they were subjected. Since independence they have also been able to develop bilateral relations with other countries. Cultural exchanges have taken place through international organizations and bilateral cultural agreements but they have also been furthered by private initiatives such as cultural foundations and scholarly institutions. Some European countries carry out a concerted cultural action abroad. France does this through the Alliance Française, and through research institutes and schools, the United Kingdom especially through the British Council, Germany through the Goethe Institutes and research institutes in Beirut and Istanbul.

I want to concentrate here, however, on those cultural relations which transcend the confines and interests of national states and which take place within a broader European or Mediterranean perspective. So I shall focus on four meetings of intercultural dialogue between Europe and its surrounding Muslim countries. I had the privilege of attending them, so that I can add some personal observations about them. "Culture" in the wider sense was at the center of these meetings; in other words, we are not dealing here with strictly scholarly or religious meetings or meetings concerned with the presence of Muslims in Europe. The conferences I will discuss are:

1. Strasbourg, 14-15 November 1991. Seminar organized by the Council of Europe on "Euro-Arab Understanding and Cultural Exchange";

2. Toledo, 4-7 November 1995. Conference organized by the European Union on "Mediterranean Society: A challenge for the three civilizations? Informal dialogue between Islam, Judaism and Christianity";

3. Amman, 3-5 April 1998. Conference organized at the University of Amman on "Arabs and the West";

4. Istanbul, 6-8 March 1998. Conference organized by the Municipality of Greater Istanbul on "Interfaith/Intercultural Dialogue".

Of these four conferences, two were organized by European bodies and took place in Europe, and the two others took place in Muslim countries thanks to local initiatives.

1. Euro-Arab Dialogue: Strasbourg 1991

A) Historical context

The so-called "Euro-Arab Dialogue" goes back to the October 1973 war between Egypt, Syria and Israel. At the time Iran and the oil-producing Arab countries increased the price of oil considerably and made an oil boycott against countries friendly to Israel. Following this, it was in Europe's interest to obtain guarantees for its oil imports from Arab countries, in exchange for greater economic and political cooperation with the Arab world. On the Arab side there was a need for development assistance but also the desire to arrive at a solution of the Palestine problem for which pressure needed to be put on the Europeans. The misery of the Palestinians in general and the wretched situation in the territories which Israel had occupied in 1967 in particular,where it had started to build Jewish settlements (against international conventions), as well as to proclaim the illegal annexation of East Jerusalem, and later the Golan Heights, were known to the Europeans but had as yet not elicited from them any coherent response.

All of this led to the first phase of the Euro-Arab dialogue, for which France took the initiative and leadership.[1] This led to negotiations between the European Economic Community (EEC) and the League of Arab States. It also opened up the area of cultural relations besides the properly political and economic relations. Its culmination may be considered the Seminar which was organized by the Cultural Committee of the Euro-Arab Dialogue, in Hamburg (11-15 April 1983).[2] Further relations in the 1980s were handicapped in particular through the exclusion of Egypt from the Arab League after the Camp David Agreement with Israel in 1978, the war between Iraq and Iran, and the continuing war in Lebanon with various international involvements. Western countries had different interests in all of this. The Palestine issue, however, came ever more on the international scene

---

1 Mustapha Benchenane, *Pour un dialogue euro-arabe,* Berger-Levrault, Paris,1983.

2 *Dialogue euro-arabe. Les relations entre les deux cultures.* Actes du Symposium de Hambourg (11-15 avril 1983). Ligue arabe et Communauté européenne, Edisud, Aix-en-Provence 1986. *Euro-Arab dialogue: The relation between the two cultures*: Acts of the Hamburg Symposium, April 11th to 15th 1983. Edited by Derek Hopwood, London 1985.

through the concerted action of different Palestinian organizations and especially when the *intifâda* started in 1989 in the territories occupied by Israel.

A second phase of the Euro-Arab dialogue started with the Gulf War of January and February 1991, after Iraq's occupation of Kuwait in August 1990. Just as the first phase was a response to the oil crisis of 1973, the second phase is to be seen as a response to the Gulf War and the turmoil in the Middle East in which Israel became more and more involved. The two wars of 1973 and 1991 were consequently instrumental in the initiation and pursuit of the Euro-Arab dialogue. Whereas the Americans after 1973 concentrated on achieving an Israeli-Egyptian settlement and after 1991 worked for a comprehensive "peace process" in the Near East, the Europeans since 1973 have been trying to cover their interests through a rapprochement with the Arab world under the title of "Euro-Arab dialogue". They were in fact marginal to the development of the “peace process”.

B) Organization

The Strasbourg seminar was a major event in intercultural relations during this second phase of the Euro-Arab dialogue. The initiative was taken by the Council of Ministers of the Council of Europe which works in particular on cultural and humane issues.[3]

The preparation of the seminar was taken care of by a Committee, chaired by Catherine Lalumière, Secretary General of the Council of Europe at that time. The Committee consisted of two Arab intellectuals living in Europe, a professor from the University of Ankara, and seven Europeans. The main theme, "Euro-Arab Understanding and Cultural Exchange", was divided into three subthemes: "The historical dimension of the Euro-Arab cultural dialogue" (report by Bernard Lewis), "Contemporary Euro-Arab perceptions and communication" (report by Hussein Ahmad Amin), and "Comparing mutual ideas and values of coexistence: the notion of democracy" (report by Şerif

[3] In May 1991 the Parliamentary Assembly of the Council of Europe had already organized a Colloquium in Paris on *The contribution of the Islamic civilisation to European culture*. Its proceedings were published as a Report of the Committee on Culture and Education (Rapporteur: Mr. Lluis Maria de Puig) with related documents by the Council of Europe in Strasbourg in 1992 (Document 6497).

Mardin).

The meeting took place in November 1991, that is to say nine months after the Gulf War of January/February of that year and one month after the Middle East Peace Conference held in Madrid in October 1991.[4]

C) The opening speeches

In her opening speech Lalumière outlined the activities of the Council of Europe in the cultural field, stressing its interest in an equal partnership and intercultural relationships between the Arab and European worlds. The relations and the dialogue between both worlds need to be improved, not only for intellectual but also for political reasons. On an intellectual level, much ignorance still exists among Europeans about the Arab countries, Arab thinking and Islam, while the Arab countries by and large are not very familiar with European thinking. On a political level there is a paradox in that the two worlds, while geographically close to each other, suffer from manifold problems in their relations with one another.

Lalumière expressed the hope that the seminar could achieve at least two aims. First of all the reasons for the bad relations which exist between Europe and the Arab world nowadays should be established. Secondly proposals should be made for how a better understanding between the two cultures could be brought about. As a next step the economic and political relations too should be improved. At the end she also expressed the hope that the meeting would contribute to an improvement in the relations between Europeans and their neighbors of Arab descent now living in Europe. These immigrants' conditions of life should also be improved.

In his opening speech the Deputy Secretary General of the League of Arab States, Adnan Omran, reminded the participants that the seminar represented an encounter between two regions which have had a

---

4 The proceedings of the Strasbourg seminar were published in three volumes under the general title: Council of Europe/Conseil de l'Europe, *Euro-Arab understanding and cultural exchange*. Euro-Arab seminar organised by the Secretary General of the Council of Europe, Strasbourg, 14-15 November 1991. The titles of the three volumes are: *Proceedings of the seminar* (156 p.), *Contributions* (190 p.) and *Summary* (50 p.). We refer here in particular to the second part of the *Proceedings* and to the *Contributions*.

common history of thousands of years. Their three monotheistic religions preached messages which implied a qualitative leap of humanity into a new era of ethics and values. These three messages had created a bridge between different peoples and furthered their mixing. After the past Gulf War (1991) attempts should be made to arrive at a new kind of society and a new international order.

Omran then highlighted one of the subthemes of the seminar, that of democracy. Complaining that this concept has been misused by some parties for specific political purposes, he explained that for the Arabs democracy implies the right to freedom and participation in decision making. This principle of freedom was given with the three monotheistic religions, but unfortunately their high values had suffered in the many conflicts which occurred in the course of history up to the 20th century. Omran mentioned as particularly fateful for freedom the practices of colonialism and neocolonialism. Unfortunately Europe furnishes examples of, on the one hand, judging a particular (Arab) country to be "undemocratic" whereas on the other hand, and at the same time, readily supporting other oppressive regimes. The Arab world expects Europe to support any group of people that, in its battle for freedom against occupation and for self-government, strives to realize values that are recognized in Europe.

Here Omran explicitly mentioned the Palestinian people. With regard to the Palestine problem he said that the Arab countries have adopted one and the same attitude, as was clear in the Madrid conference which had just taken place. In this regard Israel's attitude in Madrid and its present policies in the Occupied Territories and with regard to the rights of the Palestinian population and people in general gave no cause for optimism. International cooperation was urgently needed in order for the Palestinians to obtain international recognition. During and immediately after the Gulf War of January/February 1991 statements had been made concerning a new international order which would be founded on justice and the principles of human rights. Now a peace should be made which, under the pretext of the old theory of "secure borders", is not simply based on territorial expansion, occupation and the false legitimation of these unacceptable actions.

D) Final speeches

In his closing speech Omran stressed the consensus which had been reached on the importance of democracy and freedom in society, and on the fact that such values cannot be imposed from outside or even be awarded as a gift. True freedom and democracy can only be reached through struggling for it inside a given society. Moreover, democracy is not a fixed model to be applied generally without further ado. The precise applications and techniques of democracy are in practice pluriform. Each society is responsible for its own house and is free to construct its own legal framework in order to reach its aims.

In her closing speech Lalumière, who had presided over the seminar highlithed some points which had appeared in the discussions.

i. In the course of the history of Euro-Arab relations there have been particularly favorable moments and periods in which positive initiatives were taken on both sides, especially in the Mediterranean area. Curiously enough, these favorable periods preceded the formation of states. As a consequence it may be questioned whether the very existence of national states has furthered the cause of understanding.

ii. Euro-Arab relations h ave not improved in recent times, but rather the reverse. This movement of regression has been caused by many factors. Among the economic ones may be noted the upsurge in Europe since the 17th century, with a decline in the Arab lands at the same time. Among the political factors which have had negative effects on these relations one should note the colonization of Arab land by Europeans, the establishment of the state of Israel, and the unresolved issue of the rights of the Palestinians and of a Palestinian state. And among the cultural obstacles to good relations one should note the present-day low level of information, knowledge and understanding of each other, the existing problems to integrate Arab immigrants and their descendants in Europe, and a generally unsatisfactory presentation in the media.

iii. Among the many factors either creating a distance between the Arab and the European world or bringing them together, the first to be mentioned is the way in which the state is organized and especially the question of democracy. How can the present-day absence of democratic governments in Arab countries be explained? One should first of all look for cultural explanations. To begin with, the political organization of society was everywhere based on religion, on religious texts. Later, first in Greece and Rome and then, several centuries later, in Western Europe, philosophical thought of a non-religious nature developed. In this way the doctrines of the separation of the three powers, of the secular organization of the state, and of the separation between state and religion took shape. A way of thinking which was religio-political in its origin thus developed into a purely political way of thinking which elaborated the concept of democracy. In this way European thought followed a unique path. The Arab countries, however, at the moment find themselves in a stage in which political thinking still takes place within a religious framework.

Besides such cultural explanations for the relative absence of democratic governments in the Arab world other ones can be given as well, for instance economic ones. In the present-day struggle for economic survival in most Arab countries values other than democracy have priority. Political explanations can be given as well. The idea of democracy was brought here by the colonial powers and compromised by that fact; democratic structures were often imposed from outside or imitated from the West. On the whole, democratic experiments in Arab countries have not been very successful.

The chances of democracy in Arab countries, according to Lalumière, are difficult to estimate. In any case the simple acceptance of purely technical democratic institutions is not enough to democratize a society. Certain basic values such as freedom and justice should underpin the process. Human rights should be seen as reference values of democracy, as a foundation and orientation for it. If it is true that democracy cannot be imposed from the outside, it can at least be promoted through certain transitional measures. Lalumière mentioned as examples the promotion of human rights, the support given to found and develop free associations, the growing recognition of the role of women and their work in Arab society, and acknowledging the rights of different kinds of minorities. Arab countries should promote new ideas through intellectual exchanges and by means of the media.

iv. The Secretary General of the Council of Europe expressed the opinion that certain political problems such as the Palestine problem have to be solved as a priority. As long as this has not happened, the

Arab side logically will continue to distrust European ideas which wait for implementation.

v. To give shape to democratic ideas it will be necessary first to solve some major economic and demographic problems of the countries concerned.

vi. On an intellectual and cultural level, the Council of Europe should take new initiatives in order to strengthen the Arab intelligentsia, for instance by means of cultural exchange programs and by giving "Euro-Fellowships" allowing creative persons from Arab countries to write or do research in European countries of their choice.

E) Some suggestions of Arab participants to bridge the present-day distance between Europe and the Arab world

On their part, Arab participants made various suggestions to bridge the existing distance between the Arab world and Europe. They indicated not so much concrete measures to be taken but rather pleaded for new cultural orientations.

i. Arabs expect from their European partners a basic respect for Islam. They indicate that Muslims regard Christianity as being founded on revelation and consequently value it positively. Certain contributions, such as those by Muhammad Saïd El-Ashmawy from Egypt and also Ali Issa Othman from Jordan, referred to the spiritual values of Islam, values which are neglected both by Muslim "Islamists" who ideologically reduce Islam to a rational grid and by Western sociologists and political scientists who apply their own models of explanation to Islam. In each Euro-Arab dialogue the moral and ethical as well as the religious and spiritual aspects of Islam should be fully recognized.

ii. All Arab participants stressed forcefully the important role of intellectuals and authors living in Arab societies, in particular as bearers of creativity, voices of freedom of conscience and thought and as defenders of human rights. Mohammed Arkoun from Paris classified these intellectuals as to their attitude to the Arab political regimes in four categories:

- those who are attentive to what is said and what happens, but without responding to it;

- those who support and comment on the official statements and interpretations; they have access to the media and are allowed to participate in international meetings;

- those who carry out tactical opposition, who take a reformist attitude but who never express themselves on themes that are taboo;

- those who attack squarely what they judge to be wrong; these are a minority only but they find themselves at a deeper level in the main stream of contemporary history.

It is worthwhile to compare Arkoun's classification of the ways in which intellectuals respond to authoritarian regimes with that given by Ghayth N. Armanazi from London who distinguishes:

- those who are apologists for the regime and the persons in power;

- those who hardly deal with the situation in their own country but are more concerned with international problems, and often live abroad;

- those who have the courage to accuse the regime concerned in a direct way and who do not avoid confrontation;

- those who constitute a "loyal opposition" and try through peaceful means to bring about changes for the better in given situations.

The Arab participants clearly expected from their European colleagues and partners in the cultural field effective support for the cause of independent intellectuals and authors as well as of enlightened Muslim thinkers. Such a creative intelligentsia constitutes an alternative to those who are in power in the political field, to the established religious authorities and to the oppositional "Islamist" ideologists.

iii. Many Arab participants underlined the importance of the common history of Arab and European culture and of the common sources of these cultures. They advocated that this history in its complexity should be studied and written anew. Tahar Guiga from Tunis underlined that after the expansion of Islam the Arabs had created a cultural area which furthered exchanges with Christians and Christianity. In his own contribution he gave some historical examples of Euro-Arab cultural dialogue, for instance in Spain in the medieval period. In the course of history, however, there have also been examples of dialogue being impossible or even refused. This was the case in Algeria during French rule, when the country was made a *département* as a French province.

iv. Several Arab participants such as Mohammed Arkoun from Paris and Mohamed Sid-Ahmed from Egypt stressed the importance of the Mediterranean as an area of communication between the Arab and European worlds. The participants clearly expressed the hope that one day there would be peace in the present-day areas of tension around the Mediterranean, such as Israel, Palestine, Cyprus and Algeria, and that this inland sea would then regain its rightful central place in Euro-Arab relations. In the discussion, however, the role of those large and wealthy parts both of Europe and of the Arab world which happen not to border on the Mediterranean was not at all taken into consideration. Unfortunately, the contribution of Turkey and Greece to the Mediterranean dialogue and the role of Turkish-European and Turkish-Arab relations also fell outside the theme of the seminar.

v. Many Arab participants referred to the much needed Euro-Arab dialogue within Europe itself, given the presence of Arab immigrants and their descendants. Although this topic fell outside the scope of the seminar, it was recognized that the problem of the "internal" dialogue inside Europe cannot be dissociated from that of the "external" dialogue between Europe and its neighbors if one wants to improve Euro-Arab relations.

vi. Dialogue and understanding were not only aims of this seminar, they could also be seen as aims of the existing Euro-Arab relations. Hussein Ahmad Amin from Egypt, for instance, described these aims as part of a new world of fraternity in common humanity. Tahar Guiga from Tunis, however, warned that dialogue is not an easy matter. A cultural dialogue between peoples who equally honor their identity and love their culture, is always difficult and ambiguous. He drew attention to the mostly outside factors which have had a negative effect on attempts at dialogue in the course of history. As examples he mentioned the effects of the instinct of domination, of religious extremism and of intolerant ideologies. Dialogue implies that other people have the right to express and practice their own religious or philosophical convictions. Beyond simple tolerance, it requires on both sides attention for others as well as an open mind and an open heart.

F) Looking back at the Strasbourg Meeting

Looking back, I feel relieved that in 1991 a seminar such as the Strasbourg meeting was possible, and that such a wide variety of people participated. The theme of "dialogue" was central and there were indeed many dialogues, focusing on the cultural dimension of Euro-Arab relations. Economic, political and demographic issues were implied but not explicitly treated. The abstract nature of the theme and the prevailing good will led to much generalization; the marked differences between various groups of Arab countries as well as between the countries of Eastern and Western, Southern and Northern Europe were scarcely touched upon. Hardly any mention was made of the many forces outside the Mediterranean whose impact is felt daily, such as the USA, or of disturbing forces around the Mediterranean such as the right-wing movements on the Northern and the "Islamist" movements on the Southern side. On the other hand, many observations which were made about Euro-Arab relations are equally valid for Euro-Turkish relations, not only where Turkey is concerned but also in connection with Turkic people elsewhere.

I cannot say, however, that - at least during the sessions - the European participants engaged passionately in dialogue. There was a certain caution on their part, though not without openness. What was lacking among them was any coherent vision regarding the future. This may be explained in part by the fact that people had been overwhelmed by events. The USSR and communism had just collapsed, the Gulf War had led to an excess of Western power in the Arab world, and the Madrid Conference had not provided that breakthrough on the part of Israel which optimists had hoped for.

As far as the speakers from Europe are concerned, some papers that were submitted had little to do with the official aims of the seminar. Some of the speakers were known not to have any sympathy for Arab causes. Some old-timers with nostalgic feelings for history presented views of Arab affairs that dated from before the Suez war of 1956. More than once I was struck by antiquated views of religion and secularism, history and society which could be presented perhaps with aplomb and sometimes with wit, but had rhetorical rather than scholarly bases.

On the Arab side there were some resourceful personalities, matured through experience and with clear intellectual positions, though expressed diplomatically. Some speeches - on the Arab side too - may have been ideologically colored but they were always directed towards dialogue and so to speak waiting for an answer from their European partners. Whether the Arab participants received substantial answers from the European side remains an open question to me. One should consult the three small published booklets of proceedings of the seminar which give an excellent overview of the meetings, speakers and discussants for an answer.

In conclusion, many interesting ideas were expressed about Euro-Arab relations and their improvement, mostly with reference to the speaker's own experience. Unfortunately, neither on the Arab (mainly Egyptian) nor on the European (mainly British and French) side were clear statements made about factual realities. The words were not linked to the world of action. As a matter of fact, there were hardly any participants who played an active role in one of the existing Euro-Arab exchange programs. Consequently, the discourse moved in itself and the discussion seemed to float. But since they were free, they were revealing and informative for the attentive listener who did not want to project his own concerns, wishes or ideals on what was going on.

People on the European side had taken the subject of cultural relations and dialogue in order to manifest their desire -- but not always their capacity -- for a dialogue with Arab partners. There was discussion but only in the speaker's own language. Of the many existing cultural expressions in literature, art or scholarship, or of concrete successful examples of intercultural relations between Europeans and Arabs hardly anything was treated. The Strasbourg seminar in a way was typical of the state of Euro-Arab dialogue on an "official" level.

One aim of the seminar was to bring about an encounter of intellectuals and writers of both sides who would not necessarily solve problems but who could identify certain problems and speak about them, either in the formal sessions or more informally outside the sessions. It was perhaps less important to find common solutions for these problems. It was more important to see to what extent the two sides could enter into discussion and what kind of ideas came out of that. If anything, a certain way of pursuing dialogue seems to be easier among authors, intellectuals and artists than among other social groups. On the other hand, it has to be admitted that such creative individuals mostly occupy a rather marginal place in their societies and their meetings have little immediate practical results. However, whether living under more democratic or more oppressive regimes, in more open or more closed societies, such individuals often represent the deeper and less visible trends and orientations of societies. They sometimes suffer from their lack of visibility and in quite a few cases they are considered by others to be an "asocial" group. However, their creative potential is recognized and Strasbourg demonstrated a certain, though limited solidarity of European intellectuals with their Arab counterparts.

In this connection a few remarks are in place on the very organization of this meeting. It was set up by two organizations, the Council of Europe and the League of Arab States, which together include practically all European and Arab states. The main purpose of these two organizations is of course not so much to cultivate Euro-Arab relations as to assure and strengthen the links which exist between states within Europe and the Arab world respectively. In other words, they concentrate on certain internal aspects of the European and the Arab world, in the fields of law, society, social and cultural life.

The fact that the two organizations cooperate implies that the differences between the two worlds are taken into account realistically, without being fixed or absolutized in terms of an opposition or even an antagonism. Cooperation between the organizations and interaction between the people invited by them opens a way to overcome a Euro-Arab antagonism that has lasted for too a long time. Besides its immediate practical results which seem to have been minimal, such a seminar of intellectuals and authors consequently is a kind of manifestation with a strong symbolic value above all. The Gulf War and the Peace Conference of 1991, whatever their immediate effects, had again made the European and Arab worlds aware of the need for communication and dialogue. The different interests and intentions existing in various countries on both sides deserve careful study. Something similar seems to hold true also for the relations between Europe and the Turkic world, at this stage primarily Europe and Turkey.

2. Mediterranean Cooperation and Dialogue: Toledo 1995

Among the preliminaries of the Conference of Cooperation and Dialogue in the Mediterranean region, organized by the European Union in Barcelona on 27 and 28 November 1995, was the holding of a small informal conference in Toledo from 4 to 7 November 1995. The theme of this conference was "Mediterranean society: still a challenge for the Three Civilizations?", with the subtitle "Informal dialogue meeting between Islam, Judaism and Christianity". It may surprise the reader that an organization which is devoted to European economics and politics took an initiative to call upon representatives of religious and humanistic traditions. They were invited to engage in dialogue, less about theological or religio-legal issues than about the construction of a Mediterranean society.

A) Historical context

The initiative of this meeting is less surprising if one takes into account the historical context. Already in 1991 the President of the European Commission at the time, Jacques Delors, had invited representatives of the major European Churches to an informal meeting in Brussels, and from this developed regular meetings twice a year of an informal character. Three years later, in December 1994, M. Delors organized a similar meeting extended to a wider circle. In this way Catholic, Protestant, Orthodox, Jewish, Muslim and Humanist representatives met with the President of the European Commission, one of the topics of discussion being the possibility of holding joint Conferences. M. Jacques Santer, Delors' successor in office continued this initiative. He received the European Conference of Rabbis in March 1995 and it was apparently here that the idea emerged to organize a small conference for the major religions of the Mediterranean Basin, which resulted in the Toledo meeting.

Seen in a broader perspective, there can be no doubt that the Christian churches were interested in the construction of a new, supranational Europe from the beginning. Before the three Scandinavian countries and Austria joined and Germany was reunified, the EEC had a Catholic majority. With John Paul II's proclamation of the program to rechristianize a secularized Europe, the Vatican clearly also had an interest in what was happening in Brussels. On the Protestant side a similar effort is to be noted; the churches could not remain indifferent toward the place assigned to the religions in the new Europe. On the other hand, the European Commission and its executive organs had to remain independent of religious interests. Islam was a new feature on the religious map of Europe; the presence of some eight million Muslims in EC member states forced the EC to take into account not only the churches but also Islam and to listen to Muslim representatives. Jewish and Humanist representatives, although numerically less significant, were heard too.

B) Orientation towards dialogue

An important factor in the European Union's relations with Muslim countries has been its clear refusal of Samuel P. Huntington's idea of the - potential - clash between civilizations.[5] On several occasions, for instance in preparatory documents for the Toledo meeting, the European Union has offered intercultural exchange and dialogue as an alternative starting point to the assumptions of the American political scientist. "European construction in the sense of Monnet and Adenauer is based on the opposite assumption, that there is a possibility for countries and cultures to sit around the same table on an equal footing in order to solve together their common problems".[6]

C) Religious leaders

It must still be explained, however, why specifically representatives of religions should be involved, however indirectly, in the dialogue aims of the Barcelona conference. Here the wider international context needs to be taken into consideration. In the 1992 elections Israel obtained a Labor government, which turned out to be open to the "peace process" thought out by the USA. Especially after the so-called "Oslo Agreement" of 1993 there were high hopes of a settlement of the Israel-Palestine conflict.

---

[5] S.P. Huntington, *The clash of civilizations and the remaking of world order*, Simon & Schuster, New York, 1996.

[6] Document ML/fr (95)929.1 of 26 September 1995.

In the following mobilizaton of forces for peace, some politicians saw religious leaders as men of reconciliation and asked for their cooperation. They could for instance oppose the natural tendency to bestow a religious legitimation on conflicts of a basically political, economic or ethnic nature. Similar efforts had been made for instance by the World Council of Churches in the post-Yugoslavia conflicts. In the case of Euro-Mediterranean cooperation it was hoped that a continuing dialogue between the three monotheistic religions could not only contribute to the "peace process" in the Near East but also provide a cornerstone for building a future just and peaceful society around the Mediterranean.

D) Organization of the Toledo Meeting

This was also the mood of the Toledo meeting. I remember all the more vividly the shock caused by the news of the assassination of Yitzhaq Rabin on the very eve of the conference, 4 November 1995. Most of us realized that the meaning and significance not only of our meeting but also of the Barcelona conference itself, presupposing a "peace process" that would end in real peace, was at stake. The impulse toward real dialogue became stronger.

Participation in the conference was by invitation only and the sessions were held behind closed doors. There were 27 active participants: seven Muslims (one from Turkey, one from Tunisia, one from Algeria, two from Morocco, one from Egypt, one from Lebanon), six Catholics, six Protestants and Anglicans, three Orthodox Christians, three Jews (one from Israel) and two Humanists. Officials of the EC and observers from international organizations and national governments took part as listeners. At the end the text of a press communiqué was agreed upon. A final report of the meeting appeared in March 1997, a book appeared in 1998.[7]

The meeting lasted for somewhat less than three days and the program foresaw three round tables on the following questions:

i. Can the three monotheistic and humanist traditions develop a common vision of the future of Mediterranean society (*projet de société*)?;

[7] *The Mediterranean Society. A challenge for Islam, Judaism and Christianity.* Office for official publications of the European Communities, Kogan Page, London 1998.

ii. How can these traditions contribute to reconciliation amongst the people in the region?

iii. How do the traditions view the role of women today?

For each round table two or three short papers had been prepared by participants; they were the starting point for a more general discussion. The final session was used for an evaluation and the formulation of a press communiqué.

E) Aims and purposes

I simply give here the main points of the official letter, signed by Jacques Santer, which accompanies the final report of March 1997. He reaffirms his view that the conference has a symbolic importance not only for the Euro-Mediterranean Conference held in Barcelona a few weeks later in November 1995, but also for the construction of Europe itself. This construction, indeed, is based on the assumption that countries with different cultures can sit around the same table on an equal footing to construct peace by trying to solve common problems. Huntington's scenario of a "clash of civilizations" is clearly rejected.

Santer then affirms that the European Commission wanted to offer the religions an open space for dialogue in Toledo as a "place of European memory". In this way it wanted to contribute to the interreligious dialogue which is an essential condition for reconciliation between peoples. In doing this, the Commission was keen to listen to what the religious and humanistic traditions originating around the Mediterranean have to say to the general public about the great problems which will face society in the future. In his view, the active participation of representatives of the European humanist traditions is essential because it shows the positive fruits of the pluralism of the European cultural heritage to which he declares himself strongly attached.

Santer then ends by expressing his joy that the conclusions of the Euro-Mediterranean Barcelona Conference explicitly defended intercultural and interreligious dialogue, in the line of the conferences held in Stockholm (15-17 June 1995) and in Toledo (4-7 November 1995). In his opinion this dialogue is as important for the future as is the attention which the world of politics pays to religions at the present time.

F) Results

I may refer here to some elements of the press communiqué which was agreed upon at the end of the Toledo meeting.[8]

The conference underlined the primordial importance of a deepening of inter-religious dialogue around the Mediterranean. The monotheistic religions and the humanistic traditions show significant points of convergence such as:

- common points of reference to deal with changes in society, especially with regard to family life;
- agreement that economic forces should serve both the well-being of the individual and international justice;
- clarification of the balance between rights and responsibilities in democracy;
- "...support for the renewal of religious reflection; confronted by on the one hand both the risks and opportunities characterising secularisation and on the other by the development of extremist movements within the religions themselves, dialogue can provide the religions with the courage to question their own traditions".

The participants recognized the difficulties of dialogue. Besides underlining the need for mutual respect and recognition, and for a reassessment of history and images of the other culture, they proposed a specific project to support research on religion. This could lead to better teaching about other religions and cooperation between them:[9]

- "a concrete result would be the organisation of a trans-Mediterranean network linking autonomous research centres either already in existence or yet to be created. This network should be provided with a means of documentation and translation enabling the distribution of texts, the creation of educational outlets for the teaching on other religions and a sort of intellectual hospitality between faithful professors and students of religious science throughout the Mediterranean Basin.

The participants emphasized the responsibility of the political authorities, particularly in Europe, to support such a network and to en-

---

8 See the booklet mentioned in note 7.

9 Pp. 49-50 of the document mentioned in note 6.

sure its financial independence".

As to the question of reconciliation between peoples, the participants called attention to the situations of alienation and the signals of distress that are so visible around the Mediterranean. They had a double message to those politicians who look to the religions to provide an example of reconciliation:

- "European societies have to question themselves concerning their responsibility in the promotion of justice, the improving of the welcome accorded to immigrants, the combat of poverty, the promotion of civil society, media treatment of Islam and religion in general.

- It is impossible to call upon the wisdom of the religions without recognising the specificity of their spiritual dimension and their responses to questions of identity and otherness".

Finally, the dynamic evolution of civil society around the Mediterranean Basin and the pivotal role played by women was stressed. These women, however, "whether veiled or not" remain largely invisible in society; "in the various religious traditions they are quite removed from any major roles of authority. Recognising the full participation of women comes up not only against economic and social resistance, but also against certain perceptions on the part of the religious traditions".

The communiqué ends by mentioning several pressing causes, the implementation of which concerns both men and women, both political and religious authorities:

"A more open dialogue between couples and in society in general; the judicial entering into force of equal opportunities; reflection in and between the various denominations and humanists, based on a deepening of the interpretation of fundamental texts, having in mind the change of society and that of the religious traditions".

As to the effect of the Toledo meeting on the Barcelona conference of 27-28 November 1995, it is interesting to read in the Declaration of Barcelona adopted at the end of that conference, regarding the dialogue between cultures and civilizations:[10]

"Compte tenu de l'importance que revêt l'amélioration de la compréhension mutuelle par la promotion des échanges culturels et de la connaissance des langues, des fonctionnaires et des experts se réuni-

[10] P. 59 of the document mentioned in note 6.

ront afin de faire des propositions d'actions concrètes portant, entre autres, sur les domaines suivants:

le patrimoine culturel et artistique,

les manifestations culturelles et artistiques,

les coproductions (théâtre et cinéma),

les traductions et autres moyens de diffusion de la culture,

la formation.

Une meilleure compréhension entre les principales religions présentes dans la région euro-méditerranéenne favorisera la tolérance mutuelle et la coopération.

La tenue de réunions périodiques de représentants des religions et des institutions religieuses,

ainsi que de théologiens, d'universitaires et d'autres personnes concernées,

sera soutenue dans le but de vaincre les préjugés, l'ignorance et le fanatisme, et d'encourager la coopération à la base.

Les conférences qui se sont tenues à Stockholm (du 15 au 17 juin 1995) et à Tolède (du 4 au 7 novembre 1995) peuvent servir d'exemple à cet égard".

G) Looking back at the Toledo Conference

In looking back on the meeting in Toledo, of which I have only been able to present official statements made at the beginning and at the end, I have good memories. I vividly remember encounters with participants of quite different religious traditions who were all intent on reflecting on the problems formulated by the European Commission. It is an unusual experience to exchange experiences of ethics and religion in a meeting organized by an essentially political body. We succeeded, however, in maintaining an open dialogue with each other and resisted the temptation to accept a draft declaration which had been prepared in advance. Instead, we prepared a final press communiqué ourselves. Some elements of the discussion found their way into it, others did not.

Most of the invited participants were committed to dialogue; partly because of this, throughout the conference there was an "*esprit de corps*" and a practice of conscious self-critical dialogue which is rare in most international encounters. It may also have been connected with a common interest in the different kinds of meaning that religious and humanistic traditions can provide to their adherents in critical present-day situations.

3. The Arabs and the West: Amman 1998

From 3-5 April 1998 an international seminar took place in Amman on the theme "Arabs and the West". It was organized by the University of Jordan in cooperation with the Centre for the Study of Islam and Christian-Muslim Relations in Birmingham, England. Funding was provided, among others, by the European Union, the British Foreign Office and the Ortega y Gasset Foundation in Madrid. The Seminar took place under the patronage of Prince Hassan of Jordan.

A) Organization and subjects treated

Altogether there were 29 active participants in the Seminar, 15 from Arab countries (six from Jordan, five from Lebanon, two from Morocco, one from Tunisia, one from Qatar) and 14 from Europe (eight of whom came from the United Kingdom). Of these, 21 presented papers, ten of which were in Arabic and eleven in English. The papers were distributed to the participants on their arrival in Amman.

The papers dealt with a number of subjects concerning the relations between Arabs (mainly from the Near East) and Europeans, in imagination and reality, both in recent history and at the present time. Among the subjects treated the following may be noted: the European Union and the Arabs, the Arab-Western and the Euro-Arab dialogue, relations between particular European and particular Arab countries. There were several papers about attitudes, images and stereotypes which exist in the West about Arabs. Others treated image formation about Europe and Europeans among Arabs, and current reporting about the Muslim world in Western media. Two papers dealt with aspects of Muslim life in Britain and Denmark. Nearly all papers came from the humanities, sometimes moving to a broader cultural level; economic, sociological and political problems were hinted at but not explicitly treated. Although Arabic-English and English-Arabic translation was provided, the conference was most profitable to those participants who mastered both languages, who fortunately were the majority. All papers focused on the encounter of the European and the Arab world. The papers were published in the same year.[11]

B) Results

The final session was devoted to an evaluation and general discussion about the seminar itself and suggestions were made for further Euro-Arab cooperation in the future. Among the general recommendations adopted I just note the following:[12]

- greater cooperation between universities in the study of the history, religion and culture of both the Arab and the European world, for instance through shared research, exchange of students and lecturers, joint teaching posts;
- the need to establish teaching positions and research posts for European Studies at centres and departments in Arab universities and other Arab scholarly institutions;
- cooperation in the development of good school curricula and textbooks on both sides in the fields of history, geography, culture and religion;
- greater interaction between journalists working for European and Arabic newspapers and journals, and between journalists and scholars both in Europe and in the Arab world;
- greater exchange of literary, artistic and media production, especially to increase awareness of Arabic writing, theatre and film in Europe;
- more translations of the works of Arab writers representing different intellectual traditions into European languages to broaden the awareness in Europe of contemporary debates in the Arab world, and the other way round;
- a call for the European and Arab governments of the Barcelona conference "to increase their efforts in the dialogue of culture and civilisation and to support initiatives seeking to establish long-term coop-

11 *Arabs and the West: Mutual images*: Proceedings of a three-day seminar organized by the University of Jordan (April 3-5, 1989), Amman 1998.

12 See the report about the Amman seminar in *Campus News*, University of Jordan, (4-5/1998), pp. 3-7.

eration and continuity".

Besides these more formal recommendations, a number of individual suggestions were made in the final session, some of which may be reproduced here:

- to create a kind of "European Fullbright Program" by providing "Euro Fellowships" for Arab intellectuals, writers and artists who need to stay up to a year in Europe in a country of their choice. This should enable them to carry on with their research and writing, and to get in touch with what is going on at European scholarly, literary and artistic centers;
- to warn that a Euro-Mediterranean partnership should not eclipse the existing efforts for Euro-Arab dialogue;
- to admit more students, at least as auditors, to Euro-Arab seminars like this one;
- to organize informative workshops on Euro-Arab relations for a broader interested public;
- to ensure better media coverage of seminars like this without them being given a political color;
- to improve training in Euro-Arab relations for teachers at the elementary and secondary school level, both in the Arab world and in Europe;
- to translate the ideas of seminars like this one into practical suggestions that are easy to realize;
- to bring the ideas developed at seminars like this to the attention of decision-makers on both the Arab and the European side.

This was a highly successful conference, not in the last place because of the good quality of the papers presented by some young Arab scholars.

4) Intercultural Dialogue Symposium: Istanbul 1998

The fourth meeting to be discussed here goes back to a Turkish initiative and took place in Istanbul, from 6-8 March 1998. Originally planned to take place on a large scale in October 1997, it was then postponed and realized on a smaller scale five months later. Although the original title of "interfaith" dialogue became then that of "intercultural" dialogue, the dialogue between religions remained the focus of interest. The academic advisor for the symposium was Professor Bekir Karlığa.

A) Organization and subjects treated

The Dialogue Symposium took place in the large Cemal Reşit Rey Concert Hall in Istanbul, and was part of a broad cultural program launched by the Center for the Organization of Cultural Activities, which comes under the Municipality of Istanbul. Other activities of the program comprised invitations extended to distinguished speakers from abroad, Muslims as well as non-Muslims, to present lectures for a wider Turkish audience. The program clearly aimed to inform a cultivated public in Istanbul about international trends of thought.

Altogether 19 speakers contributed to the Symposium, of whom eight were Turkish. Of the non-Turkish participants, two were Muslims from Tunisia and Iran, and nine others came from Belgium, France, Switzerland, USA and Italy. Among them was also a Zoroastrian speaker from Iran.

The program consisted of six sessions with panels which were devoted to the following subjects:

Interfaith dialogue (Mehmet Aydın from Konya, and three foreign speakers);

Religions and living together (Ömer Faruk Harman, Y. Çetin and two non-Turkish speakers);

Religion, peace and tolerance (Z. Kazıcı, A. Yumul and one non-Turkish speaker);

4) Religion, secularism and human rights (Aytunç Altındal and one non-Turkish speaker);

5) The place and importance of religions in the world of the future (H. Hatemi and two non-Turkish speakers);

6) Evaluation (M. S. Aydın from İzmir, and one non-Turkish speaker).

In conclusion a Final Declaration, prepared by a committee ad hoc, was read out and applauded.

B) Personal appreciation

The meeting in Istanbul distinguished itself from the other three in several respects. First of all, the sessions were open to the public and had a large audience of hundreds of people who could also put questions to the speakers in the panels. Secondly, more than in the other three meetings the speakers here had an important pedagogical task to give good information to the public about the subjects assigned to them. Thirdly, there was consequently a more immediate contact between the speakers and people interested in the subject who could approach the individual speakers during the breaks between the sessions.

Given the sympathetic and open attitude of all those who attended, I consider this meeting as an important contribution to furthering the cause of dialogue not only in academic but also in broader circles in Turkey. There was an evident interest in what, not only the Turkish Muslim speakers, but also Catholic, Orthodox and Protestant Christians from Europe as well as a Shî'î *'âlim* and a Zoroastrian representative from Iran and a Muslim intellectual from Tunisia had to say about their religion, Islam and dialogue.

The Turkish historical context is well-known and should not retain us here. Since the 1980s several dialogue meetings have taken place in Turkey, in particular with Christians from the West. Several books have been published in Turkish about the relationship between Islam and Christianity. Christianity is taught at several faculties of theology in Turkey and Christian theologians have been invited here to present informative lectures about Christianity. There is an obvious desire to become better informed about Europe and Christianity; the experience of Turkish immigrants in Europe may have contributed to it. Turkish participants to international dialogue meetings elsewhere have been inspired to organize in their turn similar meetings in Turkey itself.

The situation here as well as elsewhere is complex and many factors are at play. On the one hand, recent developments in the relations between Turkey and the European Union as well as in Turkey itself (democracy and human rights, Kurdish and Alevi self-affirmation, Islamist movements) have made religion a sensitive subject. Yet, on the other hand, in the last fifteen years or so religion in general and Islam in particular have become subjects of public discourse and a certain taboo on the subject of religion is being lifted. From the amount of books which were published in Turkey in recent years on Islam and Christianity as well as other religions one may deduce that people are keen on obtaining information about the existing world religions. One way to acquire such information is through scholarship, in this case the history and sciences of religions. Another way is through direct contact with living adherents of those religions.

Against this background, the interest of the Istanbul meeting is threefold. First, it gave solid information about existing religions. Second, it showed how dialogue actually proceeds first between panel speakers and then with the public. Third, it proved clearly that such dialogue meetings can be organized profitably in a world city like Istanbul, which has a scholarly and cultural life open to other cultures and civilizations. I had the impression that everyone present at the meeting was keenly interested in the event. Continuing such meetings would be a logical sequence to the Istanbul dialogue symposium of March 1998.

5) Looking back

If the two meetings last mentioned were of a rather open nature, with participants submitting papers on their own research and interests and entering into discussion about it, the Strasbourg and Toledo meetings were organized in order to receive answers to specific problems formulated in advance. Here the organizers were international political organizations rather than academic or cultural institutions. The Council of Europe's concern was to take stock of present-day European and Arab views on Euro-Arab cooperation and discuss democracy in European and Arab -- and also Turkish -- societies. The European Union's concern was to see whether and how interreligious dialogue could be used to support cooperation and exchange between Mediterranean and other European societies and countries. Another question was whether positive changes in established religious positions could eventually be reached through interreligious dialogue and make a wider cooperation possible. The themes of the Amman and Istanbul meetings, "Arabs and the West" and "Intercultural Dialogue", on the contrary, allowed participants to formulate and treat problems as they saw them.

The selection of the participants is always crucial since the attitudes and resources of the persons invited largely determine how much can be achieved. My personal impression is that the participants of the Toledo meeting were the most promising in this respect. The discussions between them excelled perhaps not so much because of their particular expert knowledge as thanks to the exchange of concerns and insights into the human problems of their religious communities and of society at large. There were flashes of genius and intelligent solutions were proposed for weighty problems. Moreover, the leadership of this meeting was excellent.

The resources of the Strasbourg meeting were more varied, the participants including "orientalists", researchers of different disciplines, political and diplomatic figures, journalists and creative intellectuals from literature and the arts. The Arab participants were mainly liberal figures from Egypt, Lebanon and Tunisia, several living and working in Paris or London. One of the two Turkish participants was a professor from Ankara, the other a professor attached to an American university at the time. The Western scholars apparently were mostly of an older and more established generation so that fresh experience with new generations from the region and sensitivity to the shockwaves set off by the Gulf War were largely lacking. Arab appeals for assistance found little response among them. The person who visibly rose head and shoulders above the others was the intelligent and open-minded French Secretary General, Madame Catherine Lalumière.

In Amman the papers and in particular the discussions breathed more freshness. The meeting took place in an Arab country and the average age of the speakers was lower. It was an advantage to discuss relations between Arabs and the West on the other side of the Mediterranean, in the heart of the Arab world.

At the Istanbul meeting, literally between Europe and Asia, the emphasis was more on providing good information and clearly setting out one's standpoint than on making lengthy disquisitions. Given the rich program and the large audience, the speakers had to be brief and clear in their presentations if they wanted to be listened to. This was the only meeting where scholars met the general public.

Such international cultural dialogue meetings show a common structure. One ingredient is the presence, beside official dignitaries and some professors, of younger open-minded and socially-committed researchers. Another are some lively personalities who stimulate the discussion without pretending to offer anything really new. In most cases more conflictual figures or people representing what may be called “extreme” positions or "critical" countries are conspicuous by their absence. But there are surprising encounters too. Who would have expected the Istanbul meeting in March 1998 to include a discussion with both an *‘âlim* from Qum and a representative of Iran's Zoroastrian community?

One recurring question is what immediate and palpable results such meetings have. And the equally recurring answer is that the intellectual results are impossible to measure. Of course, more can be said. The results of the Strasbourg and Toledo meetings went to the political arena, and rumors about what happened afterwards remained vague. The Council of Europe, as far as I know, did not take any of the concrete measures which we had recommended to strengthen European links with intellectuals on the Arab and Turkish shores of the Mediterranean. One reason may be that the new members from Eastern Europe, including Russia, not only demand much attention and organizational skill but also considerable amounts of money so that little is left for activities further afield. As to the European Union, it seems to have had difficulties in implementing the recommendations of the Toledo meeting as well as the cultural part of the Barcelona conference. In fact, not much seems to have happend. This may have been partly due to the fact that “Islamic” matters within the European Union itself and relations between the European Union and the Mediterranean Muslim countries are dealt with in two different departments of the EU in Brussels. As far as religion is concerned, it seems to me that decision-makers are hardly aware of the existence of serious modern scholarship on religions including Islam. Their policies seem to be more affected by pressures from religious and political bodies than guided by sound knowledge of the meaning and role of religious traditions on the present-day scene. Religion is a delicate matter, even for politicians, and wrong decisions can be easily made.

My own impression is that both the European Union and the

Council of Europe not only lack the know-how but also fail to consult proper expertise on the cultural and religious dimensions of the societies of the southern and eastern shores of the Mediterranean and their immigration to Europe. In this sense, the Amman and Istanbul meetings were more appropriate in their modest set-up, arousing less weighty expectations among the organizers and the participants.

What strikes a relative newcomer in meetings such as these, is the importance of adequate communication. I do not mean here the psychological aspect, for instance the occurrence of a certain "conference fatigue" on the third or fourth day. I think rather of the continuing challenge to grasp what others really want to say, and to understand the problem for which they seek a solution as well as the solution proposed. How to escape from monologiecal discourses ad dialogue meetings?

This difficulty is still greater if one has no immediate access to the languages used. I would suggest that all speakers and active participants in such meetings should be able to handle fluently both English and Arabic or Turkish. This certainly puts a burden on the Europeans. Speakers should also be pressed not to repeat current slogans or conventional ideologies; t hey should offer some new visions and suggest solutions to deeper-seated problems. In other words, the intellectual quality of such meetings should be enhanced on both the Muslim and the European side. A certain arrogance which may perhaps be acceptable in one's own cultural circle -- British, French or German -- should certainly not be demonstrated to people of another culture. I am always struck by the unfortunate fact that certain minds, brilliant in themselves, can be so incapable of or even averse to real communication.

6. Looking forward

On the European side high-level statements of a certain political weight have been made repeatedly about the need for cooperation and dialogue with the Arab countries and Turkey. On the Arab and the Turkish side, on the other hand, serious attempts have been made by public bodies as well as academic circles to arrive at cooperation and dialogue not only with institutions in individual European countries but also with the Council of Europe and the European Union. The need for dialogue is especially emphasized after situations of conflict and in the cultural sector. In the economic and political fields serious problems have arisen, in the latter case largely because of the stagnation of the Near East "peace process" through decisions taken by the Israeli government under Mr. Natanyahu. It is significant in this context that, while the Council of Europe has always been particularly active in the cultural field, the European Union has now also started to extend its activities -- in the context of Euro-Mediterranean cooperation -- to culture and to some extent even religion.

As far as Turkey is concerned, our Workshop held in Istanbul 14-15 October 1996 on the subject of Turkish Muslim perceptions of Europe and Western Christianity with a majority of Turkish participants, has been a small step in the much needed Euro-Turkish dialogue. The very existence of the German Oriental Institute where our workshop was held, and the existence of other similar research institutes in Istanbul, testify to increasing European interests in developing closer cultural and scholarly links with Turkey.

In all four meetings which I had the privilege of attending, and which brought together Muslim and European participants, it became abundantly clear how limited the knowledge still is which we actively possess of each others' peoples and countries, their past and present. It was stimulating to meet people from the other side on a level of equal partnership, to learn from them, and where necessary to be corrected by them. I have become aware of the fact that both in Europe and in the countries around it, there are what may be called "core people" who, as individuals or as groups, are genuinely interested in people of another culture, whether European, Turkish or Arab. They want to know more about that other culture and establish contact with the people who belong to it. Beyond the efforts of international organizations, professional interests and individual adventurous life stories, the sheer presence of these interested "core people" constitutes a solid basis for further cooperation and dialogue.

There is thus a need for further cooperation between people from Europe on one hand and from Turkey and the Arab countries on the other hand. This requires on all sides the expertise of researchers who not only have carried out studies and fed the relevant data into their computers but have also the necessary language skills, an interest in social and cultural questions, an inclination toward intercultural relations, a questioning mind and that particular gift which is the ability to communicate. Better possibilities need to be created for young Europeans who want to engage in this, so that they can obtain the necessary education and instruction. And even more needed is the establishment of something like Euro-Fellowships for young Turks and Arabs, and others too, who have shown their worth in their own country and want to know Europe better. Such fellowships should be made available to creative intellectuals, writers and artists from Turkey and the Arab countries who need to spend say up to a year as "Euro-Fellows" in one ore more places in Europe to write, read and become acquainted with what is going on here. Euro-Fellow should be free to discover Europe themselves and to choose the countries they want to go.

People from the countries surrounding Europe should develop their own ideas on their own terms, Islamic or otherwise, and we should resist the lurking temptation to carry out a new European "cultural colonization. A partnership for dialogue is essentially different from a relation of domination.

Such cultural cooperation and dialogue partnership is probably simplest in the case of students and researchers. Partly because of common interests in knowledge they have a natural way to get in touch with each other. If international organizations want to promote cultural relations between Europe and Turkey or the Arab world, they should facilitate exchanges between such individuals and groups in particular. It is these people who in their turn can spread information further. As young intellectuals they should be able not only to participate in meetings of international standard as described above. They should also help in organizing workshops or informative courses for a broader interested public in their own countries. Last but not least, they may also gain access to the media where they should not only present factual data and conventional opinions but also show something of life as it is lived in other societies and countries. They can hint at the intricate nature and the broader connections of what may be called the "problems of the day", as they are seen from the other side of the Mediterranean.

In intercultural communication it seems to be the man or the woman as a person that counts. What are needed here are not monological maniacs or enthousiasts for their own ideas about a better world. The need is for people who are ready to listen to others, who dispose of a certain knowledge and experience and who want to acquire more. They should by nature be inclined to communication, while training their capacity to learn from others and making people learn from each other.

Some of these people will work together for human causes or engage in political action. Others will do research, cooperating with colleagues from the other side. Others again will work creatively as writers, artists or in the media, furthering in this way a more adequate knowledge of the other side. Some may choose to apply such positive attitudes in different kinds of exchanges between Europe and the Turkish or Arab lands, not so much as religious missionaries but rather as human and cultural explorers.[13]

[13] See also Jacques Waardenburg, *Islam et Occident face-à-face. Regards de l'Histoire des Religions*, Labor et Fides, Geneva 1998.

Le Parti de la Prospérité (Refah Partisi)

L'IMAGE DE L'EUROPE DANS SON DISCOURS POLITIQUE (1995-1997)

Deniz Vardar
Université de Marmara, Istanbul

A partir des résultats électoraux des dernières décennies en Turquie, nous pouvons constater d'emblée que le Parti de la Prospérité (Refah Partisi-RP) occupe une place de plus en plus importante sur la scène politique. En effet, la soudaine expansion de ce parti pendant les années 1980, confirmée par les élections législatives du 24 décembre 1995, a fini par le placer au premier rang des partis politiques turcs.[1] Ces résultats ont par ailleurs confirmé l'enracinement d'un parti à connotation religieuse dans le paysage électoral turc.

Le Refah Partisi (RP)

La ligne "islamiste" représentée par cette famille politique émerge sur la scène politique turque au début des années 1970. Successivement, le MNP (Parti de l'ordre National) et puis le MSP (Parti du Salut National) représentant les caractéristiques des partis de l'extrême droite classique de l'éventail politique ont fait leurs apparitions.
Le RP qui a pris le relais de cette ligne politique, a suivi une voie populiste et a glissé vers le "centre du système politique", afin d'élargir

[1] Pourtant il faut noter que certains sondages détectent une baisse chez l'électorat du RP au profit d'un parti de centre droite (ANAP) : le sondage effectué en octobre 1997, par İMV-SAM (*Siyasal ve toplumsal eğilimler araştırması* - Rapport, Istanbul 1997), ou celui de Strateji-Mori en décembre 1997.

son électorat[2]. Ceci étant dit, le RP est dissous (comme cela avait été le cas pour le MNP-MSP) par la Cour Constitutionnelle, le 16 janvier 1998, pour cause d'activité "anti-laïque"[3]. Les hauts dirigeants du parti, dont Erbakan, ont été interdits de politique pour une durée de cinq ans. Alors les cadres du ex-RP se sont précipités pour créer un nouveau parti sur cette même ligne politique - Fazilet Partisi (FP) (Parti du mérite) -. Nous pouvons donc observer que les ex-dirigeants et les cadres du ex-RP n'ont pas choisi une voie de "provocation" politique, mais ils se sont plutôt contentés d'une formule légitimant le jeu politique du système. Actuellement, nous sommes en train de suivre l'affrontement du "groupe des vieux" (voulant garder la ligne classique, se contentant d'un "adoucissement" de l'image du parti) et du "groupe des jeunes" (se présentant comme des modernisateurs à la recherche d'une démocratie musulmane, on dirait) au sein du FP. Dans ce travail, nous ne nous permettons pas de nous lancer sur ce débat qui reste encore très peu mûr.

Nous pouvons trouver les caractéristiques des partis de "droite

[2] En effet, c'est dans le sillage de la Constitution de 1961 que le premier parti de cette ligne MNP (Parti de l'Ordre National) émerge d'une scission d'un parti de centre droite (AP) en 1970. Mais il est interdit et fermé par la Cour Constitutionnelle en 1971 pour cause d'activité islamiste "anti-système". En 1972 la même tendance politique réémerge avec un nouveau parti politique, le MSP (Parti du Salut National). Un des partis charnières des années 1970, le MSP, a participé à plusieurs gouvernements de coalition. Suite à la troisième "coupure" du système politique par le Coup d'Etat militaire de 1980, le MSP est fermé (cette fois-ci, tout comme les autres partis politiques). Avec le déclenchement du processus de l'instauration de la démocratie, la ligne islamiste sera de retour avec un nouveau parti politique, le RP (Parti de la Prospérité).

Le RP a participé au deuxième gouvernement de coalition suivant les élections législatives anticipées du 24 décembre 1995 (formé le 8 juillet 1996, par le RP et le DYP -un des deux partis politiques du centre droit-, soutenu par un petit parti d'extrême droite nationaliste-islamiste, le BBP). L'accord de coalition avait prévu un système de gouvernance à tour de rôle (deux ans pour chaque tour), à commencer par le parti de la majorité relative, donc par le RP. Pourtant, vers la fin de la première année de cette coalition, une pression forte de l'armée (se proposant paradoxalement, un rôle de défenseur de la démocratie), la crise de représentativité du gouvernement a poussé les coalisés à revoir leur accord. Le premier ministre Erbakan (leader du RP) a voulu laisser sa place à Çiller (leader du DYP) bien avant la date prévue (30 juin 1997). En plus, la procédure n'a pas pu fonctionner quand le Président de la République a chargé le leader du deuxième parti politique, le ANAP (de centre droit), pour construire le gouvernement. Et ceci est suivi par le déclenchement d'un procès contre le RP, suite à une accusation d'avoir fait de la propagande "anti-laïque".

[3] *Refah Partisi kapatma davası - iddianame, esas hakkında görüş, savunma, gerekçeli karar*, Kaynak Yay., Istanbul 1998, 391 p.

radicale populiste" chez le RP[4]. Cette classification mérite toutefois quelques commentaires.

Nous pensons qu'on peut classifier le RP comme un parti de droite (même si leurs dirigeants n'acceptent pas cette classification), parce que le parti a un projet politique "organiciste". En effet, conséquence du particularisme populiste et religieux des dirigeants, leur programme politique rejette la formule égalitaire, inclusiviste/politique de citoyenneté. Ainsi, ils développent un projet exclusiviste, "mixophobe", qui se traduit dans les faits par le slogan "chacun dans sa communauté", projet qui prévoit en fait, dans un premier temps, une "reghettoïsation" sinon juridique du moins culturel de la société. On peut aisément pressentir les affinités de cette approche avec une typologie du néo-racisme[5], dont les traits saillants sont le différencialisme ou l'absolution des différences et le culturalisme, ou le relativisme culturell absolutisé. Ce néo-racisme est d'autant plus évident qu'il se présente souvent sous la forme d'un antisémitisme primaire (proche du racisme classique), soit tout simplement d'un langage teinté d'un antisémitisme à peine voilé, qui s'exprime par le biais d'un anti-sionisme intégral doublé d'un discours anti-occidental radical[6].

Nous pouvons également ranger le RP parmi les partis radicaux, dans la mesure où il rejette en bloc, surtout dans ses discours antérieurs à son "arrivée au pouvoir"[7], la totalité du système socio-culturel et politique de la Turquie. Ce parti se présente comme l'unique formation politique pouvant "purifier" radicalement le paysage politico-culturel des "éléments étrangers à lui-même" et mettre en œuvre un système économique "juste et égalitaire" qu'il appelle "l'Ordre Juste". Notons que ce concept passe bien dans une société où la redistribution des richesses est de plus en plus inégalitaire. Pourtant

---

[4] Nous inspirons de la classification de H.-G. Betz, concernant les partis radicaux-populiste de droite en Europe occidentale. Voir H.-G. Betz, *Radical right-wing populism in Western Europe*, Macmillan, London, 1994, 226 p.

[5] P.-A. Taguieff, *La force du préjugé - Essais sur le racisme et ses doubles*, La Découverte, coll. Tel, Paris, 1987, 645p ; P.-A. Taguieff, "Réflexions sur la question antiraciste", *Ligne* , no: 12, décembre 1990, pp. 15-52.

[6] Deniz Vardar, "Les exclus excluant - Le cas du RP en Turquie", Colloque - *La démocratie à l'épreuve de l'exclusion*, Istanbul, Université de Marmara - Tarabya, 3-5 juillet 1997.

[7] Le RP, au pouvoir, a produit un double message de continuité et de coupure politique et sa pratique politique allait plutôt dans le sens du premier.

dans leur conception, il s'agit bien d'un projet politique organiciste fondé sur une idée de "justice naturelle" et "anti-égalitaire".

Enfin, on peut qualifier le RP de parti populiste, dans la mesure où ce parti fait systématiquement recours à des arguments ouvertement anti-intellectuels radicaux. Autrement dit, l'activité intellectuelle, dans le sens large du terme, apparaît aux yeux des dirigeants comme synonyme d'artificialité nuisible à la culture populaire. Ils s'érigent pour cela en interlocuteurs uniques et privilégiés des classes populaires et en "protecteurs du sens commun". L'apologie de l'homme ordinaire - synonyme de naturel, pur - atteint alors son paroxysme. Ce parti fonde son populisme sur l'opposition entre centre et périphérie, qu'il représente par la dichotomie entre les "occidentalistes" (l'élite contrôlant le centre politique et les voies d'accès à ce centre, élite qui serait foncièrement coupée des valeurs du peuple) et les "islamistes" (la périphérie représentée par le RP, et qui serait le vrai centre du pays).

Par la suite, nous passons en revue quelques éléments de la position prise par ce parti par rapport à l'enjeu européen de la Turquie. Ceci est fort utile pour saisir les idées politiques de ce parti puisque l'utilisation récurrente des thèmes liés aux concepts d'"Occident" et d'"Europe", qui en fait constituent le moyen pour désigner l'"Autre", va de pair avec leur description identitaire. Ces concepts à forte charge négative font partie de l'imaginaire que ce parti véhicule.

C'est surtout le thème de l'"Europe" qui émaille les discours politiques de cette ligne politique depuis les années 1970. Concentré autour de l'"enjeu européen de la Turquie", ce thème est utilisé pour les objectifs de mobilisation politique. Dans le cadre de notre travail nous nous sommes concentrés sur le corpus concernant une période récente (juin 1995-septembre 1997) de la revue "Yörünge" (Orbite). Cette revue représente la ligne politique du RP. Dans un premier temps, nous nous proposons de présenter succinctement la spécificité de l'enjeu européen de la Turquie, puis nous situerons le RP sur la scène politique compte tenu du reflet de son approche telle qu'elle apparaît dans la revue Yörünge.

L'enjeu européen de la Turquie et le RP

Une fois que la Guerre d'indépendance est achevée et que la République est proclamée, le processus d'"importation" et d'adaptation de l'Etat-nation a suivi le chemin tracé par la politique d'"occidentalisation" de l'Empire Ottoman. Avec le choix de la voie capitaliste mixte de développement économique, l'élite politique aura besoin de se fabriquer une idéologie qui légitime ce nouveau système politique. La nouvelle formule de légitimité sera composée de divers éléments, comme par exemple un thème mobilisateur visant à donner au groupe un accès à la "première classe" des pays de la scène mondiale. Ainsi, les pays industrialisés, les démocraties libérales seront un point de référence et un modèle à suivre pour le centre politique turc à partir desquels ils formulerait sa politique. En effet, dans la période qui suit la Deuxième Guerre mondiale, toute intégration dans les organisations de l'Europe occidentale sera présentée comme une nouvelle réussite pour la nouvelle formule de légitimité, que cela se fasse dans les domaines économique (OCDE), politique (Conseil de l'Europe) ou militaire (OTAN). La recherche de relations avec l'Union Européenne (UE) s'inscrit dans la ligne droite de cette orientation[8].

Suivant ce point de vue, l'enjeu d'intégration de la Turquie dans l'UE apparaît comme "la dernière étape" pour l'accomplissement de l'objectif d'intégration de la Turquie en Europe. Ceci, perçu et présenté avec une charge affective sans commune mesure par l'idéologie officielle, est donc considéré comme la voie menant vers un ancrage définitif de la Turquie dans le groupe des pays industrialisés du Nord. Cette perspective est d'autant plus importante qu'elle vise à débarrasser la Turquie de son état de sous-développement. Ce thème reste très efficace pour mobiliser le réservoir de l'imaginaire collectif en Turquie.

Pour les mouvements qui s'y opposent, en revanche, les tentatives d'"occidentalisation" sont perçues et présentées comme le début d'une décadence qui ne peut être arrêtée que par une "purification" synonyme de "ré-islamisation". Il en découle alors un "discours identitaire" qui se concentre notamment sur les thèmes relatifs au "retour aux racines" et à la "recherche d'un âge d'or égaré dans le temps". Pour ses

[8] Deniz Vardar, "L'intégration de la Turquie en Europe et son impact", *Toplum ve Ekonomi*, no: 5, septembre 1993, pp. 147-176.

détracteurs, la formule de légitimité du centre politique a été imposée à la société, mais pas intégrée par celle-ci. Ainsi, le RP s'érige en agent politique d'une recherche d'authenticité, ce qui se traduit par un discours nostalgique véhiculé par la formule de "contre-légitimité" d'un mouvement politique contestataire.

Rappelons que depuis le début du processus d'occidentalisation de l'Empire Ottoman, ces deux tendances visaient le même objectif : le rétablissement de la puissance de l'Empire Ottoman. Les stratégies politiques d'"occidentalisation" l'avaient alors emporté sur la position anti-occidentale des "islamistes". Le RP peut être considéré comme un mouvement populiste et islamisant qui utilise le capital culturel et intellectuel de la "deuxième lignée" politique. Toutefois, afin de se faire une place sur la scène politique, ce parti n'exclut pas d'exploiter des éléments de la "formule de légitimité" du système politique existant.

Pour ce qui est de l'enjeu européen du centre politique, le RP le présente comme un danger de dissolution chez "l'autre", c'est-à-dire l'Europe judéo-chrétienne[9]. La proposition du RP consiste à déclarer une "nouvelle guerre d'indépendance", sachant que ce terme constitue un héritage collectif dont on ne peut pas se passer pour occuper une place sur la scène politique en Turquie. A cet égard, ce parti se propose, pour mener à terme une fois pour toute cette "guerre d'indépendance", de "nettoyer" la Turquie des éléments "étrangers" à elle-même. Ceci est considéré par ce parti comme une contribution à la lutte qui pourrait mener le monde musulman à devenir une force mondiale. La nostalgie de la puissance de l'Empire ottoman trouve alors son expression.

Pour le RP, chaque franchissement d'une étape dans les relations turco-UE est une nouvelle occasion pour lancer une mobilisation générale "anti-européenne". Ainsi, le dépôt de sa motion de censure contre le gouvernement en 1970 (par le Parti de Salut National à l'époque), visant à protester contre la transition de la "phase préparatoire" à la "phase transitoire" dans les relations turco-

[9] Dans leurs discours, on retrouve même une reprise de la théorie du complot juif (une réadaptation des Protocoles des Sages de Sion) : le sionisme et les juifs (termes utilisés de manière interchangeable dans les documents du parti et dans la revue *Yörünge*) auront comme projet l'établissement du "Grand Israël". Selon cette approche, la "dissolution" de la Turquie n'en serait qu'une étape.

communautaires (prévue par l'accord d'association), en est un exemple[10]. Il en sera de même lors du dépôt de la demande d'adhésion par la Turquie à la CE en 1987. Par ailleurs, le rapport de la Commission de la CE en 1989, ainsi que la procédure menant à l'achèvement de l'Union douanière avec l'UE en janvier 1996, seront largement utilisés par ce parti comme source de référence dans la construction de ses arguments de contre-légitimité. Autrement dit, chaque réussite dans les relations turco-européennes sera une occasion pour renouveler l'appel général à une déclaration de la "guerre d'indépendance". Par contre, chaque "échec ou impasse" dans ces relations sera présenté comme un phénomène de rejet par l'"organisme" d'éléments étrangers[11].

La nouvelle donne politique et le RP: continuité ou coupure ?

Dans un premier temps, nous allons étudier l'approche du parti autour des thèmes concernant l'Union Européenne. Ensuite, nous allons essayer de saisir le lien qui y est établi entre l'Europe, les Etats-Unis et Israël. Puis, nous allons donner des exemples d'alternatives proposées par ce parti face à la politique du centre. Enfin, pour terminer notre description, nous allons tâcher de l'illustrer par des exemples relevés de la politique interne. D'ailleurs, les thèmes relevés de la revue Yörünge sont des thèmes à forte récurrence dans le discours du RP.

L'Europe - l'Union Européenne

L'euro-scepticisme de ce parti, qui est en fait un sous-produit de son anti-occidentalisme intégral, se cristallise surtout lorsqu'il s'agit des relations turco-communautaires.

D'une part, la politique officielle turque vise à une adhésion à l'UE. D'autre part, l'UE étant une organisation d'intégration, faire partie de cette organisation implique un transfert progressif de la souveraineté nationale vers le centre "supranational" de cette organisation. Nous

[10] Erbakan avance que le projet d'intégration en Europe a pour but de dissoudre la "Turquie musulmane" dans l'Europe "chrétienne" qui fait partie d'un plan "sioniste juif". Discours fait par N. Erbakan au Parlement le 13 mai 1970, *Millî Gazete*, 26 novembre 1986.

[11] Deniz Vardar, "L'intégration de la Turquie en Europe et son impact", *Toplum ve Ekonomi*, no: 5, septembre 1993, pp. 147-176.

avons regroupé les thèmes abordés par le RP autour des questions comme l'achèvement de l'Union douanière avec l'UE, la "souveraineté nationale", l'"affaire chypriote" et enfin les droits de l'homme et la démocratie puisque ces thèmes concernent divers aspects des relations entre la Turquie et l'UE.

1. L'Union Douanière : c'est un événement qui est "politisé" par tous les acteurs politiques turcs. Le RP aussi l'a largement utilisé comme thème de mobilisation. Pour le RP, à l'encontre des autres acteurs politiques concernés, le fait que l'UE se montre favorable à l'Union douanière avec la Turquie est considéré comme un signe qui confirme une fois de plus les désavantages intrinsèques. Ce parti prône la révision immédiate des termes de l'unification douanière turco-communautaire[12].

Concernant l'enjeu d'adhésion à l'Europe (UE), les dirigeants du RP n'y voient pas d'issue pour la Turquie et ils utilisent cette occasion pour déclarer les "occidentalistes" comme étant des dupes[13]. Le RP est présenté par cette revue comme l'unique formation politique en Turquie susceptible de mettre fin à cette politique de dépendance vis-à-vis de l'Occident, et qui va à l'encontre des intérêts du pays[14].

A cette occasion, le RP tente de devenir le porte-parole de certains secteurs ou groupes économiques soucieux des conséquences issues des exigences de l'Union Douanière. Concernant l'Union Douanière, on y retrouve des analyses d'ordre tout-à-fait technique qui décèlent dans cette union une catastrophe potentielle pour les industries d'automobiles, de textiles et d'électroniques.

Ou alors, ils tâtonnent le terrain pour retrouver les voies d'accès aux sensibilités des travailleurs qui ont des problèmes de représentation, avec l'accent mis sur la dimension antidémocratique du système politique en Turquie. Le syndicat Hak-İş, syndicat des travailleurs de sensibilité islamique qui lutte pour occuper une place dans ces milieux, joue sur les peurs tout en dénonçant une catastrophe à venir avec l'Union douanière, qui aurait pour effet de faire diminuer le niveau de vie des travailleurs. Par contre, pour arrêter cette prétendue "ruine" on propose dans cette revue une sorte de mobili-

---

[12] *Yörünge*, no: 233, 2-8 juillet 1995, p. 5-7 ; *Yörünge*, no: 337, 27 juillet - 2 août 1997, p. 25.

[13] *Yörünge*, no: 270, 23-29 mars 1996, pp. 17-19.

[14] S. A. Emre, *Yörünge*, no: 249, 22-28 septembre 1995, p. 19.

sation nationale, afin de rattraper le niveau de développement de l'UE sans faire partie de ce dernier[15]. Ainsi on vise à récupérer le thème de "développement économique" utilisé systématiquement par "le centre politique" comme argument de l'enjeu européen.

2. La souveraineté nationale : c'est un thème utilisé souvent par le RP comme argument légitimant, toujours, sa position anti-UE mais surtout pour récupérer l'espace des nationalistes. A ce propos, la nécessité du "transfert de la souveraineté nationale" à Bruxelles en cas d'une adhésion à l'UE est systématiquement dénoncée ; elle en fait une analogie avec les capitulations de l'époque ottomane[16]. Toujours dans le même registre, cette revue soutient ouvertement le RP qui se propose comme une force politique voulant "achever la guerre d'indépendance" afin d'instaurer la souveraineté nationale, et qui montre du doigt les "occidentalistes" pour avoir causé une dégénération. L'approche de la revue Yörünge résume cette position en avançant que "se rendre à l'UE volontairement" ne ferait de la Turquie qu'un marché exposé à l'exploitation facile[17] et que les lois d'harmonisation votées pour l'unification douanière seraient le symbole du transfert, aux instances communautaires, de la souveraineté nationale et par conséquence elles seraient anticonstitutionnelles[18]. Ainsi, malgré la position anti-système de cette ligne politique, elle se présente comme le garant d'une version constitutionnelle du système politique.

3. Chypre : c'est un thème de mobilisation touchant très fortement les sensibilités nationalistes en Turquie. Le RP voulait profiter de l'occasion en récupérant ce thème. Il le place aussi dans le cadre des relations avec l'UE pour montrer à quel point les intérêts du pays y sont sacrifiés[19]. La revue Yörünge pousse son explication jusqu'à réadapter des théories du "complot juif" en avançant que l'Empire Ottoman aurait cédé l'Ile à l'Angleterre, à cause du "jeu des sionistes", avec l'aide des franc-maçons[20].

4. Les Droits de l'Homme et la démocratie : les faiblesses de la

---

[15] *Yörünge*, no: 257, 17-23 décembre 1995, pp. 40-41 ; *Yörünge*, no: 253, 28 janvier - 3 février 1996, pp. 44-45.

[16] *Yörünge*, no: 258, 24-30 décembre 1995, p. 13.

[17] Ünal Emiroğlu, *Yörünge*, no: 232, 24-30 juin 1995, p. 9.

[18] Ünal Emiroğlu, *Yörünge*, no: 236, 23-29 juillet, 1995. p. 9.

[19] *Yörünge*, no: 228, 28 mai -3 juin 1995, pp.17-19 ; no: 338, 3-9 août 1997 pp. 18-19.

[20] Ahmet Akgül, *Yörünge*, no:264, 4-10 février 1996, pp. 32-33.

démocratie et la violation des Droits de l'Homme en Turquie procurent un terrain propice aux critiques du RP. Les dirigeants du parti formulent leurs critiques selon l'ordre du jour en conséquence, il protestent souvent contre les restrictions concernant la liberté du port du foulard islamique dans les universités ou alors sur les libertés d'expression des islamistes, etc. Le problème de la "non-adhésion" de la Turquie à l'UE est présenté par les auteurs de cette revue comme un résultat des problèmes de manque de démocratisation en Turquie[21].

"Occident" = Etats-Unis, Israël - Europe

Si on décortique le concept d'"Occident" du RP, à part l'Europe, on y retrouve les Etats-Unis et Israël. Selon la conjoncture politique, ils font l'objet de mobilisation politique du RP. Nous allons l'illustrer en trois thèmes choisis comme exemples de la revue Yörünge, dont le thème de la "Force d'Intervention Rapide" (FIR) lié au thème du PKK ; les accords de coopération militaire et de sécurité signés avec Israël et le problème de l'eau; enfin, la Bosnie.

1. La Force d'Intervention Rapide (FIR) et le PKK : c'est un thème qui est traité par la revue Yörünge sous la forme d'une réadaptation des théories du "complot juif". Ici on retrouve l'équation : "l'Occident des croisés et les Etats Unis = serviteurs des projets juifs". Elle prend d'ailleurs comme cible les hommes d'affaires turcs d'origine juive, ainsi que la presse et les franc-maçons dans leur lutte contre cette "équation". Pour eux, la politique des Etats-Unis concernant le Nord de l'Irak serait, en fait, une mise en œuvre des projets du "Grand Israël". La Turquie, quant à elle, en serait réduite à une position de médiateur. "Le Grand Israël" serait en cours de construction et le PKK (dont le chef Apo qui serait par contre d'origine arménienne), ferait aussi partie de ce complot. Suivant cette fantaisie, la Force d'Intervention Rapide ne serait qu'un pont pour atteindre cet objectif, donc elle ferait partie d'une manipulation d'Israël et, une mise en œuvre des Etats-Unis

[21] "Adieu la démocratie, adieu l'Europe", *Yörünge*, no: 333, 29 juin -5 juillet, 1997, p.19. Depuis que le RP est critiqué directement par l'armée, il veut se présenter comme un acteur politique qui lutte pour la République et pour la démocratie. Selon leur conception organiciste de la démocratie, l'armée et la nation devraient constituer un tout, donc ils proposent en fait d'islamiser l'armée.

"impérialistes"[22]. Dans la revue, on soutient la position du RP proposant la nationalisation du FIR[23].

2. Les relations avec Israël et le problème de l'eau : on observe une critique systématique des accords militaires et de sécurité signés entre la Turquie et Israël[24]. Et encore une fois ils reprennent les théories du "complot juif" comme modèlle pour avancer cette fois-ci que les "sionistes", conformément à leur projet, auraient poussé la Turquie dans une impasse diplomatique[25].

Tout en présentant Israël comme un Etat terroriste, expansionniste, ils font un refus systématique des projets de transport d'eau en Israël.[26]

3. La Bosnie et l'"Occident" : la politique des "occidentalistes" turcs est désignée comme "le" responsable du manque d'initiative de la Turquie dans l'affaire bosniaque. A cette occasion, aussi, ils font référence à leurs explications calquées sur le cliché du "complot", et ils y retrouvent les indices donc d'"un jeu organisé par Israël". En fait, c'est un double complot qu'ils y détectent cette fois-ci, dont l'un serait le complot de l'"Occident chrétien" et l'autre le "complot juif". Les deux utiliseraient la Turquie pour réaliser leurs objectifs[27].

On peut souligner qu'on se sert, dans cette revue, de l'image de l'"autre" pour créer un espace d'affectivité pour la formule d'identité "organique/communautaire" de cette lignée politique et nous pouvons noter aussi que le style plutôt agressif utilisé dans la revue n'y est pas pour rien.

[22] Comme la décision prise par le gouvernement de coalition RP-DYP (Parti de la juste voie), pour prolonger la mission de la FIR, *Yörünge*, no: 265, 11-17 février 1996, p.17-19 ; le padénaire de la coalition (le DYP) est désigné comme "le" responsable, mais de même le manque d'expérience du RP y est mentionné, *Yörünge*, no: 287, 28 juillet - 3 août, p. 11, 17. Ce qui rend incontestablement peu populaire le RP au pouvoir, du côté de sa base électorale.

[23] *Yörünge*, no: 270, 23-29 mars 1996, p. 5 ; *Yörünge*, no: 243, 10-16 septembre 1995, pp. 15-20 ; Ahmet Akgün, *Yörünge*, no: 244, 17-23 septembre 1995, p. 33.

[24] *Yörünge*, no: 269, 17-23 mars 1996, p. 1.

[25] *Yörünge*, no: 275, 28 avril - 11 mai 1996, 17-19.

[26] *Yörünge*, no: 274 21-27 avril 1996, pp. 5-11, 24.

[27] *Yörünge*, no: 242, 3-9 septembre 1995, p. 40; *Yörünge*, no: 253, 19-25 novembre 1995, pp. 32-33.

"Alternatives" : ayant "diabolisé" l'"Occident",
le RP se lance à la recherche d'alternatives.

1. L'union du monde musulman : le RP accuse les "détenteurs" du système de manque d'attention porté aux intérêts du monde musulman. Pour le RP, le monde musulman constituerait une "communauté" alternative au monde occidental.

Par cette tendance islamisante, une unification du monde musulman est proposée comme alternative à l'Union Européenne en particulier et à la globalisation du monde en général[28]. La revue Yörünge vise à provoquer la panique pour soutenir cette position. Comme par exemple, on y avance des liens entre la défaite de l'Empire Ottoman depuis le deuxième siège de Vienne et le retrait continuel du monde musulman sur la scène internationale. Pour s'en sortir, ils proposent un guide[29], un "Imam" pour l'"Umma" musulmane pour se redresser[30]. C'est Erbakan qui pour eux serait capable d'en faire un guide pour faire du monde musulman une alternative face à l'union des chrétiens (UE)[31]. Dans le cadre de leur stratégie de "retour aux origines", ils avancent que la Turquie et le monde musulman pourraient ainsi retrouver leur tradition de 1000 ans (l'islam) et se sauver de l'idéologie officielle de la Turquie républicaine dont l'histoire ne remonte qu'à 70 ans[32]. En attendant, ils chargent l'organisation "Millî Görüş" ("Opinion nationale"[33]) de la protection des musulmans du monde (la diaspora)[34].

En conséquence, pour cette ligne politique qui formule une approche "essentialiste" de la "culture", les "valeurs" occidentales sont considérées comme étant imposées par la force à la Turquie. Pourtant, les années 1950 (le pouvoir du Parti Démocrate) marqueraient le déclenchement d'un processus de "retour aux origines" du pays. Ils y détectent les indices d'une "réislamisation", ce qui signifie pour eux un

---

[28] *Yörünge*, no: 248, 15-21 octobre 1995, p. 13.

[29] Mehmet Şevket Eygi, *Yörünge*, no: 271, 31 mars - 6 avril, 1996, p. 3.

[30] *Yörünge*, no:252, 12-18 novembre 1995, p. 3.

[31] *Yörünge*, no:229, 4-10 juin 1995, pp. 1, 19, 20-22.

[32] *Yörünge*, no: 252, 12-18 novembre 1995, p. 3.

[33] Voir l'article de Günter Seufert, "Die Vereinigung der religionsnationalen Sicht in Europa" dans ce volume.

[34] *Yörünge*, no: 242, 3-9 septembre 1995, pp. 26-28.

espoir impérial d'une Turquie "redevenue grande"[35]. Et d'ailleurs, ce n'est pas un hasard si les associations comme "Akıncılar derneği"[36] se présentent comme un mouvement "de retour aux origines" et qu'on y déclare la construction des mosquées en Europe comme un événement important[37].

C'est dans le cadre de cette position du RP que, dès qu'ils ont partagé le gouvernement, Erbakan a pris l'initiative pour fonder "l'association des 'D8', (8 Etats)[38]. En conséquence, la réunion des "D8" est accueillie, par Yörünge aussi, avec beaucoup d'enthousiasme. Elle est présentée, par les auteurs de cette revue, comme un nouvel espoir et comme une occasion qui se présente à la Turquie pour montrer "sa force"[39]. La signature de l'accord constituant cette association lors du sommet d'Istanbul serait, selon eux, le "précurseur d'une nouvelle face de l'Humanité" et donc une "signature historique"[40].

2. L'Extrême Orient et l'Asie : toujours dans le cadre des recherches d'alternatives de ce parti, un effort peut être détecté pour trouver une référence complémentaire au monde musulman dans l'Extrême Orient. Ainsi, le monde "riche et meilleur", retrouvé en Occident par le centre politique, se trouverait dans cette région, pour le RP. En conséquence, les visites organisées par Erbakan dans la région ont été présentées comme une réussite.[41] Nous pouvons y détecter un effort de récupération de l'idéologie développementaliste du centre politique turque.

L'"Occident"/l'"Autre" dans la politique interne

Dans Yörünge (1995-1997), on politise systématiquement certains thèmes visant à créer une atmosphère de "guerre déclarée contre l'Occident" sous la forme d'une "lutte" proposée pour l'élimination des traces d'‘occidentalisation’ dans le pays. Pour cet objectif, le thème du

[35] Arif Ersoy, *Yörünge*, no: 316, 23 février - 1 mars, 1997, p. 17.

[36] "L'association des soldats irréguliers" est une association de jeunesse islamiste.

[37] Thème repris par *Yörünge*, no: 306, 8-14 décembre, 1996, p. 25; *Yörünge*, no: 310, 12-18 janvier 1997, p. 37.

[38] A l'initiative de Erbakan, huit pays ayant une population à majorité musulmane se sont réunis pour faire une alternative aux "G7".

[39] *Yörünge*, no: 311, 19-25 janvier 1997, pp. 1, 42-45.

[40] *Yörünge*, no: 332, 22-28 juin 1997, pp. 15-16.

[41] *Yörünge*, no: 292, 1-7 septembre 1996, pp. 20-25 ; no:293, 8-14 septembre 1996, p. 43-45.

Patriarcat Grec Orthodoxe (Patriarcat Œcuménique de Constantinople) et celui de l'église Sainte Sophie ont été parmis leurs thèmes préférés.

Par exemple, ils revendiqent de "limiter l'autonomie du Patriarcat Grec Orthodoxe"[42] en la considérant comme une atteinte directe à la souveraineté nationale. A cet égard, ils avancent des arguments qui pourraient mobiliser les sentiments nationalistes de l'imaginaire social relevé de l'héritage de la "guerre d'indépendance", comme quoi ce lieu serait "une base d'espions" de l'"autre", plus précisement, de l'Occident chrétien (la chrétienté étant prise dans un sens large). Leur enjeu d'une transformation de la Sainte Sophie en mosquée[43] vise à compléter le même paysage. Il en va de même pour ce parti, avec le projet de construction d'une mosquée sur la place de Taksim (plus haute et plus grande que l'église orthodoxe grecque), présentée comme le symbole d'une présence supérieure des musulmans dans "leur" pays[44].

De la même manière qu'on retrouve ces traces d'un approche non-égalitaire, non-contractuelle de la citoyenneté, comme cela nous est montré dans la partie précédente, les acteurs de cette ligne politique ont recours à un antisémitisme systématique. Comme par exemple, les activités politiques d'un député d'un parti de centre droit, d'origine juive, sont utilisées comme objet de critiques voire d'insultes directes dans cette même revue[45].

Tous ces éléments font partie de la stratégie "identitaire" de ce parti. Une dimension de cette politique peut être comprise dans le cadre de leurs revendications de retour aux "racines" et à "l'âge d'or", ce qui signifie pour eux une réislamisation et une revendication d'"ottomani-

[42] Nous pouvons rappeler qu'avec la prise d'Istanbul (1453), la Sainte Sophie avait été transformé en mosquée. Le Patriarcat avait été transféré. Il ne s'install dans son siège actuel à Fener qu'en 1602. Le traité de Lausanne (1923) va accorder au Patriarcat un statut dépendant de l'État turc en lui laissant une autonomie interne. Ce statut va provoquer une mobilisation politique anti-gouvernemental de certains acteurs politiques aussi bien que la Sainte Sophie transformée en musée depuis 1934. Liée au débat du Patriarcat Œcuménique et de la Sainte Sophie, ces milieux (islamiste, turco-islamiste ou nationaliste tout court) y voient un "garde de front" du nationalisme grec, donc une atteinte à la souveraineté nationale et un complot anti-turc. Pour une interprétation nationaliste de l'histoire du Patriarcat, voir Süreyya Şahin, *Fener Patrikhanesi ve Türkiye*, Ötüken Yay., Istanbul 1996, 398 p.

[43] *Yörünge*, no: 277, 19-25 mai 1996, pp. 5-12.

[44] *Yörünge*, no: 286, 21-27 juillet 1996, pp. 1, 5-10 ; no: 289, 11-17 août 1996, p. 1.

[45] "... être efficace tout en s'effaçant en tant que juif", *Yörünge*, no: 327, 18-24 mai 1997, p. 46.

sation" du pays, ce qui se ferait dans un premier temps en rendant de plus en plus visible l'"identité" musulmane et du paysage quotidien. Une autre dimension de cette même politique se montre par leurs discours visant à une "purification identitaire", sinon par l'élimination de l'"autre", du moins par sa réduction à un statut secondaire dans le pays (comme cela avait été le cas dans l'Empire Ottoman avant le début de l'occidentalisation).

Dans ce même registre, autrement dit, en vue de créer un espace "non-occidental", un projet d'"ordre juste" est proposé comme une "quatrième voie", purifiée de toute trace de l'Occident (contre le communisme, le fascisme-nazisme, ainsi que contre le capitalisme). Ce qui est présenté comme "l'émancipation non seulement du monde musulman mais aussi de toute l'humanité"[46]. C'est un thème classique qui nous rappelle inévitablement les projets de "troisième voie" des partis d'extrême droite et de droite "radicale-populiste" (anti-communiste et anti-capitaliste).

Quelques remarques en conclusion

On peut avancer que le RP se sert du thème de l'Europe-l'Occident pour utiliser les malaises produits par le système politique turc. Phénomène retrouvable dans les pays qui ont "importé" leurs "Etats" rapidement et, de plus, qui sont frappés par une urbanisation rapide ébranlant les valeurs et les normes de la société. Ceci va de pair avec l'inefficacité de l'Etat providence, accompagnée par une crise du système politique et d'une crise d'identité (pouvant être classifiée comme une sorte d'"anomie"). En Turquie, si cela n'a pas abouti à la séparation complète entre la société et l'Etat[47], le succès relatif de cette tendance islamiste se présentant dans les partis d'une droite "radicale-populiste" sur l'arène politique peut être expliqué pourtant par l'existence d'un écart qui reste infranchissable entre les gouvernants et les gouvernés. Ceci étant dit, nous devons préciser que cette même tendance est loin d'être l'unique représentant de la "périphérie".

Ce mouvement contestataire préfère lutter dans le système, tout en

[46] S. A. Emre, *Yörünge*, no: 249, 22-28 septembre 1995, p. 19.

[47] Pour l'analyse des dynamiques internes et externes de la construction de l'Etat et des mouvements de contestation voir - entre autres -, D. E. Apter, *Pour l'Etat contre l'État*, Economica, Coll. politique comparée, Paris 1988, 287 p.

mobilisant les soutiens, par une formule politique anti-systémique. Pour préciser ce point, nous pouvons suivre la façon dont ils transforment "la formule communautaire" de la droite conservatrice classique en une formule "tribale". Leur formule "tribale", dont les frontières "épaisses" de la "tribu" sont toujours tracées à l'aide de l'image diabolisé de l"autre", détient forcément une charge importante d'agressivité.

Comme nous pouvons le constater, le discours "anti-occidental" (anti-européen, anti-américain, anti-sémite) du RP détient les traces saillantes d'une vision culturo-centriste, singulariste, différentialiste de l'identité. C'est ainsi que nous nous permettons de le classifier comme "néo-raciste"[48]. Ceci étant dit, nous devons rappeler peut-être que le RP n'a pas eu un passé teinté de "racisme classique"; pourtant, il reformule belle et bien le culturalisme/différentialiste des néo-racistes. Ceci signifie donc que le thème de l'"identité culturelle" à la recherche de l'"authenticité absolue" ne traverse pas la recherche d'une "pureté raciale" ; le thème de la différence va se montrer par "la hantise du contact avec les autres" et par "la phobie du mélange" qui sera complétée par "le recours à des énoncés hétérophiles". Cet aspect sera retrouvable chez ce parti mais pas la phase de hiérarchisation raciale. Et enfin, "le racisme symbolique ou indirect, qui tend à substituer au racisme direct et déclaré, opère les modes de racisation sur du sous-entendu ..."[49]. Cette spécificité sera tout à fait identifiable chez le RP, mais il faudra y ajouter la charge importante de leur antisémitisme direct. Cette dimension les séparera des néo-racistes "européens", tout en les rapprochant des antisémites classiques.

Nous avons essayé de déchiffrer ici la continuité de l'image de l'Occident-Europe véhiculée par le Parti de la Prospérité (RP) sous la forme d'un euroscepticisme. Pourtant, pendant la période de son partage du gouvernement, en tant que premier parti de la coalition, le

---

[48] Nous retrouvons chez le RP, les principales caractéristiques de la typologie du néo-racisme formulé par P.-A. Taguieff : "Le déplacement de la race vers la culture, et la substitution corrélative de l'identité culturelle "authentique" à la pureté raciale ; le déplacement de l'inégalité vers la différence ; le mépris affiché pour les inférieurs tend ainsi à laisser la place à la hantise du contact avec les autres, à la phobie du mélange ; le recours à des énoncés hétérophiles ... ; p. 38; "Réflexions sur la question antiraciste", *Ligne*, no: 12, décembre 1990, pp.15-52.

[49] P.-A. Taguieff, "Reflexions sur la question antiraciste", *Ligne*, no: 12, décembre 1990, p.38.

RP n'a pas pu changer les grandes lignes de la politique officielle de la Turquie. Il s'est contenté d'utiliser les symboles du sens collectif pour mobiliser les réservoirs de l'imaginaire turque, consistant à en vouloir à l'Occident pour la décadence de l'Empire Ottoman, ou alors, voulant récupérer la charge affective de la Guerre d'Indépendance turque pour désigner l'Occident comme l'ennemi. Autrement dit, son politique identitaire consiste à transformer la méfiance populaire envers l'Europe en un thème provoquant les sentiments de "haine" tout court.

L'image brouillée du christianisme

Etienne Copeaux
Institut français d'études anatoliennes, Istanbul

L'identité turque, actuellement, est présentée comme musulmane par le pouvoir culturel, notamment dans les ouvrages scolaires. Cette perception est l'aboutissement des événements dramatiques qui, au long du vingtième siècle, ont éliminé la presque totalité de la population chrétienne de l'Anatolie : massacres des Arméniens en 1915, expulsion des Grecs en 1922, départ de milliers de Grecs à la suite des événements de 1955. *De facto*, la république de Turquie a été construite comme un pays musulman, même s'il reste des petites minorités religieuses, même si la laïcité est une pierre angulaire de l'idéologie officielle et même si une minorité importante, les *alevi*, ne se reconnaît pas dans l'islam officiel. Tout au long du XXe siècle, l'altérité chrétienne a signifié confrontation ou conflit, même dans le cas de la «trahison» arabe de 1916, encouragée par les Anglais. La perception de l'altérité chrétienne comme entité inamicale, loin de s'estomper, a encore été renforcée par la question chypriote, surtout depuis 1974, lorsque la ligne de démarcation instituée entre les deux parties de l'île a séparé de manière durable deux peuples, deux langues et deux *religions* : la ligne de front est à la fois nationale et religieuse, entre turcité et hellénité, entre islam et orthodoxie. L'islam non arabe (bosniaque, tchétchène) de la périphérie de la Turquie est considéré par les nationalistes et les islamistes comme une variante de la turcité, ou tout au moins comme un héritage devant être protégé par l'Etat turc. De manière générale, et particulièrement durant l'année au cours de laquelle le parti religieux *Refah* a gouverné la Turquie (de juin 1996 à juin 1997), les mots *turc* et *musulman* ont été fréquemment associés l'un à l'autre. Depuis l'époque de Turgut Özal (mort en 1993), les dirigeants se sont mis à pratiquer la religion ostensiblement ; les hommes - ou femmes - politiques, les officiers supérieurs, les policiers même ont été - au moins jusqu'en 1997 - fréquemment représentés en attitude orante dans la presse. L'altérité du christianisme s'en est trouvée renforcée ; c'est, depuis 1955 surtout (si l'on excepte une très petite partie des citoyens de la Turquie), une religion d'étrangers, souvent présentés ou perçus comme des ennemis ou des adversaires, anciens ou actuels ; l'extrême-droite continue d'agiter la menace d'une nouvelle croisade chaque fois qu'une population musulmane est menacée, comme en Bosnie ou en Tchétchénie, et, depuis la chute de l'URSS et à mesure que l'affaire chypriote s'enlise, l'idée d'un complot orthodoxe mené par la Russie, la Serbie, la Grèce et Chypre revient souvent dans les éditoriaux. C'est pourquoi la vision du christianisme, chez une partie importante de la population turque, est liée à la perception d'une altérité dangereuse.

Comment, en Turquie, connaît-on le christianisme ?

Si l'on excepte quelques quartiers d'Istanbul, les Turcs, aujourd'hui, ne vivent plus côte-à-côte avec des chrétiens ; ce sont les Chypriotes du nord qui, désormais, possèdent la mémoire la plus récente de l'altérité chrétienne. D'ailleurs, plus de vingt ans après la partition de 1974, le christianisme orthodoxe, avec ses grandes églises du XIXe siècle et ses nombreux monastères, façonne toujours le paysage de Chypre du nord ; les cathédrales gothiques de Famagouste et de Nicosie rappellent de façon troublante le passé chrétien de l'île, même si elles sont transformées en mosquées depuis le XVIe siècle. En Turquie même, le christianisme continue d'avoir une présence très voyante : c'est le cas à Istanbul avec ses nombreuses églises, et dans certaines bourgades (citons par exemple Çeşme ou Gülşehir) ainsi qu'en Cappadoce. Lors des grandes fêtes musulmanes, lorsque la municipalité d'Istanbul instaure la gratuité des transports publics, les jeunes des lointaines banlieues se rendent dans le quartier de Beyoğlu, parsemé d'églises. Ils y découvrent une ville d'apparence chrétienne, sont intrigués par les églises où les plus hardis pénètrent, étonnés par les effigies du Christ et les confessionaux.

Au contraire du judaïsme, sujet de nombreux livres relayant un antisémitisme musulman actuel[1], le christianisme est à peu près absent de la littérature islamiste. Il existe du moins quelques ouvrages, peu polémiques, souvent sérieux, références de ceux qui, en Turquie, veulent connaître le christianisme.

Pour apprécier comment cette religion est connue, il importe de rappeler que la vie de Marie et de Jésus font l'objet de quatre-vingt treize versets répartis dans quinze sourates du Coran[2] ; or, comme il s'agit d'un texte considéré comme dicté par Dieu à Mohammed, ces versets ont, dans l'esprit d'un musulman croyant, une primauté indiscutable sur les Évangiles ; ainsi, la description du christianisme par les manuels scolaires, comme les propos tenus sur le christianisme par des auteurs se revendiquant comme musulmans sont généralement conformes à la vision coranique, qui ne correspond pas à celle qu'un chrétien peut avoir de sa propre religion.

On peut rencontrer pourtant une approche différente, même parmi des auteurs islamistes, qui consiste à s'appuyer sur l'exégèse chrétienne des textes évangéliques, pour tenter d'en démontrer l'invalidité et l'infériorité par rapport au Coran. Quelques éléments de ces armes critiques sont disponibles dans l'ouvrage de Maurice Bucaille, *La Bible, le Coran et la science*, publié en France en 1976, réédité une quinzaine de fois, et traduit en turc (dès 1976) comme dans les autres grandes langues de l'islam. Son propos est de démontrer la véracité « scientifique» du Coran en l'opposant à l'absence d'unité des textes bibliques. Se référant à l'exégèse chrétienne, il insiste sur les contradictions entre les quatre Évangiles, sur le long laps de temps écoulé entre la vie du Christ et la rédaction des témoignages, et sur l'importance des sources orales dans la genèse des Évangiles. Ses conclusions les font apparaître comme des textes touffus, invraisemblables et contradictoires en lesquels les chrétiens ne croiraient plus sans l'intervention de subterfuges du Vatican.

Grâce à une presse aux aguets, les Turcs pieux sont en général très attentifs aux prises de positions d'Occidentaux critiquant le christianisme, ainsi qu'aux conversions de chrétiens à l'islam, qui leur

---

1 En 1996-1997, on trouvait, même dans les librairies les plus sérieuses d'Istanbul, des ouvrages ouvertement négationnistes, ainsi que la traduction turque de *Mein Kampf*.

2 Cf M. Hayek, *Le Christ de l'islam*. Textes présentés, traduits et annotés par Michel Hayek, Paris, Seuil, 1959, pp. 29-45.

semblent, chaque fois, être une preuve de la supériorité de leur propre religion[3]. Aussi, les positions de Maurice Bucaille sur l'Évangile ne pouvaient manquer de plaire, et son livre figure parmi les sources occidentales des ouvrages turcs portant sur le christianisme[4]. A ce titre, on doit le considérer comme le vecteur d'une certaine image du christianisme.

Il est possible que la méthode de Maurice Bucaille, puisant chez des auteurs chrétiens des éléments qui, pense-t-il, peuvent prouver l'invalidité des Évangiles, ait consolidé un regard musulman indépendant du Coran sur le Nouveau Testament. S'appuyant sur des théologiens chrétiens, il a contribué à familiariser son public avec l'exégèse, de sorte qu'en Turquie il est possible maintenant de procéder à une critique des Évangiles sans se référer au Coran, en reprenant, en quelque sorte, des arguments puisés chez l'«adversaire» . Ce type de relation dialectique entre christianisme et islam, entre Occident et Orient, est très important dans la littérature polémique en Turquie, qui utilise des images réfléchies de l'islam ou de la Turquie, vues par des admirateurs occidentaux ; l'éloge de l'islam ou la critique du christianisme, dans un discours émanant de l'Occident, sont censés avoir plus de poids.

C'est ainsi qu'on peut définir deux approches du christianisme : un regard porté sur Jésus à travers le Coran, ou un regard qui tente de comprendre l'Évangile. Cependant, pour connaître le christianisme, les musulmans ne peuvent en aucun cas se contenter du Coran puisque celui-ci - pas plus que les Évangiles - n'évoque le dogme, bâti par l'Eglise et les conciles. Dans tous les cas, leur regard provient d'une religion présentée comme simple et rationnelle : la complexité des croyances chrétiennes et de leurs mystères ne peut que provoquer l'étonnement.

---

[3] Le commandant Cousteau occupe une place de choix dans ces représentations ; une rumeur lui attribue le mérite d'avoir prouvé, par ses explorations sous-marines, la véracité scientifique du Coran. Il est présenté comme musulman par les milieux islamistes, mais les reportages sur ses obsèques à Notre-Dame de Paris, en 1997, ont semé un certain trouble.

[4] C'est le cas pour Mehmet Aydın et Osman Cilacı, *Dinler tarihi*, Konya, 1980, et Suat Yıldırım, *Mevcut kaynaklara göre Hıristiyanlık*, Izmir, 1996. Dans ce dernier ouvrage, les pages 140-144 ne sont qu'une simple traduction de M. Bucaille, o.c., pp. 80-84.

Le christianisme dans les manuels d'enseignement religieux

L'enseignement religieux est obligatoire depuis 1980, imposé par les militaires qui pensaient en faire un rempart contre le communisme. Dans ses grandes lignes, il est conçu pour un public musulman, ce qui est le plus souvent le cas, puisque ce qu'il reste de «minoritaires» en Turquie fréquente plutôt des établissements communautaires ou étrangers ; l'importante population *alevi*, dont le dogme et surtout les pratiques sont différentes de ceux du sunnisme, n'est pas considérée comme une «minorité» religieuse [5]. Dans les manuels, qui s'intitulent en fait *Culture religieuse et science morale*, la religion n'a pas l'exclusivité, puisqu'une large place est consacrée à une morale sommaire, et surtout aux principes du kémalisme, parmi lesquels la laïcité. C'est donc, en principe, dans une optique «laïque» que les religions sont présentées aux élèves, dans les cours destinés aux collèges (*ortaokul*) et aux lycées.

Dans les manuels pour *ortaokul*, le christianisme est sommairement exposé en une seule page[6]; la représentation de Jésus y est conforme au Coran : homme de naissance miraculeuse, mais homme comme les autres (cf sourate de Marie, 31-33). Les Évangiles sont vus comme un livre saint envoyé par Dieu à Jésus, qui aurait subi tellement de modifications par les hommes d'Église qu'il fallut, lors du concile de Nicée (İznik), mettre de l'ordre et choisir quatre versions parmi les dizaines existantes. Le reste de la leçon évoque, sans s'y étendre, le dogme, et les trois grandes divisions du christianisme actuel. Les auteurs ne cherchent pas à expliquer à leur public d'enfants les mystères du dogme, comme la Trinité, le péché originel, l'eucharistie, démarche pédagogique évidemment difficile.

---

5 Le mot «minorité» (*azınlık*) a un sens très précis en Turquie : il ne peut désigner que les minorités définies par le traité de Lausanne, c'est-à-dire les populations non musulmanes autrefois organisées en *millet* dans l'empire ottoman : *Rum* orthodoxes, Juifs, Arméniens. Un *alevi* ne saurait être considéré comme «minoritaire», *a fortiori* un Kurde sunnite.

6 Abdülkadir Şener et Orhan Karmış, *Ortaokullar için Din Kültürü ve Ahlâk Bilgisi*, Ankara, Ministère de l'Education Nationale, pp. 3-4 ; ce manuel a été constamment réédité de 1982 à 1996. Depuis l'automne 1997, les *ortaokul*, équivalentes aux collèges français, n'existent plus ; ce cycle a été intégré au cycle primaire qui dure désormais huit ans. Cette réforme a été imposée par le Conseil de Sécurité Nationale, c'est-à-dire l'armée, dans le but de gêner le développement des écoles privées pour imams et prédicateurs (*imam hatip liseleri*).

Dans les manuels pour lycées, la leçon sur le christianisme est plus fournie et existe, selon les maisons d'édition, en des versions d'esprit très différent qui vont nous permettre de retrouver les deux approches, coranique ou évangélique, définies plus haut[7]. La version du manuel dirigé par Rami Ayas, édité par le Ministère de l'Éducation Nationale, est dépourvue d'intention polémique ; les auteurs insistent dès l'abord sur les points communs entre le christianisme et l'islam et sur les différences avec le judaïsme. Leur ouverture d'esprit se traduit par un élément linguistique qui m'a déjà permis, antérieurement, d'évaluer le degré de laïcité d'un discours portant sur la religion : en effet, il existe en turc deux temps du passé ; l'emploi de l'un (le parfait de non constatation en *-miş*) infère que le locuteur n'a pas assisté à l'événement ; l'autre (le parfait de constatation en *-di*) infère, dans un discours historique, une reconnaissance par l'auteur de la réalité de ce qu'il rapporte. Il est intéressant de noter, dans ce contexte, que les miracles opérés par Jésus sont narrés au parfait de constatation (*-di*). De plus, les auteurs n'hésitent pas, à l'occasion, à s'associer aux chrétiens et à l'humanité en employant un *nous* (*biz*) englobant, qui les fait s'exprimer en tant qu'hommes et non en tant que musulmans. Rami Ayas et Günay Tümer, en énonçant les valeurs prônées par Jésus dans ses sermons, comme le volontarisme, la rectitude morale, le pardon, le devoir d'aide, la bonté et l'amour, les présentent comme des valeurs positives universelles[8]. En ce qui concerne le sort terrestre de Jésus, ils prennent soin d'expliquer qu'il existe une version évangélique et une version coranique, en soulignant l'importance capitale, pour le dogme chrétien, de la passion et de la résurrection. L'évolution ultérieure du christianisme est rapidement évoquée par le concile de Nicée, rendu nécessaire par une série de graves désaccords ; le grand schisme et la Réforme sont présentés comme le résultat d'une incapacité du christianisme à maintenir son unité. La suite expose, sans commentaire, l'essentiel du dogme. C'est une leçon dont l'esprit d'ouverture est remarquable, surtout si on la compare au discours scolaire historique, aujourd'hui grandement in-

[7] Ayas Rami & Tümer Günay, *Liseler için Din Kültürü ve Ahlâk Bilgisi*, vol. 1, Ankara, Ministère de l'Education Nationale; 1996, pp. 39-45 ; Çelebi İlyas et al., *Liseler için din Kültürü ve Ahlâk Bilgisi*, vol. 1, Istanbul, Salan Yay., 1995, pp. 38-46.

[8] Ayas, o.c., p. 41.

fluencé par la «synthèse turco-islamique», idéologie qui, sans rejeter ouvertement le laïcisme kémaliste officiel, intègre l'islam parmi les autres valeurs du nationalisme turc[9]. Le point de vue n'est pas vraiment laïc, puisqu'il reconnaît implicitement le miracle comme un fait d'ordre historique, mais il est au moins pluraliste car il n'oppose pas le christianisme, comme une croyance fausse, à l'islam, vraie religion.

L'ouvrage dirigé par İlyas Çelebi peut servir d'exemple de manuel conçu dans un autre esprit. La leçon sur le christianisme commence en effet par exposer le point de vue coranique sur Jésus (quatre citations du Coran contre une seule de l'Évangile). Comme dans d'autres ouvrages, les Évangiles sont perçus comme une «révélation» qui aurait été apportée à Jésus lors de sa trentième année, puis dispersée en de nombreuses versions. Les auteurs exposent également les deux versions, évangélique et coranique, de la mort de Jésus. Mais lorsqu'ils utilisent le pronom *nous*, c'est pour désigner *les musulmans*. La leçon s'adresse donc implicitement à cette communauté religieuse, et non à un public d'élèves qui pourraient être des fidèles de n'importe quelle religion, ou des incroyants. Néanmoins, le dogme est clairement exposé ; pour faire comprendre la Trinité, ce qui n'est pas facile même à des enfants chrétiens, l'auteur emploie une formule poétique et pédagogique : «[La Trinité est comme] le feu, la lumière qu'il émet et la chaleur qui en émane». Comme dans l'ouvrage précédent, la leçon insiste sur les valeurs morales du christianisme, «qui a atteint un niveau plus avancé que les dix commandements», comme l'esprit de conciliation, la soif de justice, la clarté du cœur, le pacifisme, etc., et sur la méfiance envers les biens matériels.

Cependant, l'intention polémique n'est pas absente ; le péché originel est présenté en termes de droit comme une responsabilité collective, à laquelle l'auteur oppose le droit musulman, conforme, lui, au droit moderne, puisqu'il ne retient que la culpabilité personnelle de l'individu. Le texte de la leçon se termine sur une citation de

9 Sur cette idéologie, voir mon livre *Espaces et temps de la nation turque*, Paris, CNRS-Editions, 1997, pp. 75-101, ainsi que «La synthèse turco-islamique en Turquie», Actes du colloque «Idéologies islamiques contemporaines » Lausanne, 6-7 décembre 1993, *Cahiers du département interfacultaire d'histoire et de sciences des religions*, Lausanne, n° 3, mai 1995, pp. 25-51.

Matthieu (VI, 25-29), mais le chapitre est clos, en réalité, par une calligraphie du *kelime-i tevhid* : «Il n'y a d'autre dieu que Dieu et Mohammed est son prophète», et les textes qui suivent la leçon sont entièrement composés d'extraits du Coran[10].

En somme, l'examen de ces chapitres permet d'évaluer non seulement la position (ou les positions) du système éducatif vis-à-vis du christianisme, mais aussi de cerner des représentations dans lesquelles un chrétien ne reconnaîtrait pas sa propre foi. Ces points de désaccord porteraient sur la vision coranique de la vie de Jésus et sur la nature des Évangiles. Pour le premier point, le caractère central de la passion et de la résurrection du Christ, dans la foi chrétienne, ne peut s'accorder avec la vision coranique : il existe une incompatibilité théologique qui, dans un discours scolaire, devrait être soulignée. Pour le second point, la version musulmane de l'histoire du christianisme estime que les Évangiles sont un texte révélé, puis partiellement perdu et déformé. C'est également un point de désaccord important, car le discours musulman étudié en tire, explicitement ou non, des conclusions sur une plus grande rationnalité de l'islam : le Coran, révélé directement par Dieu, aurait une supériorité décisive sur les Évangiles, dans lesquels on ne peut avoir confiance en raison du long laps de temps - jusqu'à un siècle - qui s'est déroulé entre leur «révélation» à Jésus et leur rédaction. Ces éléments s'ajoutent à d'autres (comme la simplicité du dogme musulman) pour former l'image d'une religion plus rationnelle, plus simple, sans mystère, dont la *doxa* n'a pas été déformée par des versions successives du texte sacré.

Le christianisme dans le récit historique

Nous pénétrons ici dans un autre type de représentation du christianisme, qui peut faire partie des programmes d'histoire à plusieurs titres ; d'une part, en tant que religion, les principales phases de son histoire peuvent être étudiées pour elles-mêmes, au titre des connaissances générales ; d'autre part, sous la forme de diverses puissances politiques, la chrétienté est l'une des principales altérités adverses rencontrées par les Turcs au cours de leur passé.

---

10 Çelebi et al., o.c., pp. 40-46.

Depuis le début du xxe siècle, on est passé de programmes calqués sur le système éducatif français à une vision de l'histoire beaucoup plus «turquiste» , un récit conçu selon la notion d'ethnicité et, en conséquence, tourné vers un passé asiatique. La part de l'histoire des grandes civilisations non turques et non musulmanes a fortement diminué, sinon disparu des programmes. Il en est ainsi de l'antiquité méditerranéenne, dont on n'a conservé, depuis le début des années quatre-vingt-dix, qu'une petite part «anatolienne» , à savoir l'histoire des cultures hittite, phrygienne, lydienne et ionienne. Il n'y a plus de leçon portant proprement sur Rome ; pour trouver quelques éléments sur la naissance du christianisme, il faut se reporter au chapitre consacré à la naissance de l'islam, qui débute par un tableau de «la situation générale du monde au moment de la naissance de l'islam»[11]. Dans le cadre d'un long *flash-back*, les auteurs décrivent en une petite page la naissance et le développement du christianisme ; c'est une présentation très factuelle qui ne comporte aucune indication sur l'enseignement de Jésus ou les dogmes de l'Église. L'importance de l'Anatolie comme cadre géographique du développement du christianisme n'est pas soulignée[12]. L'enfant et l'adolescent turcs peuvent néanmoins situer le christianisme dans son historicité ; mais ils ne peuvent comprendre, d'un point de vue historique, de quelle manière l'islam naissant se définit en partie par rapport aux autres religions révélées.

Les croisades

Le récit historique centré sur les Turcs et l'islam se doit d'évoquer les croisades, confrontation majeure entre l'islam et la chrétienté. Elles ont un rôle important dans la rhétorique, puisqu'elles sont présentées comme un événement de l'histoire occidentale provoqué par l'arrivée des Turcs en Anatolie. Aussi, toutes les conséquences positives des

---

[11] K.Y. Kopraman et al., *Tarih 1,* Istanbul, M.E.B. Devlet Kitapları, 1994, p. 72.

[12] Dans un certain discours *externe*, destiné à l'Europe, il arrive au contraire qu'on impute le mérite de la pensée chrétienne à une sorte de génie chthonien de l'Anatolie; l'ancien président de la République Turgut Özal, dans un livre publié alors qu'il était premier ministre (*La Turquie et l'Europe*, Paris, Plon, 1988), qualifie Saint Paul de «notre compatriote» ; dans cette optique (qui a été sévèrement critiquée en Turquie), les Turcs seraient *aussi* les héritiers de l'esprit des premiers chrétiens - et méritent donc d'entrer dans l'Europe.

croisades pour l'Europe seront présentées comme redevables aux Turcs, par le recours à une fausse causalité[13]. Les croisades sont aussi l'un des éléments qui permettent d'affirmer que la Turquie est le bouclier de l'islam. Toutefois, comme on le verra plus loin, l'idée même de croisade reste, dans l'inconscient collectif, la métaphore de toute menace grave de la part de l'«Occident chrétien».

Les manuels d'histoire récents qualifient de croisade toutes les expéditions européennes de la fin du Moyen-Age et de la Renaissance dirigées contre les Turcs. Alors que les historiens occidentaux n'insistent pas beaucoup sur l'habillage religieux de la résistance des puissances balkaniques à l'avancée ottomane, les manuels turcs étudient les événements à travers ce prisme, ce qui permet de désigner constamment l'ennemi par le mot de *croisés*. C'est un fait important car il permet de situer ces épisodes militaires dans la continuité des croisades des xiie-xiiie siècles, et alimente, dans le discours politique sur les événements de l'ancienne Yougoslavie, le fantasme d'une nouvelle croisade, très fréquemment exprimé. Les «croisés» du xve siècle veulent «jeter les Turcs hors des Balkans» [14], comme ils le feront au xixe siècle, et comme cherchent encore aujourd'hui à le faire les « nouveaux croisés» envers les «frères musulmans » de Bosnie, puis du Kossovo. Accoler systématiquement l'étiquette de «croisés» aux coalitions européennes du Moyen-Age tardif et de la Renaissance n'est pas une opération anodine. Elle contribue à transmettre l'obsession de la croisade aux jeunes ; inversement, leur perception de la croisade en histoire ne peut être que troublée par l'usage politique du mot.

Lors des graves difficultés du xixe et du début du xxe siècles, le point commun de tous les adversaires de l'empire ottoman est d'être chrétiens, ou soutenus par des puissances chrétiennes. Les vicissitudes subies par les Turcs ont facilité la formation du stéréotype d'«Occident chrétien», si fréquent de nos jours dans le discours nationaliste.

Les chrétiens étant ressentis, dans le récit historique, comme des ennemis extérieurs (les croisés, l'Occident) ou intérieurs (les Grecs et Arméniens de l'empire), les instances de l'éducation turque n'ont pas encore conçu, à la fin du xxe siècle, un récit historique leur accordant

[13] Cf mon article «*Hizmet* : a keyword in the Turkish historical narrative», *New Perspectives on Turkey*, 14, 1996, pp. 97-114.

[14] Par exemple, Köymen et al., *Lise II*, 1990, p. 180; Yıldız et al., *Lise II*, 1989, p. 156.

leur place dans le passé de l'Anatolie. Les auteurs de manuels ne peuvent admettre que difficilement que cette terre fut pendant des siècles le cadre des civilisations arménienne et byzantine. Aussi, tous les épisodes chrétiens de l'histoire de l'Anatolie sont-ils plus ou moins gommés du récit historique ; le millénaire byzantin est résumé en une page ou moins, et l'histoire arménienne médiévale (royaume Bagratide, royaume de Petite Arménie en Cilicie), qui était faiblement présente dans les manuels jusque vers 1980, a disparu depuis cette date[15]. Ces observations ne sont pas surprenantes ; cependant, la réticence à prendre en compte le passé chrétien de l'Anatolie empêche l'élaboration d'un récit historique complet de la terre sur laquelle vivent les enfants turcs, à qui on ne facilite pas la compréhension, dans beaucoup de régions dont celle d'Istanbul, de leur environnement monumental.

La Réforme

Dans les programmes d'histoire de 1997, il ne subsiste qu'une leçon où le christianisme est évoqué pour lui-même ; elle porte sur la Réforme, qui est l'un des éléments inamovibles de l'histoire de l'Europe telle qu'elle est vue par les manuels turcs ; même lorsque celle-ci est réduite à peu de choses, la Réforme continue d'être exposée. Ce fait a sans doute une signification. D'une part, la leçon sur la Réforme est l'occasion d'exposer, invariablement, l'image d'un catholicisme dégradé, avili, dont les prêtres ne pensent qu'à s'enrichir et à s'amuser, et dont la hiérarchie catholique vit dans le luxe ; un catholicisme qui a oublié l'enseignement spirituel des Évangiles, dont le texte est inconnu du peuple, misérable, exploité et opprimé par les gens d'Église. L'affaire des indulgences occupe une place importante dans le récit et surtout dans les représentations populaires du christianisme, où elle est devenue un stéréotype, selon lequel les chrétiens seraient persuadés qu'ils peuvent acheter leur place au paradis. Cette leçon acquiert donc une fonction religieuse ou culturelle dans la mesure où elle infère une idée de décadence et de division du christianisme, opposée à la vigueur de l'islam qui, à la

15 Seuls quelques paragraphes subsistent sous le sous-titre «La question arménienne», à la fin des leçons sur l'empire ottoman, destinés à réfuter l'existence d'un génocide en 1915 ; cf *Espaces et temps de la nation turque*, pp. 322-338.

même époque, est guidé par les Turcs ; elle diffuse des stéréotypes négatifs sur le catholicisme, qui restent vivants dans les mentalités et réapparaissent à l'occasion dans des écrits polémiques de la presse religieuse ou d'extrême-droite.

D'autre part, la leçon induit aussi l'idée qu'une religion est réformable ; la représentation du protestantisme comme un perfectionnement du christianisme, qui l'a sauvé de la décadence et l'a rapproché du p euple, est tellement v ivante qu'il est ass ez courant de qualifier, dans les années quatre-vingt-dix, de «protestantisme musulman» le mouvement qui cherche à retourner aux valeurs coraniques débarrassées des superstitions.

Le christianisme comme thème politique : Croisés et missionnaires

Les observations qui précèdent portent sur la présence de discours (idéologique) dans le récit (historique). Il existe également des kystes de récit historique dans le discours politique. On peut observer, comme partout, un va-et-vient entre les deux formes d'énonciation, et le discours politique s'appuie souvent sur un savoir historique communément partagé, diffusé par l'école. La croisade en est le meilleur exemple, puisque le terme est aujourd'hui plus politique qu'historique, et les passerelles entre récit et discours sont parfois construites par les auteurs de manuels eux-mêmes : «Depuis les croisades jusqu'à la lutte de libération nationale [1922], on a cherché à nous jeter hors de l'Anatolie, et cela continue par des moyens politiques. Les mouvements qui cherchent à diviser notre pays, ceux qui les soutiennent ou qui entravent le développement de notre économie, continuent à faire vivre l'esprit de croisade»[16].

La tendance à incruster, dans le discours politique, des éléments du récit historique est forte et constante ; on peut l'observer à la lecture de quotidiens comme *Türkiye* (ultra-nationaliste) ou *Zaman* (religieux). Les exemples évoqués ci-dessous sont des stéréotypes dont j'observe l'évolution depuis plusieurs années[17]. Dans le discours nationaliste, qu'il s'agisse de la mouvance dite «synthèse turco-

16 Yıldız, o.c., id.

17 Cf mes articles dans les *Cahiers d'études sur la Méditerranée orientale et le monde turco-iranien (CEMOTI)*, n° 13, 1992, pp. 45-68 ; n° 14, 1992, pp. 31-52 ; *Hérodote*, n° 64, 1992, pp. 183-193 et n° 67, 1992, pp. 151-159.

islamique» ou de la mouvance plus religieuse du parti *Refah*, l'emploi du mot «croisade» est constant, pour désigner tout ce qui agresse la Turquie ou l'islam. Il s'est renforcé au cours des dernières années pour désigner un ennemi encerclant ; il est révélateur de la fièvre obsidionale qui existe en Turquie depuis un siècle. Le thème des croisades est évoqué lors de chaque crise chypriote (comme en été 1996), puisque le passé même de Chypre renvoie à ce thème historique[18]. L'idée de croisade évoque ainsi le conflit par excellence, et l'opposition entre la chrétienté et l'islam apparaît comme irréductible.

Dans la longue histoire de l'affrontement gréco-turc, le conflit entre les deux nationalismes est souvent lu comme conflit inter-religieux. L'ennemi grec, c'est l'ennemi chrétien ; le Grec, en caricature, est souvent représenté par un pope agressif et méprisable, agent de propagande, éventuellement armé. Inversement, la confusion entre la nation et la religion peut aboutir à une certaine confusion des cibles : à la suite des graves incidents de l'été 1996 à Chypre et en Thrace occidentale, c'est devant le patriarcat orthodoxe de Constantinople, et non devant le consulat de Grèce, que des membres de l'organisation *Nizam-i alem* (organisation de jeunesse religieuse et ultra-nationaliste) sont allés manifester. Les slogans proférés à cette occasion mêlaient des éléments religieux (récitation de la formule *Allahuekber*) et historiques («Aujourd'hui nous sommes le 9 septembre, c'est le jour où, à Izmir [en 1922], nous avons jeté à la mer nos ennemis lors de la Guerre de Libération. Cette nation [la Grèce] ne se redressera pas, nous les repousserons jusqu'à l'Adriatique»)[19]. La confusion entre nation et religion, il est vrai, est complaisamment entretenue par les Etats protagonistes, où les lieux de culte sont volontiers pavoisés des drapeaux nationaux. L'image de l'«ennemi chrétien» , alimentée par l'histoire de la fin de l'empire ottoman, continue de l'être par l'actualité ; dans la relation des événements de Bosnie et dans les commentaires de la presse

[18] Ainsi, la manifestation de motocyclistes grecs sur la ligne de démarcation entre les deux parties de Chypre, le 11 août 1996, a été qualifiée de «tentative de 10e croisade» ; Ayhan Songar, «Onuncu Haçlı Seferi denemesi», *Türkiye,* 13 août 1996. On peut comparer ces représentations des croisades avec celles des pays arabes, cf Emmanuel Sivan, *Mythes politiques arabes*, Paris, Fayard, 1995.

[19] Cf *Yeni Yüzyıl*, 10 septembre 1996.

nationaliste, le mot « Serbe» est souvent co-occurrent de « chrétien» (*vahşi hıristiyan Sırpları*) ; c'est non seulement aux Serbes, mais aussi à l'Occident chrétien qu'on impute la responsabilité du nettoyage ethnique[20].

Comme dans tout discours de ce type, l'ennemi extérieur (le croisé) s'appuie sur des agents infiltrés. En Turquie, c'est encore une métaphore religieuse, celle des « missionnaires», qui prévaut. Le plus dangereux est le missionnaire caché, l'enseignant, le membre d'une institution occidentale, l'orientaliste. La qualification de ces «agents secrets» par un terme renvoyant au christianisme est significative de l'image négative de celui-ci dans les représentations nationalistes. Loin d'être le signe d'un manque de confiance en la force de l'islam, il révèle la peur d'une déculturation, car le «missionnaire» désigné est vecteur de manières d'être et de vivre, plus encore que d'une religion : « Le mode de vie chrétien est présenté [par les missionnaires] comme le mode de vie contemporain, le mode de vie de la modernité et du progrès» [21]. Les agents de l'étranger ont leurs complices : par exemple, les Turcs étudiant dans les établissements étrangers, ou dans les écoles religieuses (dites les « Saints» à Istanbul). Selon l'éditorialiste Necati Özfatura, tout film occidental est une leçon de christianisme ; le triple but de la télévision serait de faire de la propagande chrétienne, de détruire les valeurs nationales, spirituelles et la culture des musulmans, et de leur imposer, de la naissance à la mort, une vie sociale calquée sur celle des chrétiens et qualifiée de «vie moderne »[22]. Cette perception n'est pas seulement celle de quelques journalistes vindicatifs ; elle est partagée par la frange la plus nationaliste de la p opulation, les sympathisants du *Refah* et des partis d'extrême-droite, qui formaient en 1995 environ un quart de l'électorat.

En raison même de l'évocation fréquente de la croisade, la perception du christianisme est fortement connotée de l'idée d'intolérance. C'est là un thème qui fait efficacement contrepoint au

---

20 Interview d'habitants turcs de Krefeld (Allemagne), *Türkiye*, 9 novembre 1992.

21 Necati Özfatura, «Misyoner faaliyetleri», *Türkiye*, 22 janvier 1992.

22 *Türkiye*, 23 décembre 1991. Depuis, des chaînes plus «nationales» et plus «musulmanes» ont vu le jour, comme TGRT et Samanyolu. En 1990 , la diffusion du film français *Jeux interdits* a dû être interrompue car des crucifix sont visibles au cours de certaines scènes.

thème de la tolérance musulmane et turque. En effet, selon le discours historique officiel, les Turcs auraient de tout temps, dès avant l'islam, été porteurs de cette vertu ; ce sont eux qui l'auraient apportée au monde musulman. Grâce à l'éducation historique et par l'effet répétitif de très nombreux énoncés dans les *media*, il est vraisemblable que la plupart des Turcs sont sincèrement persuadés qu'ils sont les champions de la tolérance. Des épisodes comme la bataille de Mantzikert (1071, victoire des Seldjoukides sur Byzance), la prise de Constantinople (1453) ou la victoire sur les Grecs en 1922 sont censés apporter la preuve même de la magnanimité des Turcs[23]. La tolérance est perçue comme caractérisant le mode de relation entre les Turcs et le reste du monde. Le système de la *dhimmitude*, si sévèrement critiqué dans certains ouvrages récents[24], est présenté comme une preuve de la tolérance de l'islam.

Il est donc tentant, pour les polémistes, de présenter au contraire les chrétiens comme particulièrement intolérants. Certains faits historiques, comme l'Inquisition, le procès de Galilée, acquièrent une fonction stéréotypée dans ce discours ; l'opposition entre ces cas de persécution et le Sermon sur la montagne permet de souligner l'hypocrisie chrétienne, jusque dans *Cumhuriyet*, quotidien de centre-gauche, kémaliste et laïque[25] ; ainsi, l'utilisation de ce thème dépasse largement les milieux islamistes ; il sert la fierté nationale turque, notamment lorsqu'elle est mise à mal par des critiques venant de l'Occident.

Un moment paroxystique : Noël et nouvel-an

Dans les perceptions turques du christianisme, la fête de Noël occupe une place de plus en plus importante, à mesure que s'impose la mode des illuminations de fin d'année, celle du père Noël et celle du sapin de Noël, ainsi que la célébration du nouvel-an. Ce phénomène est particulièrement sensible à Istanbul. Il s'agit d'une authentique occi-

23 Cf mon article «Les prédécesseurs médiévaux d'Atatürk», *Revue de la Méditerranée et du Monde Musulman (REMMM)*, Aix-en-Provence, à paraître en 1998. [Ce texte fut rédigé en 1997, *Réd.*]

24 Cf Bat Ye'or, *Juifs et chrétiens sous l'islam. Les dhimmis face au défi intégriste*, Paris, Berg International, 1994, 420 p.

25 Yavuz Gör, «Galileo Galilei», *Cumhuriyet*, 5 janvier 1996.

dentalisation par copie d'un ensemble de traditions qui n'avaient jamais eu cours en Turquie.

Comme tout progrès de l'occidentalisation, la célébration de Noël et du nouvel-an provoque des réactions. A Sincan, ville nouvelle de la banlieue d'Ankara, la municipalité a été jusqu'à interdire la vente de dindes ; à Beykoz (commune riveraine du Bosphore, sur la rive asiatique), une banderole proclamait, le 31 décembre 1995 : «Les Serbes, les Arméniens, les Russes, les *Rum* fêtent le nouvel-an ; ne le fêtez pas!». La presse islamiste et nationaliste, en décembre de chaque année, met son lectorat en garde contre les coutumes importées, et certains commentaires sont révélateurs d'une certaine vision du christianisme par les militants islamistes. L'un des plus caractéristiques est un texte d'A yhan Songar, homme de l ettres et chroniqueur du quotidien nationaliste *Türkiye*, publié le 27 décembre 1995 [26]. Après avoir manifesté sa réprobation devant le luxe, la pompe et l'ostentation affichés lors de la messe de Noël à Saint-Pierre de Rome, diffusée par la télévision italienne, Ayhan Songar fait part de quelques-uns de ses étonnements, et décrit cette cérémonie et les croyances catholiques comme typiquement polythéistes et idolâtres.

Des jugements semblables on été diffusés, dans la même presse, par İsmet Miroğlu, ancien directeur des archives de l'Etat et co-auteur de manuels d'histoire [27] : la fête de Noël est idolâtre, critiquée même par les chrétiens pieux ; la diffusion de coutumes comme celle du père Noël est le résultat des entreprises des agents missionnaires qui viennent dans les pays musulmans et font de la propagande chrétienne. Ainsi, les Occidentaux cherchent à éloigner les musulmans de leur religion pour les christianiser. De tendance plus religieuse, *Zaman* adresse également des avertissements à ses lecteurs : «Les fêtes de fin d'année sont devenues une tradition. Les bienheureux minoritaires s'en vont à l'étranger avec des valises pleines de devises. Les héros écologistes ont oublié leurs protestations contre les sacrifices du *Kurban Bayramı* [désignation turque de l'*Aïd el Kebir*] et vont tuer des dindes chez eux. Nous vivons une déculturation (*yabancılaşma*) ; où va la Turquie ? Sois toi-même, ne deviens pas un étranger ! Marche dans la lumière de ton cœur ; parcours les pages du

---

[26] Ayhan Songar, «Bir Noel âyininin düşüdürdükleri», *Türkiye*, 27 décembre 1995.

[27] İsmet Miroğlu, «Noel ve yılbaşı», *Türkiye*, 1 janvier 1996.

Livre. (...) Tiens-toi à l'écart des appels de cette nuit!»[28].

La presse de gauche est plus discrète sur ces fêtes. Généralement, de petits reportages sur la messe de minuit à Saint-Antoine, au centre d'Istanbul, mettent en avant l'idée de tolérance tout en présentant un aspect un peu exotique de la ville. Mais des réflexions sérieuses sur la place de Jésus dans la vie musulmane peuvent s'exprimer à cette occasion, comme celle de Niyazi Öktem dans le quotidien de centre-gauche *Yeni Yüzyıl*[29]. Rejetant la critique de la presse de droite qui qualifie les fêtes de fin d'année de *gavurluluk* (mécréance), de *zındıklık* (athéisme), de *yozluk* (abâtardissement), l'auteur réexamine les sources coraniques sur Jésus ; il s'interroge sur les raisons de l'inquiétude musulmane à propos de la célébration de Noël et ne voit pas pourquoi, lors de cette fête, les musulmans ne liraient pas la *mevlud* en l'honneur de Jésus, ni pourquoi les mosquées ne seraient pas illuminées : « Ainsi, peut-être, pourra-t-on renforcer le dialogue, la tolérance et la paix.»

Altérité mineure, altérité majeure ?

L'ensemble des observations présentées ici peut paraître hétéroclite, mais il m'a paru intéressant d'essayer de percevoir les osmoses entre des discours différents par nature. Les représentations évoquées sont partagées au moins par un quart de la population turque, lorsqu'il s'agit du discours nationaliste-religieux, et par une plus grande partie, certainement, pour ce qui est du discours scolaire. Cet examen m'incite à définir deux modes d'altérité du christianisme.

On peut parler d'altérité mineure lorsque le christianisme est perçu dans sa vision coranique : l'islam est la seule religion qui admet la validité d'une partie du christianisme et révère ses grandes figures. La condition de *dhimmitude* est perçue comme une composition bienveillante avec les autres religions révélées, et le système ottoman du *millet* comme un équilibre qui a permis la cohabitation, durant des siècles, de communautés religieuses différentes dans une relative harmonie. Ce rapport *mineur* avec l'altérité chrétienne tient dans le mot

---

28 Nihat Dağlı, «Yabancılaşmanın tavana vurduğu gece ve vicdan ritimler », *Zaman*, 31 décembre 1995.

29 Niyazi Öktem, «Müslümanlar Noel'i kandil gibi kutlayabilir», *Yeni Yüzyıl*, 24 décembre 1995.

hoşgörü, tolérance. Le chrétien est un voisin proche ; le musulman éclairé se plaira à discuter des différences de croyances ; malgré les incompatibilités théologiques portant sur la nature divine ou humaine du Christ, et sur la signification centrale de sa mort pour les chrétiens, malgré aussi un sentiment de supériorité, pas toujours exprimé, de chaque côté, il existe un terrain d'entente, une possibilité de discussion. La transformation d'églises en mosquées, par exemple, est un processus important dans la conscience des rapports entre les deux religions. Il s'agit d'une manifestation de respect des lieux de culte, de l'acceptation du christianisme en tant qu'altérité mineure ou partielle, compatible dans une certaine mesure avec sa propre identité; église ou mosquée, le lieu de culte reste maison de Dieu.

Le mode *majeur* d'altérité est complexe et inquiétant, car il peut aboutir à des actes déplaisants, sinon violents. Il résulte de la rémanence de traumatismes historiques comme les croisades et la colonisation, ou d'un phénomène d'uniformisation - qu'on l'appelle mondialisation, américanisation ou impérialisme - qui aboutit toujours à la diffusion d'une culture chrétienne ou perçue comme telle. L'un des principaux problèmes des perceptions croisées provient du caractère réducteur des regards, qui ont tendance à l'amalgame ; il importe de casser les images dépourvues de nuances et de proclamer clairement qu'être chrétien - ou d'éducation chrétienne, ou encore simplement occidental - ce n'est pas approuver les exactions serbes (ou chypriotes grecques en 1963), ni se sentir descendant des croisés, et qu'être musulman, ce n'est pas être islamiste extrémiste.

Le mode majeur d'altérité résulte aussi de la confusion, entretenue par les Etats ou gouvernements, des deux côtés de la mer Égée, entre l'identité religieuse et l'identité nationale. En raison de cette confusion entre l'ennemi - ou supposé tel - et sa religion, le nationalisme a tendance à prendre pour cible les signes extérieurs de la religion de l'adversaire. Certes, les très nombreuses églises de Turquie sont généralement respectées, et pas seulement parce qu'elles représentent un capital touristique. Cependant, il faut bien constater qu'en cas de crise, les actes de violence sont tournés vers le religieux. Lors des pogroms anti-grecs de septembre 1955, déclenchés par la fausse nouvelle d'une agression contre la maison natale d'Atatürk à Thessalonique, les ultra-nationalistes turcs s'en sont pris aux boutiques rum de Beyoğlu, mais aussi aux pierres tombales, aux églises, à la personne des popes. J'ai signalé plus haut les manifestations concernant le problème chypriote devant le patriarcat orthodoxe de Constantinople ; à l'automne 1996 encore, des croix ont été brisées au cimetière rum de Heybeliada (Istanbul).

Mais le plus impressionnant est le spectacle de la partie nord de Chypre, territoire majoritairement orthodoxe avant la partition de 1974, où l'ensemble des cimetières a été profané : croix abattues, tombes éventrées d'une manière systématique. Il ne fait aucun doute que cette destruction massive a été faite avec l'approbation au moins tacite de l'armée turque[30] ; la population chypriote turque vit, depuis plus de vingt ans, avec le spectacle de croix brisées ; dans le cimetière dévasté de Geçitkale (Lefkoniko) on a installé un petit terrain de football pour enfants. Les églises qui n'ont pas été transformées en mosquées servent d'étables ; elles ont été entièrement pillées et sont souvent profanées. La signification d'un tel ensemble d'actes est claire : il s'agit de frapper l'ennemi dans ce qu'il a de plus intime, son rapport au sacré, son rapport à sa terre et à ses ancêtres. La dévastation d'un cimetière manifeste l'irrespect non seulement pour l'individu enseveli, mais pour sa famille et ses proches vivants[31], ou pour la communauté à laquelle il a appartenu. La portée à long terme d'une familiarité de vingt ans entre une population et des signes de profanation est plus difficile à cerner ; la population, et surtout les jeunes, sont incités à cultiver le ressentiment ; le respect de l'altérité ne peut qu'en être affecté ; l'effet éducatif est évidemment désastreux.

Ici, l'altérité religieuse est irréductible justement parce qu'elle n'est plus religieuse mais nationale. L'exemple des émeutes de 1955 à Istanbul, et celui des cimetières de Chypre, sont révélateurs de certains réflexes qui peuvent encore fonctionner en cas de crise. Les actes qui en résultent démontrent à quel point la confusion est établie entre nation et religion, sans que les Etats - la Grèce et la Turquie - ne découragent ce type de perception ; ils démontrent aussi que la volonté de nuire s'exerce plus volontiers à l'encontre de l'élément

---

30 Le cimetière orthodoxe de Paşaköy (Askeia) portait en 1998 des signes très récents de dégradation (bris de croix, profanation des tombes) ; il est situé à quelques centaines de mètres d'un important camp militaire.

31 Un des plus forts désirs des Chypriotes turcs avec qui j'ai conversé est de pouvoir retourner sur la tombe des leurs, au sud, avant de mourir.

sacré de l'altérité, qui touche les tréfonds de la conscience bien plus que les symboles de la nation, qui sont pourtant sacralisés. On comprend, à la vue de ces cimetières, à quel point le nationalisme a besoin de l'élément religieux pour sacraliser la nation et les objectifs nationaux ; il profite de la force de la religion dont il utilise des éléments.

Mode mineur, mode majeur de l'altérité chrétienne : les différends théologiques peuvent être discutés et disputés ; mais l'image du christianisme est brouillée par l'histoire, par le différend gréco-turc et la question chypriote, et par le maintien de la Turquie hors du «club chrétien» qu'est encore l'Europe ; lorsque la religion recouvre un antagonisme national, les accusations de traîtrise, d'entente avec l'ennemi empêchent tout débat. C'est pourquoi le rapprochement islamo-chrétien pourrait et devrait aussi passer par la déconstruction des discours nationalistes, par la démystification de cette confusion entre nation et religion, ainsi que par la recherche d'un regard dépassionné sur l'histoire.

East is East, and West is West

Remarks on Muslim perspectives on Europe and Christianity

Ali Köse
Türkiye Diyanet Vakfı, İslam Araştırmaları Merkezi, Istanbul

East is East, and West is West,
and never the twain shall meet.
Rudyard Kipling

Abstract

This paper evaluates the need for dialogue between the Western and Islamic worlds and discusses the areas that would need to be dealt with as part of such a dialogue. Firstly, the history of the relations between the East and West are briefly outlined and the bad feeling that has been created explained. Such topics as the Crusades, imperialism and colonialism, and Western media accounts of the contemporary Islamic world are covered. More importantly, this paper presents the views of Muslims too -- how the Western media's portrayal of Muslims is seen as insulting, how the lack of decisive assistance to the Muslims in Bosnia is seen to indicate a Western double standard, and how the marginalization of religion in the West causes anxiety in the East as new Western values and secularization spread more widely around the world. This paper concludes that the need for dialogue exists but that greater understanding will be hard to achieve before problematic issues are worked through.

How have the West and the Islamic East viewed each other over the many years that they have been in contact? What events and policies have led to current tensions? Are the earlier stereo-types being overcome or are new ones being developed? Are secularization and new values in the West affecting Muslims? These are some of the questions that this paper tries to answer.

The perceptions derived from the past

The interaction between Europe and Islam dates from 710 A.D., only 80 years after the death of the Prophet Muhammad, when powerful Arab and Berber armies crossed the straits of Gibraltar and invaded Spain. The Spanish converted to Islam until 1492, when the Spanish regained control and Spain became Christian again. By that time there was further Muslim expansion elsewhere under the Ottoman Turks[1], who eventually extinguished what was left of the Byzantine Empire, occupied its capital, Constantinople, and expanded into Eastern and Central Europe. As late as the seventeenth century they were able to occupy the island of Crete and threaten Vienna. Similarly, Islam infiltrated many European countries long ago and remains until the present day. The fact that Islam is found in many East European countries is because the indigenous populations converted to Islam under the rule of the Ottoman Turks. The relationship between Muslims and European Christians, however, was not based only on war, but also on trade across the Mediterranean and the interaction of ideas.[2]

It was during the Middle Ages that the Western perspectives of Islam were formed. At first, the more commonly held view was that Islam was a heresy of Christianity.[3] During and after the Crusades, the European image of Islam and Muslims was slowly formed on misinformation about Islam, leading to Islam being described as a form of polytheistic idol worship. The West also perceived the East as a dangerous region where Islam flourished and monstrous races multiplied.[4] Turks were portrayed as the incarnation of horror, cruelty,

---

[1]Western history does not seem to have detached the Turks from the other Islamic ethnic groups of the Middle East such as the Arabs and Iranians although their origins and cultures, for example, differ. See K. Aydın, Western images of the Muslim Turks prior to the 20th Century, *Hamdard Islamicus* XVI, 4 (1993), p. 103. This might be so due to the fact that it was the Turks who spread Islam westward.

[2] W.M. Watt, *The influence of Islam on medieaval Europe,* Edinburgh University Press, Edinburg 1972, pp. 2-4, 10; Albert Hourani, *Islam in European thought*, Cambridge University Press, Cambridge 1991, pp. 7-8.

[3] N. Daniel, *Islam and the West,* Oneworld, Oxford, 1993, p. 209.

[4] R. Kabbani, *Europe's myths of Orient,* MacMillan, London 1988, p. 14.

revenge, or passion, not so much because of their race but because they represented Islam.[5] Islam was also held responsible for ordering the Saracens "to rob, to make prisoner and to kill the adversaries of God and their Prophet, and to persecute and destroy them in every way."[6] Apparently, in the Christian world the stereotypes which developed during the Crusades have led to hostility towards Islam which has survived to the present day.[7] This may be in order to justify Europe's later changes in attitude towards the outside world which came with its discoveries of new lands.

While Europe's hostile view of Muslims can be traced back to the Crusades, Muslims' negative perceptions of Europe derive from the later period of Europe's discovery of the outside world. Muslims in medieval times generally regarded Europe as simply a land of non-believers.[8] The Turks then, like the Arabs, did not perceive Europeans as violent in the way Europeans viewed them, despite the fact that they knew about the Inquisition Courts[9] in Europe where heretics were severely punished or even burnt to death.

It was in the late seventeenth and eighteenth centuries when Europe became more expansionist, that Muslims changed their view of it, now seeing it as imperialistic. Thereafter, even Christian missionaries were identified with imperialism.[10] Thus, the Christian West, once viewed from a religious standpoint, was now viewed in a non-religious way due to imperialism and colonialism.

By the eighteenth century Muslims were travelling to Europe, embassies were established, and some Muslims went to the West to study. This interaction enabled Muslims to gain a closer and more realistic view of the West and Western Christianity.[11] By the early nineteenth century, though, there was no need for Muslims to travel to Europe to learn more about Europe and Europeans because they now faced Eu-

5 Aydın, p. 106.

6 Watt, p. 75.

7 R.W. Bulliet, Process and status in conversion and continuity, in *conversion and continuity*, M. Gervers & R.J. Bikhazi (eds), Pontifical Institute of Medieval Studies, Toronto 1990, p. 2.

8 B. Lewis, *The Muslim discovery of Europe*, W. W. Norton, New York 1982, p. 301.

9 Lewis, pp. 179-80; H. Goddard, *Muslim perceptions of Christianity*, Grey Seal, London 1996, p. 57.

10 Goddard, pp. 59, 85.

11 Lewis, pp. 302-303.

ropeans as invaders in Muslim lands.

More recent perceptions

After the Second World War a new era began in terms of Muslims' views of Europe. This time Europe was viewed much more positively. With Muslim emigration to Europe it came to be regarded as a land of abundance. Information about the advent of new technologies was conveyed to the home countries, and those back home formed an image of a Europe where people lived in great luxury. This image has, to some extent, remained up to the present day, although it is not as strong as it used to be. Thanks to the mass media, the Muslim world seems to have grown out of this perception. Also, the growing technological capacity of Muslim countries themselves has helped to change this image.

Today, the Muslim world, especially the Turks, view the West more positively than the Western world views them. Muslims under the influence of Westernization have largely wiped out their previous more negative images of the West. A look at the recommendations to Muslims in many of the old books of exegesis reveals how much things have changed. In such books, for example, the interpretation of the nineteenth verse of Surah 31 of the Qur'an, about being modest in bearing or one's walk and about speaking in a subdued voice, urged Muslims not to walk with the fast pace of Jews nor with the slow pace of Christians but to walk at a moderate pace.[12] Now some Western norms and even conduct have been adopted by many Muslim societies.

In spite of these changes, one cannot deny the history of past conflicts and hostility. Resolving hostility that has lasted for more than a thousand years will not be easy. The granting of permission to construct a mosque in Rome, the largest in Europe, by Italian officials was a positive step forward. However, at the opening of the mosque in 1995, the way the past can overshadow the present was made clear. The opening ceremony was boycotted by some of Italy's highest officials. Moreover, the Speaker of the Italian lower house, Irene

12 See for example, Abu'l Barakat al-Nasafi, *Tafsir al-Nasafi* (or *Madarık al-Tafsir...*), Vol. III, Istanbul, 1984, p. 282.

Pivetti, instead of taking part in the opening ceremony which she was invited to attend, went to a nearby church in order to make amends for the opening of the mosque. There she joined others in a service honouring a sixteenth century battle which broke the naval might of the Ottomans.[13] Thus, an attempt to promote dialogue between the two religions provoked some counteractions.

Another example of the past being resurrected in the present involves remarks made by the Serbian leader Radovan Karadzič during an interview broadcast by the BBC. He said that it was the Serbs who protected Europe from the Turks for over 500 years. This statement came in answer to the BBC presenter's question of why the Serbs insisted on committing atrocities against the Bosnian Muslims. What Karadzič was trying to imply was that Muslims are, in fact, an enemy for Europe rather than for themselves.

A much more serious example of the past influencing the present is the possible way that an "us" versus "them" attitude has developed in Europe and the Western world towards the Muslim world. Due to the European colonialism and imperialism it seems that the Western world has come to see itself as superior to all other nations, with a right to dominate the world. This attitude is even reflected in Western nineteenth and twentieth century novels. Also, one can easily find the same "us" and "them" mentality among contemporary novelists like Graham Greene, particularly in his novel *The Quiet American.*[14] Unfortunately, this superiority complex and the pattern of interaction it creates still continues, and since Muslims are included among the "others," they deserve to be ruled or punished when they "misbehave" or "rebel." This phenomenon might be labelled "ultra-nationalism or racism" or "national or racial narcissism." Individuals who have taken on these attitudes tend to see their own nation as perfect, peace-loving, and cultured, for example, while "other" countries are the opposite. Narcissistic nationalism encourages people to notice only the virtues of their own nation while noticing only the vices of the "other." We often witness the mobilization of narcissistic nationalism in the lead up to war. In a sense, it makes a nation psychologically ready for war.

---

13 J. Hooper, When in Rome, do as the Muslims, *The Guardian*, London, 29.6.1995.

14 See Edward Said, *Culture and imperialism*, Vintage, London 1993, pp. xvi-xi.

When this narcissism takes over, reason disappears.[15] In other words, not only are the old views of the Islamic world created at the time of the Crusades still causing problems, but so are the views caused by the superiority complex still not thrown off by the Western world.

If we assume that a minority of Europeans have progressed beyond the old attitudes, we are still faced with the majority that have not. So how are the old stereotypes to be overcome? What are Europeans taught about Islam? What they seem to know is nothing more than secondary school information such as the story of Richard the Lion Heart and Salahaddin. Most ordinary Europeans have not even heard about the presence of Islam in Spain until the fifteenth century and the great effect it had on Europe.

The portrayal of the Islamic world in the Western media

Another source of information about the Islamic world comes from the media. Unfortunately, what it presents to the West is Muslims as terrorists waiting to shoot tourists in Egypt or bomb innocent civilian Jews in Israel, and Muslims as barbarians who yearn for the execution of Salman Rushdie in Britain. This creates the idea in the West that all Muslims are potential terrorists and leads to an atmosphere in which Muslims are viewed with suspicion. No doubt the remarks of a Swedish citizen, Erik Hörstadius, after the Gulf War are due to the mistrust that has been created by the media. He said, "I would feel nothing if a hundred thousand Arabs die, but I feel sympathy for the soldiers of the Allies and their families because I am terrified of Arabs."[16] As this example illustrates, Islam is represented as a threat to the West, and therefore to Christianity, whereas, as Esposito puts it, Islam is not a threat but a challenge.[17] In my opinion, it is time to dispel the medieval perception of Islam as a mortal threat.

This view greatly insults and humiliates Muslims. It may also cause problems for some of Europe's other "others" as well. An English pro-

---

15 Erich Fromm, *Greatness and limitations of Freud's thought*, Abacus, London 1982, pp. 52-53.

16 Cited by Ingmar Karlson, *İslam ve Avrupa <Islam och Europa, tr.>*, Cem Yay., Istanbul 1996, p. 11.

17 John Esposito, The threat of Islam, in *Islam: a challenge for Christianity,* H. Küng & J. Moltmann (eds.), SCM Press, London 1994, p. 45.

verb says, "Give a dog an ill name and hang him!" Unfortunately, this is what most Muslims believe the West does in order to pursue its interests. For instance, Americans need someone like Saddam Hussein. He is someone they can call names and punish. What happens is that "others," innocent people, suffer. The ultimate aim of the U.S. or the West in the Middle East is control. Of course, Saddam is just an excuse. This has always been the policy of the West. It resembles the way in which Americans systematically vilified the American Indians as savages in order to clear the new world of them.

As for the European press, Islam and Muslims are presented not only as dangerous but also as primitive and even deranged. One can easily find vivid examples of this in articles in the British tabloids. Even the more serious British papers in writing about the wedding in May 1995 of Pakistan's well-known former cricketer Imran Khan and Jemima, the daughter of billionaire financier James Goldsmith, took the position that Jemima faced a life of hell in Pakistan. An article confirming the negative effect that the media is having on Westerners appeared in the U.S. publication *Newsweek.* It printed an article in 1996 that mentioned a French opinion poll in 1994 in which both Muslims and non-Muslims in France were asked to choose from several words and phrases the three that most closely corresponded to their idea of Islam. They picked "democracy", "justice" and "liberty." Non-Muslims, picking from the same list, chose "fanaticism" by a wide margin. Then came "submission" and "rejection of Western values."[18]

Muslims discover a double standard

Not mentioned in the *Newsweek* article but of great importance is that Muslims today view the West as applying a double standard-- one for themselves and another for Muslims. Westerners, who claim to be civilized and possess concepts like *democracy* and *human rights* , will, on the one hand, demand to see democracy and human rights as a part of their interaction with some countries but, on the other hand, they support non-democratic rulers in the Middle East. It was the ethnic cleansing faced by Muslims in Bosnia while the West looked on that for

18 *Newsweek*, 29.5.1996, p. 14.

Turks, especially, revealed the existence of the double standard. Whatever doubts that might have been felt about this before were destroyed. No event in Europe has effected Muslims throughout the world as much as what happened in Bosnia.

Besides Bosnia, the West's encouragement or even backing of the Algerian army when it stepped in to prevent a party supporting Islamic values from rightfully taking power, its fickle attitude towards the Kurdish problem in Turkey, its political games in Cyprus, and its approach towards Palestine are regarded by the Muslim world as hypocritical. The words of the U.S. State Department spokesman who urged both sides, the Israelis and Palestinians, to be calm after about 70 Palestinians were killed in 1995 instead of condemning the killing are not forgotten by Muslims. Muslims today believe that the West does not put enough effective pressure on those preventing greater democracy in the Middle East. In fact, there often seems to be support for the anti-democratic forces.

The marginalization of religion in the West and how this afects Muslims

Another problematic area is the way the West treats religion and the way this affects Muslims. Today, the fundamentals of modern Western culture are said to be post-Christian because modern culture is gradually losing the marks of Christianity that have shaped it for so long. This does not mean that Christianity has become irrelevant, but that it has become marginal for many people. To think and act in secular terms and even be indifferent to religion has become the norm. This has given birth to a secular culture, and religion has been relegated to the edges of modern consciousness. Consequently, individuals in advanced societies become members of an increasingly secular society.[19]

Since the West dominates the Muslim world in many aspects of life, the Western attitude towards religion is indirectly imposed on Muslims. Islam, unlike Christianity, is bound to affect society. In fact, it is a stabilizing force. Islam does not change its rules to suit changes in society nor to follow secular needs. In fact, Muslims do not want their

[19] G. Vahanian, *The death of God,* George Braziller, New York 1967, pp. 152, 228; B. Wilson, *Contemporary transformation of religion*, Clarendon, Oxford 1976, p. 85.

religion to be eroded by secularization. They want to maintain their Islamic culture. Here, what Muslims oppose is not Christianity but current Western values that are under the influence of modern liberal thought. Muslims blame modernization, which is sometimes called Westernization, and therefore the West for the weakening of religious observance among younger generations of Muslims. This problem is greater in the case of Muslim immigrants living in the West.[20] Muslim parents and the community in general fear that their children will soon adopt Western standards and ideas and that they will lose their religion as well as their cultural heritage. Muslim children educated in the generally liberal *"think-for-yourself"* atmosphere of Western schools find themselves at the centre of cultural conflict.[21] In a recent survey almost half of the Muslim parents, 47%, and 41% of young Muslims surveyed felt that Muslim children were being influenced by Christianity.[22] This indicates that Christianity is also being blamed for the present circumstances in the Muslim world.

Muslims also believe that the West is not far from collapse since it has lost its religious and moral values. They see the church as being too permissive towards modern day demands. Promiscuity, drug use, and crime among other behaviours are cited as indicators of the West's social malaise. Since Muslims strongly oppose such behaviours they feel that they have to oppose the West. It is true that there is some degree of misinformation among Muslims regarding the social and moral problems in the West. There is tendency for people to think, for example, that most Europeans, in one way or another, are involved in drug use or that most women are available all the time. In his article, "The problem of Christianity in the Muslim Perspective," the late David Kerr discusses the moral permissiveness of Christianity as viewed by Muslims and observes that Muslims are gravely concerned about the matter. He writes that "evidence of the failure of Christianity in the West is further adduced from what many Muslims see to be the rampant moral permissiveness, which, they argue, is the inevitable

20 Ali Köse, *Conversion to Islam,* Kegan Paul, London 1996, p. 8.

21 Muhammad Iqbal, The Muslim community in Britain, in *Islamic Education and single sex schools*, Union of Muslim Organizations, London 1975, p.10; I. Wilkinson, Muslim beliefs and practices in a non-Muslim country, *Research Papers: Muslims in Europe* 39 (1989), p. 18.

22 Muhammed Anwar, *Young Muslims in a multi-cultural society,* The Islamic Foundation, Leicester, 1986, pp. 15-16.

consequence of secularism. The majority of criticism made on this issue can be grouped under three interrelated categories: the devaluation of the dignity of women through commercial exploitation of sex, resulting in the disintegration of the family of which the mother is the traditional pivot, resulting in juvenile delinquency (drugs, alcohol, etc.).[23]

Developing greater understanding through dialogue

In order to provide better information and promote understanding between Muslims and Westerners there are those on both sides who advocate dialogue. In fact, dialogue of some sort has been one of the major topics raised in religious and political circles within the last two or three decades. It is clear that advocates of dialogue believe, at least in principle, that the need for it is great. Despite the innumerable differences, it is hoped that dialogue can bring about a spirit of peace and meet the challenge that arises from these differences.[24]

One noticeable difference between the Christians in the West interested in inter-faith dialogue and the Muslims aware of these Christians' interest is that the Christians seem to be quite confident about planning for such a dialogue while the Muslims are somewhat suspicious and unsure of the intentions of the Christians. Their anxiety is not due to concern that the people with whom they will be in dialogue are Christians. Rather, they are concerned that they are Westerners. Given past political and economic imperialism and the fear of cultural imperialism today, Muslims are suspicious of hidden agendas. Muslims want to be able to identify whether or not those proposing dialogue are motivated by imperialistic tendencies. In other words, Muslims are of the opinion that an inter-faith dialogue between them and, say, Nigerian Christians would be more fruitful than one between Muslims and Western Christians. Another worry is that, given such influences as pluralism and post-modernism, Westerners have lost their belief in religious truth and hope that Muslims will do the same.

---

23 D. Kerr, The problem of Christianity in the Muslim perspective, *International Bulletin of Missionary Research* 4 (1981), p. 158.

24 H. Küng & J. Moltmann, Editorial, in *Islam: A Challenge for Christianity*, p. vii.

Conclusion

To conclude, it is quite normal for there to be different views when there are different phenomena. The problem is whether the differing views represent the truth. To discover the truth about each other Westerners and Muslims will need to do their best to scrutinize and overcome whatever old distorted images they hold. Only then will better understanding develop. As a Turkish proverb states "man is an enemy of whatever is unfamiliar to him."

However, in the context of a dialogue, the negative perceptions mentioned before represent the areas that need to be dealt with if better understanding is to be reached. To summarize, I see four major areas that need to be tackled. The first involves being more objective about the long history of rivalry and hostility that exists between the Western and Islamic worlds. The second has to do with the perceptions each hold of the other's religion. Christianity does not seem to have come to terms with the fact that Islam, which claims to complete or perfect every monotheistic religion, has spread so widely, while Islam still perceives Christianity as historically distorted and corrupted. The third is that Muslims are suspicious of imperialism and links between Christianity and imperialism while Western Christians view Islam as a religion of the barbaric masses. The fourth area is that Muslims believe that Christianity has become secularized and the church too permissive, causing it to lose its grip on moral values while Christians think that Muslims see the world from too religious a perspective. Working through these areas will not be easy.

Conflictual images of Turkey and Europe

Ali Murat Yel[1],
Bilgi University, İstanbul

"Whenever an educated Turk dipped into western histories of civilisation or books on Turkey, he ran into unpleasant passages about his own people" remarked Bisbee referring to the countless prejudiced portrayals of Turks in existing Western literature (Bisbee 1951; 7, quoted in Aydın 1993; 105). For example, when Pierre Belon du Mans (1518-1546) a French botanist and historian of nature, visited Egypt in order to find some plants and herbs to cure his patients, he observed that the Egyptians and the Turks were quite different from each other: "car les Turcs sont naturellement mornes, lents, & paresseux" (Voyage en Egypte de Pierre Belon du Mans 1547, Paris 1555, fol. 110b-110a). Since I am not a historian or a student of literature, it is not my intention to delve into the depth of a large number of accounts written in various Western languages to find and bring back light into such prejudices. Yet, I definitely think that the contemporary negative image of Turks and Turkey held by Western people dates back to these earlier representations. If one has ever seen an old map of the world, one will surely remember some ridiculous monster drawings on others' - rather, 'unknown' - lands (see R. Kabbani 1986). Of course one cannot be sure of the mapmaker's real intention in putting monsters on foreign lands, but such a negative attitude clearly shows the kind of hostile feelings held toward people whom one does not know. Most importantly, the Western attitude towards the people who live today in these unknown lands remains unchanged. Anthropology, a modern science which tries to overcome such feelings, I feel, is not successful in improving these attitudes, since the dominating and colonialist disposition of the anthropologist toward his or her field sub-

[1] The author wishes to thank Lisa Isaacson for her help in proofreading this text.

jects has enhanced the hostility between two culturally different worlds: the anthropologist's modern and technologically advanced world and the field subject's culture of a Third World country. Nevertheless, if and when anthropologists have adopted a relativist attitude toward other people's cultures; in other words, when they consider all the cultures of the world population to be valid and coherent in themselves, the condescending attitude of Westerners towards others would begin to change.

What I shall try to elaborate on in this article are the modern attitudes of both Western and Turkish cultures towards each other. Throughout this paper I will use the terms Islam, Muslim, and Turk interchangeably since I believe that historically and socially the image of the Turk has been identified with Islam.[2] Likewise, the terms West (in which I include the United States of America and Canada) and Europe will also be used homogeneously and, as the roots of American and European civilisations are grounded on the same ancient Greek philosophy, I do not think that the Westerners and Europeans will object to this usage.[3] I must also stress here that I am aware that these two entities are not homogeneous in themsel-

2 "The word 'Turk' was mainly used in two ways, as a generic name for an Islamic state with its own characteristic institutions of government and military; and as a description of behaviour or character - the Turk being of nature cruel and heartless" Shepherd, Simon, *Marlowe and the politics of Elizabethean theatre*, 1986, p. 142, quoted in Aydın 1992, p. 104. In fact, the term used for the people who lived in the Islamdom (I borrow this usage from Hodgson) was "Saracens". Metlitzki (1977; 3) defines the term broadly so as to include in it various religious groups as well: "They were Greeks, Persians, Indians, Copts, Nestorians, Zoroastrians, and Jews, whole populations living in a vast expanse of territories extending from the Indian Ocean to the Atlantic which the spread of Islam from the heart of the Arabian peninsula had engulfed with lightning speed". The epithets Turk and Saracen were also used in Elizabethan plays interchangeably as Rana Kabbani (1986; 20) has pointed out: "The Saracen, the Turk, ... were key villains in the drama of the period, crudely depicted as such by the lesser play-wrights, but drawn with more subtle gradations by a Marlowe or a Shakespeare".

3 On the other hand, Muslims use the term Majus for the Europeans the same generic way. According to an Arab source the first 'Saracens' who arrived at a British island gave their impressions as follows: "This is a great island in the encircling sea in which there are flowing waters and gardens, and between it and the mainland are three days which is three hundred miles, and in it are Majus whose number cannot be counted and near this island are many islands, small and big, whose population is all Majus, and some the mainland belongs to them also. The size of their country is several days' journey. They are Majus and to-day they adhere to the Christian law" D. M. Dunlop, The British Isles according to Mediaeval Arabic authors, *Islamic Quarterly* 4 (4/1957), pp. 12-14, quoted in Metlitzki 1977, p. 121.

ves; that is, one cannot reduce all the different European and American cultures under one all-encompassing heading of "West"; likewise, the term "Turk" is also a 19th century construct in the "ethnic" sense as a result of the nationalistic movements around the world in general and that of a shift from traditional states to nation-states particularly in Europe. Yet, the historical developments of the West's representation of itself and the nationalist consciousness of the Turkish people in defining themselves as "Turks" require such thorough research that must be dealt with elsewhere. This paper is organised in the following way: First I will talk about my personal experience of Europe as a student and then about attitudes of Europeans towards myself as a Turk and a Muslim then, I shall look at the Turkish attitudes towards Europe and Europeans.

I left Turkey towards the end of 1988 by bus. I may have flown as well but consciously I chose travelling by bus, thinking in this way I could "see" more of Europe; perhaps I should cross out the word "see" and put "have a glimpse" instead. The Balkan countries (Bulgaria and Yugoslavia) were, apart from being under the Communist yoke, a result of which they showed themselves as collective entities, especially so in agricultural fields since there were no field boundaries, rather familiar to me. In Turkey farmers would grow different crops in accordance with their own will, but in these communist countries one could see as far as the horizon the same crop - whether wheat or barley - in the fields.

After crossing the Channel from France, I arrived at my destination: England. Having spent a few days in London, I went to Oxford to attend an English language school. My classmates were all Europeans except for one Japanese student. Sometimes we discussed several issues in the class; almost invariably our teacher would ask me and the Japanese student to present our ideas about the topic of discussion. She would ask me about latest developments in Turkey, such as whether we, in Turkey, had capital punishment, or about Human Rights or the status of women. I realised that at home I had been led to believe that Turkey was a "European" country and part of Europe, but I became aware of the fact that this was not the case, as my teacher would ask me and the Japanese friend about the issues which were considered as the same in other European students' countries. As she did not see any point in inquiring about the matter in other "European" lands through the other students, I was always excluded from the Europeans. Other students were curious about my country as well; they would ask me whether we had electricity or television broadcasting in Turkey. One day I told my classmates that in Turkey we travelled by camels and that I had seen a television set for the first time in my life in England. I meant these comments sarcastically, but they all liked them because they perfectly fitted with their image of Turkey.

In the meantime I travelled in various Europeans countries. The main problem was at the borders; as a Turkish citizen I needed visa for all European countries. Having checked my passport the custom officials would busy themselves with searching my car; I will never forget the day when some French officials stopped me after crossing the Spanish border a few miles into France. They asked me to show them the drugs I was carrying from Morocco. I told them in vain that I was just a student and had never been to Morocco in my life, but they did not believe me and searched my car for several hours. Although they could not find what they were looking for, their faces revealed that they still were not satisfied, but could not keep me there any longer.

Later on I went to Portugal to do field research for my Ph. D. thesis. The "field" was a Catholic pilgrimage town called Fátima, and there I suffered numerous discriminations, both religious and racial: The Portuguese clergy and pilgrims were convinced that I was a spy, or at best, an author who would "write a book *against* Fátima"; several times I was asked to leave the shrine grounds since I was not a Catholic; a very pious old lady asked me whether I had not been baptised before giving me an interview, and upon receiving a negative answer just walked away; the clergy had, on more than one occasion, refused to grant me an interview as "they didn't like the non-Catholics"; a Portuguese policeman, checking my driving licence and seeing the 'crescent and star' on it, took me for an Iraqi and associated me with terrorism as he imitated the sound and gesture of using a machine gun. As my Portuguese had improved I tried to read the classics in this language. One of them, perhaps the best literary work in the Portuguese history, was *Os Lusíadas* of

Luís de Camões, the national hero of Portugal, who would mention Turkey (in the 16th century there was no Turkey!) and Turks on several occasions, but always in a condescending manner. At Fátima I would introduce myself as a Turkish student but upon hearing the word 'Turk', people would immediately associate me with Mehmet Ali Ağca, who was a Turk that attempted to assassinate the Pope. What this incident very clearly shows is that the image of a Turk is that of a terrorist and an enemy of Christians. I suppose I do not need to remind the readers of the cartoons in Western newspapers depicting Muslims as terrorists and hijackers in the Middle East. For unknown and groundless reasons Western opinion is alarmed about incidents of violence or authoritarian regimes[4] that seem to be generated by Islam more than they are by other similar cases stemming from various other religions. If these incidents are covered by the media they are all attributed to Islam and the alarm becomes fiercer. These are some examples of my experiences in, not of Europe. Although I have received advanced degrees from the London University, and have participated in an acculturation process which transmitted an admiration for European values, I still insist that East in general and Turkey in particular should remain Eastern.

The question that should be posed here is this: "Why is Islam in general and Turks in particular represented as bad?" One may extend this mis-perception back to the times of the Crusades in the Middle Ages and the very discipline of Oriental Studies which is, in my opinion, an apparatus used to show Islam as a kind of primitive religion that blocks the rationality. Oriental Studies reduce Muslims to the status of people who need to be studied and then dominated by Western superpowers; in this way Oriental Studies symbolised the era of inferiority and intellectual guardianship that the East was passing through (Edward Said 1978). I now have a better understanding of the traditional Orientalist who "when addressing a Western audience simplifies, popularizes, and cheapens the substance of what he knows" (Djaït 1985; 52). I myself as an anthropologist have studied a Western religious folk culture, and in order to represent that culture to my audience I had to draw a simple picture of Portuguese Catholicism since it is a subject to which most Turkish

[4] In particular, Saddam Hussein in Irak and Ayatollah Khomeini in Iran are seen as ruthless dictators persecuting their own peoples.

people have not paid any attention so far. Therefore, I needed to give the audience the simple basics of Catholicism, as I myself have understood it. Yet, my case is different from that of an Orientalist in many ways; for example, I am one of the first examples of an Occidentalist, and since Occidentalism has not been established fully in Eastern societies, I may be excused. The second reason why I must be excused is more important, as the relationship between the West and the rest of the world is a history full of intentions to colonise whereas an Occidentalist has no chance of putting a Western culture under his or her hegemony.

After the Enlightenment and the Industrial Revolution in the 18th century onwards, the West advanced particularly technologically, and the Muslims who lagged behind this technological advance felt inferior to the West. For the last two centuries the roles have changed: now the West was the 'dominator', if we consider the cultural, economic and technological colonisation of many Muslim countries by the West, and the Muslims were the 'dominated'. The West introduced itself as the yardstick by which the progress of humanity could be measured.[5] The Turkish intelligentsia have been misled to believe this ethno-, rather, Euro-centric scheme of humankind's history. This has resulted in the conviction that the West should be imitated on the Turkish part. Muslims, specifically Turks have been fascinated by the "success" of Europe with its industrial and imperial might; some others have been attracted by its humanism and liberalism. An example of the Turkish official propaganda which still survives today is that in Turkey almost everybody knows the impressions of an Ottoman official who had visited the Versailles palace in the last century and when he saw its wonderful gardens he recited a *hadith* (the sayings of the Prophet) which could be translated as follows: "This world is the hell of the Muslim and the paradise of the non-Muslim". In my opinion this passage was taken from his book of travels in order to show the Turkish public the advanced level of Europe, which was the aim of the first Turkish Republicans to be achieved, and the fatalistic atti-

5 "It was one of the impulses for the creation of the science of anthropology: the study of certain societies which still existed but stood at a lower stage of the development through which more advanced societies had passed". Hourani 1990; 250.

tude of the Muslims. The idea they were trying to give the people was that we should work very hard to reach that level of welfare, and give up the traditional Islamic fatalistic attitude.

Prior to preparing this paper I had wished only to describe the present condition of Europe and Turkey, but later on I decided that this was not enough; I had also to try to pinpoint the socio-cultural dynamics of the de facto situation. What are these dynamics? First and foremost, they involve the so-called liberal ideology of the West today, which claims to be more humanist than any other ideology. Second, the West is not honest enough to admit that it tries to dominate the rest of the world by means of categorising them into specific groups such as "Third World", "developing" or "underdeveloped" countries. In fact, this classification means "those so-called developing countries are behind the level of civilisation that the West has already reached and they are advised to catch up with that civilisation". The West claims to have inaugurated various schemes for the underdog and underprivileged, such as the Universal Declaration of the Human Rights, but today in the West Blacks, Muslims, Asians, and others are still treated as second-class human beings. The West, on the one hand, appears to be the guardian of human rights, but on the other hand, it acts hypocritically.[6] This double standard of the West puts all the possibilities of dialogue in doubt, not only with the Islamic world but with others as well. The dishonest policy of the West gives feedback to the radicals in Muslim countries who see their heads of states as the "puppets" or "slaves" of their Western masters, and therefore, are critical of their

6 Here I wish to cite an example of such hypocrisy from the earlier contacts of Muslims and Christians in history. Pope Gregory VII wrote a letter to a Muslim prince in Algeria called al-Nasir in 1076 aknowledging the spiritual closeness between the two religions: "There is a charity which we owe to each other more than to other peoples, because we recognise and confess one sole God, although in different ways, and we praise and worship Him every day as creator and ruler of the world"; text in Patrologia Latina, vol. 148, J.P. Migne (ed.) Paris 1853, pp. 450-52, quoted in Hourani 1990, p. 228. This letter attracted the attention of various scholars and it has been suggested that the Pope wrote such a letter in order to protect some shrinking Christian minorities in North Africa. He was not sincere in his views of Islam in the mentioned letter since "in other letters, written to Christians, Gregory wrote of Muslims and Islam in harsher ways". Hourani 1990; p. 228. Similarly, the proceedings of the Second Vatican Council mentions Muslims and Islam in a favourable way but to what extent are the Church officials sincere about their views of Islam and its adherents is debatable, see Flannery, *Vatican Council II*, Nostra Aetate, pp. 739-80.

states' dealings with the West. For example, the indecent attitude of the West towards Iraq and Kuwait during the Gulf War and the genocide in Bosnia have endangered a possible friendly relationship between the West and the Islamic world: Today who, among the Turkish politicians, could suggest an integration of Turkey into the European Union after the Bosnian crisis? It is really difficult for a political leader to explain the contradictory attitudes of the West.

The Serbian genocide of the Albanians in the former Yugoslavian republic of Kosovo has opened a new black page in European history. Although the mentioned genocide is taking place right before European eyes, they have not attempted to stop this ugly conduct. Perhaps the statement by Dr. Radovan Karadzič, the former leader of the Bosnian Serbs, that the Serbs had always been a wall against the Turkish intrusion into Europe is relevant here. In the past they were the defenders and guards of the European civilisation against Turkish attacks and today they are the people who cleanse Europe of the Muslims, and anybody else historically related to the Turks. The Turkish public believes that the administration of the United Nations and NATO is in the hands of Westerners who are preventing these institutions from taking any measures against the Serbian attacks. To the ordinary Turkish citizen, the Westerners are turning a blind eye on the Serbian attempts to realise the Greater Serbia dreams at the expense of Muslims.

The reasons and dynamics of the Crusades[7] are beyond the scope of this paper, but on the basis of the historical facts we may assume that there has been a conflict between Christianity and Islam since the very early times of these great world religions. Here I may suggest that two very similar phenomena most of the time considered the other as a possible enemy; like the international conflicts between two very similar cultures such as Greece and Turkey, and Spain and Portugal. Perhaps this is due to the fact that one needs an "other" in order to ascertain his or her own identity. Why has the West needed an enemy, or at least, an "other"? Perhaps the West is not sure about the perfection of its civilisation and has suffered

[7] In 1998a group of European people mainly consisting of children, is visiting Turkey for the purpose of apologising to the Turkish public for what their ancestors did during the Crusades. They are wearing t-shirts with a message on it, which reads in Turkish "we are sorry for what our ancestors did to your country".

from a kind of inferiority complex after experiencing a number of defeats against the Muslims and Turks in its history. In order not to be influenced by the Islamic civilisation Westerners had to represent it in as bad a light as possible, and in turn *they* have tried to influence the rest of the world.

Such a fear, which originating in uncertain sources of the "European Culture and Civilisation" with regard to the Islamic world, has been conceived by the Europeans as a Muslim threat to themselves.[8] Against this so-called threat they decided to form a European Union like the "Holy League"[9] against the Turks on the 7th October 1571 at Lepanto, and finally, Europeans united against the Turks when they stood at the gates of Vienna in 1683. One can hardly find another example of uniting the Europeans in history; the West could unite only against a common enemy, for instance, the Nazis of Hitler in the Second World War or Saddam Hussein in the Gulf War. In modern times the Europeans have formed another union (EC), which is nevertheless, first and foremost an economic union, since the cultural influence and impact of the EC is still debatable. I do not want to discuss here the reasons why Turkey as a

---

8 According to a "certain" source, in the 8th century Alvaro, the famous bishop of Cordova (Spain), despaired of the future of Christian youth as they were able to speak Arabic better than Latin: "My fellow-Christians delight in the poems and romances of the Arabs; they study the works of Mohemmedan theologians and philosophers, not in order to refute them, but to acquire a correct and elegant Arabic style. Where today can a layman be found who reads the Latin Commentaries on Holy Scriptures? Who is there that studies the Gospels, the Prophets, the Apostles? Alas! The young Christians who are most conspicuous for their talents have no knowledge of any literature or language save the Arabic; they read and study with avidity Arabian books; they amass whole libraries of them at a vast cost, and they everywhere sing the praises of Arabian lore. ... The pity of it! Christians have forgotten their own tongue, and scarce one in a thousand can be found able to compose in fair Latin a letter to a friend! But when it comes to writing Arabic, how many there are who can express themselves in that language with the greatest elegance, and even compose verses which surpass in formal correctness those of the Arabs themselves!" Alvari Cordubensis Indiculus Luminosus in Migne, *Patrologia Latina* 121, cols. 555-56. Quotation in English from R. Dozy, *Spanish Islam in* London, 1972, p. 268.

9 When Sultan Selim II (1566-74) demanded the surrender of Cyprus in 1570, the Venetian senate appealed to Pope Pius V. "The Pope succeeded in organizing resistance to the Moslems and assembled a fleet to meet at Messina in 1571 under the command of Don Juan of Austria, half-brother of Philip II of Spain. Spain would pay one-half, Venice one-third, and the Pope one-sixth of the total expense of the operation. Of a total 206 galleys, Venice furnished 108, Naples 29, Genoa 14, Spain 13, the Pope 12, and Malta 3." Heffernan 1981; p. 665.

Muslim country has and must have been excluded from this entity.[10]

Today several political scientists and researchers from other social sciences argue that after the demolition of Communism and the end of the so-called Cold War, the West has found a new enemy - Islam. This does not mean that the West ceased to perceive the Turks and Muslims as enemies after the Crusades or after the First World War, which was a turning point in the history of Muslim peoples as they had radically undergone a process of being colonised, but Muslims and Turks were seen against the background of Communism and they remained potential enemies. Furthermore, I personally believe that the Cold War between the two blocks has not come to an end yet. Erstwhile the USSR was a threat to the West, but today it has become especially an economic burden. The West should be very careful in dealing with Russia today; it is not supposed to help Russia to the extent of enabling it to become a new superpower by strengthening its economy, but at the same time it cannot allow Russia to starve, as it may then resort to an attack on its neighbours.

In any case Communism, as its main state has lost its influence, is no longer the "archenemy" of the West. So, the need for an "other" has emerged. That "other" is Islam, and the Turks because of their long history of conflicts with Europe were adapted easily into this new image. This new enemy is no other than an old nemesis (memory) resurrected. After Communism was run out of town, a number of Turkic republics appeared on the scene. The Soviet threat gave way to that of a new bloc, that is, the Turks. Let me explain this new phenomenon. The possibility of a united Turkish - or Turkic - existence in the world and the possibility of setting up a Turkish Commonwealth and of Turkey's becoming the leader of Turkish republics and the Muslim world is something the West utterly abhors. An economically strong Turkey supported by other republics and the Muslim countries in general would bring about a new kind of Ottoman Empire. Yet, in my opinion, Turkey has lost this historic chance since it failed to unite and integrate the ex-re-

[10] At the beginning of 1998 the European Economic Council excluded Turkey from other candidate countries which were invited for negotiations to become full members.

publics of the Soviet Union and could not play an important role in the Bosnian crisis. Therefore, the West should not fear a second siege of Vienna, at least not in the near future.

Apart from these historical facts, I wish to touch now upon the current situation in terms of Turco-European relations. After the First World War and the establishment of the Turkish Republic at the beginning of this century, the relations between both entities seem to have been slowed down for several decades. However, the Second World War destroyed many European countries, and as they lacked manpower, they began to accept foreign workers. In the 1960s there was a vast immigration from Turkey to certain European countries. The Federal Republic of Germany was the main European country to receive Turkish immigrant workers, besides France, the Netherlands, Belgium and Austria. This was the beginning of a new era in terms of Turco-European relations. Many Turks preferred Germany, despite the fact that it had a rather different immigration policy from other European countries (see Mandel 1990). Another, perhaps the most important, reason for the Turkish workers' preference of Germany was that it had no record of aggression or hostility against Islam and the Turks, did not have a colonialist relationship with any Arab or Muslim country, and most importantly, it was the enemy of Islam's enemies. In short, it was an ally of Turkey, as in the First World War. Even today the Turkish public has a good opinion of Germany despite all the bad treatment Turkish guest workers have received in that country. During the first years of this immigration things seemed to be going well, but later on, when Turkish families began to settle down, especially in Germany, and their children's preference of Germany to Turkey was established, problems arose. Specifically after the re-unification of East and West Germany the Turks in this country became a target (of some groups like Neo-Nazis or skinheads) since they were seen the basic cause of unemployment. The Germans began to argue that the Turkish culture was incompatible with theirs; for them the most distinguishing characteristics of the Turkish migrant community as "other" is their religion, that is, Islam.

The structural marginality, denigration and stigma attached to Turkishness in Europe have made the Turks resort to forming a kind of exclusive community, usually a religious one, where one feels respected and not discriminated against. I suggest that this is the reason why ethnic minorities tend to cluster around a religious community. The increasing religiosity of the Turks in Europe has become another burden for them since some Europeans cannot bear to see a head scarfed Turkish girl or woman on the street. This kind of behaviour is perceived by Europeans as a protest to Western values, and many Europeans have become involved in a hot debate over whether the head scarf is bad, ugly, etc. It is quite significant that a Turkish researcher, Yalçın-Heckmann seems to share this view. She quotes a German person who sees the rejection of wearing a head scarf as a manifestation of integration: "these Turkish women were well integrated, they did not even have head scarves" (Yalçın-Heckmann, 1994; 189). Yet, what they seem to forget is that European tourists are welcome in Turkey and that their values are respected. When the European tourists are in Turkey they do not do as the Turks do. A Westerner is welcomed in Turkey with her bikini or she even might feel free to the extent of sunbathing topless, but no Turk interferes with her clothes, or rather with her being without any clothes at all, although this is shocking to a Turk's eyes in terms of ethics and family values. These sorts of incidents support the traditional view of the Westerners by the Turks, who were led to believe that the Westerners are quite permissive or even promiscuous, and some Turks are afraid this permissiveness will creep into the Turkish culture and way of life. If national identities are defined according to the differences between oneself and others it becomes quite understandable that, if one cares to guard his or her own identity, one should keep it intact. This sort of fear could also be encountered today among the peoples of the EEC, especially after the Council's attempt to unite the European country. The local people are almost sure that this unification will be the cause of losing local cultures. If and when the Europeans are afraid of losing their local cultures themselves, then the Turks should be tolerated against this threat of losing their cultural unity as the European culture is much more different to Turks than their cultures among themselves.

The Turkish culture is not incompatible with the European

one.[11] This is illustrated well by the identification of Turkish immigrants in Europe as Alamancı (German-ish, German-like). This redefinition shows that these Turks have been Europeanised; immigrant Turks are called "new Turks" in Turkey and they are caught in between, neither Turk nor European. They try to do *uyum* (adoption) but are not appreciated; for example, on 29 May 1993 five Turkish people (women and children) were murdered through arson. Had this event happened to a citizen of any other European country, there would be an international upheaval. As a good example of *uyum* Lale Yalçın-Heckmann argues that Turks willy-nilly have adopted German New Year's Day fireworks even if they are considered to be un-Islamic.

As I mentioned earlier in this paper people in Turkey were, and still are, led to believe that they are European. A very simple and casual observation of Turkish TV broadcasting would give us some clues on this subject: First of all, almost all of the films, documentaries, and series, which are shown on TV, are originally produced in the West; this means the country is exposed to the Western style of life. From time to time it is heard that the folk people of Anatolia would give their children the names of the TV series' heroes, like Melissa, Esther and Samantha. Second, there is a weather report af-

---

[11] Mark Sykes, the spokesman of the British Empire at the turn of the century observed during his visit to the Ottoman Empire in 1902/3 that the Turks would make good Europeans. He, playing the role of an anthropologist, argued that "in speech the Turks are expressionless, quiet and laconic [compare the account of Pierre Belon given at the beginning of the article], using few gestures or similes [sic.]; but with Arabs it is almost possible to follow an argument while not comprehending a word of the language. I have heard a person, who could speak with authority, state there could never be an amalgamation between Turks and Arabs, and I think there is no doubt this is true. A Turk will understand an Englishman's character much sooner than he will an Arab's; the latter is so subtle in his reasoning, so quick-witted, so argumentative and so great a master of language that he leaves the stolid Osmanli amazed and dazed, comprehending nothing. The Turk is not, truth to tell, very brilliant as a rule, though very apt in assuming Western cultivation. This may sound extraordinary but is nevertheless true so far as my experience carries me. Every Turk I have met who has dwelt for a considerable period in any European country, although never losing his patriotism and deep love for his land, has become in manners, thoughts and habits an Englishman, a German or Frenchman. This leads one almost to suppose that Turks might be Europeanised by an educational process without any prejudicial result, for at present they have every quality of a ruling race except initiative, which is an essentially European quality". Mark Sykes, *Dar-Ul-Islam: A record of a journey through ten of the Asiatic provinces of Turkey*, quoted in Glass 1990, p. 78.

ter each news bulletin on TV channels. On these weather reports, the main Turkish cities' forecasts are given first, and immediately after that the viewer is informed about some major European cities' weather conditions. Of course these reports use a map and Turkey is always shown just next to Europe; the continent takes its place in the centre of the screen. Yet, when I was in a European city, I often watched the TV news bulletins of various European countries, and on these reports they would show a map of Europe just cut at the eastern frontiers of Greece. One could not see Turkey on these maps; it was as if Turkey did not exist at all. The European continent would be shown like an island cut off from the rest of the world. Another casual observation of the ordinary Turkish public reveals the failure of the attempt of the official ideology that Turkey belonged to Europe. People would make such statements in their ordinary daily lives: "Next week I am going to Europe" (they never say simply 'I am going to Berlin, Bern or Bonn') or "I bought these clothes in Europe". This everyday talk gives us some clues that the public still does not feel European or that their country is in Europe; one would not go to Europe if one were living in Europe.

As has been discussed throughout this paper the mutual misunderstanding of Westerners and Turks resides in the lack of efforts to understand each other; in other words, both sides are and have been trying to make the opposite party "other". If and only if the sides give up creating an "other" and accept each other as simple human beings who have different cultures, religions, and worldviews from oneself, then the opportunity of creating a context in which a process of a possible dialogue would begin. In order to create such an ambience we must first put aside the age-old prejudices towards each other. In this respect, the Christian clergy should give up treating Islam as if it is trying to sweep Christianity away from the world; the best example of such an attitude shows itself in a recently edited issue of the journal *Concilium* by the leading theologians Hans Küng and Jürgen Moltmann: *Islam: A challenge for Christianity*. When one looks at history one would realise that for various historical circumstances (here I have in mind the history of the Ottoman Empire and its warfare relations with the West) the West has had more reasons to hold prejudices against the Turks which resulted from a fear of the Ottoman Empire. Therefore, what remains for the West to do is to overcome such a fear because the "Grand Turc" no longer poses a threat to their dearly loved values. As Hïchem Djaït has pointed out: "The old conflicts between Islam and the West are now especially outdated because a unified Islam has ceased to exist, while the West is perceived and by this time perceives itself as a heterogeneous composite, and today's modernity has a different meaning from yesterday's" (1985; 168).

I would like to conclude, then, with a statement from a Martiniquean psychiatrist who had become an Algerian militant through the Algerian Revolution of 1954-1962, Frantz Fanon. He says that "for Europe, for ourselves and for humanity, we must turn over a new leaf, we must work out new concepts, and try to set afoot a new man" (quoted in Gendzier 1973; 270).

In sum, as I have tried to show throughout the paper, the non-existence of a dialogue between the West and the Islamic world is the result of the West's falsely created image of the others. As long as the West does not come to terms with the reality, which is quite different from their current perceptions, and stop acting hypocritically, any attempts to establish a possible dialogue between the two blocs seem to be in vain. As an anthropologist who has studied a part of Western religious folk culture I realise that there are differences and similarities among the world cultures. I have found out that if one tries to emphasise the differences he or she will definitely succeed in this attempt, but that it is more important to reveal the similarities. If and when such studies begin to appear, everyone will realise how similar the foundations on which their cultural backgrounds had been built really are.

As was pointed out by Hugh Goddard, who has produced a well-researched work among the writings of Muslims, that a sort of positive improvement in the dialogue between these two world views is recorded, especially when Muslim authors write about Christianity, and that they tend to treat that religion with more positive terms if they "have individual Christian friends and some of them at least have been involved in formal dialogue between Christians and Muslims. This has clearly had a significant impact on both their knowledge of and their attitude towards Christianity" (Goddard 1996; 173-174). Therefore, it is the task of intellectuals of both sides to improve their relationships with each other through organising formal dialogues like symposia, panels, discussion groups, or teaching other religions in their respective schools.

References Cited

Aydın, Kamil: Western images of the Muslim Turks prior to the 20th century, *Hamdard Islamicus*, XVI (4/1993), pp. 103-125.

Bisbee, Eleanor: *The New Turks*, University of Pennsylvania Press, Philadelphia 1951.

Belon du Mans, Pierre: *Les Observations de plusieurs singularitez & choses mémorables, trouvées en Grèce, Asie, Iudée, Egypte, Arabie, & autres pays étranges, redigées en trois liures, par Pierre Belon du Mans*, Cairo: L' Institut Français d' Archéologie Orientale du Caire, Caire <1555> 1970.

Camões, Luís de: *Os Lusíadas*, Instituto de Alta Cultura, Lisboa, 1972.

Djaït, Hichem: *Europe and Islam*, University of California Press, London 1985.

Dozy, R.: *Spanish Islam*, Frank Cass, London <1913> 1972.

Flannery, Austin (ed.): *Vatican Council II*, The Liturgical Press, Collegeville <1975> 1992.

Gendzier, I. L.: *Frantz Fanon*, Pantheon Books, New York, 1973.

Glass, Charles: *Tribes with flags*, Picador, London <1990> 1992.

Goddard, Hugh: *Muslim perceptions of Christianity*, Grey Seal Books, London 1996.

Heffernan, J. B.: "Lepanto, Battle of", *New Catholic Encyclopedia*,

VIII, <1967> 1981, pp. 665-666.

Hourani, Albert: "Islam in European thought", in *The Tanner Lectures on human values XI*, G.B. Peterson (ed.), University of Utah Press, Salt Lake City 1990, pp. 223-287.

Kabbani, Rana: *Europe's myths of the Orient*, Macmillan, London 1986.

Küng, H. & Moltmann, J. (eds.): 1994. *Islam: A challenge for Christianity*, the issue of *concilium*, 1994/3 SCM Press, London 1994.

Mandel, Ruth: Shifting centres and emergent identities: Turkey and Germany in the lives of Turkish Gastarbeiter in *Muslim travellers: pilgrimage, migration, and the religious imagination*, D. F. Eickelman. & J. Piscatori (eds.): Routledge, London 1990, pp. 153-171.

Metlitzki, Dorothee: *The matter of Araby in medieval England*, Yale University Press, London 1972.

Said, Edward: *Orientalism*, Penguin Books, Harmondsworh <1978> 1985.

Yalçın-Heckmann, L.: "Are fireworks Islamic? Towards an understanding of Turkish migrants and Islam in Germany", in *Syncretism/antisyncretism*, *C.* Stewart, C. & R. Shaw (eds.), Routledge, London, 1994, pp. 178-195.

Ein Behörde im Spannungsfeld von Religion und Staat

DAS PRÄSIDIUM FÜR RELIGIÖSE ANGELEGENHEITEN

İsmail Kara
Marmara Üniversitesi

Von den Osmanen zur Republik *

Sei es im Hinblick darauf, daß die Osmanen die Diskussion begannen, sei es, daß sie bereits erste Reformschritte unternahmen; die *Reformen* (inkılâp) der Republik Türkei haben ihre Wurzeln in den heute circa hundert Jahre zurückliegenden Verwestlichungsbemühungen des Osmanischen Staates. Das gilt für die politischen und bürokratischen Neuordnungen genauso wie für die juristischen und soziokulturellen, und das gilt auch für das Verhältnis von Staat und Religion. "Viel mehr als ein Traum"[2], unter diesem Titel veröffentlichte 1912 Kılıçzâde Hakkı Bey[3] in der Zeitschrift İctihad einen wegweisenden Artikel[4]. Der Autor schrieb unter dem Pseudonym *Zeichen der Hoffnung* (Timsâl-i Emel), und die 18 Punkte, die er auflistete, lesen sich wie eine Vorschau auf die Reformen der Republik. Ein Auszug:

"... 4. Die Frauen kleiden sich, wie es ihnen beliebt und achten nur darauf, nicht verschwenderisch zu sein. (...) Der Şeyh ul-İslâm hat ebensowenig wie die anderen Autoritäten das Recht, eine Kleiderordnung vorzuschreiben. (...)

6. Die Derwischkonvente und ihre Niederlassungen (tekâya ve

[1] * Deutsch von Günter Seufert, Anmerkungen in [] vom Übersetzer.

[2] [Das Original der notwendigerweise freien Übersetzung: Pek uyanık bir uyku.]

[3] Nach dem Gesetz zur Einführung der Familiennamen als Hakkı Kılıçoğlu in der dritten und vierten Legislationsperiode, von 1872 bis 1959, Parlamentsabgeordneter.

[4] Der Artikel wurde im darauffolgenden Jahre ein zweites Mal abgedruckt, siehe *İctihad*, No. 51, vom 21. Februar 1328, S. 1226-1328 und *İctihad*, No. 57, vom 7. Februar 1329, S. 42-62. Unter dem Titel *Traum* fand eine überarbeitete Version Eingang in das Buch des Autors *İtikadât-ı bâtılaya ilan-ı harb*, Istanbul 1329, S. 42-62; vgl. auch die Edition des Artikels in Dücane Cündioğlu, *Bir siyasî proje olarak Türkçe ibadet*, İstanbul Kitabevi, Istanbul 1999, S. 161-172.

zevâya), die heute nur noch Orte von Trägheit und Müßiggang sind, werden allesamt geschlossen. (...)

7. Alle bestehenden Medresen werden geschlossen. Anstelle der Süleymaniye Medrese wird eine 'Geisteswissenschaftliche Hochschule' (Ulûm-i Edebiye Medresesi) nach dem Vorbild des Collège de France eröffnet und die Fatih Medrese wird von einer Sultanats-Hochschule nach dem Muster der Ecole Polytechnique abgelöst. (...)

8. Grabstättenverehrung wird untersagt, und die an diese Stätten gehenden Spenden fließen der Flotte und den *Gesellschaften zur nationalen Verteidigung* (müdafaayı milliye cemiyetleri) zu.

12. Wie andere Ministerien und Dienststellen wird auch das Şeyh ul-İslâm-Amt (Daire-i Muallâ-yı Meşihat) aufgelöst und die dort tätigen Beamten entlassen (...) die Freitagspredigten erhalten eine zeitgemäße inhaltliche Ausrichtung und werden auf Türkisch vorgetragen."
Tatsächlich baut die frühe Republik in vieler Hinsicht auf den Verwestlichungsbestrebungen des Osmanischen Staates auf. Doch diese richtige Verallgemeinerung darf nicht den Blick dafür verstellen, daß insbesondere ab 1923 zu radikalen Maßnahmen gegriffen wurde, die sich nicht einfach als Fortschreibung der osmanischen Modernisierung fassen lassen, die jedoch gleichwohl für viele der heutigen Probleme verantwortlich sind.

Die Unterschiede zwischen der osmanischen Verwestlichung und den republikanischen Reformen liegen im Folgenden: In den ersten Phasen der osmanischen Verwestlichungspolitik spielte das Bestreben, zu einer neuen Interpretation der Religion zu gelangen, religiöses Verständnis und religiöse Praxis umzuwälzen, nur eine sekundäre Rolle. Die Änderung der herrschenden Religionsauffassung und die Entwicklung eines modernen Islam-Verständnisses waren kein Ziel an sich. Sie wurden eher als eine Bedingung dafür angesehen, die zu Beginn in der Gesellschaft nur als 'notwendiges Übel' akzeptierten Modernisierungsschritte durchzusetzen. Beispiele sind der Transfer und die Akzeptanz moderner Technologie und die damit verbundene räumliche und soziale Mobilisation. Die anschließenden Phasen der osmanischen Verwestlichungspolitik waren durch drei Prozesse gekennzeichnet: durch die Übernahme europäischer Institutionen, wie Parlament, Verfassung und Konstitutionalismus; durch die allmähliche Aneignung von grundlegenden philosophischen und politischen Begriffen wie Freiheit, Gleichheit (müsavat), Sozialvertrag (mukavele-i ictimaiye), Fortschritt (terakki) und die Reinterpretation von Begriffen wie *millet* und *vatan* im Sinne des europäischen Nationen- und Nationalstaats-Verständnisses; sowie durch die schrittweise Legitimierung und Anerkennung neuer Verhaltensmuster wie etwa die positive Bewertung von individueller und gesellschaftlicher Veränderung.

Wesentlich ist, daß die Träger der osmanischen Verwestlichungsbemühungen stets darauf achteten, jeden Schritt -- direkt oder indirekt -- im Rahmen eines religiösen Weltbildes nachvollziehbar und verständlich zu machen, vollkommen unabhängig davon, ob ein solches Vorgehen der Logik des von ihnen beförderten Vorgangs entsprach. Folge war, daß der Abgrund, welcher sich zwischen dem modernen/modernisierten und dem traditionell religiös symbolisierten gesellschaftlichen Bereich aufzutun drohte, überdeckt und nicht als gefährlich wahrgenommen wurde. Es war durchaus beabsichtigt, daß die Modernisierung in gewisser Weise eine Neubelebung religiösen Denkens und Erlebens mit sich brachte. Damals entstand eine 'neue Islam-Interpretation', die bisweilen als *Islamische Moderne* bisweilen als *Islamismus* bezeichnet wird und die ausnahmslos alle intellektuellen und politischen Strömungen in den muslimischen Ländern -- vom Nationalismus bis zum Sozialismus -- befruchtet aber auch inhaltlich begrenzt hat.[5] Inwieweit die damals entwickelten Perspektiven und Ansätze noch *islamische* und *religiöse* sind, ist eine ganz und gar offene und diskussionswürdige Frage; allein, sie war damals von untergeordneter Bedeutung; ging es doch darum, den Bestand eines Staates zu sichern, mit dessen Überleben das Überleben des Islams gleichgesetzt wurde und der deshalb seine Struktur zwangsweise ändern mußte. Aus diesem Grunde erschien es viel passender, die neuen Lösungsansätze in religiöser Verpackung zu präsentieren, als an einem 'Eigentlichen' festzuhalten.

Von dieser Leitlinie, Modernisierung und Neubelebung der Religion grundsätzlich zusammen und im Einklang miteinander zu verfolgen, hat sich die Republik nach 1923 verabschiedet. Wohl hat auch die Republik eine religiöse Neubelebung betrieben -- weiter unten

[5] Vgl. zur ersten Welle des Islamismus im Osmanischen Staate: İsmail Kara (Hrsg.), *Türkiye'de İslâmcılık düşüncesi,* Band I und II, Risale Yay., 2. Auflage, Istanbul 1987 und 1989; vgl. zur Vorreiterrolle der osmanischen Diskussion für die Islamische Welt: Mümtaz'er Türköne, *İslâmcılığın doğuşu*, İletişim Yay., Istanbul 1991.

wird darauf näher eingegangen werden -- doch vertrug sich die republikanische Politik einer religiösen Neubelebung nur schlecht mit der historischen Ausgangslage der Türkei. Diese Neubelebung wurde nie zur politischen Leitlinie, und sie wurde aus diesen Gründen auch nicht durchgehalten. Die Religionspolitik der Republik beschränkt sich darauf, die Religion als Legitimation für ihre politischen Ziele und als Mittel zur Beeinflussung der Bevölkerung zu nutzen.

Die Gründe für diesen Bruch der Republik mit der osmanischen Form der Verwestlichung und die Bedingungen dafür, sind offensichtlich nicht nur innenpolitischer Natur. Innenpolitische Gründe allein können nur schwerlich erklären, warum sich die politische Klasse in Ankara im kurzen Zeitraum von nur drei bis vier Jahren einem so radikalem Wandel unterwarf, der die politischen Institutionen der Republik genauso betraf wie ihre Gründungskader und der eine vollkommene Kehrtwendung im politischen Diskurs, im politischen Handeln und in den öffentlichen Stellungnahmen erforderte. Die Erklärung, die ausschlaggebenden Akteure hätten nur günstige Umstände zur Verwirklichung eines von vorneherein gefaßten Reformplans abgewartet,[6] erscheint zumindest unvollständig, wenn nicht naiv.

Intellektuelle Umbrüche und politische Instabilität zwangen das Regime, seine lange ungeklärte Legitimation, welche in der Rivalität zwischen Ankara und Istanbul ihren Ausdruck fand[7], zu Entscheidungen, die weder durchdacht noch ausreichend diskutiert worden waren, die jedoch seine Stellung im Ausland stärkten. Diese Entscheidungen erwiesen sich im weiteren Verlauf freilich als untauglich für die Etablierung von Werten und Normen, welche von den unterschiedlichen gesellschaftlichen Gruppen hätten geteilt werden können. Bei den betreffenden Entscheidungen handelt sich um die Trennung des Sultanats vom Kalifat und die Reduzierung des letzteren auf ein Amt ohne tatsächliche Kompetenz; um die Auflösung der Ersten Nationalversammlung, die in der Tradition der Osmanischen Konstitution stand, den *Befreiungskrieg* (Millî Mücadele) geführt hatte, viele demokratische Elemente enthielt und aus diesen Gründen hohes Ansehen genoß; sowie um die Aufnahme von Artikeln in den Vertrag von Lausanne,

[6] Erklärungen in dieser Richtung finden sich in M. K. Atatürk; *Nutuk 1919-1927: CHP'nin 15-20 Ekim 1927 tarihleri arasında toplanan 2. Büyük Kongresi'nde söylenmiştir*, Atatürk Araştırma Merkezi, Ankara 1997.

[7] Man darf nicht vergessen, daß die ausländischen Botschaften erst in der Dreißigern nach Ankara umzogen.

welchen von der Ersten Nationalversammlung niemals ratifiziert worden wären. All das erscheint als das Ergebnis übermäßiger Eile, die ein Abwägen von Vor- und Nachteilen unmöglich machte.

Der große Skeptiker Kazım Karabekir, der erst in der Opposition zum Konservativen wurde, schreibt in seinen Memoiren, das Motto "der Islam behindert den Fortschritt" sei von heute auf morgen in Ankara aufgetaucht. Er ist sich sicher, daß es sich um eine Empfehlung aus Lausanne handele und trägt dies İsmet İnönü mit der Begründung vor, Atatürk habe sich in seinen Ansprachen noch gestern hinter den Koran, den Propheten und das Kalifat gestellt.

Karabekir bezieht sich auf die *Freitagspredigt* (hutbe), die Mustafa Kemal am 7. Februar 1923 in der Paşa Camii im nordwest-anatolischen Balıkesir gehalten hatte. Nach dem Mittagsgebet und nach einem weiteren Gebet für die Gefallenen hatte Atatürk die Kanzel bestiegen, und seine Ansprache mit folgenden Worten begonnen:

"Landsleute! Es gibt nur einen Gott, Allah, der Ruhmreiche! (...) Unser verehrter Prophet ist von Gott berufen und beauftragt worden, den Menschen die *Wahrheiten der Religion* (hakayık-i diniye) zu lehren. Ihr wißt alle, daß unsere *Verfassung* (Kanun-ı Esasi) mit den Vorschriften des Korans übereinstimmt. Unsere Religion hat den Menschen eine fortschrittliche Geisteshaltung beschert und ist die einzige immergültige und vollkommene Religion. Denn unsere Religion entspricht der Vernunft und befindet sich in völliger Übereinstimmung mit der Realität."[8]

Die Antwort İnönüs ist ganz von der Art, die Zweifel Karabekirs zu bestärken, der in seinen Memoiren schreibt:

"(...) İnönü erklärte mir daraufhin, daß die Ungarn und Bulgaren, die an unserer Seite gegen die Entente gekämpft und verloren hatten, ihre Unabhängigkeit der Tatsache verdankten, daß sie Christen sind, und daß man uns die Unabhängigkeit nicht zugestanden hätte, weil wir Muslime sind. Obwohl wir nach jahrelangen Kämpfen jetzt die Unabhängigkeit gewonnen haben, würden die Kolonialstaaten und insbesondere die Engländer, solange wir am Islam festhalten, immer gegen uns Stellung beziehen und unsere Unabhängigkeit bedrohen. (...) Ich [Karabekir] erwiderte darauf, daß ich diese Sicht der Dinge

[8] Der Text dieser berühmten *Balıkesir-Predigt* und Belegstellen in: Dücane Cündioğlu, *Türkçe Kur'an ve Cumhuriyet ideolojisi*, İstanbul Kitabevi, Istanbul 1998, S. 185-187.

aus folgenden Gründen nicht teile: 'Nach diesen Überlegungen zu handeln, das hieße, die Nation einem noch stärker unterdrückerischen und noch mehr Unheil bringendem Regime zu überantworten. (...)'

(İsmet İnönü): 'Solange wir die Ulema nicht entmachten, sind uns die Hände gebunden'."[9]

Tatsächlich stehen fast alle Reformen der Republik in Bezug zur Religion. Noch die Verfassung von 1982 führt in Artikel 174 diejenigen *Revolutionsgesetze* (inkılâp kanunları) auf, die den Laizismus bewahren und "die türkische Gesellschaft auf das moderne Zivilisationsniveau heben"[10] sollen:

das Gesetz zur Vereinheitlichung des Unterrichtswesens;[11]

die Verpflichtung zum Tragen eines Krempenhutes;[12]

die Schließung der Ordenskonvente;[13]

der § 110 des Türkischen Zivilgesetzbuches, der die Zivilehe und die Trauung vor dem Standesbeamten vorschreibt;[14]

die Einführung der internationalen Ziffern;[15]

die verpflichtende Einführung der türkischen Buchstaben;[16]

das Verbot bestimmter Ehrentiteln und Anredeformen;[17]

das Verbot bestimmter Kleidungsformen,[18]

In dieser Liste nicht enthalten, aber den religiösen Bereich betreffende Regelungen und Verbote sind die Schließung der Scheriat-Ge-

---

[9] *Kazım Karabekir anlatıyor*, Uğur Mumcu (Hrsg.), Tekin Yay. Istanbul 1990, S. 95-97.

[10] *T.C. Anayasası*, Der Yay. Istanbul 1995, S. 145-146.

[11] [1924, Schließung der Medresen, mittelfristig Einstellung aller religiösen Erziehung].

[12] [1925, Verbot des Fez, der seinerseits 1828 verpflichtend geworden war und Einführung des europäischen Krempenhutes]

[13] [1925, bedeutete zusammen mit dem Verbot religiöser Kleidung ein Unter-Strafe-Stellen aller Ordensaktivitäten]

[14] [1926]. Der genannte Paragraph lautet: "Falls die (vom Standesbeamten ausgestellte) Heiratsurkunde nicht vorliegt, darf keine religiöse Trauung stattfinden. Für die Gültigkeit der Trauung bedarf es keiner religiösen Zeremonie." Der § 237 des StGB sieht Gefängnisstrafe für denjenigen vor, "der ohne Vorlage einer standesamtlichen Trauungsurkunde die religiöse Trauung vollzieht."

[15] [1928, d.h. die Einführung der lateinischen Schreibweise der arabischen Ziffern]

[16] [1929, d.h. die Einführung der Lateinschrift mit einigen türkischen Sonderzeichen]

[17] [1934] § 1 des Gesetzes nennt folgende Titel: Ağa (Großgrundbesitzer), hacı (Pilger), hafız (Koranvortragender), hoca (Lehrer), molla (Geistlicher), efendi (Herr), bey (Herr), beyefendi (hoher Herr), paşa (General), hanım (Dame), hanımefendi (geehrte Dame), hazretleri (Eure Heiligkeit). [Außer dem letzten Titel sind alle theoretisch verbotenen Anreden noch heute Elemente der Umgangssprache.]

[18] [1934, in der Praxis richtete sich das Verbot gegen alle Kleidungsstücke und Accessoires, die auf die (islamische) Religion des Trägers schließen lassen.

richte, die Verlegung des wöchentlichen Ruhetags von Freitag auf Sonntag, die Übernahme des christlichen Kalenders und der europäischen Uhrzeit.

Die Redefinition des Religiösen

Am 3. März 1924 verabschiedete das Parlament nach nur kurzer und hastiger Beratung drei Gesetze, die das zukünftige Verhältnis von Staat und Religion bestimmen sollten.

Das erste dieser Gesetze brachte die Aufhebung des Kalifats. Es bedeutete das Ende für eine Institution, die bereits in der konstitutionellen Periode viel von ihrem Einfluß verloren hatte[19], durch die Trennung des Kalifats vom Sultanat zu einer rein geistlichen Autorität herabgesunken war und sich darüberhinaus ihrer Abhängigkeit von der neuen Hauptstadt Ankara voll bewußt war. Das Gesetz bedeutete darüberhinaus, die vollständige Absage des Staates an seine religiöse Identität[20] und -- vielleicht noch wichtiger als dies -- die Entfernung des zentralen Scharniers, das die neue Türkei mit der Islamischen Welt verband. Die Republik Türkei hat es seit dieser Zeit weder vermocht noch versucht, tragfähige Beziehungen mit der Islamischen Welt aufzubauen, deren Teil sie -- ob sie will oder nicht -- in geopolitischer, geokultureller und strategischer Hinsicht nun einmal ist und auf deren Unterstützung sie im Grunde nicht verzichten kann. Die Türkei hat die Islamische Welt verloren, ohne daß sich ihr eine neue Welt aufgetan hätte, zu der sie gehören könnte.

Das zweite der Gesetze, die das Religiöse neu bestimmen sollten, war das *Gesetz zur Vereinheitlichung des Bildungswesens* (Tevhid-i

[19] Vgl. zur Lage des Kalifats in der konstitutionellen Periode: İsmail Kara, *İslâmcılar'ın siyasî görüşleri*, İz Yay. Istanbul 1994, S. 156-164.

[20] 1924 lautet Artikel 2 der Verfassung (Teşkilat-ı Esasiye Kanunu): "Die Religion des türkischen Staates ist der Islam", und in den Beratungen der Zweiten Nationalversammlung am 16. März 1924 war dieser Artikel einer der wenigen, die ohne Aussprache angenommen wurden. Vgl. A. Ş. Gözübüyük & Z. Segin, *1924 anayasası hakkındaki meclis görüşmeleri*, SBF İdarî Bilimler Enstitüsü Yay. Ankara 1957, S. 100-101. Der betreffende Artikel wurde 1928 gestrichen doch erst 1937 wurde das Laizismus-Prinzip in der Verfassung verankert. 1924 dagegen erklärte die Verfassung in ihrem Artikel 26 das Parlament für "die Durchsetzung der Bestimmungen der Scheriat" verantwortlich". Änderungen der Verfassung vom 9. April 1929 ersetzen die Formel "Bei Gott" (vallahi), die bei der Vereidigung der Abgeordneten und des Staatspräsidenten gesprochen wurde, durch "bei meiner Ehre" (namusum üzerine söz veriyorum).

tedrisat kanunu). Es unterstellte die Medresen dem *Bildungsministerium* (Maarif Vekâleti), welches sie trotz zahlreicher Proteste umgehend schloß.

Dabei hatte sich Mustafa Kemal noch im März 1923 auf einer Reise nach Konya in der dortigen Kalifats-Medrese in einer Weise anerkennend über die Arbeit in den Medresen geäußert, die stark an seine Predigt in Balıkesir erinnert:

"Ich sehe mit großer Zufriedenheit, daß Unterricht und Studium ganz im Sinne der Religion vor sich gehen. Inschallah werden aus euch, den Studenten, moderne Ulema und tugendhafte Professoren hervorgehen, die unserem Land und unserer *Nation* (millet) neue Kraft geben und sie wiederbeleben. Richtigen und aufrechten Ulema gebührt hohes Ansehen. Die Bemühungen unserer Ulema und die Belehrungen unserer Gebildeten werden, inschallah, dazu führen, daß aus unserer Nation Ibn Ruschds, Ibn Sinas, Al-Farabis und Imam Gazalis hervorgehen, die -- ausgestattet mit dem Wissen um die Errungenschaften unseres Jahrhunderts -- eine *Erneuerung der Religion* (ihya-yı hakikat-ı diniye) bewirken. Ich gratuliere Aksekili Ahmed Hamdi Efendi (der damalige Erziehungsdirektor des Scheriat- und Stiftungsministeriums) und bedanke mich bei ihm. Was ich gesehen habe, läßt mich für die Zukunft unseres Landes hoffen."[21]

Tatsächlich hatten sich die Medresen seit 1914 in großem Maße gewandelt und es vermocht, sich den modernen, weltlichen *Schulen* (mekteb) in vieler Hinsicht anzupassen. Doch obwohl § 4 des genannten Gesetzes die Eröffnung von Berufs- und Hochschulen zur Ausbildung von Theologen (din mütehassısı) vorsah, wurde der Unterricht generell von religiösen Inhalten gesäubert und legte den Schülern ein ganz und gar säkulares Weltbild nahe. Der schulische Religionsunterricht selbst wurde schrittweise abgebaut und 1933 eingestellt. Die ausserschulische religiöse Bildung (z.B. die freien Koran-Kurse) kam so-

[21] Zitiert nach der Zeitschrift *Hakimiyet-i Milliye*, No. 771 vom 23. März 1339. Auf der gleichen Reise benutzt Atatürk die Formel von den Ibn Ruschds, Ibn Sinas, Al-Farabis und Imam Gazalis ein zweites Mal, jetzt in der Konya Sultanisi [Medrese]. *Atatürk'ün söylev ve demeçleri*, Band II, 4. Auflage, TTK Yay., Ankara 1989, S. 159.

fort zum Erliegen.[22] Dem Gesetz folgend wurden auch die Medaris-i İlmiye geschlossen, Schulen, die, 465 an der Zahl, bereits während der Republik "per Entscheidung der Ersten Nationalversammlung mit dem Ziel eröffnet worden waren, für den Dienst in Dörfern und Provinzstädten Vorbeter und Prediger heranzuziehen".[23] Die hinter diesem Vorgehen stehende Logik wurde 1947 auf dem Parteitag der Republikanischen Volkspartei[24] von Yusuf Ziya Kösemen, Delegierter der Provinz Kocaeli, mit folgenden Worten zum Ausdruck gebracht:

"Parteifreunde! Euch ist bekannt, daß 1924 das Gesetz zur Vereinheitlichung des Erziehungswesens, das noch heute in Kraft ist, erlassen worden ist. Es hat die religiöse Ausbildung und die Ausbildungsstätten dem *Nationalen Erziehungsministerium* (Millî Eğitim Bakanlığı) unterstellt, das sich deshalb der sittlich-religiösen Erziehung unserer Bürger anzunehmen hat. Doch aus der Befürchtung heraus, das Laizismusprinzip könnte Schaden nehmen, bleibt diese wichtige Aufgabe unerledigt."[25]

Das dritte Gesetz, um das es hier geht, betrifft die Gründung des *Präsidiums für religiöse Angelegenheiten* (Diyanet İşleri Başkanlığı). Diese Behörde wirkt auf den ersten Blick wie die republikanische Entsprechung des einstigen osmanischen Şeyh ul-İslâm-Amtes oder doch zumindest wie die Fortführung des kurzlebigen *Scheriat- und Stiftungsministeriums* (Şeriye ve Evkaf Vekâleti) welches seinerseits bereits eine Hervorbringung der Republik und von ihrem Verständnis bestimmt gewesen war. Das *Präsidium* jedoch hat einen niedrigeren Status und untersteht direkt dem Ministerpräsidenten. In der Gesetzesbegründung heißt es:

"Die Vermengung der Religion und des Militärs mit politischen Interessen und Strömungen ist in vieler Hinsicht von Übel. Diese Überzeugung wurde zum Leitsatz aller zivilisierten Nationen und ihrer Re-

[22] Zur generellen Würdigung des Gesetzes vgl. İhsan Sungu, Tevhid-i tedrisat, *TTK Belleten*, No. II/7-8, 1938, S. 379-431.
Das Gesetz unterstellte auch die Militärschulen dem Erziehungsministerium, doch führte der Widerstand von Marschall Fevzi Çakmak bereits nach kurzer Zeit dazu, daß diese aufs neue dem Generalstab unterstellt wurden und damit das Gesetz nur kurz nach seinem Erlaß gebrochen wurde.

[23] Aus dem von Ahmed Hamdi Akseki in seiner Eigenschaft als Präsident des *Präsidiums für religiöse Angelegenheiten* am 12. Dezember 1950 vorgelegten Bericht mit dem Titel: Dinî müesselerimiz hakkında bir rapor, zitiert nach Kara, *Türkiye'de İslâmcılık düşüncesi*, Band II, 3. Auflage, S. 362 bis 379, hier S. 367.

[24] [Cumhuriyet Halk Partisi, CHP]

[25] *CHP Yedinci Kurultay Tutanağı*, Ankara 1948, S. 462.

gierungen. Unter diesem Aspekt betrachtet, war es nicht sinnvoll, das *Scheriat- und Stiftungsministerium* und das *Generalstabsministerium* (Erkân-ı Harbiye-i Umumiye Vekâleti) in die Struktur der politischen Institutionen der Republik Türkei zu integrieren, in die politische Struktur eines Landes, das sich eine vollkommen neue Existenz aufbauen will. Deshalb empfiehlt sich die Aufhebung des Scheriat- und Stiftungsministeriums und die Schaffung einer Stiftungsverwaltung, die der Übertragung aller Stiftungen in das Eigentum der Nation Rechnung trägt. (...)"[26]

In seiner Rede vor dem Parlament, die er am 1. März 1924 hielt, benutzte Mustafa Kemal eine ganz ähnliche Argumentation:

"(...) Der Islam, dem untrennbar zuzugehören, uns über alle Maßen glücklich macht, wurde über Jahrhunderte in den Niederungen der Politik mißbraucht. Für uns steht außer Zweifel, daß es gilt, ihn über diese zu erheben. Unsere heiligen und göttlichen Glaubens- und Gewissensüberzeugungen sofort und endgültig vor der Politik und allem was damit zu tun hat, vor diesem Streit der niedrigsten Begierden und Interessen zu retten, das ist eine für das diesseitige und jenseitige Wohlergehen unserer Nation unabdingbare Notwendigkeit. Nur so kann die wahre Bedeutung des Islams hervortreten."[27]

Das Zusammenspiel des Gesetzes zur Vereinheitlichung des Erziehungswesens mit dem Gesetz, das zum Präsidium für religiöse Angelegenheiten führte, schuf die unseres Wissens nur in der Türkei bestehende Regelung, nach der dem *Präsidium* zwar die Leitung des religiösen Lebens obliegt, jedoch die Religionserziehung dem Nationalen Erziehungsministerium vorbehalten ist und auf diese Weise beide Bereiche vollständig voneinander getrennt sind. Das galt für die Zeit vor der Einstellung aller religiösen Ausbildung und das gilt für die Reaktivierung religiösen Unterrichts und religiöser Bildung nach 1949. Nicht unter die Kompetenz des *Präsidiums*, sondern unter die des Nationalen Erziehungsministeriums fielen damit in der frühen Republik

---

[26] TBMM Zabıt Ceridesi, Devre: 2, Band. VII.

[27] Ebenda, S. 6

Dasselbe Gesetz, welches das Scheriat- und Stiftungsministerium ins *Präsidium für religiöse Angelegenheiten* (Diyanet İşleri Riyaseti) umwandelte, wandelte -- mit der gleichen Begründung, d.h. der Trennung der Religion und des Militärs von der Politik -- das Generalstabsministerium in das *Generalstabspräsidium* (Erkân-ı Harbiye-i Umumiye Riyaseti), den heutigen *Generalstab* (Genelkurmay Başkanlığı) um. Es wäre aufschlußreich, die weitere Entwicklung dieser beiden Institutionen zu verfolgen, die damals zur gleichen Zeit und durch dasselbe Gesetz entstanden sind.

die *Vorbeter- und Predigerschulen* (İmam Hatip Mektebleri), die bereits 1930 geschlossen wurden, und die Theologische Fakultät an der noch aus osmanischer Zeit stammenden *Hochschule* (Darulfünun), die erst 1933[28] den Lehrbetrieb einstellen mußte. Nach 1949 leitete das Nationale Erziehungsminsterium die neu eröffnete Theologische Fakultät und die später neu gegründeten Vorbeter- und Predigerschulen sowie die *Hohen Islam-Institute* (Yüksek İslâm Enstitüleri). Daß die *Frommen Stiftungen* (evkaf-ı hayriye) bei der Abwicklung des Scheriat- und Stiftungsministeriums nicht dem *Präsidium*, sondern einer davon getrennten *Stiftungsgeneraldirektion*[29], die ebenfalls dem Ministerpräsidenten untersteht, zugefallen sind, verdient besonderes Interesse. Diese Regelung entzieht die Stiftungen und ihr Einkommen dem vom Stifter festgelegten Stiftungszweck und verletzt somit grundlegende Rechtsprinzipien. Mehr noch, indem sie das *Präsidium* seiner natürlichen finanziellen Quellen beraubt, schränkt sie seine Tätigkeit auf die Zuweisungen aus dem Staatsbudget ein.

Die Aufgaben des Präsidiums *und seine Rechte*

Nachdem auf diese Weise die historische Entwicklung des Verhältnisses von Staat und Religion umrissen und die Perspektive des republikanischen Regimes auf die Religion grob gezeichnet worden sind, kann sich die Analyse jetzt dem Präsidium für religiöse Angelegenhei-

[28] Das Gesetz zur Vereinheitlichung des Erziehungswesens sah die Einrichtung einer Theologische Fakultät an der Darulfünun vor, [für die alsbaldige Schließung dieser Fakultät gab es keine gesetzliche Grundlage. Die Neueröffnung einer Theologischen Fakultät in Ankara 1949 folgte rein politischen Erwägungen.] Professor Alberte Malche, dessen Bericht die 1933 erfolgte erste Gründung einer Universität nach westlichem Vorbild vorbereitete, hatte sich [bereits damals] für einen Thologischen Studiengang an der Geisteswissenschaftlichen Fakultät der neuen Universität Istanbul ausgesprochen, doch blieb sein Votum unberücksichtigt. Nach Malche sollte eine solche Fakultät aus sechs Lehrstühlen bestehen: 1. Metaphysik und Religionsphilosophie, 2. Geschichte des Korans und Koranauslegung, 3. Islamische Religions- und Rechtsgeschichte, 4. Arabisch, 5. Persisch, 6. Überlieferungsgeschichte (hadis). Vgl. Albert Malche, İstanbul Üniversitesi hakkında raport, S. 44 der Übersetzung, zitiert nach Rahmi Karakuş, *Felsefe serüvenimiz*, Seyran Yay., Istanbul 1995, S. 309, Fußnote. 229; vgl. auch Horst Widmann, *Atatürk Üniversite Reformu*, Cerrahpaşa Tıp Fak. Yay., Istanbul 1981, S. 50, Fußnote 2. [das deutsche Original: *Exil und Bildungshilfe in der Türkei*, Frankfurt/Main u.a. 1974].

[29] [Dessen heutige Bezeichnung lautet Vakıflar Genel Müdürlüğü]

ten selbst zuwenden.[30]

Einen möglicher Rahmen für diese Analyse stellt die Entwicklung des Verhältnisses von Staat und Religion in der türkischen Geschichte dar, bzw. die Frage danach, welche historische Institution das *Präsidium* ablösen, bzw. ersetzen sollte. Häufig wird vorgetragen, das *Präsidium* stände in der Tradition des Şeyh ul-İslâm und -- in der Republik -- in der Tradition des *Scheriat- und Stiftungsministeriums* und bildete daher eher eine Kontinuität im Verhältnis von Staat und Religion als einen Bruch ab. Bisweilen hat man den Vergleich noch weitergetrieben und behauptet, daß mit der Gründung des *Präsidums* so recht keine wesentliche Veränderung vor sich gegangen sei. In der Absicht, dies zu belegen hat man darauf hingwiesen, daß, ganz so wie seinerzeit der Şeyh ul-İslâm vom Padischah ernannt wurde und ihm verantwortlich war, heute der Präsident des *Präsidiums* vom Ministerpräsidenten (mit Zustimmung des Staatspräsidenten) ernannt wird und ihm verantwortlich ist. Solche Gedankenspielerei entbehrt freilich jeder historischen Grundlage und läßt jedes Augenmaß vermissen.

Was Ansehen und Einfluß betrifft, kam das Amt des Şeyh ul-İslâm im Osmanischen Reiche gleich nach dem Kalifen und dem Padischah sowie dem Amte des *Großwesirs* (sadr-ı azam).[31] Seine Kompetenzen in den Bereichen Gesetzgebung, Verwaltung und Justiz sind nur schwerlich mit denen irgendeines anderen Amtes vergleichbar. Bis zum 19. Jahrhundert waren Gebiete wie Erziehung, Justiz und Stiftungen ausschließlich seine Domäne. Viele Aufgaben, die heute den Stadtverwaltungen obliegen, wurden von Kadis ausgeführt, die Angehörige der Ulema waren und dienstrechtlich dem Şeyh ul-İslâm unterstanden.

---

[30] Die einzige auf Türkisch vorliegende Abhandlung ist İ. B. Tarhanlı, *Müslüman toplum laik devlet - Türkiye'de Diyanet İşleri Başkanlığı*, Afa Yay., Istanbul 1993, eine Dissertation im Fach Öffentliches Recht, deren religionspolitische Dimensionen nur schwach entwickelt sind. Eine holländische Dissertation fokussiert die aktuelle Situation des *Präsidiums* in der Türkei und in Europa und wertet dafür primär die Fetwas seines *Hohen Rats für religiöse Angelegenheiten* (Din İşleri Yüksek Kurulu) aus: Jak den Exter, *Diyanet, een reis door de keuken van de officiele Islam*, Beverwijk 1990. Eine Besprechung dieser Arbeit ist: A. Yüksel & İ. Clasz-Coockson, Diyanet üzerine Hollandaca bir kitap, *Tarih ve Toplum*, No. 113, Mai 1993, S. 63-64.

[31] Vgl. Hezarfen Huseyin Efendi, *Telhisü'l-beyan fi kavanîn-i Âl-i Osman*, S. İlgürel (Hrsg.) TTK Yay., Ankara 1998, S. 197: "Malum ola ki bu Devlet-i Aliyye'de makam-ı Şeyh ul-İslâm, mertebe-i vekâlet-i kübra yani vezaret-i uzma'dan a'lâ değil ise bari beraber ve bazı hususa nazar olunsa ondan bâlâterdir."

Auch wenn das Scheriat- und Stiftungsministerium, das zwischen 1920 und 1924 in Ankara seinen Sitz hatte, sich im Vergleich zum Şeyh ul-İslâm-Amte mit geringeren Kompetenzen begnügen mußte, so war es letzten Endes doch eine Institution im Range eines Ministeriums. Es war direkt verantwortlich für religiöse Zeremonien, religiöse Veröffentlichungen sowie für die Medresen und die Stiftungen. Sein Minister nahm im Ministerrat Platz, es war in der *Scheriat-Kommission* (Şeriye Encümeni) des Parlaments vertreten und spielte seine Rolle im Prozeß der Gesetzesformulierung. Die Persönlichkeiten, die ihm vorstanden, waren -- wie Mustafa Fehmi Efendi[32] und Mehmed Vehbi Efendi[33] -- Angehörige der Ulema, Parlamentsabgeordnete und darüberhinaus einflußreiche Mitglieder des [jungtürkischen] Komitees *Einheit und Fortschritt* (İttihat ve Terakki), die aktiv am Befreiungskrieg teilgenommen hatten. Im Protokoll des Ministerrats hatte der Scheriat- und Stiftungsminister -- ähnlich wie seinerzeit der Şeyh ul-İslâm -- seinen Platz gleich nach dem Parlaments- und dem Ministerpräsidenten.

Ein systematischer Vergleich der Kompetenzen und Verantwortlichkeiten, die dem Präsidium für religiöse Angelegenheiten übertragen wurden, mit den Kompetenzen seiner beiden Vorgänger-Institutionen macht deutlich, daß hier weniger von historischer Kontinuität als von einem radikalen Bruche gesprochen werden muß.

Die Auseinandersetzungen, die am historischen 3. März 1924 anläßlich der Beratung des Gesetzes zur Umwandlung des Scheriat- und Stiftungsministeriums ins Präsidium geführt worden waren, werfen ein Licht auf die Natur dieser Veränderung. Lange drehte sich die Diskussion um einen bestimmten Begriff. Im Gesetzesentwurf lautete die amtliche Bezeichnung des zu gründenden Präsidiums *Umûr-u Diyaniye Reisliği*[34] was Einspruch und den Vorschlag hervorrief, die Bezeichnung *Umûr-u Diniye Reisliği* zu verwenden, ein Vorschlag, der auf der Gegenseite Empörung auslöste. So fragte etwa Tunalı Hilmi empört: “Was soll das ‘Umûr-u Diniye’ wo doch ‘Umûr-u Diyaniye’ vorgesehen ist? Bei der Auseinandersetzung um *Umûr-u Diniye* gegenüber *Umûr-u Diyaniye* (gleich *Din İşleri* gegenüber *Diyanet İşleri*) ging es um mehr als Wortklauberei: Es war eine ernsthafte Auseinan-

[32] Mit dem späteren Familiennamen Gerçekler.

[33] Mit dem späteren Familiennamen Çelik.

[34] [reisliği = riyaset = başkanlık, Präsidium / umûr = emirler = işler, Angelegenheiten]

dersetzung darüber, wie in Zukunft die Religion und das Religiöse verstanden werden sollten und in welche Richtung die Religion sich entwickeln sollte; mit allen politischen Konsequenzen. Die Ernsthaftigkeit dieser Auseinandersetzung spricht aus der Argumentation, die Samih Rifat, Abgeordneter aus Biga, in derselben Sitzung vortrug:

"(...) Die *islamische Rechtswissenschaft* (fıkıh) unterscheidet klar zwischen *din* und *diyanet*. Der Begriff *din* schließt alles ein, die [religionsgesetzlich relevanten Bereiche, die der] *Rechtsprechung des Kadis* [unterliegen] (kazaî), das *Fetwa-Wesen* (iftaî), den [religionsgesetzlich legitimierten] *Erlaß von Verboten* (muamelât-ı nasa), [Religions]-*Gesetze* (ahkâm), die *Kultvorschriften* (ibadat) und die *Glaubenswahrheiten* (itikadât). Doch all die Bereiche der Religionsgesetze, des Fetwa-Wesens, des Kultes und der Glaubenswahrheiten, die *außerhalb der religionsrichterlichen Kompetenzen* liegen, bilden nach der islamischen Rechtswissenschaft einen eigenen Interpretationszusammenhang und werden unter dem Begriff *diyanet* zusammengefaßt. Alle Werke der islamischen Rechtswissenschaft trennen nach *kazaen* und *diyaneten*. Der Begriff *din* assoziert *Befehl* (imaret) und *Regierung* (hükumet) und umfaßt *die Wirtschaft* (iktisadîyat), *das Soziale* (ictimaîyat), *die öffentliche Ordnung* (inzibat) sowie *das Unterrichtswesen* (tedrisat). Alle diese Bereiche sind von der Regierung [der jungen Republik] bestimmten Behörden zugeteilt worden. Was übrig bleibt, das ist der Kult, das sind die Glaubenswahrheiten und die religiösen Regeln, die unter das Fetwa-Wesen fallen, und genau diese Bereiche gehören zu einem *Präsidium für religiöse Angelegenheiten* (Umûr-u Diyaniye Riyaseti), und genau das wird mit dem Begriff *diyanet* ausgedrückt."[35]

Nun wird deutlich, wie oberflächlich eine Gleichsetzung des heutigen *Präsidiums* mit dem Amte des Şeyh ul-İslâm ist. Der osmanische Staat war dadurch gekennzeichnet, daß der religiöse Bereich vom Kalifen und der politische[36] Bereich vom Padischah repräsentiert wurde und daß beide Bereiche im Sultanat zusammenfielen. So wie der Großwesir den Sultan im politischen Bereich vertrat, so der Şeyh ul-İslâm im religiösen und in manchen Sektoren der Verwaltung. Wird von dieser Dimension der Stellvertreterschaft abgesehen, bleibt das Verhältnis von Padischah und Şeyh ul-İslâm mit seinen Dimensionen

---

[35] TBMM Zabıt Ceridesi.

[36] [im Sinne von direkt herrschaftlich, Macht und Herrschaft tatsächlich ausübend]

von Kompetenz und Verantwortung nur mangelhaft bestimmt. Hinzu kommt, daß der Osmanische Staat, der seinen Şeyh ul-İslâm ernannte, letzten Endes ein religiös legitimierter Staat mit dem Kalifen an der Spitze war, während die Republik ein laizistischer Staat ist, die für ihr *Präsidium* einen Präsidenten gerade so wie andere leitende 'Beamte' ernennt. Das läßt sich in schöner Regelmäßigkeit anläßlich der Beratungen des *Präsidiums*-Haushaltes verfolgen, wo stets darauf hingewiesen wird, daß sein Präsident verwaltungsrechtlich mit dem Generaldirektor der Kataster-Ämter auf einer Stufe steht. Man kann deshalb nicht behaupten, daß die Behörde wirklich religiöse Autorität repräsentierte.

Tatsächlich wird das *Präsidium* schließlich als *Diyanet* İşleri Başkanlığı gegründet, und der ihm zugewiesene Wirkungskreis und die zugesprochene Kompetenzen verbleiben exakt in den Grenzen dieses Begriffs. Das bereits genannte Gesetz No. 429 bestimmt in seinem § 1:

"In der Republik Türkei obliegt *der Erlaß und die Durchführung der bindenden Vorschriften* [die aus dem religiösen Recht gewonnen werden] (muamelât-ı nâsa dair olan ahkâmın teşri ve infazı) der Großen Türkischen Nationalversammlung [dem Parlament] und der von ihr gebildeten Regierung. Für die Regelungen und Angelegenheiten der geoffenbarten Religion, die darüberhinaus in den Bereichen Glaubenswahrheiten und Kult bestehen, wurde ein *Präsidium für religiöse Angelegenheiten* (Diyanet İşleri Reisliği) gegründet, das auch die Verwaltung der religiösen Anlagen übernimmt und seinerseits der [Regierung der] Republik verantwortlich ist."[37]

Ein 1965, mehr als vierzig Jahre später, erlassenes *Gesetz über die Gründung und die Aufgaben des Präsidiums für religiöse Angelegenheiten* mit der Nummer 633 bestimmt in seinem § 1:

"Für die Erledigung der Aufgaben, die im Zusammenhang mit Fragen des Glaubens, des Kultes und der Sittlichkeit im Islam anfallen, für die Aufklärung[38] der Gesellschaft in religiösen Fragen und für die Verwaltung der religiösen Anlagen wurde ein Präsidium für religiöse Angelegenheiten gegründet, das dem Ministerpräsidenten unter-

[37] Die gleiche Aufgabenbeschreibung des *Präsidums* durch seinen dritten Präsidenten Ahmed Hamdi Akseki in *Türkiye'de İslâmcılık düşüncesi*, Band II, S. 366.

[38] [aydınlatmak = aufklären; es ist kein Zufall daß der Begriff gewählt wurde, der im Türkischen auch für "die Aufklärung" steht.]

steht."[39]

Auch in diesem Gesetz finden sich die drei von Akseki genannten Aufgabenbereiche: Anleitung in Fragen des Glaubens, des Kultes und -- zusätzlich -- der *Sittlichkeit* (ahlâk); Verwaltung der Gebetsstätten und Aufklärung der Bevölkerung in religiösen Fragen.

Auffallend ist, daß der *Bereich der bindenden Verhaltensvorschriften* (muamelât) (des religiösen Rechts) vollkommen beiseite gelassen und der Erlaß sowie die Durchführung von Regelungen in diesem Bereich dem Parlament und mehr noch der jeweiligen Regierung übertragen werden. Geht man von der Überlegung aus, daß im Islam Glaube, Kult und Sittlichkeitsfragen nicht von der Regelung konkreten Verhaltens zu trennen sind, liegt die Vermutung sehr nahe, daß das Zentrum der politischen Macht den Glauben, den Kult und die Sittlichkeit weder auf der Ebene der Überzeugungen noch auf der Ebene des konkreten Verhaltens einer ihrer Natur entsprechenden [und eigendynamischen] Entwicklung überlassen wollte. Die Praxis bestätigt diese Vermutung. Interessant ist ferner, daß 1965 der Begriff *Sittlichkeit* in den Text des neuen Gesetzes No. 633 aufgenommen worden ist, obwohl er in der von der Regierung eingereichten Gesetzesvorlage nicht enthalten war. Verantwortlich dafür war der Beratende Ausschuß und um die Aufnahme des Begriffs wurde im Parlament heftig gestritten. Eine verwaltungsjuristische Analyse kommt in dieser Sache zu folgendem Schlusse:

"Weder auf der Ebene von öffentlicher Dienstleistung noch auf der von öffentlicher Kontrolle lassen sich Aufgaben der Verwaltung in bezug auf 'Sittlichkeit' juristisch legitimieren"; und: "Die Zuweisung von Aufgaben, die auf 'Sittlichkeitsvorstellungen' beruhen, bedeutet die Erteilung juristisch nicht definierbarer Aufträge und läuft allenfalls auf einen Staat hinaus, der sich eine religiöse Ideologie zu eigen gemacht hat."[40]

[39] Vgl. zur rechtlichen Lage des *Präsidiums* und zu den Verwaltungsvorschriften: Nail Aslanpay; *Diyanet İşleri Başkanlığı - kuruluşu, çalışması ve birimlerinin tanıtılması, 1924-1973*, Diyanet İşleri Başkanlığı Yay., Ankara 1973; ferner Ahmet Uzunoğlu, *En son değişikleriyle Diyanet İşleri Başkanlığı Mevzuatı*, 2. Auflage, Istanbul 1978, vgl. auch *Açıklamalı Diyanet İşleri Başkanlığı Mevzuatı*, Ankara 1989 und Tarhanlı 1993.

[40] Tarhanlı 1993, S. 98 und 159. Eine Zusammenfassung der Parlamentsdebatte findet sich ebenda, S. 72-73 und S. 96-98. Vgl. zur Debatte auch Bahri Savaşçı; Diyanet İşleri teşkilatının gelişmeleri, *A.Ü. Siyasal Bilgiler Fakültesi Dergisi*, No. XXII/3, November 1997, S. 99 und 101.

Im Grunde reicht die politische Auseinandersetzung um das Verhältnis von diyanet und Sittlichkeit bis zum 7. Parteitag der Republikanischen Volkspartei im Jahre 1947 zurück. Auf ihm wurde die Frage des Laizismus lang und breit diskutiert, denn eine ganze Reihe von Abgeordneten und Delegierten gaben ihren Befürchtungen über die soziale und gesellschaftliche Desintegration dieser Tage Ausdruck und verwiesen auf die sittliche Dimension der Religion, d.h. des Islams, die solchen Entwicklungen einen Riegel vorschieben könnte. Sie forderten einen Ausbau des *Präsidiums*, die generelle Wiedereinführung des Religionsunterrichts sowie die Eröffnung von theologischen Studiengängen.[41] Nur einer derer, die in dieser Debatte das Wort ergriffen, vertrat insofern eine moderne/säkulare Position, als er nicht von einem notwendigen Zusammenhang zwischen religiöser Erziehung und Sittlichkeitserziehung ausgehen wollte: Fazıl Ahmet Aykaç, Abgeordneter von Diyarbakir. Sich gegen die allgemeine Stimmung auf dem Parteitag wendend, führte er aus:

"(...) Unsere Freunde sind Opfer einer heillosen Begriffsverwirrung. Sind doch überall auf der Welt Religionserziehung und Sittlichkeitserziehung verschiedene Sachen. (...) Wäre dem nicht so, wie könnten wir heute Atatürks Vermächtnis preisen. Sowohl die Geschichte als auch die Wissenschaft formen unser Gewissen und unsere Sittlichkeit in äußerstem Maße. Wer unvoreingenommen ist, findet dafür zahlreiche Beispiele."[42]

Im Grunde beschränkten sich 1924 die Kompetenzen des *Präsidiums*, wie sie in den ersten beiden Paragraphen des damaligen Gesetzes genannt worden sind, auf die Verwaltung der Moscheen. So vermochte sein erster Präsident Rifat Börekçi auf die Frage eines Journalisten, "Besteht Ihre Aufgabe ausschließlich darin, die Imame zu überwachen?" nur ausweichend zu antworten: "Unsere Aufgabe besteht in der Absetzung und Ernennung der Imame. Darüberhinaus beschäftigen uns religiöse Fragen."[43] Tatsächlich hatte das *Präsidium* noch bis

[41] Vgl. *CHP Yedinci Kurultay Tutanağı*, Ankara 1948, S. 448f, 451 und 454. Einige Redner machten detaillierte Vorschläge zum Fächerkanon und wollten Gegenstände wie 'Islamische Geschichte', 'Islamische Philosophie' und 'Vergleichende Religionsgeschichte' berücksichtigt wissen.

[42] Ebenda, S. 465.

[43] Türkçe namaz, *Vakit* vom 20 Şevval 1344 (3. Mai 1926). In einem anderen Interview spricht Börekçi von der "Befriedigung der religiösen Bedürfnisse der Einwohner", Namazda Türkçe Kur'an okunabilir mi?, *Vakit* vom 26. Cemazyiyelevvel 1345 (22. Dezember 1927).

vor kurzem hinsichtlich der Errichtung, Förderung und Ausstattung von Moscheen genauso wenig Kompetenzen wie hinsichtlich ihrer Bedarfsfeststellung und Planung. Heute ist die Inventar-Direktion (Donatım Müdürlüğü) des *Präsidiums* für die Verwaltung der Moscheen zuständig. 1998 erlassene Neuregelungen zur Ausweitung seiner Kompetenzen in Bezug auf die Planung und Eröffnung von Moscheen und Gebetsräumen zielten jedoch nicht auf seine Aufwertung, sondern wurden im Rahmen der *"Gesetzesänderungen zur Einschränkung der religiösen Reaktion"* (irtica yasaları) beschlossen. Es ging einzig und allein darum, Initiativen der Bevölkerung zum Bau vom Moscheen, die durch eine allmähliche Ausweitung des öffentlichen Raumes möglich geworden waren, zu kontrollieren. Eines der Gesetze, welches unter der parallel zu den Vorgaben des Nationalen Sicherheitsrates an die Macht gelangte Regierung Mesut Yılmaz[44] verabschiedet wurde, trug den Titel "Die Errichtung und Verwaltung von Moscheen obliegt dem *Präsidium*".[45] Kurz darauf erließ der Kassationsgerichtshof ein Urteil, das die Moscheen generell als "öffentliches Eigentum" bestimmte.[46] Soweit aus den Bekanntmachungen zu ersehen ist, wird die "Errichtung und Verwaltung von Moscheen durch das *Präsidium*" folgender Prozedur unterworfen sein: Die natürlichen und privaten juristischen Personen, welche die Errichtung einer Moschee beabsichtigen, reichen die entsprechenden Pläne beim *Präsidium* ein. Dieses prüft, ob in der Umgebung Bedarf besteht und der vorgesehene Ort für einen Moscheebau geeignet ist. Sind beide Kriterien er-

[44] [Im Amte vom Juni 1997 bis zum Dezember 1998]

[45] Vgl. die Presse vom 23. und 24. März 1998.

[46] "Der Kassationsgerichtshof hat entschieden, daß die Moscheen nur Eigentum öffentlicher Institutionen sein können und ihr Besitz durch natürliche oder private juristische Personen wie Stiftungen oder Vereine nicht rechtsmäßig ist. Desgleichen darf auch die Verwaltung und Leitung der Moscheen nicht in den Händen natürlicher oder privater juristischer Personen liegen. Der 1. Senat des Kassationsgerichtshof unterstrich, daß die Moscheen Gebetsstätten der Muslime sind und deshalb der Öffentlichkeit zur Verfügung stehen müßten. Aus dieser Eigenschaft der Moscheen ergebe sich, so das Urteil, daß es sich bei den Moscheen um öffentliches Eigentum handele. Das Urteil nimmt auf die neuesten Änderungen des *Gesetzes über die Gründung und die Aufgaben des Präsidiums für religiöse Angelegenheiten* (Diyanet İşleri Başkanlığı'nın kuruluşu ve görevleri hakkındaki kanun) Bezug und führt aus, dieses Gesetz bestimme, daß Moscheen nur mit Erlaubnis des *Präsidums* eröffnet werden dürften und von ihm verwaltet werden müßten. Das Gericht erinnert außerdem an eine weitere Vorschrift desselben Gesetzes, nach der die Verwaltung und Leitung der Moscheen, welche von natürlichen oder privaten juristischen Personen eröffnet worden sind, innerhalb von drei Monaten dem *Präsidium* zu übertragen seien." Yargıtay'ın kararı: Camiler kamu malı, *Yeni Şafak* vom 23. Februar 1999, S. 2.

füllt, bestimmt das *Präsidium* die konkrete Ausführung des Baues.

Seine Vorschläge und Vorgaben für die werktäglichen Predigten sowie für die, welche Freitags- und Feiertags gehalten werden, sowie seine Veröffentlichungen ermöglichen dem *Präsidium* eine indirekte Einflußnahme auf die Ausgestaltung der Glaubenswahrheiten und Kultvorschriften. Der Religionsunterricht und das, was als originär religiöse Erziehung in den Predigerschulen, die dem *Präsidium* einen Teil seines Personals heranziehen, gelehrt wird,[47] liegt vollkommen in der Kompetenz des Nationalen Erziehungsministeriums; die Theologischen Fakultäten sind über die Universitäten dem *Rate für das Hochschulwesen* (Yüksek Öğretim Kurumu, YÖK) unterstellt.[48] Das bereits angeführte Gesetz über die Gründung und die Aufgaben des Präsidiums für religiöse Angelegenheiten mit der Nummer 633 bestimmt in seinem § 5, Abs. J. lediglich, die Hohe Kommission für religiöse Angelegenheiten des *Präsidiums* habe zu den berufsbildenden Fächern der Schulen, welche der Verwaltung des *Präsidiums* Fachkräfte ausbilden, und zu den Lehrbüchern, den Curricula und den Stundenplänen des Religionsunterrichts an allgemeinbildenden Schulen Stellung zu nehmen und gegebenenfalls mit den zuständigen Behörden zusammenzuarbeiten. Was den Inhalt, die Curricula und die Stundenpläne für religiöse Erziehung betrifft, besitzt das *Präsidium* keine finale Kompetenz.

Ähnlich verhält es sich mit der Gestaltung der religiösen Programme in den öffentlichen Radio- und Fernsehkanälen. Auch hier ist das

[47] Von einer *religiösen Erziehung*, die hinsichtlich ihres Inhaltes, ihrer Perspektive und ihrer Funktion diesen Namen verdiente, läßt sich in der Türkei nicht sprechen. Man kann höchsten sagen, daß innerhalb einer durch und durch säkularen Erziehung Religionsunterricht erteilt wird. Bereits 1927 hat der erste Präsident des *Präsidiums* Rıfat Börekçi die Überzeugung geäußert, "daß uns eine Berufsakademie Not tut". Vgl. *Vakit* vom 26. Cemazyiyelevvel 1345 (22. Dezember 1927).

[48] Eine gewisse Kompetenz in der Religionserziehung hat das *Präsidium* nur in den Koran-Kursen, die von ihm selbst ausgerichtet werden, jedoch ebenfalls der Kontrolle des Nationalen Erziehungsministeriums unterliegen. Man darf dabei jedoch nicht vergessen, daß die Koran-Kurse, auch wenn sie Katechese enthalten, mit ihrem Ziel, den arabischen Vortrag des Korans zu vermitteln, stark praxisbezogen sind, besonders wenn die Ausbildung den *freien Rezitator des Korans* (hafız) zum Ziel hat. Ebenfalls dem *Präsidium* unterstehen die sogenannten *Ausbildungszentren* (Eğitim Merkezleri), die primär berufliche Kurzzeit-Fortbildung betreiben. 1976 wurde das *Ausbildungszentrum Haseki* gegründet, das ebenfalls dem *Präsidium* untersteht. Es bildet Muftis und *Prediger* (vaiz) fort und sein Programm kann, sowohl was die zweijährige Dauer dieser Fortbildung als auch was ihr arabisches Quellenstudium betrifft, als orginär *religiöse Bildung* bezeichnet werden. Vgl. zu den Koran-Kursen und *Ausbildungszentren* Ahmet Uzunoğlu 1978, S. 84-98 und 337-338.

Votum des *Präsidiums* nicht ausschlaggebend. Dies kritisierte einer seiner früheren Präsidenten, Tayyar Altıkulaç, mit folgenden Worten: "Ist die *Staatliche Radio- und Fernsehbehörde* (TRT) etwa ein zweites Präsidium für religiöse Angelegenheiten, daß sie religiöse Programme gestaltet und versucht, 'die Gesellschaft in religiösen Fragen aufzuklären'[49]? Das ist nicht hinnehmbar. (...) Wie kann eine laizistische Institution eines laizistischen Staates Programme ausstrahlen, die vom Präsidium für religiöse Angelegenheiten, d.h. von der Behörde, die von Rechts wegen für religiöse Angelegenheiten zuständig ist, weder gestaltet noch abgesegnet sind? Das ist unerhört. Das ist gegen die Verfassung."[50]

Diese Beschneidung der inhaltlichen Kompetenzen des *Präsidiums* wird verstärkt durch seine finanzielle Abhängigkeit, die sich, wie erwähnt, aus der Abkoppelung der *Frommen Stiftungen* vom *Präsidium* ergibt. All dies trägt zur Entstehung einer Situation bei, deren Problematik schon sehr früh, nämlich 1947 auf dem Parteitag der Republikanischen Volkspartei zur Sprache gebracht worden ist:

"Jawohl, wir haben heute einen Präsidenten für religiöse Angelegenheiten. Aber seine Verwaltung ist außerstande, der jungen Generation die Religion zu vermitteln. Sie kann lediglich einige Beamte auf freiwerdende Mufti- und Vorbeterstellen berufen, sonst nichts." (Abdülkadir Güney, Delegierter aus Çorum)

"Sie (die nichtmuslimischen Gemeinden) haben die Verwaltung ihrer Stiftungen behalten, aber den muslimischen Gemeinden hat man ein Präsidium für religiöse Angelegenheiten vor die Nase gesetzt; und hat diese Institution doch gleichzeitig aller Möglichkeiten beraubt, wirklich tätig zu sein. Das einzige, was der Präsident dieser Behörde tun kann, ist, sich den lieben langen Tag mit der Gebetskette zu vertreiben." (Sinan Tekelioğlu, Abgeordneter aus Seyhan.)

"Das Präsidium für religiöse Angelegenheiten müßte sich eigentlich mit dem Religionsunterricht befassen. Man muß ihm erlauben, sich dieses für das Land ganz und gar wesentlichen Problems anzunehmen

[49] [Altıkulaç wählt hier wörtlich die Wendung, die im Gesetz No. 633 zur Bestimmung der Aufgaben des *Präsidum* benutzt wird.]

[50] Ahmet Ersöz, Dr. Tayyar Altıkulaç ile ..., (Reportage), *Zaman* vom 10. September 1998, S. 8. Seit November 1997 hat das *Präsidium* im 4. Kanal des Staatsfernsehens seine eigene Sendung, die Diyanet Saati, die sich jedoch von den früheren 'religiösen' Freitag-Abend-Sendungen des staatlichen Fernsehens in keinster Weise unterscheidet.

und die Prediger und Vorbeter auszubilden, die an allen Ecken und Enden fehlen." (Hamdullah Suphi Tanrıöver, Abgeordneter aus Istanbul)[51]

1927 wurde die Freitagspredigt auf Türkisch gehalten, 1932 wurde das Türkische für den Gebetsruf, den *Totenruf* (salâ), das Ritualgebet sowie für das *Bekenntnis der Allmacht Gottes* (tekbir) verbindlich, und 1934 wurde die Ayasofya-Moschee[52] in ein Museum umgewandelt. Bei all diesen Schritten handelt es sich um Entscheidungen des politischen Zentrums, das entweder von vorneherein darauf verzichtete, die Stellungnahme des Präsidiums in diesen durch und durch religiösen Angelegenheiten einzuholen oder sich ostentativ über seine gegensätzliche Stellungnahme hinwegsetze, mehr noch, es zur Ausführung der neuen Regelungen zwang.

Die Aufgabe des *Präsidiums*, "die Gesellschaft in religiösen Fragen aufzuklären" beschränkt sich in der Praxis auf die Formulierung der Freitagspredigten, auf die Beantwortung von Fragen in Zusammenhang mit der Religion (das Fetwa-Wesen) und auf die Herausgabe religiöser Veröffentlichungen wie Bücher, Zeitschriften, Kalender und Casetten. Die Qualität der Veröffentlichungen und ihr Bezug zu der Aufgabe, "die Gesellschaft in religiösen Fragen aufzuklären" ist ein Thema für sich, das ich an anderer Stelle abgehandelt habe.[53] Selbst der spätere CHP-Abgeordnete Dr. Lütfi Doğan, der als der 'laizistischste' Präsident gilt, den das *Präsidium* je hatte, meinte: "Das *Präsidium* ist beauftragt, die Gesellschaft in geistigen Fragen aufzuklären, doch mit dem Status, den es heute besitzt, ist dies schlechterdings unmöglich."[54]

Das Regime erhoffte sich von den Veröffentlichungen des *Präsidiums* denn auch zweierlei: die "Säuberung der Religion von abergläubischen Vorstellungen und Praktiken" und die Versöhnung der Religion mit den republikanischen Reformen und der republikanischen Ideologie. In diesem Sinne äußerste sich Hamdi Şarlan, Abge-

[51] *CHP Yedinici Kurultay Tutanağı*, S. 449, 450, 469.
[52] [die Hagia Sophia]
[53] Vgl. İsmail Kara, Cumhuriyet Türkiyesi'nde dinî yayıncılığın gelişimi üzerine birkaç not, *Toplum ve Bilim*, No. 29-30, Frühling-Sommer 1985, S. 153-177; Mehmet Bulut, Diyanet İşleri Başkanlığı yayınları bibliografyası 1924-1997, *Diyanet-İlmî Dergi*, No. XXXIII/4, Oktober-Dezember 1997, S. 85-128; Tarhanlı 1993, S. 76-79, 92-95; vgl. auch Uzunoğlu 1978, S. 99-104, 310-320.
[54] Eski başkan Lütfi Doğan'dan eleştiri, *Hürriyet* vom 1. September 1989, S. 3 und 21.

ordneter der Republikanischen Volkspartei für Ordu anläßlich der Beratungen über das Budget des *Präsidiums* im Rahmen der Haushaltsdebatte 1949:

"(...) Es ist dringend notwendig, daß das Präsidium für religiöse Angelegenheiten zwei wöchentlich erscheinende Zeitschriften herausbringt, eine für das Volk und eine für die Gebildeten. Diese Zeitschriften sollen eine von abergläubischen Vorstellungen gereinigte Religion lehren und gleichzeitig zum Schutze des Staates und seiner Reformen beitragen. Sie sollen dem gläubigen Bürger klar machen, daß er sich in der Ausübung seines Glaubens innerhalb der Grenzen der [republikanischen] Reformen zu bewegen und auf Andacht und Sittlichkeit zu beschränken hat."[55]

Es ist offensichtlich, daß die republikanische Ideologie keine Trennung von Religion und Staat, bzw. Religion und Politik nach westlichem Muster vorsah, ja eine solche Trennung sogar als gefährlich erachtete. Berücksichtigt man die Tradition der politischen Vorstellungen des Landes und das Verhältnis des republikanischen Regimes zur Religion und zu den Muslimen, wird man nicht umhinkönnen, diese Haltung nachvollziehbar, mehr noch, strategisch richtig zu finden. Die am türkischen Laizismus-Prinzip ausgerichtete Umsetzung dieser an und für sich nachvollziehbaren und richtigen Haltung jedoch führte dazu, daß die Kompetenzen des Präsidiums für religiöse Angelegenheiten äußerst niedrig gehalten wurden, und daß auf der anderen Seite das politische Machtzentrum den religiösen Bereich zunehmend einengte und sich sogar des religiösen Alltagslebens bemächtigte. Dieses Verhältnis von Staat und Religion, daß sich nur als Unterwerfung der Religion und Eingrenzung des religiösen Bereichs bezeichnen läßt, führte dazu, daß *Religion* entweder 'Bedrohung für den gesellschaftlichen Frieden' oder -- in einer säkularen und national-türkischen Version --'Mittel politischer Legitimation' ist, in jedem Falle aber zum Objekt der Politik wird.

[55] 50. Sitzung, gehalten am 23. Februar 1949, *TBMM Tutanak Dergisi*, No. XVI, S. 447. Läßt man die Sondernummer zum Ramadan 1956 außer Acht, wurde die *Zeitschrift Diyanet* (Diyanet Dergisi) erst 1960 ins Leben gerufen. Vgl. die Themenlisten der *Zeitschrift Diyanet* [die für das Volk erscheint] und der *Wissenschaftlich/theologischen Zeitschrift Diyanet* (Diyanet İlmî Dergi) [die sich an die Gebildeten wendet]: Mehmet Bulut, Diyanet Dergisi/Diyanet İlmî Dergi: genel fihrist ve indeksi, *Diyanet İlmî Dergi* No. XXXIV/4, Oktober-Dezember 1998, S. 1-180.

1970 reichte die Einheitspartei[56] eine Verfassungsbeschwerde gegen das Gesetz No. 633, die gesetzlich Grundlage des *Präsidiums*, mit der Begründung ein, sein Bestehen widerspreche dem Laizismus-Prinzip der Verfassung. Die Urteilsbegründung des Verfassungsgerichts scheint die Position des Regimes in aller Deutlichkeit zum Ausdruck zu bringen und erhellt deshalb den Gegenstand unserer Abhandlung:[57]

"Das Präsidium für religiöse Angelegenheiten *ist keine religiöse Organisation*, sondern *eine Verwaltungseinheit*, die nach Abs. 154 der Verfassung Teil der allgemeinen Staatsverwaltung ist. (...) Es besteht kein Zweifel daran, daß die Verankerung des Präsidiums für religiöse Angelegenheiten in der Verfassung und die Verbeamtung seiner Bediensteten (...) *notwendige Folge bestimmter historischer Konstellationen, spezifischer Bedingungen und spezifischer Notwendigkeiten dieses Landes* ist. Daß die Religion von Staats wegen kontrolliert wird und daß die Religionsbeamten gründlich ausgebildet werden, hat seine Begründung darin, *religiösen Fanatismus zu verhindern und die Religion als ein Mittel sittlicher und moralischer Festigung der Gesellschaft zu erhalten und die Türkische Nation auf diese Weise zu adeln und der modernen Zivilisation zuzuführen.* (...) Deshalb kann die diesbezügliche Unterstützung des Staates und die Verbeamtung der Religionsbediensteten nicht als Förderung und Gestaltung der Religion verstanden werden, sondern nur als Antwort auf spezifische Bedingungen und Notwendigkeiten."

[56] [Birlik, Partisi, BP, später Türkiye Birlik Partisi (TBP), eine Partei mit deutlich alewitischen Tendenzen, gegründet im Oktober 1966, die erste Partei in der Geschichte der Republik, die sich unverhohlen an die Mitglieder einer Konfession wandte.]

[57] Esas: 1970/52, Karar: 1971/76, vgl. *Resmi Gazete* vom 15. Juni 1972, zitiert nach Uzunoğlu 1978, S. 61-62, Fußnote 1, Hervorhebungen İ.K. Vgl. auch die Bewertung in Tarhanlı 1993, S. 107 ff. Anläßlich seines Verbotes der *Huzur Partisi* (Partei der Ausgeglichenheit) hat das Verfassungsgericht eine ganz ähnliche Stellung bezogen: "Laizismus ist ein Prinzip, welches das Verhältnis von Religion und Staat regelt. Es ist deshalb nur natürlich, daß seine Ausgestaltung in einem gegebenen Lande durch die von der jeweiligen Religion vorgegebenen Bedingungen beeinflußt wird und je nachdem, wie stark die Harmonien und Gegensätze sind, unterschiedlich ausfällt. (...) Christentum und Islam geben unterschiedliche Bedingungen vor, weisen verschiedene Glaubenswahrheiten auf und stellen unterschiedliche Anforderungen, weshalb die Ausgangsbedingungen und das Ergebnis in unserem Lande andere sind als die in einem westlichen Lande. Wenn so die Religion und das Religionsverständnis eines Landes vollkommen unterschiedlich ist, kann nicht erwartet werden, daß es den Laizismus im gleichen Sinne versteht, wie ein westliches Land, auch dann nicht, wenn das betreffende Land, der westlichen Zivilisation gegenüber prinzipiell offen ist." Esas: 1983/2, Karar: 1983/2, in *Resmi Gazete* vom 15. Oktober 1984, zitiert nach Tarhanlı 1993, S. 161-162.

Tatsächlich hat sich das *Präsidium* im Verlauf seiner Geschichte, die mit der der Republik nahezu identisch ist, als eine Institution erwiesen, die sich stets innerhalb der ihr gezogenen Grenzen bewegt hat, sich mehr der 'Religion des Staates' als der 'Religion der Muslime' angenommen hat, eine Institution, deren Interpretation von Religion sich freiwillig oder gezwungenermaßen staatlichen Tendenzen anpaßte und die bestrebt ist, das Religionsverständnis des Volkes umzuwälzen.

Die ihm zugewiesenen Kompetenzen zeigen, daß das Präsidium für religiöse Angelegenheiten in den Augen des Regimes niemals besonderes Ansehen genoß. Vom Volke jedoch sollte der Behörde Achtung entgegengebracht werden, denn nur in diesem Falle konnte sie als Mittel zur Einflußnahme benutzt werden und nur in diesem Falle konnte -- mit dem Verweis auf ihr bloßes Bestehen -- der nach wie vor unangefochtene Status von traditionellen religiösen Autoritäten wie die Ulema und die Scheichs der Derwischorden geschwächt werden.

"Unsere republikanische Regierung verfügt über ein Präsidium für religiöse Angelegenheiten. In ihm arbeiten eine ganze Reihe angesehener und verbeamteter Muftis, Prediger und Vorbeter. *Ein jeder weiß um den hohen Kenntnisstand und um die Tugend der dort Tätigen.* Doch sehe ich immer wieder welche, die obwohl sie dort kein Amt innehaben, fortfahren, im gleichen Gewand wie die Amtsträger aufzutreten. *Ich selbst habe unter ihnen viele Unwissende und Ungebildete, ja sogar Analphabeten angetroffen.* Gleichwohl genießen diese *Dilettanten* manchenorts ein Ansehen, als wären sie die natürlichen Vertreter des Volkes. Sie benehmen sich ganz so, als wollten sie verhindern, daß direkt mit dem Volke in Kontakt getreten wird. Ich würde diese Subjekte gerne fragen: 'Wer hat euch eine solche Aufgabe gegeben und euch eine solche Kompetenz zugesprochen? (...) Dem Volke möchte ich einschärfen, daß es nicht angebracht ist, diesem Treiben tatenlos zuzusehen."[58]

Ein Mittel zur Überwindung dieses Widerspruchs zwischen den begrenzten Kompetenzen des *Präsidiums* einerseits und dem angestrebten Ansehen der Behörde andererseits war stets, Persönlichkeiten mit hoher Reputation an seine Spitze zu berufen. Der erste Präsident der

[58] Mustafa Kemal in seiner Rede vom 30. August 1925 in Kastamonu, *Atatürk'ün söylev ve demeçleri*, Band II, S. 225-226.

Behörde, Rıfat Börekçi, stand ihr von 1924 bis 1941 vor. Börekçi war lange Jahre Mufti in Ankara und einer der wichtigsten Persönlichkeiten im Befreiungskrieg. Er stellte sich offen gegen die Fetwa des in Istanbul verbliebenen Şeyh ul-İslâm, die den Befreiungskrieg verurteilte, und er war darüber hinaus einer der hohen Ulema unter den Abgeordneten des ersten Parlaments. Der zweite Präsident der Behörde, Şerefeddin Yaltkaya, hatte das Amt zwischen 1942 und 1947 inne. Der Ordinarius, der auch an osmanischen Medresen gelehrt hatte, galt als herausragender Dogmatiker. Seine umfassende Kenntnis der arabischen Literatur bescherte ihm darüberhinaus Anerkennung in akademischen Kreisen. Besonders aufschlußreich ist 1947 die Ernennung des dritten Prädienten Ahmet Hamdi Akseki durch İsmet İnönü. In der Zweiten Konstitution[59] war Akseki einer der führenden Theoretiker der islamistischen Strömungen. Er war in der Bevölkerung hoch angesehen und hatte bereits seit 1924 einen Platz in den hohen Rängen der Behörde.[60] Seine Ernennung fiel in die letzten Jahre der Einparteienherrschaft, die Vorbereitungen zur Etablierung eines Mehrparteiensystem waren bereits im Gange, und die Opposition setzte der Regierung besonders in religiösen Frage zunehmend stärker zu. In diesem Klima, in dem die innen- und außenpolitischen Parameter auf eine liberalere Religionspolitik und eine Ausweitung der religiösen Erziehung hindeuteten, ist die Entscheidung İnönüs für Akseki leicht nachzuvollziehen.[61] Nicht übersehen werden darf, daß alle drei während der Einparteienperiode ernannten Präsidenten, wenn auch nicht von Rechts wegen so doch faktisch, auf Lebenszeit berufen worden waren und im Amte starben.

Mit dem Übergang zum Mehrparteiensystem fand dieser Brauch sein Ende. Jetzt zeigte auch die Spitze des *Präsidiums* verstärkt Unbeständigkeit und Opportunismus, und sein Ansehen schwand weiter.

Siehe die Liste der Amtszeiten auf der folgenden Seite! ➔

[59] [1908-1913]

[60] Vgl. zur Biographie Aksekis und zu seiner Tätigkeiten in der früheren Republik: İsmail Kara, Bizden biri olarak Ahmet Hamdi Akseki, in: ders. Şeyhefendi'nin rüyasındaki Türkiye, İstanbul Kitabevi, Istanbul 1998, S. 23-30.

[61] Ganz ähnlich gelagert war 1949 -- wiederum durch İsmet İnönü -- die Ernennung Mehmet Şemsettin Günaltays, eines weiteren Islamisten der Zweiten Konstitutionsperiode, zum Ministerpräsidenten.

Präsident	Amtszeit	Dauer:	Jahre,Monate
Rıfat Börekçi	04. 04. 1924	05. 03. 1941	17,00
Şerefeddin Yaltkaya	14. 01. 1942	23. 04. 1947	5,03
Ahmet Hamdi Akseki	29. 04. 1947	09. 01. 1951	4,08
Eyüp Sabri Hayırlıoğlu	02. 04. 1951	10. 06. 1960	9,00
Ömer Nasuhi Bilmen	29. 06. 1960	06. 04. 1961	0,09
Hasan Hüsnü Erdem	06. 04. 1961	13. 10. 1964	2,05
Tevfik Gerçeker	15. 10. 1964	16. 12. 1965	1,01
İbrahim Elmalı	17. 12. 1965	25. 10. 1966	0,11
Ali Rıza Hakses	25. 10. 1966	15. 01. 1968	1,02
Lütfi Doğan (Stellv.)	15. 01. 1968	25. 08. 1972	4,07
Dr. Lütfi Doğan	26. 08. 1972	26. 07. 1976	4,00
Doç. Dr. Süleyman Ateş	28. 07. 1976	07. 02. 1978	1,06
Tayyar Altıkulaç	09. 02. 1978	10. 11. 1986	8,09
Doç. Dr. Sait Yazıcıoğlu	17. 06. 1987	02. 01.1992	4,06
Mehmet Nuri Yılmaz	02. 01. 1992	zur Zeit im Amte[62]	

[62] Vgl. bis zur Amtszeit Dr. Lütfi Doğans: Aslanpay 1973, S. 93 und bis zur Amtszeit M. Sait Yazıcıoğlus: *Diyanet İşleri Başkanlığı teşkilat albümü 1924-1989*, Diyanet İşleri Başkanlığı Yay., Ankara 1989, S. 31., ferner: İrfan Yücel, *Diyanet İşleri İslâm Ansiklopedisi*, No. IX, S. 460. Hinsichtlich der Tage und Monate finden sich in den Werken kleinere Unstimmigkeiten.

Die Tabelle ist in mehrerer Hinsicht aufschlußreich. Die Regierung der Demokratischen Partei (DP) hielt an der von den CHP-Regierungen übernommenen Praxis fest, sie beließ Ahmet Hamdi Akseki im Amte und entließ auch den von ihr selbst eingesetzten Eyüb Sabri Hayırlıoğlu nicht.

Die erste Abberufung wurde sofort nach der Militärintervention von 1960 vorgenommen. Hayırlıoğlu mußte sein Amt an den Mufti von Istanbul, Ömer Nasuhi Bilmen, abgeben, der seinerseits bereits nach neun Monaten entlassen wurde.

Dessen Nachfolger Hasan Hüsnü Erdem wurde umgehend in den Ruhestand geschickt, als er sich weigerte, ein gegen die Nuristen gerichtetes Pamphlet im Namen des *Präsidiums* zu veröffentlichen. Autor des umstritten Textes war sein kurz vorher ernannte Stellvertreter, der pensionierte Vizeadmiral Sadettin Evrin, der gleichzeitig Mitglied eines Derwischorden war.[63] Der Text wurde anschließend mit dem Titel "Über den Nurismus"[64] in der Broschüren-Reihe des *Präsidiums* veröffentlicht, ohne daß ein Verfasser genannt wurde. Im gleichen Jahre brachte das *Präsidium* zwei weitere anonyme Streitschriften heraus, deren Aufmachung der Anti-Nuristenschrift gleicht. Eine, als deren Verfasser ebenfalls Hasan Hüsnü Erdem gilt, war gegen den Orden der Biberiye[65] gerichtet, und eine weitere trug den Titel:"Islamische Argumente gegen den Kommunismus"[66]. Die drei Veröffentlichungen bilden gewissermaßen die politische Frontstellung der 60er Jahre auf der Ebene des *Präsidiums* ab. Sie richten sich gegen die beiden 'Hauptfeinde' der Republik, die 'religiöse Reaktion' (irtica) und den 'Kommunismus'.

İbrahim Elmalı, einer der darauffolgenden Präsidenten geriet über die Ernennung eines Mitarbeiters in Auseinandersetzung mit dem zuständigen Staatsminister Refet Sezgin, er wurde im Amte beleidigt und

[63] Der abberufene Präsident Hasan Hüseyin Erdem hat den Vorgang später öffentlich gemacht, vgl. Eşref Edip, Sabık Diyanet İşleri Başkanı'nın tekaüde sevki nasıl oldu? *Yeni İstiklâl*, No. 196, vom 12. Mai 1965, S. 3. Zu seinem Kontrahenten Sadettin Evrin vgl. Mustafa Kara, Doğumunun 100. yıldönümünde mutasavvıf bir general: Sadettin Evrin, *İLAM Araştırma Dergisi*, No. II/1, Januar-Juni 1997, S. 55-81. Vgl. auch Diyanet İşleri Başkanlığı'nda Hurufîlik hareketleri: Sadettin Evrin Kur'an âyetlerini ebced hesabına vurarak siyasî hadiselerle bağlantılar kuruyor, *Yeni İstkilâl*, No. 196, vom 12. Mai 1965, S. 3.

[64] *Nurculuk hakkında*, Ankara 1964. Ein Gegenpamphlet trägt den Titel *Diyanet İşleri Reisliği Nurculuk hakkında ne diyor?*, Uhuvvet Yay. Izmir 1964.

[65] *Biberiye tarikatı hakkında*, Ankara 1964.

[66] *Komünizm karşısında İslâmî görüşler*, Ankara 1964.

abgesetzt.

Nimmt man Tayyar Altıkulaç, der auf eigenen Wunsch in den Ruhestand ging, und M. Sait Yazıcıoğlu, der an die Universität zurückkehrte, aus, läßt sich formulieren, daß seit 1951 alle Präsidenten von den politischen Autoritäten abberufen oder in den Ruhestand versetzt worden sind und daß es dabei in der Regel zu unschönen Vorfällen gekommen ist. Das zeigt, wie sehr das *Präsidium* und sein Präsident zum Zankapfel der Politik geworden sind. Zur Verdeutlichung hier die Stellungnahmen zweier ehemaliger Präsidenten:

“Die Verstimmungen, mit denen wir im *Präsidium* fast täglich zu kämpfen haben, resultieren daraus, daß die politische Autorität die Kompetenzen, die seinem Präsidenten per Gesetz zustehen, in ihrem Sinne zu nutzen versucht. (...) Es fehlt ohne Zweifel an religiöser Autorität. Grund dafür ist, daß das *Präsidium* als verlängerter Arm der Politik erscheint und daß bestimmte Kreise diese Situation ausnutzen.”[67]

“Das *Präsidium* ist eine lendenlahme Institution, mehr noch es ist die lendenlahmste Institution in der Türkei. (...) Im Grunde liegt das an seiner rechtlichen Verfaßtheit. (...) Die Ungereimtheiten in der Bestimmung des Laizismus wirken auf das *Präsidium* zurück. Das Verhältnis von Politik und *Präsidium* ist nach wie vor unbefriedigend. (...) Auch in der Vergangenheit war dieses Verhältnis meist problembeladen.”[68]

Nach 1971 kam zum Einfluß der Regierung auf das *Präsidium* noch der Einfluß der einzelnen Parteien, nach 1973 insbesondere der der *Nationalen Heilspartei* (Millî Selamet Partisi, MSP), die in diesem Jahre an der Regierunsskoalition beteiligt wurde und den für das *Präsidium* zuständigen Staatsminister stellte. Damals wurde sein bis dahin ‘laizistischster Präsident’ Dr. Lütfi Doğan durch Süleyman Ateş abgelöst und der seinerzeitige Stellvertretende Präsident Tayyar Altıkulaç, welcher der MSP immer fern stand, wurde ins Nationale Erziehungsministerium abgedrängt und dort zum Chef des *Generaldirektoriums*

[67] Tayyar Altıkulaç, Daha yürekli bir Diyanet, *Altınoluk*, No. 93, vom November 1993, S. 20-21.

[68] M. Sait Yazıcıoğlu, Diyanet en sancılı muessese, ebenda, S. 16 und 18.

für Religionserziehung (Din Eğitimi Genel Müdürlüğü) ernannt.[69] Seit dieser Zeit kann sich diese politische Strömung des Vorwurfs, die Religion für ihre Zwecke zu instrumentalisieren, noch weniger als früher erwehren. Nach der Wahl von 1977 kehrte Tayyar Altıkulaç mit der Unterschrift des neuen Ministerpräsidenten Bülent Ecevit, als ihr Präsident an die Behörde zurück. Nach dem Putsch von 1980 spielte Altıkulaç eine zentrale Rolle in der Religionspolitik der Militärregierung und vermittelte insbesondere zwischen den verschiedenen muslimischen Gemeinden und Strömungen auf der einen und der Regierung auf der anderen Seite.[70]

Wie sehr das Präsidium in die politischen Auseinandersetzungen verstrickt ist, ist auch an den politischen Biographien eines guten Teils seiner Präsidenten ablesbar. Rıfat Börekçi war vor seiner Amtszeit Abgeordneter der Ersten Nationalversammlung und Mufti von Ankara. Eyüb Sabri Hayırlıoğlu war Abgeordneter der Zweiten Nationalversammlung für die CHP. İbrahim Elmalı war Mitglied der *Nationspartei* (Millet Partisi, MP) und später Abgeordneter für die *Demokratische Partei* (DP). Lütfi Doğan war in verschiedenen Legislaturperioden Abgeordneter für die MSP, die RP und schließlich für deren Nachfolgerin, die *Tugendpartei* (Fazilet Partisi, FP). Sein akademischer Namensvetter Dr. Lütfi Doğan war Abgeordneter für die CHP und unter der Zweiten Regierung Ecevit der für das *Präsidium* zuständige Staatsminister. Daß Tayyar Altıkulaç auch Abgeordneter für die DYP war, ist bereits erwähnt worden.

Die Liste zeigt außerdem, daß fünf der bisherigen Präsidenten des *Präsidiums*, circa ein Drittel der Amtsinhaber, nur weniger als zwei Jahre und sieben weitere nur weniger als fünf Jahre tätig sein konnten. Ein großer Teil ihrer Vorsitzenden leitet diese für die Türkei wichtige Institution ohne die Zeit zu haben, ihrer tatsächlich Herr zu werden,

---

[69] Sowohl in der CHP-MSP-Koalition als auch in den Regierungen der *Nationalen Front* (Milliyetçi Cephe) stellte die MSP den kleineren Koalitionspartner. Trotzdem vermochte die Partei Erbakans es damals, den für das *Präsidium* zuständigen Staatsminister zu stellen. Daß die neue Partei Erbakans, die *Wohlfahrtspartei* (Refah Partisi, RP), obwohl sie sich mittlerweile zur größten Partei gemausert hatte, es in ihrer Koalition mit der *Partei des rechten Weges* (Doğru Yol Partisi, DYP) nicht vermochte, diesen Posten erneut zu besetzen, hat sicher mit ihrem Verhalten Anfang der 70er Jahre zu tun.

[70] Aufschlußreich ist jedoch, daß es Tayyar Altıkulaç unter der RP-DYP-Koalition nicht gelungen ist, zu dem für das *Präsidium* zuständigen Staatsminister zu werden, obwohl er damals als Abgeordneter für die DYP im Parlament saß.

eigene Vorstellungen zu entwickeln und sie in die Tat umzusetzen. Die extrem kurzen Amtszeiten sind gleichzeitig ein Hinweis auf die mangelnde Sicherheit, die für eine gestalterische Tätigkeit Voraussetzung ist. So richtig es ist, daß das Problem extrem kurzer Amtszeiten die gesamte Bürokratie der Türkei belastet, so sehr ist der Verweis auf die ganz anderen Gepflogenheiten gerechtfertigt, die andernorts in Fragen der Leitung großer Religionsgemeinschaften herrschen.

Zum Abschluß der Erörterung über die Präsidenten des *Präsidiums* sei noch auf zwei, unseres Erachtens wichtige, Einzelheiten hingewiesen: Darauf, daß die Präsidenten -- beginnend mit Tayyar Altıkulaç -- heute den ehemals genau beachteten Brauch, die Übernahme des Amtes nach außen mit dem Tragen eines Vollbartes zu symbolisieren, aufgegeben haben und darauf, daß die Regel, Akademiker zu berufen, die sich mit der Amtsübernahme Dr. Lütfi Doğan etabliert hatte, mit der Ernennung des heutigen Präsidenten Mehmet Nuri Yılmaz fallengelassen wurde.

Schlußbemerkung

Ahmed Hamdi Başar, der einige Jahre als Wirtschaftsberater Kemal Atatürks tätig war, schildert in seinem Buch eine Episode aus dem Jahre 1930: Nach der Schließung der *Freien Republikanischen Partei* (Serbest Cumhuriyet Fırkası, SCF)[71] hätten Mustafa Kemal und er die kemalistischen Prinzipien und darunter auch den Laizismus diskutiert. Nachdem er, so Başar, auf grundlegende Unterschiede zwischen Christentum und Islam hingewiesen habe, habe er zu Kemal Atatürk gesagt:

"(Anders als das Christentum) kennt der Islam keine Trennung der Religion von der Welt und von weltlichen Angelegenheiten. Besser gesagt, der Islam geht von den weltlichen Gegebenheiten aus, er bezieht sich auf die Vernunft und erkennt die Volkssouveränität genauso an wie eine Änderung der gesellschaftlichen Ordnungsregeln im Laufe der Zeit. Er etabliert keine Dogmata und schreibt vor, die Vernunft zu gebrauchen. [Doch] das Wesen des Islams wurde entstellt und es entstand eine eigene religiöse Klasse [die Ulema]. Die von dieser Klasse hervorgebrachten Institutionen haben der Gesellschaft schweren

[71] [Nach sechsmonatigem Bestehen am 18. Dezember 1930 verboten.]

Schaden zugefügt. [Im Grunde] gibt es heute keine [originäre] Religion mehr. *Wir sollten unter Laizismus nicht die Trennung der Religion von der Welt verstehen, sondern die Notwendigkeit, zu verhindern, daß die Religion in den Händen einer eigenen Klasse zu einer Reihe von Dogmata wird und diese Klasse die weltlichen Angelegenheiten unter ihre Herrschaft nimmt.* Alles was wir im Namen des Laizismus verfolgen, das können wir guten Gewissens auch im Namen des Islams unternehmen. *Aber wenn wir versuchen, die Religion von der Welt zu trennen, entfernen wir uns unweigerlich vom Islam und betreiben letztendlich Atheismus.* Das Christentum kann getrennt von der weltlichen Ordnung existieren, der Islam nicht. (...)"[72]

Başar schreibt weiter, daß er auf der gleichen Reise dem Abgeordneten Dr. Reşit Galib[73], mit dem er -- wie er schreibt -- hinsichtlich des Laizismus gleicher Meinung war, folgendes gesagt habe:

"In der Form, in der wir heute den Laizismus anwenden, ist er nichts anderes als Atheismus. Im Islam bedeutet die Trennung der Religion von der Welt nun einmal Atheismus. So opponiert die Religion denn auch gegen alles, was wir unternehmen. Sie tragen einen europäischen Krempenhut, in den Augen der Religion werden Sie zum Ungläubigen. Die Schriftreform, die neuen Gesetze, kurz und gut, alles war wir zur Modernisierung unternehmen, bewegt sich außerhalb der Religion. Und jene, welche das veranlassen, gelten als Ungläubige. Das führt dazu, daß diejenigen im Volke, die gläubig sind, der Regierung und dem Staate mißtrauen. Das Volk entbehrt entweder der Religion oder der Regierung. (...) Wenn wir den Laizismus in der jetzigen Form beibehalten, opfern wir den Islam und haben nichts, was wir an seine Stelle setzen könnten. (...)

Es gilt nicht, die Religion aus der Gesellschaft zu vertreiben, sondern die Religion zu erhalten, indem wir sie in den Dienst der kemalistischen Reformen stellen. Wir erreichen unsere Ziele nicht dadurch, daß wir die Moscheen leer stehen lassen oder abreißen und uns statt dessen in den Volkshäusern (Halk Evleri) versammeln. Wir müssen das Volk da ansprechen, wo es ist, in der Moschee. Es ist durchaus möglich, aus den Moscheen moderne Volkshäuser zu machen, die

---

[72] Ahmed Hamdi Başar, *Atatürk'le üç ay ve 1930'dan sonra Türkiye*, Istanbul 1945, S. 49, Hervorhebungen İ. K.

[73] Galib, der 1934 starb, wurde 1932 Chef des Nationalen Erziehungsministeriums und ist einer der Architekten des Projekts "Nationalreligion".

Klasse der Religionsgelehrten abzuschaffen und alle [Parteimitglieder] im Namen der Religion und der Welt sprechen zu lassen. So betrachtet ist der Islam die modernste und fortschrittlichste Religion überhaupt."[74]

Fast scheint es so, als hätte sich die Religionspolitik der frühen Republik die Vorschläge Ahmed Hamdi Başars zu Herzen genommen.

[74] Başar 1945, S. 51, Hervorhebungen İ. K.

Cemaleddin Kaplan's Union of Islamic Societies and Communities

THE İCCB IN GERMANY

Fulya Atacan
Marmara Üniversitesi, Istanbul

International migration is a universal fact in the twentieth century. After World War II, industrialised European countries started to accept people from different countries in order to fill the vacuum of labour force. Later on, a new type of immigration began in which people were looking for jobs abroad without the permission of the host countries.

Turkish workers also have migrated to Germany under the framework of the bilateral agreement between Turkey and Germany. The numbers of Turkish workers in Germany rose rapidly between 1968 and 1973. Even though recruitment ended in 1973, the number of immigrants continued to grow and today Turks are the largest immigrant group there. Most of the Turkish immigrants are Muslim -- Sunni and Alevi. At the beginning they were guest workers and they planned to stay only for a short period. They tried to fulfill their religious duties and needs in small rooms, since Islam in Germany has not had an official structure. But particularly after family reunion and when it became clear that they were going to stay in the country, the immigrants started to establish mosques on their own initiatives.

Islam has become visible in European countries. In this process not only have Muslim immigrants created new types of Islamic organisations under the legal structure of the host European countries --even though most of these organisations have some connections with their mother organisations in the home countries -- but their way of interpreting Islam has also changed.

The policies of the host countries towards immigrants and foreigners, the legal structure in this respect, and the immigrants' situation in these countries have resulted in different experiences in different countries. In this process the social structure of the immigrants has varied according to their education and occupation.

Against this background the *Union of Islamic Societies and Communities* (İslami Cemiyetler ve Cemaatler Birliği, İCCB) was established by Cemaleddin Kaplan (Hocaoğlu) in Cologne, Germany, in 1985. As a result of internal conflict, a group of members broke away in 1987 and again in 1989. The Union changed its name to *Union of Islamic Communities* (İslami Cemaatler Birliği, İCB) in 1990.

The leader of the group: Cemaleddin Kaplan (Hocaoğlu)

Cemaleddin Kaplan was born in a small town called İspir in the province of Erzurum in 1926. He started to receive religious education from his father at a very early age. Kaplan first worked as an imam (preacher) for eleven years in a small village called Kong and later in Erzurum. After completing his military service, he passed the exams and followed primary, secondary and lycee education as an external student. In 1961 he enrolled in the Faculty of Theology in Ankara. After graduation in 1965, he worked for the *Directorate for Religious Affairs* (Diyanet İşleri Başkanlığı, DİB) as an inspector.[1] Working as a mufti in Adana between 1966 and 1981, he established good relations with the military government and played an active role in the elimination of the Süleymancıs[2] at that time.[3]

He stood as a candidate of the *National Salvation Party* (Millî Sela-

---

[1] C. Hocaoğlu (Kaplan), *Tebliğcinin el kitabı*, Tebliğ Yay., Köln 1986.

[2] Süleymancıs are a sub-group of the Naqshbandi order in Turkey. They are well organised in Turkey and among the Turks in Europe. About this group see H. Algar, Der Nakşibendi-Orden in der republikanischen Türkei, in *Jahrbuch zur Geschichte und Gesellschaft des Vorderen und Mittleren Orients 1984*, J. Blaschke, M. van Bruinessen (eds.), Express Ed., Berlin 1985, pp. 182-185; Ruşen Çakır, *Ayet ve slogan*, Metis Yay., Istanbul 1990, pp. 125-139; F. Atacan, Anadolu Gazetesi ve 'Süleymancılar', *Toplumbilim* 2, 1993, pp. 135-152.

[3] Uğur Mumcu, *Rabıta*, Tekin Yay., Istanbul 1987, p.11, Çakır 1990, pp. 130-131.

met Partisi, MSP)[4] in Erzurum for the 1977 elections to the National Assembly but he did not win. A complaint was made against him and two of his friends in 1978 because of his political activities and an investigation was opened. After the military coup in 1980, fearing that he would be penalised he retired from the *Directorate* on his own initiative in 1981.

Just after retirement Kaplan emigrated to Germany in December 1981. He worked for *Avrupa Milli Görüş Teşkilatı* (AMGT)[5], in short Millî Görüş, and was appointed as Head of the Commission of Guidance and Fetwa of this association, a post he occupied until 1983.

It has been claimed that Cemaleddin Kaplan was sent to Germany by Necmettin Erbakan, the leader of the National Salvation Party until 1980 and later the leader of the Welfare Party, because of internal fragmentations of the AMGT, with instructions to put it in order.[6] While he was answering a question concerning his way of arrival to Germany and his relations with the MSP at that time, Kaplan partly rejected this claim and said that after the military coup in 1980, he thought about his students' position in Turkey and decided to take them to Europe. He said: "I came to Berlin before and I knew that there is freedom of thought in this country. So I thought that I could bring my students here and raise them as I wish. I made my prepara-

4 The National Salvation Party was established as the successor of the National Order Party (Millî Nizâm Partisi, MNP) in 1972. It was -- like all other political parties -- forced to dissolve after the coup d'etat of 1980 but in 1983 it reappeared as Welfare Party. See Binnaz Toprak, *Islam and political development in Turkey*, Brill, Leiden 1981; A.Y. Sarıbay, *Türkiye'de modernleşme, din ve parti politikası,* Alan Yay., Istanbul 1985.

5 AMGT started to be organised in the 1970s in Germany. It was recognised officially in 1985. It has about 400 branches including women's and youth sections all over Europe. It is a member of the *Islamic Federation* which was founded in 1981 and has been striving for the recognition as an *Organisation of Public Law* (Körperschaft des öffentlichen Rechts) in order to be able to conduct Islamic education in Berlin. AMGT dominates the *Islamic Federation* which also has German, Iranian, Iraqi and other Arab member-organisations. AMGT was closely related to the National Salvation Party and now is related to the Welfare Party. See: AMGT Genel Sekreteri Ali Yüksel ile röpörtaj, *Dava* 26, May 1992, pp. 23-29; H. Thomä-Venske, The religious life of Muslims in Berlin, in *The new Islamic presence in Western Europe*, T. Gerholm & Y.G. Lithman (eds.), Mansell Publ., London 1988, p.81; A. Gitmez & C. Wilpert, A micro-society or an ethnic community? Social organization and ethnicity amongst Turkish immigrants in Berlin in Immigrant associations in Europe, J. Rex, D. Joly & C. Wilpert (eds), Gower, Brookfield, 1987, pp. 119-120.

6 T. Hacıkadiroğlu, *Kaplan'ın tükenişi*, Yeni Yay., Ankara,1989, pp. 95-99, 107-109.

tions. I had a green passport.[7] While I was preparing for my trip, a friend of mine called me and asked me to go to Ankara. I went to Ankara and he said that Mr. Erbakan would send Mr. ... to Europe and they needed another person. He asked me to go to Germany. I said I was going anyway. I came to Germany with Mr. ... That is how we got here. And then AMGT looked after us. We found a mess here. We tried to sort it out and gave sermons.... The reason for my coming was to educate my students. But here we were faced with the visa problem. Some of my students came here [without a visa] and they were sent back. We could not succeed in our aims."[8]

Establishment of the Kaplan group

Because of his radical approach and his relations with Iran, Kaplan came into conflict with AMGT and his group broke away from it in 1983. Kaplan's followers distributed a proclamation in which they discussed ways of taking over the state through political process or by the way of a call. This happened on 13 August 1983 in the Barbaros Mosque in Cologne. This proclamation created serious conflict and fights between Kaplan's followers and other Milli Görüş members. The incident was considered by the members as "the opening of a new era that is suitable to the soul of the *şeriat* (the Islamic law) and the beginning of a bright future."

The group prepared statutes and elected Cemaleddin Kaplan as *emir* (commander of the faithful) of the group for life. The group was officially organised under the name *Union of Islamic Societies and Communities* in 1985.[9] It has established branches among the Turkish immigrants in Germany, Holland, Belgium, France, and Denmark. The group has a very small number of followers in Turkey and it seems that these followers are mainly the relatives of the Turkish immigrants in Europe.

At the beginning the Union had a great number of members but in

---

7 Since he worked as a senior state employee at the Directorate for Religious Affairs he had a right to have this sort of a diplomatic passport.

8 From his tape cassette called *Yazarlarla sohbet*.

9 Founders of the Union were Cemaleddin Kaplan, Ahmet Polat, Selahattin Yazıcı, Hasan Hayri Kılıç, Seyfettin Özkan, Süleyman Aslan, Mustafa Özçelik, İbrahim Kaba, and Hilmi Elgünlü. Mumcu, p. 13.

the course of time it lost many of them and has become really small compared with the other Islamic groups and organisations which have been active among the Turkish immigrants in Europe. Internal conflicts and close relations with Iran at that time played an important role in this decline.

The first conflict occurred in 1987. A group of people headed by Ahmet Polat left the Union. They claimed that Cemaleddin Kaplan was receiving assistance from Iran in the form of financial aid and that he obeyed orders from Iran. But the main subject of conflict was money. Kaplan was accused of taking money which had been collected from the members. Bank accounts belonging to the group had been opened in the names of Cemaleddin Kaplan and other leading members like Ahmet Polat or Hasan Hayri Kılıç. In this context, the way of spending money collected from the members has always been a main subject of dispute.

Among the members one group claims that they fully trust their commander, another group admits that misuse of collected money is possible. Since most of the members of this group have a low income, working in unskilled jobs or being unemployed, it is understandable that money is a sensitive issue. Money is a problem for many members and since their average income is more or less known, they are aware of who earns enough money and who does not. If, then, someone starts to spend much or has a relatively comfortable life, the question of how and where he finds the money for it comes to people's minds and they start to gossip.

A second important conflict and breakaway was experienced in 1989. This time, it had an ideological content. A group of people headed by Hasan Hayri Kılıç criticised Kaplan, claiming that he had no real knowledge of Islam, that he harmed some imams in the group, that he stole money and used it for his private needs, etc. And Kaplan's followers claimed that Kılıç and his friends were strict followers of Iran and that they had converted to the Shia and been bought off by Iran. The real reason behind this conflict was relations with Iran.

The discourse of Kaplan's group and his position in the group are very similar to Khumaini's. The similarities and even identical features between the Islamic constitution which was published by the group and the constitution of the Islamic Republic of Iran have been shown in detail.[10]

Cemaleddin Kaplan himself visited Iran in 1982 and later some group members also went there. Group members could not obtain visas from Saudi Arabia for the pilgrimage in 1988. It is said that the group's sympathy for Iran was the reason for this.

The group members own books which are published by the Propagation Centre of the Islamic Republic of Iran in Turkish. Iran sends a journal called "İslam'a Çağrı" (Call to Islam) to the group members regularly.

It is also claimed that Kaplan has received money from Iran. The group members have denied this accusation and one of the members told me: "Some people claim that the Hoca [Cemaleddin Kaplan] is supported by Iran. But he has said that our approach to Iran is the *Ehl-i Sünnet* (Sunni) approach. Of course it was an Islamic revolution and we should support it, but we cannot follow their path. They help a lot but the Hoca says that they help today and they will ask to change our *mezheb* (confession) tomorrow. They will try to convert us to Shia. They do not help without any expectation. Some people from the Iranian embassy came here. Here, I mean my house. They met with the Hoca. Previously they had invited some learned men from Turkey and other places. The Hoca went to the Iranian embassy. When they talked there, they offered him 30 000 DM but he refused it." It is clear that at the beginning the group had relatively good relations with Iran but later these relations broke down or took a more indirect form.

Iran is the first country in the world to have carried out an Islamic revolution. Consequently, it became a kind of centre of attraction for the radical Islamic groups all over the world just as the U.S.S.R., as the first country which carried out the Socialist revolution, did for communist or socialist groups. On the one hand Iran, as an isolated country, tried to export her revolution to other countries or at least tried to establish good relations with other Islamic movements which were and are mainly in the opposition in their home countries. On the other hand the appealing side of the Islamic revolution made many Islamic groups look towards Iran even when they did not have any direct contact with the Iranian government. But soon after the very deep-

10 Mumcu, p. 47-60.

rooted conflict, namely that between Shia and Sunni, came to the surface. The *mezheb* dimension of the Islamic revolution in Iran was questioned.

It seems that the *mezheb* dimension of the Islamic revolution alienated many Sunnis except very few radical groups. Even most radical Sunni groups prefer to follow Sunni leaders like Sayyid Qutb, Mawdudi, or Fathi Yakin rather than Khumaini. It seems that Kaplan, realising this problem, denied his relations with Iran and started to criticise her. It is not possible for an academic to know the real content of this relationship.

It has been claimed that the group consisted of about 12 000 or 15 000 members in Europe and in Turkey in the 1990s. But it seems to have been getting smaller particularly after the death of Cemaleddin Kaplan in 1995. Since his death his son, Metin Kaplan, has headed the group.[11]

The ideology of the Kaplan group

According to Cemaleddin Kaplan, Islam has the power to answer all questions human beings have and will have. Islam consists of four main parts; *itikad* (conviction), *ibadet* (worship), *muamelat* (this world, state and politics) and *ukubat* (punishment). He claims that in Turkey people can partly practise the first two parts of their belief but they are not allowed to practise and even to talk about the other ones.[12]

Kaplan insists that Islam is not only a religion but also politics. That is why he considers that Islam without politics and a state is unthinkable. Consequently, he calls those who propose and defend the separation of state and religion *kafir* (unbeliever), and *mürted* (apostate).[13]

The aim of the group is to establish an Islamic state in which the Quran will be the constitution and the *şeriat* will be the law. Accord-

11 After Cemaleddin Kaplan's death the struggle for the leadership led to another split in the group in 1996.

12 C. Hocaoğlu (Kaplan), *Tüm İslami kuruluşlara tebliğ*, one of the communiqués written by Kaplan, photocopied and delivered by the group. Kaplan gave it to the author of this article in 1990 in Germany.

13 C. Hocaoğlu (Kaplan), *Tebliğ ve metod*, Tebliğ Yay., Köln 1986, pp. 17-20.

ing to Kaplan, since sovereignty belongs to God, most of the current states in Muslim countries are in the stage of *cahiliye* (ignorance). That is why people must act against them. He insists that there is no place for concessions in this struggle. The source of the movement is the Quran and the example for it is the prophet Muhammad.

To prepare to reach this aim Muslims must be educated in three different places, namely the *medrese* (religious school), the *tekke* (dervish lodge) and the *kışla* (barracks). In the medrese they will learn the şeriat; in the tekke they will learn the *tarikat* (sufism) and in the barracks they will learn how to use a gun. Only after this education, he claims, one can be a proper human being.[14]

The method to reach the group's aim is to call people to Islam. The group members must call people everywhere and in every condition to Islam. They must start with their closest friends and relatives. On the one hand they will carry the propaganda of their ideology in face to face relations and on the other hand they will utilise all means of the mass media.[15]

Kaplan indicates that the group members will face many difficulties while they are trying to invite people to Islam, but he says: "God will not give you an Islamic state without you being made prisoner, being beaten, or being killed (*şehit olmadan*). He asks "Did God give it to the Prophet and his companions without these difficulties?"[16] One of the group members writes the following; "It is not easy to go to heaven. On the road to heaven there are prisons, exiles, hospitals, tortures, leaving behind all your property and unhesitatingly giving your life when it is necessary."[17]

According to the group, humanity is divided into two *camps* (*hizib*), the camp of God and the camp of Satan. A person is either in the first camp or in the second. These two camps are completely different. Only those who get on the road of God and live under his flag are brothers.[18] At this point, the group members must first struggle

[14] C. Hocaoğlu, Barbaros Hareketi ve bir dönüm noktası, *Ümmet-i Muhammed,* 15-31 August 1988, p. 8.

[15] *Tebliğcinin el kitabı,* p. 94.

[16] *Yazarlarla sohbet.*

[17] S. A. A. Settaroğlu, İslam Devletine giden yokuşlar çilelerle aşılır, *Tebliğ,* 15 January 1988, p. 3.

[18] Biz hangi safda bulunuyoruz? *Ümmet-i Muhammed,* 1 December 1990, p. 2.

with their own selves, and must get organised. The group calls this process *cihad* (fight in favour of religion).

According to the Kaplan group, *cihad* is an order of God. So the punishment for those who neglect this duty is to go to Hell. *Cihad* will continue until all the people in the world accept the sovereignty of God. The group claims there are five different types of *cihad; cihad* made with property; *cihad* made with the call; *cihad* made with education; political *cihad*; and *cihad* as an armed struggle.[19]

Kaplan says that today's conditions are not suitable for armed struggle. That is why the group members must only propagate Islam to other people. At this stage they should not be involved in any terrorist acts. But when the conditions are right for armed struggle to establish an Islamic state in Turkey, the group must engage in it. Kaplan claims that it is not possible to come to power by way of election in a democratic society, because this is not written in God's law.

According to the Kaplan group, two conditions are necessary to start the armed struggle. First the group must have a great number of followers and then it needs educated cadres. Kaplan claims that those who have been having religious education in the group will be the ministers, mayors and officers of the coming Islamic state. In answer to some critics who indicate the group members' lack of secular education, he says, "Education is not needed. Who had a university degree among the Companions of the Prophet? As long as they have conscience and conviction they can have the knowledge later."

It is clear that this approach promises them a very high social status in the future Islamic state, which is just the opposite of their low social status today. Therefore one needs to work hard now.

The aim of the Kaplan group is to establish an Islamic state in Turkey. It has a long term plan for this, in which the struggle starts with one's own self and continues to an armed struggle via a process of exhortation of others.

19 İşte davamız, *Ümmet-i Muhammed,* 15 April 1990, p. 5.

Democracy and communism

Kaplan's group rejects democracy and communism as political systems. According to Kaplan there are two idols at the world agenda. Communism, which rejects God, has collapsed but democracy is still standing. He claims that even though democracy does not deny the existence of God, it takes the right of sovereignty from God and gives it to the people. So there is no difference between the two in essence. Communism is openly a *tagut* (false god) but democracy is "an insidious, hypocritical, and mischiefmaking system and is consequently a non-Muslim regime.[20]

The differences between Islam and democracy are explained in the group's magazine called *Tebliğ* (announcement), as follows; in democracy there is a division of power and responsibilities. But in Islam "responsibility belongs only to the governor and he is accepted as the only responsible person. "In other words, in the state structure responsibility belongs to the head of the state (*halifa*) and in the process of community building, responsibility belongs to the leader of the community (*emir*). In a democracy, the majority of the people can make decisions and the head of the state does not have the right to change or to disapprove them. But in Islam, the head of the state has the right of decision making. He may take into consideration the opinion of the majority, or minority, or only himself. In democracy every issue is on the agenda of society and may be discussed. However in Islam, if an issue is considered and explained in a verse in the Quran, in a hadith or in Islamic law, it cannot be discussed. Everybody must obey the rules of Islamic law. Only subjects which are not considered in Islamic law can be discussed. Even in this condition, the ultimate authority to decide on the subject belongs to the head of the state. In a democracy the head of state is elected for a period of time but in Islam he is elected for life."[21]

One of the group members explains democracy like this "According to the ideologues of democracy only the majority of the people has the right to make a new law, to declare something forbidden (*haram*) or permissible (*helal*). If the majority of the people says that

20 C. Hocaoğlu, Dünya'yı fesada veren iki put, *Ümmet-i Muhammed*, 15 October 1990, p. 3.

21 Demokrasi ve İslam, *Tebliğ*, 15 January 1988, p. 3.

using heroine is free, no one can stop its production and consumption. Or if the majority decide that the law of God cannot be applied, the application of religious law becomes a crime, and the people who insist on applying religious law will be punished."[22] One of its members claims that the group will never follow the decision of the majority because they are not democrats. They believe in the sovereignty of God, and they accept only the guidance of the ulema.[23]

Cemaleddin Kaplan believes that democratic systems will collapse as communism has. But the necessary conditions for this are to hate democracy like many people hated communism and to avoid participation in party politics and elections.[24]

Islam and other religions

Since Islam is the last revealed religion and the Quran is the last book of God, Muslims believe that Christianity and Judaism are not as perfect as Islam. Muslims consider that the holy books of Christianity and Judaism have been changed and the original text could not be preserved. This also explains the need of the Quran to correct the errors which were created by people in the course of the history of religions.

Members of Kaplan's group, too, believe that Christianity and Judaism have been corrupted and their adherents have to be invited to accept Islam. For this reason Cemaleddin Kaplan published open letters to the Christian and Jewish religious establishments in the group's magazines. In these letters he said that some parts of the Old and New Testament have been changed while only the Quran has remained unchanged until today. He explained that the Old Testament was valid until the next holy book was revealed to humanity and then it lost its validity. But the Quran is the last book of God and another holy book will not be revealed, as is clearly declared. He said that the Quran was sent to all mankind, not to any particular nation or race, so he called

22 M. Z. Hoca, Asrın tuzağı, *Ümmet-i Muhammed,* 15 June 1990, p. 8.

23 ibid.

24 Dünya'yı fesada veren iki put, p. 3.

on Christians and Jews to convert to Islam.[25]

If the publications of this group and the attitudes of its members are examined, it becomes clear that they define Jews, not Christians, as their enemy. It is well known that animosity towards Jews is very widespread among Islamist movements. This animosity is closely related with the Palestinian problem. The fact that Israel controls Jerusalem is unacceptable to many Islamists.

Among the Kaplan group, this animosity towards Jews is very clear. When the group members have any problems, they blame Jews and start to talk about a "Jewish or Zionist conspiracy". They believe that Jews have shaped the internal and external policies of the U.S.A. This situation also holds good for Turkey and Europe. They claim that Jews in Turkey are the richest people in society and that they run the country. When I told them that the Jewish population in Turkey is very small and that there are poor Jews too, they said, "You don't know anything. Look at America. Look what Israelis are doing to Muslims. You don't realise that they are running the world."

The members of the group believe that Israel will be destroyed one day. One of them said, "While the Jews are controlling Jerusalem, I cannot live comfortably. Israelis do not have any chance. They will disappear. There is a *hadith* saying that the Israelis will disappear. There is no other way."

The social base of the group

Turkish immigrants came to Germany as *guestworkers* (Gastarbeiter) to fill the need of labour force for postwar Germany. Their aim was to save enough money in order to establish a secure future in Turkey. But in the course of time it became clear that they would not go back. When they decided to stay in Germany permanently, their status as guestworkers became a problem for them.

As Mandel indicated "...guests are by definition temporary, and are expected to return home. Guests are bound to rules and regula-

---

25 C. Hocaoğlu, Kilise mensublarına tebliğ, *Ümmet-i Muhammed,* 15 December 1990, p. 8, C. Hocaoğlu, Kilise mensuplarına tebliğ, *Ümmet-i Muhammed,* 15 Febru-ary 1991, p. 10; C. Hocaoğlu, Yahudiler'e tebliğ, *Ümmet-i Muhammed,* 15 December 1990, p. 9; C. Hocaoğlu, Yahudiler'e tebliğ, *Ümmet-i Muhammed* 15 Februar 1991, p. 11.

tions of hosts. Whatever the intentions, guests rarely feel at home in foreign environs. The second half of the compound word..., worker refers to the economic and use value of the migrant determined solely in relation to his or her labor... Their identity as defined by the German term reduces the migrants to their functions."[26]

Germany does not consider herself a country of immigration. "Access to citizenship is not a basic right open to foreign workers as a whole. It is always decided on a case-to-case basis. The German concept of citizenship is inseparable from nationality. Nationality, based on jus sanguis, is hereditary. As a result, birth on German territory does not guarantee the right to citizenship. Hence, guestworker migration has resulted in a specific form of legal marginality which permits the legitimacy of the instutionalization of the status of a foreigner over two and more generations."[27]

The social base of the Kaplan group consists of Turkish immigrants in Europe. They are active in Germany, Holland, Belgium, France, and Denmark. The group recruits its members from unskilled workers with low status jobs or even unemployed. It is possible to find first and second generation immigrants among the group members. The second generation members are mostly the sons and daughters of the group's members.

These people represent the lowest social strata and live in ghettos[28] of Western European cities facing discrimination and racism all the time in their everyday life. They share living space with German marginal groups who are also alienated from their own society. In this sense, these Turkish immigrants are angry and anxious because they have been experiencing conflicts and tensions all the time.

The open or covered discrimination lead them to withdraw to their own community and develop solidarity in their own religious groups. The Union of Islamic Communities provides a solidarity network, which is ready to be used by the members whenever needed. This network may provide legal advice in the case of a work permit or a

26 Ruth Mandel, Turkish headscarves and the 'foreign problem': constructing difference through emblems of identity, *New German Critique*, Winter 1989, pp. 28-29.

27 Gitmez & Wilpert, p. 89.

28 The concept is taken from Sema Köksal, *Refah toplumumda "getto" ve Türkler*, Teknografik Matb. 1986, pp. 11-12, 32-47. Ghettos are places where the newcomers of the industrial society, the low status immigrant groups, have settled down in the urban spatial structure.

staying permit; it may also provide financial help. The network provides a sense of security at a psychological level. At this level the group's fatalistic approach gives them the courage to resist against the discrimination and rejection in European societies.

These experiences force them to reconsider their experience of immigration. In this framework, the worldview developed by the Kaplan group on the one hand gives sacred meaning to their experience of immigration, and on the other hand, it emphasises a fatalistic approach towards the discrimination they are facing in Western societies.

When the group's Islamic discourse is examined, it becomes clear that the group uses a radical Islamic approach very similar to other radical groups all over the world. Their ultimate aim is to establish an Islamic state in Turkey via an Islamic revolution. But this radicalism covers a fatalistic worldview which has been developed and used in the context of the host country.

Providing a *mücahid* (fighter for Islam) identity creates a resistance point against the pressure and discrimination coming from outside. Being a *mücahid* is an honourable position, which can not be compared with the actual social status. It is not important for the group members that Germans do not understand this honourable position. The important point is that they are defining themselves as *mücahid* and not as guestworkers, as a second class Turkish worker, cleaner or unemployed.

This definition gives the members of the Kaplan group an opportunity to change their identity. The new identity not only gives them a resistance point against the outsiders but also justifies their opposition to the circle of intellectuals in Turkey. In this context, clothing and a way of life which is defined, as "Islamic" became an important and sensitive issue.

As mentioned above, this group is based on Turkish immigrants who have no proper education, who work in unskilled jobs or who are unemployed. One aspect of their worldview is very fatalistic which helps the members to ignore the difficulties they are facing in their daily life in Western Europe. Another aspect of their worldview is very radical and promises them to be the rulers of the coming Islamic state in Turkey.

The anger, which emits from the conditions they are living in

Western societies, is reflected on another level that of the home country to which it is almost impossible or very difficult to go back.[29] The group considers Turkey as a place where *asr-ı saadet* (the era of felicity) is going to be realized. Even though parts of the second generation do not speak proper Turkish, do not know very much about Turkish political history and the current situation, they believe that they will establish an Islamic state in Turkey. They create an image of Turkey, which does not really correspond with the real Turkey. In their own image of Turkey, they define the brothers whom they can cooperate with and the enemies whom they have to fight with. But this does not necessarily mean that the brothers they considered, are supporting them in Turkey. Since they do not have a substantial number of followers in Turkey, this situation widens the gap between the real Turkey and the Turkey of their imagination.

It is known that the migration process has an effect on the people's religious interpretations.[30] In other words, the religious discourse which immigrants brought with them has changes in the context of the new country. The interpretation of Islam by the group has also effected the meaning of immigration, particularly for the second generation members. According to many first generation members, people immigrated to Western Europe because of poverty. Their only aim was to earn money. But this fact of immigration actually had a deeper meaning, which was understood by the members later. They found Islam in this process. The interpretation of this fact by the first generation is quite different from that by the second generation.

Second generation members are aware of the fact that going back to Turkey is almost impossible or extremely difficult. Being aware of this, they are trying to find a place in Western societies and they also try to explain their current position in Western societies. In this framework, some groups that are also organised on the base of Islam try to get a better position with the help of education. These people who have better education and mix with Germans, ask for equal status and respect. They are involved in the problems of immigrants and they

29 Similar reflection can be observed among the Pakistani immigrants in Britain. See J. Rex, The urban sociology of religion and Islam, in *The new Islamic* ..., pp. 217-218.

30 See W. Schiffauer, Migration and religiousness, in *The new Islamic* ... , pp. 155-156.

develop new projects to solve them.

But the Union of Islamic Communities makes a clear distinction between Muslims and non-Muslims. According to this group, it is not sensible to expect to receive equal treatment and equal status in a non-Muslim society, because there is a severe struggle between Muslims and non-Muslims in the world. Christians and particularly Jews do not want Islam to become a power centre in the world. That is why they develop all sorts of tricks to block it. The prophet himself experienced cruelty and sufferings during the *cahiliye* period, as the group members are experiencing now. But he was patient. Now like the prophet, the group members must be patient and accept the difficulties. One of them said, "If Allah wanted us to have an easy life, would Allah have led the prophet Muhammad to experience those sufferings?" In other words Muslims have to suffer until they seize power and establish an Islamic state. They are at the stage of suffering at the moment.

One of the group's members explained this situation like this; first he said he tried different life styles and then he found out about Cemaleddin Kaplan and became his follower and then "After many readings I told myself that I was sent here by Allah. There is a reason for that. My destiny is to live Islam here and call the other people to Islam. We are working for the ruling of Islam. But this is a very difficult and long way, we know. All our hope is they -- he showed his children. They will establish an Islamic state. We have risked everything. If my prophet suffered and if his tooth was broken, it is forbidden (*haram*) for me to have a comfortable life".

To project a sacred meaning to the problems the members are facing means to tell people who experience many problems and feel that they face injustice to be patient and to accept the treatment they are getting from the society. They have to behave like this because the Prophet did the same. They have to postpone their demands to the future Islamic state.

This approach not only prevents lower class Turkish immigrants to demand to be treated as equals in Western societies but it also prevents them to defend their existing rights. It also justifies an open or covered discrimination with a sacred discourse.

Experiences in Germany

It is possible to hear many experiences about the difficulties and discrimination they are facing as Turks in Germany. Some of them are as follows:

"After marriage I covered myself under the influence of my husband. We looked for a flat for a long time. They do not rent a flat to Turks. I decided to go back to Turkey and my husband had to stay here. I did not want to do it but I had no other choice. My husband sent his German friend from his working place to rent a house. He managed to rent a flat. But as soon as they discovered that we, Turks, are going to live there, they changed their mind. Finally a Turk who owned a building rented us a flat. Of course life in Germany is easier than life in Turkey. That is why many people do not want to go back. But Germans treat us badly. They are shouting "Turks out" behind us. They are writing this slogan everywhere."

"The teacher made fun of my daughter in the class because she covers her head. The teacher said in front of the whole class that she looked like an Arab. She does not want to go to school any more."

"Turks who immigrated to Germany either work in the dirtiest jobs or they do cleaning. You may have worked here for many years but if you get sick, they try to send you back. Our sons do not want to do these jobs. They are looking for the better ones. But this time they cannot find a job and become unemployed. What can they do? They start to get unemployment benefits, and Germans get angry. The German government tries to make it more difficult to get unemployment benefits. In short, they try everything to send us back."

"I applied for German citizenship. Do you know what they are asking? How many times do you go to theatre in a month? I wonder how many German workers go to the theatre not in a month, but in one year?"

A female member of the group said: "All my brothers and sisters are working in Europe. My sister brought me to Germany to look after her children. My husband's family is a distant relative of us. They saw me in my sister's house and liked me. Anyway finally we got married. My husband was not religious at that time. At the beginning he brought me clothes which were not modest. I told him that I grew up in a village. I could not wear them. He insisted. He wanted me to be like these European women. Then he started to go to the mosque and read Islamic books. This time he said that I should stay at home, not go out. I asked why, because I used to take the kids to the park. He said I had to pray five times a day. I had not been used to it. It was a little bit difficult for me but I started to pray. Sometimes I miss a prayer but I am praying more often than in the past. Then he insisted that I had to wear chador. I said I could not do it. I was ashamed of it. But he said he would otherwise divorce me. So I accepted. In short, we followed the fashion of short sleeves first. It is over now. At the moment we are practising this fashion. We will see what will happen."

A 27 year old group member explained his experience of immigration like this "My father immigrated to Germany because of poverty. Some of our villagers went to Germany. On holidays they used to come to the village. They told my father that he could earn money here. First my father came, then my mother and finally me. We came here because of poverty, otherwise why should we leave our country? The place is not important for us. The world belongs to us. If we leave Germany, we will go to another place. But Turkey is our fatherland. Of course we miss Turkey. Look, I am not allowed to go there for six years. I missed my places. I have pain in my heart. I told the Turkish Consulate that I am not a Muslim in the passport. They can take my passport if they wish, I do not care. I did everything in this society. I had many German girlfriends. I used to smoke hashish. I know Germans better than anyone. I experienced their badness and evil actions. I know their culture and I have no intention to imitate them. On the contrary, God is my witness, I hate them and their culture."

The most interesting example is that the slogan of "Turks out" was written on the wall of an apartment where Cemaleddin Kaplan lived.

Conclusion

The Union of Islamic Communities is a small radical Islamic organisation which recruits its members among the unskilled or semiskilled, less educated and unemployed Turkish immigrants living in the ghettos of Western Europe. The members feel a strong sense of discrimination and anger and they reflect this to their home country.

The open or covered discrimination these people faced lead them to withdraw from society and against these problems the Kaplan group inculcates in its members to be patient like the Prophet. Giving a sacred meaning to their immigration experience the group members interpret their problems in this framework and develop a fatalistic world-view. The radical discourse, actually aiming at Turkey, covers this fatalistic approach.

The Union of Islamic Communities has a modern organisational structure. Even though it tries to justify this structure by basing it on Islamic concepts, it is a new and modern organisation which grows among the Turkish immigrants in the conditions of Western Europe.

Die Türkisch-Islamische Union der türkischen Religionsbehörde (DİTİB)

Zwischen Integration und Isolation

Günter Seufert
Institut der Deutschen Morgenländischen Gesellschaft, Istanbul

Einführung

Das Engagement des staatlichen türkischen Präsidiums für religiöse Angelegenheiten (Diyanet İşleri Başkanlığı, kurz Diyanet)[1] in Europa ist ein relativ neues Phänomen. Beim Abschluß der Anwerbeverträge hat der türkische Staat sich nicht für die Regelung der religiösen Betreuung seiner Staatsangehörigen stark gemacht. Erst in den 80er Jahren wurde die Religionsbehörde aktiv, und heute sind in allen europäischen Ländern mehr türkische Religionsbeauftragte als türkische Lehrer tätig.[2] Ob der sich in den sechziger Jahren noch stärker laizistisch verstehende Staat damals bewußt auf die religiöse Betreuung seiner Staatsangehörigen verzichtete, oder ob sich die türkischen Stellen genausowenig wie die Aufnahmeländer über die langfristigen Folgen der als vorübergehend eingestuften Arbeitskräfteentsendung im klaren waren, kann hier nicht entschieden werden.[3] Jedenfalls hat der türkische Staat die religiöse Betreuung der Diasporagemeinden erst nach dem Putsch von 1980 begonnen, der dem Ausland gegenüber

1 Die Religionsbehörde ist die Nachfolgeeinrichtung des 1924 abgeschafften şeyh ül-İslam, der höchsten theologischen Autorität im Osmanischen Reich. Die Behörde ist heute von ihrem Range her einem Staatssekretariat vergleichbar und untersteht direkt dem Ministerpräsidenten. Zur Geschichte und Struktur der Diyanet vgl. İ.B. Tarhanlı, *Müslüman toplum, "laik" devlet*, Afa Yay. Istanbul 1993.

2 Fikri Sağlar, Paris'te kültür çıkarması, *Yeni Yüzyıl* 21.2.1996, S. 12.

3 Auffallend ist jedoch, daß andere Länder, z.B. Griechenland, von vorneherein Regelungen in dieser Hinsicht getroffen haben.

auch mit dem Anwachsen der 'religiösen Gefahr' begründet wurde,[4] weshalb das Engagement der Religionsbehörde primär als Reaktion auf den organisatorischen Erfolg nichtstaatlicher muslimischer Gruppen in der Diaspora zu verstehen ist.

Tatsächlich schöpft der türkische Staatsislam in der Diaspora seine Existenzberechtigung und sein Selbstverständnis primär aus seiner Ablehnung konkurrierender türkisch-muslimischer Gruppen. In einem Informationsblatt seines bundesdeutschen Ablegers, der Türkisch-Islamischen Union der Anstalt für Religion (DİTİB), heißt es im März 1992: "Es wird uns mit der Zeit gelingen, hier in Köln, dem Hauptzentrum aller extremistischen Strömungen religiöser Prägung, noch bessere Resultate zu erzielen."[5] Die Warnung vor den muslimischen Gruppen jedenfalls, die "den falschen Weg"[6] gehen, ist regelmäßig Teil von öffentlichen Stellungnahmen der Behörde. Man geht bisweilen soweit, anderen muslimischen Gruppen ihr Muslimentum abzusprechen, auf jeden Fall bezichtigt man sie — wie im Falle von AMGT[7] — der Ausnutzung religiöser Gefühle für den eigenen politischen und wirtschaftlichen Vorteil.

Die Zielsetzung der Behörde in der Diaspora und die Art und Weise ihrer juristischen Institutionalisierung in den Einwanderungsländern.

Wie sehr die Einrichtung der Religionsbehörde in der Diaspora sich von dem Ziel hat leiten lassen, die türkischen Muslime im Ausland zu kontrollieren, soll hier über eine kurze Analyse der rechtlichen Struktur des deutschen Ablegers der Diyanet geschildert werden, deren

---

[4] Karl Binswanger, Türkei, in *Der Islam in der Gegenwart*, W. Ende & U. Steinbach, (Hrsg.), Beck, München 1984, S. 212-220, hier S. 212.

[5] Zitiert nach M.S. Abdullah, *Was will der Islam in Deutschland?* GTB, Gütersloh 1993 S. 60.

[6] Gespräch mit Sami Uslu, stellvertretender Präsident des Präsidiums für Religiöse Angelegenheiten, Ankara 29.3.96.

[7] AMGT = Avrupa Millî Görüş Teşkilâtı, auf deutsch: *Verband der Religionsnationalen Weltsicht in Europa*, eine der ehemaligen Wohlfahrtspartei und der heutigen Tugendpartei der Türkei sehr nahestehende europaweite Organisation, die heute unter dem Namen IGMG = *Islamische Gemeinschaft Millî Görüş* tätig ist. Die ehemalige deutsche Eigenbezeichnung der Organisation *Vereinigung der Neuen Weltsicht* wird hier nicht übernommen, weil sie zum einen den türkischen Namen nicht wiedergibt und zum anderen eben den religions*nationalen* Charakter des Verbands verschleiert.

Kölner Zentrum für ganz Europa zuständig ist.[8]

Die DİTİB Köln wurde offiziell am 5.7.1984 gegründet und beschränkte sich in ihrer ersten Satzung auf die türkischen Muslime in Köln. Von Beginn an ist die "Zusammenarbeit mit dem Erziehungsministerium der türkischen Republik und dem Präsidenten des Amtes für Religiöse Angelegenheiten" eines der in § 2 der Satzung geregelten Hauptanliegen des Vereins.[9] Von Anfang an auch erhalten der Präsident der Diyanet in Ankara, "der Generalkonsul der Republik Türkei in Köln oder ein von ihm Beauftragter" und die "vom Amt für Religiöse Angelegenheiten für die europäischen Länder beauftragten Sozialräte (Räte für Religiöse Angelegenheiten)" das "Recht zur Aufnahme in den Verein."[10] Der Mindestbeitrag wurde 1984 auf DM 10,-- festgesetzt und seitdem nicht erhöht. Organe des Vereins sind die Mitgliederversammlung, der Vorstand und der Beirat.

Aus der dem Beirat eingeräumten Rolle erschließt sich der Charakter der DİTİB: "Der Beirat besteht aus fünf Religionsbeauftragten. Vorsitzender des Beirates ist der Präsident des Amtes für Religiöse Angelegenheiten ... Im Falle seiner Verhinderung wird der Vorsitz von seinem Vertreter im Amte geführt. Der türkische Generalkonsul von Köln kann ebenfalls Beiratsmitglied sein. ... Bei Ausscheiden eines Beiratsmitgliedes ernennen die verbliebenen Beiratsmitglieder dessen Nachfolger." (§ 11 Abs. 1 u. 2)[11]

Die Befugnisse dieses von den muslimischen Migranten vollkommen unabhängigen Beirates sind außerordentlich groß: Satzungsänderungen müssen von ihm genehmigt werden (§ 8, Abs. 5e)[12], nur er schlägt die Kandidaten für den Vorstand vor, und er hat daneben das Recht, falls erforderliche Mehrheiten nicht zustandekommen, Vorstandsmitglieder einfach zu ernennen (§ 9, Abs. 2 u. 3).[13] Der Beirat bestimmt desweiteren bei einer eventuellen Auflösung des Vereins den

---

8 Unabhängig von der jeweiligen juristischen Form der Institutionalisierung des türkischen Staatsislams in den einzelnen europäischen Ländern läßt sich die Intention der Diyanet-Zentrale in Ankara an der Art und Weise der rechtliche Gestaltung der Organisation in nur einem europäischen Land deutlich aufzeigen.

9 Amtsgericht Köln, *Vereinsregister*, 25.1.96, Blatt 3.

10 AG Köln 25.1.96, Blatt 4.

11 AG Köln 25.1.96, Batt 10.

12 AG Köln 25.1.96, Blatt 7.

13 AG Köln 25.1.96, Blatt 8.

gemeinnützigen Empfänger des Vereinsvermögens.

Mit dieser Satzung ist die DİTİB nichts anderes als die vereinsrechtliche Einkleidung der staatlichen türkischen Religionsbehörde. Denn ohne den ausschließlich aus Amtsträgern des türkischen Staates bestehenden Beirat kann die Mitgliederversammlung weder einen Vorstand wählen, der die Geschäfte des Vereins führt, noch seine Satzung ändern. Umgekehrt haben jedoch weder die Mitgliederversammlung noch der Vorstand irgendeinen Einfluß auf die Zusammensetzung des Beirats oder auf seine Entscheidungen.[14]

Zum nicht stimmberechtigten Ehrenvorsitzenden wählte die Gründungsversammlung des Vereins den damaligen Präsidenten des Amtes für Religiöse Angelegenheiten der Republik Türkei. Jedoch nicht Tayyar Altıkulaç, der das Amt seinerzeit bekleidete, wurde zum Ehrenvorsitzenden bestimmt, sondern diese Würde wurde dem Amte verliehen, welches er innehatte. Damit versteht sich die DİTİB auch auf symbolischer Ebene als Teil der Religionsbehörde.

Erst mit der Satzungsänderung vom 26.4.87 weitete die DİTİB Köln ihre Aktivitäten auf das gesamte Gebiet der Bundesrepublik aus. Im § 2 Abs. 2 präsentiert sich die Union jetzt als Dachverband mit kontrollierender Funktion: "Der Verein hat als Dachorganisation die schon gegründeten oder noch zu gründenden türkisch-islamischen Kulturvereine in der BRD, die der Türkisch-Islamischen Union der Anstalt für Religion (DITIB) Köln angeschlossen sind, zu beaufsichtigen, in allen, insbesondere in religiösen, sozialen, kulturellen und gemeinnützigen Fragen zu unterstützen und ihnen Gründungshilfe zu gewähren." Er "überwacht speziell die Rechte und Pflichten dieser Vereine."[15]

Damit kennzeichnet ihre Satzung die DİTİB als Kontrollorgan des türkischen Staates über die Moscheegemeinden der Migranten. Diese Kontrolle erfolgt jedoch nicht nur durch die Eingliederung der Moscheegemeinden in die Verwaltungshierarchie der Religionsbehörde, sondern auch durch den - weithin erfolgreichen - Versuch der DİTİB, sich den Grundbesitz der Moscheegemeinden anzueignen: "Um die

14 Der erste Beirat bestand aus dem Präsidenten der Diyanet, dem türkischen Generalkonsul in Köln, den Botschaftsräten in Brüssel und Den Haag, dem Stellvertretenden Präsidenten der Behörde in Bonn und einem ihrer Religionsbeauftragten aus den Niederlanden.

15 AG Köln 25.1.96, Blatt, 17.

genannten Vereine zu schützen, kann der Verein Grundbesitz erwerben oder Spenden der genannten Vereine entgegennehmen", heißt es euphemistisch in § 9, Abs. 9 der geänderten Satzung.[16] Wie beschränkt Geschäftsfähige zwar Schenkungen entgegennehmen aber nichts veräußern dürfen, ist nach der neuen Satzung auch der Vorstand der DİTİB berechtigt, Schenkungen anzunehmen - "Sollte jedoch Grundbesitz veräußert werden, so ist vorher die Einwilligung des Beirates einzuholen."[17]

Eine weitere Satzungsänderung vom 5.7.87 erlaubt im Katastrophenfall die Überführung von Spendengeldern in die Türkei, allerdings nur an die Diyanet selbst. Gleichzeitig wird festgelegt, daß die angeschlossenen Vereine keine größere finanzielle Unterstützung von der DİTİB erhalten dürfen als diese von ihnen entgegennimmt.[18] Eine zusätzliche Satzungsänderung vom 28.3.92 legt fest, daß die einzelnen Moscheegemeinden jeweils stimmberechtigte Mitglieder in der DİTİB sind, die Mitglieder der Moscheegemeinden dagegen sind Mitglieder ohne Stimmrecht.[19]

Nach eigenen Angaben will die DİTİB 1987 drei Jahre nach ihrer Gründung 520, bis 1988 640 und bis 1993 700 Moscheegemeinden in der BRD organisiert haben.[20] Abdullah indes schreibt ohne nähere Begründung, daß von höchstens 400 angeschlossenen Gemeinden ausgegangen werden könne.[21] Zu dem 'Wie' dieses Organisationserfolgs gibt es unterschiedliche Stellungnahmen. Von Seiten ihrer Konkurrenten wird der DİTİB vorgeworfen, sie habe sich die Beitritte erkauft. Lier/Piest kommen in ihrer Studie allerdings zu dem Schluß, daß die Initiative zum Beitritt der einzelnen Gemeinden von diesen selbst ausgegangen sei.[22] Diese Version verträgt sich sowohl mit der starken Staatsfixierung der türkischen Muslime als auch mit der angeführten DİTİB-Satzung, aus welcher klar hervorgeht, wie sehr in der Türkei noch der Gedanke einer unterstützenden und redistributieren-

16 AG Köln 25.1.96, Blatt 17.

17 § 9, Abs. 9, AG Köln 25.1.96, Blatt 18.

18 AG Köln 25.1.96, Blatt 20.

19 AG Köln 25.1.96, Blatt 34.

20 T. Lier & U. Piest, *Muslimische Vereinigungen und Moscheen in Köln*, Manuskript, Köln 1994, S. 19.

21 Abdullah 1993, S. 61.

22 Lier & Piest 1994, S. 10.

den Dienstleistungsverwaltung hinter dem der Kontrollverwaltung zurücksteht. Wie erfolgreich die Bemühungen der DİTİB um die Übernahme der Grundstücke und Gebäude der Moscheegemeinden wirklich gewesen sind, kann hier nicht beantwortet werden. Becker schreibt, daß sich von den 600 bis 700 der DİTİB angeschlossenen Moscheevereinen nur die Grundstücke und Gebäude von ca. 200 Gemeinden im Besitz der Kölner Zentrale befinden.[23] Der ehemalige Präsident der Behörde hat dem Autor dieser Studie gegenüber indessen erklärt, die Immobilien seien "in der Regel" in der Hand der Zentrale.[24] In Holland begann der Ableger der Religionsbehörde, dort im rechtlichen Gewand einer Stiftung, bereits Ende 1982 mit der Konzentrierung der Gemeindeimmobilien in seiner Hand.[25]

Die Gesamtzahl der über die angeschlossenen Moscheegemeinden in Deutschland bei DİTİB organisierten Muslime beträgt nach Angaben der Organisation circa 90 000.[26]

Image der Behörde

Vor allen Dingen unter der genannten Perspektive von 'der Eindämmung extremer islamischer Gruppen' befürworten auch europäische Behörden und Beobachter die Existenz der Diyanet in Europa. Die Verwestlichung der staatlichen Institutionen und der Gesetze der Türkei unter dem Staatsgründer Mustafa Kemal Atatürk wurde primär über die Zurückdrängung der Religion aus den genannten Sphären erreicht. Das Wissen darum führte in Europa dazu, daß weite mit Einwanderern beschäftigte Kreise die unter Aufsicht des verweltlichten Nationalstaates ausgearbeitete und propagierte Islam-Version der Reli-

23 Hildgard Becker, Dialog ja - aber mit wem? Referat auf der Tagung *Muslime in Deutschland*, Ostakademie Königstein, 11.-12.11.95 (Manuskript), S. 4.

24 Unterhaltung mit dem ehemaligen Präsidenten der Behörde Tayyar Altıkulaç am 5.5.1996 am Rande der Deutsch-Türkischen Gespräche der Körber-Stiftung in Bonn-Königswinter.

25 Jacques Waardenburg, The institutionalization of Islam in the Netherlands in *The new Islamic presence in Western Europe*, T. Gerholm & Y.G. Lithman (Hrsg.), Stockholms Universitet, London 1988, S. 8-31, hier S. 26.

26 Becker 11.-12.11.95, S. 4.

gionsbürokratie[27] des Landes ungeprüft für moderat, liberal und auf Verständigung mit dem Westen und dem Christentum gerichtet erachten. "Sie vertritt ein 'laizistisches' Islam- und Gesellschaftsmodell....", schreibt beispielsweise Abdullah[28] über die Religionsbehörde und wiederholt damit die weitverbreitete Überzeugung, daß in der Behörde ein Islam ohne politische Komponenten gelehrt werde, der gemäß der atatürkschen Reformen von gesellschaftspolitischen Vorstellungen der Religion nichts wissen wolle und von staatspolitischen Konsequenzen religiösen Lebens schon gar nichts. "Damit garantiert DİTİB, daß an den ihr angeschlossenen Moscheevereinen die herrschende laizistische Religionsauffassung gewahrt bleibt", heißt es unisono auch bei anderen Autoren.[29] Solche Einschätzungen legen den Schluß nahe, eine enge Kooperation mit der DİTİB trage dazu bei, die türkischen Muslime zu einem eher moderaten Verständnis ihrer Religion zu bewegen und damit den 'Integrationsprozeß' zu fördern.

Selten nur wird Kritik an der DİTİB geübt und die Vermutung geäußert, daß in den Moscheen der Religionsbehörde in Europa keine grundsätzlich andere Version des Islams gepredigt wird als bei den explizit politischen muslimischen Gruppen. So meint Becker, daß auch die DİTİB "Amtsgeistliche" besoldet, "die nicht verschweigen, daß sie gegen die Wiedereinführung des islamischen Rechts in der Türkei nichts einzuwenden hätten."[30] Die vorsichtige Formulierung muß überraschen, denn viele Führer der Organisationen, mit deren Aktivität die DİTİB ihre Arbeit in der Diaspora begründet, kommen aus der Behörde selbst. Cemalettin Kaplan, der verstorbene Führer des iranorientierten und hyperpolitisierten *Verbandes islamischer Vereine und Gemeinden e.V. in der BRD* (ICCB) war vor seinem Engagement

---

27 Zur Religionsbürokratie der Türkei gehört nicht nur die Religionsbehörde mit den ihr angeschlossenen Institutionen im In- und Ausland, den Mufti-Ämtern, Moscheen, Koranschulen und den zivilrechtlichen Gründungen in der Diaspora, sondern auch das *Direktorium für Religionserziehung*, Din Eğitimi Müdürlüğü, im *Nationalen Erziehungsministerium*, Millî Eğitim Bakanlığı, das die Theologischen Fakultäten, die Predigergymnasien sowie die Religionslehrer an den Allgemeinbildenden Schulen beaufsichtigt.

28 1993, S. 95.

29 Lier & Piest S. 19 und Faruk Şen, (K)ein Weg in die Schule, *Das Sonntagsblatt*, Hamburg 5.7.96, S. 24.

30 Becker 11.-12.11.95, S. 4.

für die Muslime in der Diaspora Mufti von Adana.[31], Ali Arslan, einst Vorsitzender der Fetwa-Kommission von AMGT, war bevor er dieses Amt bekleidete, Mufti im ostthrakischen Tekirdağ[32], Osman Yumakoğulları, Gründungsmitglied und langjähriger Vorsitzender der AMGT, war mehrere Jahre Oberprediger in Istanbu[33]. Selbst der Generalsekretär des Verbandes, Ali Yüksel, arbeitete vor seinem Aufenthalt in Deutschland u.a. als stellvertretender Direktor der Entwicklungsabteilung in der Religionsbehörde in Antalya.[34] Der ehemalige türkische Minister für Kultur, Fikri Sağlar, meint gar, daß sich die Religionsbehörde in ihrer praktischen Arbeit in der Diaspora insofern nicht von der Auslandsorganisationen der pro-islamischen türkischen *Wohlfahrspartei* (Refah-Partisi) unterscheide, als beide die Migranten geradezu in eine islamische Identität drängen würden.[35]

Andere Kritiker der Behörde fragen eher danach, welche Interessen die Institution eines Staates wohl bei der religiösen Betreuung ihrer Staatsangehörigen im Ausland verfolgen möge.[36] Es läßt sich jedenfalls formulieren, daß bei den Auslandsgliederungen der Diyanet die Tendenz besteht, die in Europa lebenden türkischen Muslime primär über ihre Zugehörigkeit zur türkischen Nation und zum türkischen Staat anzusprechen. Oft stehen nicht die konkreten Lebensverhältnisse der Muslime in der Diaspora im Mittelpunkt, sondern die Notwendigkeit, den Zusammenhalt innerhalb der türkischen Nation zu sichern und ihren Staat zu stärken.[37]

---

31 Abdullah 1993, S. 68.

32 Binswanger 1984, S. 219.

33 Osman Yumakoğulları, Avrupa'da İslam'ın geleceği parlak, *AMGT Bülten* (4/1995), S. 16-17 (Interview), hier S. 16.

34 Gespräch mit Ali Yüksel in Köln im Januar 1994.

35 Sağlar 21.2.96, S. 12. Die Wohlfahrtspartei wurde 1997 auf Betreiben der Militärs vom Verfassungsgericht verboten. Ihre Nachfolgernin, die *Tugendpartei* (Fazilet Partisi) ist heute ebenfalls vom Verbot bedroht.

36 Ozan Ceyhun vom Einwandererbüro im hessischen Familienministerium beispielsweise sagt, die DİTİB vertrete "eher die türkische Staatslinie als die Interessen der Muslime in Deutschland", zit. nach F.M. İlhan, Experten und intelligente Studien über Muslime in der Zeitschrift *Millî Görüş* (11/1995), S. 42-43, hier S. 43.

37 Vgl. dazu die Berichte über öffentliche Veranstaltungen der Diyanet-Auslandsgliederungen, beispielsweise *Türkiye Gazetesi* vom 16.1.96, S. 18 und vom 18.1.96, S. 18 (Deutschlandausgaben).

Das Islamverständnis der Religionsbehörde

Zur Eruierung der tatsächlich innerhalb der Religionsbehörde vertretenen Islamauffassung gilt es, sich mit den Publikationen der türkischen Religionsbürokratie im Allgemeinen und der Diyanet im Besonderen zu befassen. Zwar kann hier keine auch nur annähernd repräsentative Prüfung des Schrifttums der Religionsbürokratie vorgenommen werden, doch bereits ein kurzer Blick in einige aussagekräftige Quellen wird Auskunft über grundlegende Orientierungen geben können.

In den Organen der Religionsbürokratie lassen sich die Stellungnahmen zu *Europa als vom Christentum geprägter Ort* und zu *Europa als die größte Diasporaregion für türkische Muslime* ohne Mühe in zwei Kategorien einteilen. Da sind zum einen Schriften prinzipieller Art, die den Charakter von Fetwas, religiösen Gutachten, tragen und die sich in ihrer Argumentation auf den Koran, die Sunna des Propheten oder auf andere autoritative Schriften wie die Werke der Gründern der großen Rechtsschulen und anderer wichtiger Theologen stützen. Und da sind zum anderen Aufsätze, in denen die eben genannten Quellen so gut wie keine Rolle spielen und in denen die Argumentation auf einer ganz anderen Art von Wissen gründet, auf populären Überzeugungen und Einstellungen, auf Bruchstücken pädagogischer, psychologischer und soziologischer Theorien, auf religionswissenschaftlichen Theoremen und endlich auf Nationalstaatsideologien und politischen Zweckmäßigkeitserwägungen. Ich werde Bei-träge beider Art vorstellen und abschließend prüfen, welche von ihnen das praktische Handeln der Religionsbehörde stärker bestimmen.

Theologische Schriften im engeren Sinne

Als erstes sollen einige Stellungnahmen referiert werden, die sich auf originär religiöse Quellen stützen: In Beiträgen dieser Art ist der Ausgangspunkt für die Überlegungen über das Verhältnis der muslimischen Völker und ihrer Staaten zu Europa und für die Diskussionen über Rechte und Pflichten der Muslime in der europäischen Diaspora stets die Feststellung, daß es sich bei den europäischen Aufnahmeländern ausnahmslos um Gebiete handelt, die nie zur islamischen Welt gehörten. Sie sind deshalb nicht dem dar ül-İslâm (Haus des Islams), sondern dem dar ül-harb (Haus des Krieges) zuzurechnen, das auch dar ül-kafir (Haus der Leugner) genannt wird.[38] Die "religiösen, gottesdienstlichen und moralischen" Pflichten der Muslime sind im 'Land der Islamleugner' dieselben wie im dar ül-İslâm, doch in Bezug auf das Verhältnis der Muslime zu den Individuen einer mehrheitlich nichtmuslimischen Gesellschaft in der Diaspora gelten teilweise andere Rechtsvorschriften als für die Muslime untereinander im dar ül-İslâm.[39] So ist es den Muslimen im Dar ül-harb nach hanefitischer Rechtsschule beispielsweise erlaubt, von Nichtmuslimen Zins zu nehmen und ihnen Alkohol oder Schweinefleisch zu verkaufen.[40]

Auch in anderen Fragen ist die hanefitische Rechtsschule in der Diaspora eher großzügig. Das von Christen geschlachtete Fleisch darf solange ohne Bedenken verzehrt werden, solange man nicht sicher wissen könne, daß der Schlachter kein gläubiger Christ sei und daß er sich bewußt geweigert habe, beim Töten des Tieres Gottes zu gedenken.[41] Die Arbeitsaufnahme bei Nichtmuslimen ist für die Hanefiten kein Problem und der daraus gezogene Verdienst fällt unter das Er-

---

38 Vgl. Hayreddin Karaman, *Erlaubtes und Verwehrtes* <Haram ve helal, dt> Türkische Stiftung für Religion <Türk Diyanet Vakfı>, Ankara 1990, S. 24-26. Karaman gilt als der bedeutendste Rechtsgelehrte *(fakih)* der Türkei. Ferner Ahmed Şahin, *Sualli/cevaplı dinî bilgiler*, 4. Auflage, Cihan Yay., Istanbul 1991, S. 177. Das Werk von Ahmed Şahin ist als Ratgeber in Frage und Antwort-Form konzipiert und wird wie das Karamans in den Läden der DITİB verkauft.

39 Hier wird eine der grundlegenden Unterscheidungen im islamischen Recht relevant, die Abhebung des Tanrı Hakkı, *das Recht, das Gott dem Menschen gegenüber hat*, vom Kul Hakkı, *das Recht, das der Mensch seinen Mitmenschen gegenüber hat.*

40 Şahin 1991, S. 177, Karaman 1990, S. 45, der Autor schließt jedoch die Zinsnahme aus, weil davon indirekt auch das Geld der Muslime, welches diese beispielsweise auf deutschen Banken deponiert hätten, betroffen sei; ebenda S. 26.

41 Şahin 1991, S. 140-141. Mit dieser Entscheidung macht der türkische, hannefitische Rechtsgelehrte seinen Landsleuten das Leben in der Diaspora wesentlich einfacher als es beispielsweise die Rechtsgelehrten anderer Konfession aus Pakistan und Indien ihren Diasporagemeinden in England machen. Dort besteht man ausdrücklich auf der Schlachtung durch Muslime und nach islamischem Ritus, vgl. M.Y. McDermott & M.M. Ahsan, M.M., *The Muslim guide*, The Islamic Foundation, Leicester u.a. 1993, S. 36.

laubte (helâl).[42] Auch im Bezug auf die rituellen Vorschriften zur Trennung der Geschlechter sind beispielsweise die Schafiiten strenger als die Hanefiten, denen die türkischen Muslime angehören. Denn zumindest einige der hanefitischen Gelehrten erlauben den Händedruck zwischen Mann und Frau, so keine Begehrlichkeit im Spiele ist, und eine Berührung der Frauenhand hebt bei den Hanefiten nicht die rituelle Reinheit auf.[43] Doch hat die christliche Ehefrau eines Muslimen auch bei den Hanefiten weder ein Recht auf das Erbe ihre Mannes noch bei Scheidung ein Recht auf Sorge für das gemeinsame Kind.[44]

Genauso wesentlich wie einzelne rechtliche Bestimmungen ist jedoch, wie das Verhältnis der türkischen Muslime zum Aufnahmeland und seiner Gesellschaft als Ganzes definiert wird. Dazu heißt es beispielsweise: "Einige Rechtsgelehrte des Islams sind der Meinung, daß die Muslime nur zur Verteidigung Krieg führen, daß der Krieg nur etwas Akzidentielles ist und daß es im Grunde darum gehe, in Frieden zu leben. Doch die Mehrzahl der Rechtsgelehrten glaubt, daß der Islam sich mit allen nichtmuslimischen Gesellschaften im Kriegszustand befinde und zwar deshalb, weil er 'die Gerechtigkeit aufrichten, religiöse Unterdrückung verhindern und die Bedingungen für die Verkündung des Islams schaffen' muß."[45]

Aus dieser markigen Positionsbestimmung eines Theologieprofes-

---

42 Şahin 1991, S. 181. Bis heute wurde jedoch kein Versuch unternommen, aus der Fülle der Einzelvorschriften für das muslimische Alltagsleben einen Katalog mit Forderungen an die Aufnahmeländer zur muslimgerechten Gestaltung ihrer öffentlichen Institutionen zu entwickeln. Themen wie der Schwimm- und Turnunterricht für Mädchen, die Möglichkeit gemeinsamen Fastenbrechens im Ramadan, Räumlichkeiten und Pausen für die Verrichtung des Ritualgebetes, Beachtung der Gebote zu koscherem Essen und die Notwendigkeit islamischer Betreuung in Krankenhäusern und Gefängnissen, mit denen beispielsweise in England und Holland die öffentliche Verwaltung von Seiten unabhängiger Muslimgruppen konfrontiert wird, werden von der Religionsbehörde weder systematisiert noch zur Sprache gebracht. Vgl. dazu für England McDermott & Ahsan und für Holland W.A.R. Shadid & P.S. van Koningsveld, Institutionalization and integration of Islam in the Netherlands, in *The integration of Islam and Hinduism in Western Europe*, W.A.R. Shadid & P.S. van Koningsveld (Hrsg.) Kok Pharos P.H., Kampen 1991, S. 89-121. Zu sehr wohl widerspräche ein solch offensives und forderndes Auftreten der Tradition der türkischen Religionsbehörde, die gewohnt ist, die Perspektive der Regierenden zu teilen.

43 Karaman 1990, S. 100-101, Şahin 1991, S. 55.

44 Şahin 1991, S. 189-190.

45 Hayreddin Karaman, Yurt dışında Müslümanlar, *Diyanet Dergisi* (Zeitschrift der Religionsbehörde) (3/1975), S. 133-139, hier S. 134.

sors im Organ der Religionsbehörde, die für sich genommen als Aufruf zur Errichtung einer islamischen Staatsordnung auch in den Ländern der Diaspora verstanden werden könnte, werden jedoch keinerlei Konsequenzen für den einzelnen in Europa lebenden Muslimen gezogen. Die Pflicht, zur Überwindung der nichtislamischen Ordnungen aktiv zu werden, besteht nur für das Gemeinwesen der Muslime als Ganzes, für ihren Staat und nicht für jeden Einzelnen. Statt die Muslime zur politischen Aktivität im Namen der Scheriat aufzurufen, geht der Autor dazu über, erst einmal die Anwendbarkeit von in der Scheriat klar formulierten Sanktionen, sogenannte hadd-Strafen, in nicht-islamischen Ländern zu diskutieren. Er referiert u.a. den Gründer der hanefitischen Rechtsschule, Ebû Hanîfe, der die Verurteilung nach - und die Vollstreckung von Scheriat-Strafen in der Diaspora mit der Begründung ausschließt, daß dort keine islamische juristische oder administrative Autorität besteht, die dazu allein berechtigt wäre.[46] Damit wird die Anwendbarkeit des islamischen Rechts vom Bestehen einer islamischen Herrschaft abhängig gemacht und auf diese Weise für die *Länder der Leugner* verneint. In dieser Argumentation kann nur die Führung der Muslime, das Haupt ihres Gemeinwesens, sprich der Staat, im Namen des Islams handeln, niemals jedoch der einzelne Muslim. Was das Verhältnis des Letzteren zu den nichtmuslimischen Einwohnern des Aufnahmelandes betrifft, legt der Autor strenge Maßstäbe an. Entschieden tritt er Meinungen entgegen, nach denen es den Muslimen gestattet sei, Nichtmuslime zu übervorteilen und zu schädigen. Er interpretiert die einem Muslim erteilte Einreiseerlaubnis des fremden Staates als Vertrag, in dem sich der Muslim verpflichtet, den Einwohnern dieses Landes keinen Schaden zuzufügen. Selbst der Prophet Mohammed habe sich immer an sein Wort gebunden gefühlt, welches er Nichtmuslimen gegeben hatte. Der Artikel schließt mit den Worten: "Buchstaben und Geist der islamischen Gesetzgebung sind von den Prinzipien Rechtsgebundenheit, Vertragstreue und (dem Streben nach, GS) Gerechtigkeit durchdrungen."[47]

Auch bei der Bewertung des von Muslimen mit Nichtmuslimen einzugehenden Verhältnisses spielt die Vorstellung von Gerechtigkeit eine zentrale Rolle. Hier beruft man sich auf den Koran 5/52, wo es

---

46 Karaman (3/1975), S. 138.

47 Karaman (3/1975), S. 139.

heißt: "Nicht verbietet euch Allah gegen die, die nicht in Sachen des Glaubens gegen euch gestritten oder euch aus euren Häusern getrieben haben, gütig und gerecht zu sein. Siehe, Allah liebt die gerecht Handelnden."[48] Gegensätzliche Vorschriften beträfen allein den Fall, daß die Ungläubigen den Islam und die Muslime angriffen.

Die gleiche Linie verfolgt ein weiterer in der Fachzeitschrift der Diyanet veröffentlichter Beitrag über "Die Haltung des Islams zu anderen Religionen und das Verhältnis zu ihnen."[49] Sein Autor schreibt, daß die Muslime verpflichtet seien, den Nichtmuslimen menschlich zu begegnen, ihnen Gutes zu tun und sie freundlich aufzunehmen. Auch er beruft sich auf den Koran und zitiert 9/6 und 4/90: "Und wenn einer von den Heiden dich um Schutz angeht, dann gewähre ihm Schutz, damit er das Wort Gottes hören kann! Hierauf laß ihn dahin gelangen, wo er in Sicherheit ist." und "... wenn sie sich von euch fernhalten und nicht gegen euch kämpfen und euch ihre Bereitschaft erklären, sich friedlich zu verhalten, gibt euch Gott keine Möglichkeit, gegen sie vorzugehen."[50]

Der Autor faßt seine Untersuchung zu diesem Thema mit folgenden Worten zusammen: "Ohne Zweifel zögert der Islam keinen Augenblick, einem jeden, gleich welcher Nation, Religion, Konfession und Überzeugung, für die Verwirklichung von Gerechtigkeit und Sicherheit, für die Ausbreitung der Ordnung, für die Verhinderung von Blutvergießen und Ehrverletzung und zur gegenseitigen Hilfeleistung seine Hand zu reichen."[51]

Was die Christenmission betrifft, bekennt man sich zwar allgemein zur Bemühung um die Ausbreitung des Islams, doch wird mit Bezug auf Koran 2/256 jeder Zwang ausgeschlossen und unter Anführung von 10/99 und 11/118 daran erinnert, daß es Gott gefallen habe, daß es neben den Gläubigen auch Ungläubige gibt, was die Bekehrungshoffnungen auf ein realistisches Maß zurückschraubt. Auch in 28/56 hieße es: "Du kannst nicht rechtleiten, wen du gerne magst. Gott ist es vielmehr, der rechtleitet, wen er will. Er weiß am besten, wer sich

---

48 Zit. nach Karaman 1990, S. 171.

49 Abdullah Draz, İslâm'ın diğer dinlere karşı tutumu ve onlarla ilişkisi, *Diyanet Dergisi* (3/1994), S. 59-67.

50 Draz (3/1994), S. 66, zitiert in der Übersetzung von Paret, Rudi: *Der Koran*, 3. Auflage, Kohlhammer, Stuttgart 1979.

51 Draz (3/1994), S. 67.

rechtleiten läßt."[52]

Die auf religiösen Quellen fußenden Beiträge der Diyanet vertreten wohl den "orthodox-sunnitischen Islam hanefitischer Rechtsschule"[53], doch sie legen mit einer solchen Orientierung dem Verkehr zwischen Muslimen und Nichtmuslimen in der Diaspora keine unüberwindlichen Hürden in den Weg. Der orthodoxen Lesart der Quellen entspricht, daß kein politischer Aufruf an den einzelnen Muslim ergeht, sich (islam-)politisch zu betätigen, was nach türkischem Verständnis heißen würde, sich in Staatsgeschäfte einzumischen und die Macht herauszufordern. Im Gegenteil, die Beiträge propagieren eher noch den Untertanen als den Bürger, auf jeden Fall aber den unpolitischen Muslimen, der nicht ohne die Anweisung seiner (islamischen) Staatsautorität handelt und ansonsten sich (einer jeden, auch der des Aufnahmelandes) staatlichen Autorität zu beugen hat.[54]

Bis zu einem gewissen Grad wird das Christentum als ein Stück des Weges zur Wahrheit anerkannt,[55] Kooperation zwischen Christen und Muslimen gefordert und die Verantwortung der Muslime für ein gedeihliches Zusammenleben hervorgehoben.

Theologische Schriften im weiteren Sinne

Die bis jetzt behandelten Schriften bauen vollständig auf religiösen, ja auf sogenannten 'klassischen' Quellen auf, und eine etwaige spezifische Wahrnehmung der konkreten gesellschaftlichen Verhältnisse, mit ihren politischen Konstellationen, wirtschaftlichen Verflechtungen, kulturellen Einflüssen und sozialen Strukturen spielt in ihrer Argumentation so gut wie keine Rolle. Gänzlich anders liegt der Fall jedoch bei den Schriften des zweiten Typs, in dem, wie angeführt, zeit-

52 Draz (3/1994), S. 66, zitiert in der Übersetzung nach Paret 1979.

53 K. Binswanger & F. Sipahioğlu, *Türkisch-islamische Vereine als Faktor deutsch-türkischer Koexistenz*, Rieß, Benediktbeuern 1988, S. 75.

54 Daß der orthodoxe sunnitische Islam von seinen Gläubigen Anstrengungen zur Errichtung eines islamischen Staatswesens fordere, ist eine Mär, welche erstmals die islamistischen Theoretiker Anfang dieses Jahrhunderts den kolonialisierten bzw. unter absolutistischen Herrschern lebenden Muslimen erzählten. Vgl. zum Komplex Staat und Religion im Islam Sami Zubaida, *Islam, the People and the State*; London 1992.

55 "Die Unterrichtung, die die göttlichen Religionen auf diese Weise dem Menschen in seinem Entwicklungsprozeß angedeihen lassen, ist Ausdruck eines wohlüberlegten und allmählichen Vorgehens der göttlichen Gnade." Draz (3/1994), S. 63.

genössische Begriffe und Konzepte verschiedenster theoretischer Provenienz das Denken strukturieren. Zum Ausgangspunkt der Analyse von Schrifttum dieses Typs wähle ich ein Buch, das auf den ersten Blick nicht in diese Kategorie zu gehören scheint. Es richtet sich an den Nachwuchs der Religionsbehörde, die Schüler der Predigergymnasien und trägt den Titel *Religionsgeschichte: Die göttliche Philosophie in der Erschaffung des Menschen*.[56]

Von einer auch nur annähernd objektiven und vorurteilsfreien Darstellung des Christentums kann in diesem Buch keine Rede sein. So beginnt etwa die Vorstellung der Bibel in dem Kapitel, das das Christentum nicht im Lichte des Koran widerlegen, sondern aus dem Abschnitt, der es lediglich darstellen will, folgendermaßen: "Das heilige Buch des Christentums besteht aus der Thora, die 'Das Alte Testament' genannt wird, und dem Evangelium mit dem Namen 'Das Neue Testament'. Doch obwohl die Christen die Thora heiligen, halten sie sich nicht an ihre Lehre und an ihre Vorschriften. Weil sie mit der Thora, wie sie sie von den Juden übernommen haben, nicht nach Belieben verfahren konnten, haben sie deren Dogmata in ihren Geistlichen Konzilien verändert oder sie dem christlichen Glauben gemäß ausgelegt."[57]

Hier wird der aus der islamischen Theologie bekannte Vorwurf der Schriftverfälschung angedeutet, explizit jedoch eine absichtlich falsche Interpretation der Heiligen Schrift behauptet. Die Vorstellung der "Grundlegende(n) Dogmata des Christentums" beginnt mit ihrer modern und positivistisch[58] anmutenden Verurteilung: "Dieser Teil ist der wichtigste und umstrittenste Aspekt des Christentums. Die Dreifaltigkeit, die um der Sündenvergebung der Menschheit willen durchgeführte Kreuzigung Jesu und das jüngste Gericht, alles Dinge, die sich mit keiner Logik und mit keinem Wissenschaftsverständnis vereinbaren lassen, bilden seit Jahrhunderten die wichtigsten Glaubensgrund-

56 Ahmet Kahraman: *Dinler tarihi: İnsanın yaratılışındaki ilahi felsefe*, Marifet Yay. Istanbul <1966> 1988. Das Werk wurde an der Theologischen Fakultät der Universität Marmara als Lehrbuch für die Abschlußklassen der Predigergymnasien vorbereitet und vom Nationalen Erziehungministerium zugelassen. Es erlebte 1988 seine 5. Auflage und wird noch heute in den Läden der Diyanet-Moscheen in Europa vertrieben.

57 Kahraman, S. 161.

58 Ein Beispiel dafür, daß der Westen in der Auseinandersetzung mit der heutigen islamischen Welt sich selbst gegenübertritt.

lagen des Christentums."[59]

Im Abschnitt "Die großen Konfessionen des Christentums" wird deren Entstehung damit erklärt, daß die Christen von der Wahrheit abgewichen seien, was letztendlich zur Entwicklung getrennter Religionen geführt habe: "Das Christentum entfernte sich von seinem Ursprung, und man richtete Geistliche Konzilien aus, um die eigentliche Lehre zu bestimmen. Doch es kam zu Meinungsverschiedenheiten, und daraus entstanden verschiedene Konfessionen. Die wichtigsten dieser Konfessionen, die heute als Manifestationen unterschiedlicher Religionen erscheinen, sind der Katholizismus, die Orthodoxie und der aus der Reformation geborene Protestantismus."[60] Bereits aus diesen wenigen, jeweils einleitenden Passagen, die ja nicht aus der — im Buch ebenfalls enthaltenden — Polemik gegen das Christentum stammen, geht hervor, daß es an den Bildungseinrichtungen des laizistischen Staates um den Einfluß einer unabhängigen vergleichenden Religionswissenschaft schlecht bestellt ist.

Prinzipiell unabhängig von der Frage der theologischen Wahrheit der anderen Religion ist die Bewertung der Rolle, die das Christentum und seine Institutionen, die Kirchen, in der Geschichte Europas besonders in dessen Verhältnis zur nichteuropäischen Welt gespielt hat. Für deren Beurteilung zitiere ich wiederum einleitenden Sätze des genannten Buches, diesmal die des Abschnitts über die "Christlichen Missionseinrichtungen": "Als die Christen merkten, daß sie mit Waffengewalt ihre Religion nicht ausbreiten und den Islam nicht verdrängen konnten, änderten sie ihre Methode. Jetzt benutzten sie die Predigt, den 'wohlmeinenden' Rat, das Buch und die Broschüre, die Schule und das Krankenhaus. Dabei beschränkten sie sich nicht auf religiöse Einflüsterung und auf die Christianisierung. Neben der religiösen Propaganda ist[61] ihr eigentliches Ziel, die christliche Kultur auf den Trümmern der Kulturen der Völker (oder Nationen = milletler) zu errichten und die Völker (oder Nationen) von ihren volkstümlichen (oder nationalen = millî) Werten abzubringen. Dabei trieben sie es oft bis zur Landnahme. Die Kolonien der christlichen Staaten in Afrika und vielen (anderen, GS) Teilen der Welt sind dafür beredte

59 Kahraman, S. 166.

60 Kahraman, S. 178.

61 Man beachte den Wechsel des Tempus.

Beispiele."[62]

Mir erscheint hier weniger die Betonung der historisch gesicherten Tatsache der imperialistischen Nutzung des Christentums durch die Europäer bemerkenswert, sondern die Art und Weise der Darstellung, in der die europäische Expansion als direkte Folge des Christseins der Europäer erscheint. Dadurch nämlich, daß die Religionsbehörde den expansionistischen Charakter Europas an dessen Christlichsein bindet, leistet sie einem ausschließlich religiösen Lesen der Geschichte Europas und der Dritten Welt Vorschub und *bestätigt* damit letzten Endes das Weltbild der Islamisten, deren Einfluß *zurückzudrängen* sie doch angetreten sein will. Zwar besteht kein Zweifel daran, daß sich dieses Wahrnehmungsmuster auch ohne Zutun der Religionsbürokratie in weiten Kreisen des Volkes findet.[63] Doch die Publikationen staatlicher Institutionen nehmen es auf, verstärken es, und wenden seinen Focus von 'den Muslimen' weg, hin zum laizistischen Staat. Man schlägt den Bogen von der Kolonialzeit zum Heute und funktionalisiert gleichzeitig die antiwestlichen und antichristlichen Ressentiments im Volke für die Legitimation des Staates. Deshalb erscheinen am Schluß des genannten Abschnitts die christlichen Kirchen als ausgemachte Feinde der Republik Türkei und der türkischen Nation. Denn durch Landkäufe in West- und Südanatolien bereiteten die Kirchen die Zerstückelung des Landes vor, doch: "Dieses Land gehört uns und bleibt unser. Jeder Türke, der sein Vaterland und seine Nation liebt, ist ein Freiwilliger in diesem Kampf. Ob hier oder im Ausland, wer uns schief ansieht, der verliert sein Augenlicht. Anatolien, unsere paradiesgleiche Heimat ist das letzte und ewige Stück Land unseres großen Volkes (oder Nation = millet). Es kann sich keiner davor drücken, die Märtyrer, die in diesem Boden ruhen, vor neuen Kreuzzügen und neuen Feindseligkeiten zu schützen. Wer nicht mit uns ist, ist gegen uns. Ein jeder muß wissen: Dies ist eine religiöse und nationale Pflicht."[64]

---

62 Kahraman, S. 201-202; exakt die gleiche Argumentation findet sich auch in einer Publikation der Religionsbehörde, siehe Osman Cilacı: *Hıristiyanlık propagandası ve misyonerlik faaliyetleri*, Diyanet İşleri Başkanlığı, Ankara 1992, S. 9-10.

63 Vgl. zu religiös konnotierten Wahrnehmungsmustern und Haltungen der türkischen Bevölkerung Günter Seufert, Religion und Politik in der Türkei, BTS-Franz Steiner, Stuttgart und Istanbul 1997.

64 Kahraman, S. 213.

So endet das Kapitel über das Christentum, welches hier nur in zweiter Linie religiös - nämlich als Irrlehre - beschrieben und in erster Linie als Mittel der ideologischen Kriegsführung Europas präsentiert wird. Im Grunde läßt sich die Aussage, die die Religionsbürokratie mit diesem und ähnlichem Material nahelegt, auf folgenden Satz zuspitzen: Als Religion ist das Christentum keiner weiteren oder keiner eingehenden Auseinandersetzung wert, doch weil Europa das Christentum als ideologische Waffe benutzt, ist diese Religion gefährlich für unser Land. Dabei ist die Politik in der Argumentation der Religionsbürokratie die eigentlich wichtige Sphäre, und religiöse Fragen werden auf den zweiten Rang verwiesen. Einer politologischen und soziologischen Betrachtung des Handelns einer nationalstaatlichen Institution mag dieser Befund nahezu selbstverständlich erscheinen, doch für die Beurteilung der Religionsbehörde als Partner im Integrationsprozeß muslimischer Minderheiten in der europäischen Diaspora ist er zweifelsohne bedeutsam.

Die Beurteilung der Diaspora

Im vorangegangenen Beispiel ist das gleichzeitig nahe und ferne *Europa* in der Wahrnehmung der türkischen Muslime ein aus unentwirrbaren religiösen (christlichen) und weltlichen (die europäische Expansion) Komponenten bestehender Gegenstand, der mit starken Bedrohungsgefühlen besetzt ist. Ich glaube, daß auch die muslimische Wahrnehmung der Diaspora durch eine ähnliche Verbindung einer religiösen (christlichen) und einer weltlichen Dimension charakterisiert ist, wobei ich in diesem Fall die weltliche Dimension als die spezifische Säkularität der europäischen Gesellschaften und ihrer Institutionen ansehe. Es ist die Spannung zwischen diesen beiden Dimensionen, die den Muslimen Unbehagen bereitet und die es ihnen so schwer macht, Stellung zu beziehen.

Europa als Hort des Christentums

Wählen die Muslime der Diaspora die religiöse Dimension Europas, seine Christlichkeit, zum Ausgangspunkt für ihr Verhältnis zu ihm, dann läßt sich formulieren, daß sie sich mit einer christlich-konservativen europäischen Gesellschaft, in der eine traditionelle Sittlichkeit herrschte, leichter abfinden könnten als mit einer säkularen christlichen Gesellschaft, die alle ihre konkreten Handlungsnormen unter Hinweis auf moderne Ideologien von der Notwendigkeit absoluter Freiheit des Menschen relativiert.

Wählen die Muslime der Diaspora indes die säkulare (für sie oft gleich einer laizistischen) Dimension Europas zum Ausgangspunkt für ihr Verhältnis zu ihm, dann kann gesagt werden, daß sie sich wohl eher mit einem wirklich laizistischen Europa arrangieren könnten, in dem die Trennung von Kirche und Staat gewährleistet und dessen Kultur nicht von christlichen Begriffen durchdrungen wäre, als mit einer Gesellschaft, die anscheinend keinen Widerspruch mehr sehen will, zwischen ihrer säkularen Modernität und der oft christlichen Symbolisierung ihrer grundlegender Werthaltungen.

Ich beginne die Konkretisierung der oben getroffen allgemeinen Aussagen mit der Zeichnung des zweiten Bildes der Muslime von Europa, des Bildes von Europa als einem Ort, der sich weltlich geriert und doch ein Hort christlicher Kultur bleibt.

Die Frage, die es zu beantworten gilt, lautet, was macht die Religionsbehörde aus dieser Spannung? Deshalb stammt das Material, mit dessen Hilfe ich mich dem Komplex nähere, aus der Feder von Mitarbeitern der Diyanet, die sich mit den Problemen der türkischen Muslime in Europa beschäftigen und die teilweise selbst mehrere Jahre für die Behörde in Europa tätig waren. In einem solchen Beitrag schreibt der Autor[65], daß die Kinder in Belgien sowohl in den staatlichen, besonders aber in den Konfessionsschulen das ganze Jahr über an ihr Christsein erinnert würden. Er fährt folgendermaßen fort:

“Wie kann das sein, in einem europäischen Land?’, mag sich der eine oder andere fragen. Denn davon ist (in der Türkei, GS) nicht viel berichtet worden. Im Curriculum ist das alles (die christlichen Elemente, GS) gar nicht einzeln vermerkt. Doch es gibt (immer wieder, GS) Anlässe, die dazu führen, daß die christliche Atmosphäre aufrechterhalten wird. So sind z.B. innerhalb eines Schuljahres in Belgien 41 Tage schulfrei, nur einer davon anläßlich des Endes des Zweiten

65 Abdullah Sevinç hat seine Erfahrungen in der europäischen Diaspora als Religionslehrer in Belgien und als Religionsattaché in Holland gemacht. Zum Zeitpunkt der Veröffentlichung seiner Artikels in der Fachzeitschrift der Diyanet war er in der Publikationsabteilung der Religionsbehörde tätig.

Weltkriegs. Die Gründe für die restlichen vierzig sind ausschließlich religiöser Natur, sind Festen geschuldet wie Sinter Klaas, Noel, Drie Koningen, Hemelvaartsdag und Paasfest."[66]

Auf diese Feste würde die Schule, so der Autor, ihre Schüler oft schon einen Monat vorher vorbereiten. Ein auf diese Weise stets präsentes Christentum grenze zwangsläufig muslimische Schüler aus, bei denen sich oft das Gefühl der Mangelhaftigkeit einstelle und sich daraus resultierend der Wunsch bilde, auch Christ zu sein.[67] Eine solche mittelbare religiöse Beeinflussung durch die christlich geprägte Kultur Europas finde jedoch nicht nur in der Schule, sondern auch über die Massenmedien, insbesondere das Fernsehen, statt, wo nicht nur Gottesdienste und Messen übertragen, sondern darüberhinaus in Spielfilmen und Serien tagtäglich christliche Bräuche, Sitten, Verhaltensnormen und Wertorientierungen popularisiert würden.[68] Die geschilderte *Entdeckung* dieser starken christlichen Prägung der europäischen Gesellschaften und ihrer Kultur durch die türkischen Muslime ist ein immer wieder zu beobachtender Vorgang[69] und gleichzeitig ein in der innertürkischen Auseinandersetzug gegen Laizisten und Säkularisten häufig vorgebrachtes Argument.[70]

Doch für die Beobachter aus der Religionsbehörde bleibt es nicht bei einer solchen, eher indirekten Einflüsterung des Christentums, und die Beschuldigung ausnahmslos alle christlicher Kirchen und Sekten würden Mission unter den Muslimen betreiben, sind fester Bestandteil eines jeden Beitrags der Religionsbehörde über die Situation in der Diaspora.

"Für die Christen ist die Mission eine Grundlage ihrer Religion,

66 Abdullah Sevinç, Türkiye Avrupa Ekonomik Topluluğu'na girerse ..., *Diyanet Dergisi* (1/1989), S. 105-120, hier S. 108.

67 Sevinç (1/1989), S. 116-117; gleichlautend İrfan Başkurt, *Federal Almanya'da din eğitimi*, Marmara Üniv. İlahiyat Fak. Vakfı Yay., Istanbul 1995, S. 117. Nahezu unmöglich gemacht würde die Identifikation des Kindes mit dem Islam, wenn zum schädlichen Einfluß der christlichen Umwelt auch noch der ebenso schädliche eines nicht-muslimischer Elternteils hinzukomme, vg. Abdullah Sevinç, Nesli korumak, *Diyanet Dergisi* (2/1991), S. 117-127, hier S. 218.

68 N.Y. Aşıkoğlu, *Almanya'da temel eğitimdeki Türk çocuklarının din eğitimi*, Türkiye Diyanet Vakfı, Ankara 1993, S. 71-72.

69 Başkurt 1995, passim, Şükrü Özbuğday, Misyonerliğin dünü-bugünü, *Diyanet Aylık Dergi* (populäre Monatsschrift der Religionsbehörde) (11/1995), S. 38-39.

70 Vgl. Günter Seufert, Wie aus Freunden Fremde werden, *Das Sonntagsblatt*, Hamburg 24.2.95, S. 7-9.

und sie sehen es als eine Gnade Gottes an, daß Angehörige anderer Religionen in ihre Länder kommen, Menschen, die sie christianisieren können."[71] Noch immer geht man in der Behörde davon aus, daß die Christen sich den Muslimen in erster Linie in bekehrender Absicht nähern würden, und läßt bei dieser Vermutung keinen Unterschied zwischen den Großkirchen und missionarischen evangelischen Freikirchen oder Sekten, wie den Zeugen Jehovas, gelten.[72]

Die Autoren der Religionsbürokratie empfehlen als Antwort auf all diese Gefahren in der Regel die Selbstisolierung der Muslime und ihre Abschottung von der Gesellschaft des Aufnahmelandes. Konkrete Ratschläge in dieser Richtung sehen folgendermaßen aus: "Die Kinder sollten sofort nach der Grundschule in die Türkei geschickt und vor allen Dingen religiös unterrichtet werden."[73]

So das nicht zu machen ist, sollte die Erziehung der türkisch-muslimischen Kinder in der Diaspora weitestgehend unter türkischem Einfluß stattfinden: "In Deutschland sollten die Kinder vier Tage in die türkische und zwei Tage in die deutsche Schule gehen. Man muß ihnen unbedingt Türkisch beibringen und die türkische Geschichte muß so vermittelt werden, daß sie sich mit ihr identifizieren können. Die Eltern in Deutschland müssen sich mehr um die Kinder kümmern ... und unser (das türkische, GS) Nationales Erziehungsministerium muß die Lehrinhalte der Schulen kontrollieren."[74] "Wir müssen erreichen, daß die Erziehung unsere Kinder unter unserer Kontrolle abläuft. Deshalb sollten Heime eröffnet werden, in denen türkische Pflegerinnen Dienst tun. So kann es nicht zu der Tragödie kommen, daß

71 Sevinç (1/1989), S. 117; christliche Missionierungsversuche beklagen auch Kahraman 1984, S. 210; M.N. Yılmaz, (Präsident der Religionsbehörde): Misyonerlik faaliyetler üzerine, *Diyanet Aylık Dergi*, (11/1995), S. 1 und Başkurt 1985, S. 116 und Osman Cilacı, Yurtdışındaki işçi çocuklarının dinî problemleri açısından Türkiye'ye uyumları meselesi, *Diyanet Dergisi* (3/1985), S. 54.

72 Uslu 29.3.96.

73 Cilacı (3/1985), S. 51

74 Ebenda. Das Bestreben der Religionsbürokratie, Einfluß auf die Sozialisation der Migrantenkinder ausüben zu können, läßt sich auch an den Diskussionen über die Erteilung eines muslimischen Religionsunterricht an deutschen Schulen ablesen. Nachdem die türkische Botschaft gegenüber dem nordrhein-westfälischen Landesinstitut für Schule und Weiterbildung, das die Curriculumentwicklung betreibt, erst betonte, daß es für solche Aktivitäten deutscher Stellen keinen Bedarf gäbe, hat sie sich in den folgenden Jahren darum bemüht, Einfluß auf die Arbeiten zu nehmen. Dokumentiert bei Aşıkoğlu 1993, S. 56-81.

unsere Kinder zusammen mit fremden Kindern in einen Kindergarten gehen und dort unter den religiösen Einfluß von Pfarrern und Nonnen geraten..."[75]

An den genannten Artikeln aus der Fachzeitschrift der Religionsbehörde fällt auf, daß jemand, der die Frage stellen würde, was es denn auf theologischer, auf rein religiöser Ebene, für Eltern in der Diaspora bedeute, wenn sie ihr Kind nicht zu einem guten Muslimen erziehen, keine Antworten finden würde. Auch Hinweise darauf, was es denn über die Verantwortlichkeit eines muslimischen Kindes zu sagen gibt, das unter den so geschilderten Umständen in der europäischen Diaspora fast zwangsweise dem Christentum anheimfällt, finden sich nicht. Dem Pathos, mit dem die religiöse Gefahr beschworen wird, steht der Verzicht auf jegliche theologische Reflexion dieser Gefahr oder ihrer Folgen gegenüber. Wenn von den Konsequenzen christlicher Einflüsterung und christlicher Kultur auf die türkischen Muslime die Rede ist, dann primär - und hier läßt sich der Bogen zu dem bereits angeführten Buch über die Geschichte der Religionen schlagen - in politischen Parametern. Dann ist die Rede von den Folgen, die die Christianisierung der Migranten für den türkischen Staat und seine Nation hat.

Welche sind das? Ganz allgemein drohen Staat und Nation ihrer Menschen verlustig zu gehen, und noch 1985 zeichnete die Fachzeitschrift der Religionsbehörde folgendes Schreckensgemälde: "Eine der größten Gefahren für unsere Kinder besteht darin, daß die Deutschen sie dazu bringen, die deutsche Staatsangehörigkeit anzunehmen .. "[76] Doch selbst wenn sich die türkischen Muslime in ihrem jeweiligen Aufnahmeland nicht naturalisieren lassen, verlieren sie für die Religionsbehörde mit ihrem Glauben auch jeglichen Nutzen für Staat und Nation. Den Zusammenhang zwischen Glaubensverlust und Schwächung der Nation stellt Mehmet Nuri Yılmaz, Präsident der Religionsbehörde her: "Die entsprechenden Gesetze haben unserem Präsidium die Aufgabe erteilt, die Gesellschaft in Fragen der Religion zu unterrichten. Unser Präsidium wird ... nicht zulassen, daß der Islam geschwächt oder gar zerstört wird, der die Grundlage der Nationalkultur unserer Nation ist, die zu 99% aus Muslimen besteht. Diese Angele-

[75] Cilacı (3/1985), S. 57.

[76] Cilacı (3/1985), S. 56.

genheit hängt eng mit unserer nationalen Geschlossenheit zusammen und ist deshalb von besonderer Wichtigkeit."[77]
Mit dieser Haltung, in der die Religion primär als Kitt für die Geschlossenheit der türkischen Nation erscheint, übernimmt die Religionsbürokratie die Vorgaben der sogenannten Türkisch-Islamischen Synthese. Diese Ideologie von einer einheitlich türkisch-sunnitischen Religionsnation wurde Anfang der 80er Jahre zur offiziellen Leitlinie der Bildungs- und Kulturpolitik der Republik Türkei und schließt die Anerkennung von unterschiedlichen ethnischen Gruppen unter ihren Bewohnern genauso aus, wie die Anerkennung unterschiedlicher Konfessionen.[78] Auch der Autor, der oben mit seinen Vorschlägen zu einer vom türkischen Staat zu steuernden und zu kontrollierenden Sozialisation der türkischen Kinder in Westeuropa angeführt wurde, bezieht sich in seinem Beitrag ausdrücklich auf die entsprechende Vorlage 'Nationalkultur' des Staatlichen Planungsamtes *(Devlet Planlama Teşkilâtı)*, in der sich diese Ideologie ausformuliert findet und in der auf das Recht des Staates zur Kulturlenkung hingewiesen wird.[79]

Die so einfachen wie grundlegenden Thesen dieser Ideologie zusammenfassend schreibt er: "Die Religion des Islam formt uns und macht aus uns das, was wir sind. Unsere Nation hat zwei Grundlagen, unsere Religion und unsere Sprache, nur mit beidem sind wir Türken."[80] Weil in diesem Raster religiöse und nationale Identität untrennbar miteinander verwoben sind, muß dem Einfluß einer christlichen Umwelt nicht nur mit einer Erhöhung der Dosis religiösen Wissens begegnet, sondern auch das nationale Bewußtsein gestärkt werden. Um aus Diaspora-Geschädigten taugliche Staatsbürger zu machen, wird empfohlen, Rückkehrerkindern ein Jahr lang Sonderunterricht zu erteilen, in welchem ihnen (in dieser Reihenfolge) "Liebe zu den Großen des türkischen Volkes, zum Vaterland, zur Nation, zur Fahne und zur Religion"[81] beigebracht werden soll. Folgerichtig

77 Yılmaz (11/1995), S. 1

78 Vgl. zum Inhalt dieser Türk-İslam-sentezi Seufert 1997, S. 182-191.

79 Cilacı (3/1985), S. 48. Vgl. Devlet Planlama Teşkilâtı: *Millî Kültür*, Ankara 1983; siehe zur Anerkennung dieser Ideologie durch den Staat: B. Güvenç, G. Şaylan, İ. Tekeli, İ. Turan: *Türk-İslam sentezi*, Sarmal, Istanbul 1991.

80 Cilacı (3/1985), S. 49.

81 Cilacı (3/1985), S. 54. Vgl. die Betonung des nationalen Elements durch die Religionsbürokratie auch in der Diskussion um den Religionsunterricht in der bundesdeutschen Diaspora, Aşıkoğlu 1993, S. 65-68.

sprechen Autoren der Religionsbehörde und der übrigen Religionsbürokratie selten nur von der Religion, sondern in der Regel von "religiöser *und* nationaler" "Kultur", "Beeinflussung", "Sitte" und "Liebe"; von "religiösem *und* nationalem" "Wissen" und "Brauchtum" und von "religiösen *und* nationalen" "Werten". Denn: "Wir dürfen nicht übersehen, daß eine Nation, die ihre religiösen und nationalen Werte verliert, ihrer Lebenskraft verlustig geht."[82]

Für die Religionsbehörde liegt die Gefahr demnach primär darin, daß die europäisch-christliche Umwelt den islamischen Glauben der türkischen Staatsbürger schwächt, diese damit in ihrer türkischen Identität schädigt und sie damit dem Staate entfremdet, der sich türkisch (und zunehmend auch islamisch) definiert. Folge einer solchen Entfremdung sind — in den Parametern der Religionsbehörde — soziale Verwerfungen, Unruhe und Unfrieden, in weniger moralisierenden Begriffen ausgedrückt ist es die Gefahr politischer Opposition.

Europa als Hort des Säkularismus

Die Wahrnehmung der Religionsbehörde von Europa und vom Christentum wird somit zu einem guten Teil durch ihren Charakter als Institution eines jungen Nationalstaates und durch ihren spezifischen Auftrag gezeichnet. Die Analyse dieser Wahrnehmung bliebe jedoch unvollständig, würde nicht auch die zweite oben angesprochene Dimension von Europa reflektiert, das Bild von Europa als Inbegriff der säkularen Moderne.

Anders nämlich als die oben referierte Phobie vor christlichem Einfluß in Kindergarten, Schule und Massenmedien nahelegen könnte, wird das offensichtliche Schwinden des kirchlichen Einflusses in den europäischen Gesellschaften insbesondere im Hinblick auf den damit einhergehenden Verfall unzweideutiger Sittlichkeitsvorstellungen offen beklagt. Es ist vor allen Dingen das Ineinanderfließen ehedem klar voneinander geschiedener geschlechtsspezifischer Rollenvorschriften und damit die Auflösung der patriarchal strukturierten Familie, die unter den Muslimen den Eindruck entstehen läßt, daß die ordnende Kraft der Religion im sozialen Leben der europäischen Gesell-

82 Cilacı (3/1985), S. 57

schaften am Erlöschen ist.[83] Denn im Unterschied zu den modernen Christen Europas verhandeln die Muslime aus den Anwerbeländern den Bereich innerfamilialer Moralität nach wie vor in religiös konnotierten Begriffen und erscheint ihnen deshalb die Auflösung der gewohnten familialen Beziehungen als Verflüchtigung der Religion.[84]

Mit allen muslimischen Gruppen teilt die Religionsbehörde die Sorge um die Bindung der Frau an die Familie und damit über die Kontrolle ihrer Sexualität in der so anders strukturierten Diaspora.[85] Diese Sorge drückt sich am augenfälligsten in den Kopftuchdebatten aus, die in nahezu allen Aufnahmeländern geführt worden sind. Tatsächlich hat keine muslimische Organisation Schwierigkeiten mit folgendem Satz aus der Zeitschrift der Religionsbehörde: "Es ist eine bekannte Tatsache, daß Religionserziehung und Sittlichkeitserziehung nicht zwei voneinander verschiedene Dinge sind."[86] Als Sittlichkeitserziehung hat Religionserziehung zu verhindern, daß sich die Familien der muslimischen Migranten den europäischen Familien angleichen. Denn diese sind in Auflösung und Degeneration begriffen, was nach einem weiteren Artikel eines bereits angeführten, europaerfahrenen Autoren für Homosexualität, AIDS, Drogenmißbrauch, Alkoholismus und Inzest verantwortlich ist.[87]

Doch wie eng für die Muslime die Verbindung von Sittlichkeit und Religion auch immer sei, die Moralität ihrer Gläubigen ist der Religionsbehörde in letzter Instanz wieder nur Mittel zum bereits bekannten Zweck: zum Schutz des türkischen Staates und seiner Nation. Die Familie ist die Keimzelle der Nation,[88] und wer sie schwächt, der tut dies in den Augen der *Religionsbehörde* allein deshalb, um die Sitten

83 Daß sich patriarchale Moralität in religiösen Begriffen äußert, ist der wichtigste gemeinsame Punkt zwischen dem protestantischen Fundamentalismus vom Anfang dieses Jahrhunderts und dem sogenannten islamischen Fundamentalismus, vgl. Martin Riesebrodt, *Fundamentalismus als patriarchalische Protestbewegung*, Mohr, Tübingen 1990.

84 Daraus resultiert die Bereitschaft islamischer Staaten, in Familienfragen eine gemeinsame Front mit dem Vatikan zu bilden, zuletzt geschehen auf der Welt-Wohnraumkonferenz HABITAT II von 3. bis 14. 6. 96 in Istanbul.

85 So nennt Cilacı in seinem Aufsatz als einziges *konkretes* Problem muslimischer *Kinder* die zu lange Schulzeit für Mädchen, siehe (3/1985), S. 50.

86 Cilacı (3/1985), S. 51

87 Sevinç,(2/1991), S. 121.

88 Sevinç, (2/1991), S. 118.

der Türken zu verderben und der türkischen Nation zu schaden: "Ein (nicht näher genannter türkischer, GS) Schriftsteller behauptet 'Die Revolution in der Familie beginnt damit, daß die Frau ihre sexuelle Freiheit erlangt.' Wer da so zur Verirrung und Verwirrung beiträgt, sollte sich darüber klar sein, daß er mit der Entartung der Familie denen zuarbeitet, die die muslimisch-türkische Nation vernichten wollen."[89] Dabei sei die türkische Familie von Natur aus gesund. In Quellen aus vorislamischer Zeit heiße es, daß die Frau, die auf ihren in die Fremde gegangenen Mann wartet, nicht einmal einer männliche Fliege erlaube, sich auf sie zu setzten. Wie damals der Schamanismus sichere heute der Islam, daß die hohe Sittlichkeit der Türken von Generation zu Generation weitergegeben werde.[90]

Wieder tritt der Schutz von Nation und Staat als die Achse hervor, um die sich das Denken in der Religionsbehörde dreht.[91] Nachdem dies herausgearbeitet wurde, kann jetzt ein Zitat vollständig angeführt werden, das oben nur teilweise verwendet wurde, weil nicht ersichtlich gewesen wäre, wie seine einzelnen Sätze inhaltlich zusammenhängen: "Es ist eine bekannte Tatsache, daß Religionserziehung und Sittlichkeitserziehung nicht zwei voneinander verschiedene Dinge sind. Religionserziehung ist systematisch nur in der Schule leistbar. Für jede Nation ist die Religion wie ein schützendes Schild."[92]

In dem von der Religionsbürokratie produzierten Schrifttum der zweiten Kategorie, in den *Publikationen, in denen nicht originär theologische, sondern primär Versatzstücke säkularer Weltanschauungen*

89 Sevinç (2/1991), S. 124. Der Autor führt außerdem das 'Zitat' eines christlichen Geistlichen namens G. Simon an, der die Zerstörung der Sitten und moralischen Werte unter den Türken als Schritt zur Verbreitung des Christentums und der Herrschaft Europas über die Muslime beschwöre. Der gleiche Topos, vom christlichen Geistlichen, der über die Vernichtung der Sitten und der Kultur der Muslime diese letzen Endes schwächen und unterwerfen will, findet sich auch bei Özbuğday (11/1995), S. 39. In der Person der sittenuntergrabenden christlichen Geistlichen gelangen die beiden Bilder von *Europa als Hort des Christentums* und von *Europa als Ort der säkularen Sittenlosigkeit* zur Deckungsgleichheit.

90 Sevinç (2/1991), S. 118-119.

91 Tatsächlich bringen es aus der Türkei eingeflogene Referenten fertig, noch beim Thema Suchtmittelmißbrauch der türkischen Jugendlichen in Deutschland darauf hinzuweisen, daß der Alkoholismus eine ganze Nation zerstören kann, und daß genau das die Feinde der Türkei beabsichtigen. So etwa Rabi Baştürk im Januar 1996 auf einer Veranstaltung von neun der DİTİB angeschlossenen Moscheegemeinden, vgl. *Türkiye Gazetesi*, 18.1.96, S. 18, Deutschlandausgabe.

92 Cilacı (3/1985), S. 51.

die zentralen Konzepte bilden, erscheint das Islamverständnis der Religionsbehörde als inhaltsleer. Die Religion wird ausschließlich im Hinblick auf die Möglichkeiten betrachtet, die sie zur Stärkung des Staates und zur Vereinheitlichung seiner Nation bietet, ist eher Mittel als Zweck und führt kein Eigenleben. Der Islam, wie ihn die Religionsbehörde in diesen Schriften präsentiert, spricht den einzelnen Gläubigen nicht an, sondern die Gruppe und ruft diese zu steter Vorsicht und Abschottung auf. In der Diaspora, so der Islam der Religionsbehörde, zieht sich der Gläubige am besten auf sich und seine Gruppe zurück, denn überall lauern Gefahren für ihn selbst und für Staat und Nation. Ein solches Religionsverständnis muß passivierende Wirkung haben. Es provoziert keine Fragen, die Religion stellt dem Einzelnen keine Forderungen und ruft ihn nicht zur Aktivität. Ein solches Religionsverständnis lädt den Gläubigen nicht zum Nachdenken ein, denn was der Islam von ihm will, steht von vorneherein fest: bleiben, was er ist, ein Türke in der Fremde *(gurbet)*, seiner Nation verbunden und seinem Staate gehorsam.

Ergebnis

Während der *orthodoxe sunnitische Islam*, wie er in den Publikationen aufscheint, deren Argumentation *auf religiösen Quellen* aufbaut, *im Prinzip* eine Fülle von Verständigungsmöglichkeiten zwischen Muslimen und Christen eröffnet und - wiederum *im Prinzip* - viele Ansatzpunkte für gemeinsames Handeln bietet, ist der *Islam im Dienste des Nationalstaates* und des Nationenbaus in der Diaspora auf Abgrenzung fixiert. Der *orthodoxe Islam* konfrontiert den Gläubigen zwar mit bisweilen strikten konkreten Verhaltensnormen und bindet ihn damit immer wieder an seine Gemeinschaft zurück. Er stellt ihm jedoch auch ethische Forderungen, die ihm nahelegen, sich in der Gesellschaft, in der er lebt, mit Nichtmuslimen auseinanderzusetzen. Der *orthodoxe Islam* lädt dazu ein, die Position des anderen im Lichte der eigenen Wahrheit zu prüfen und ist deshalb auch ein Mittel intellektueller Verarbeitung neuer Situationen. Der *Islam des Nationalstaates* verfügt weder über Verhaltensnormen noch über ethische Forderungen. Denn beide werden stets von einem Wir-Gruppen-Interesse relativiert, dessen aktuelle Form von der Staatsbürokratie bestimmt wird.

Der *Islam des Nationalstaates* ist damit intellektuell ähnlich unfruchtbar wie die Ideologie des Nationalismus. Es spricht vieles dafür, daß sich im praktischen Handeln der Religionsbürokratie im In- und Ausland, in der islamischen Welt und in der europäischen Diaspora der *Islam des Nationalstaates* eher wiederfindet als der *orthodoxe Islam*.

So wird auch bei Gesprächen in der Zentrale der Diyanet in Ankara betont, daß es die Aufgabe der Behörde sei, den Muslimen in der Diaspora bei der Bewahrung ihrer "*nationalen und* religiösen Identität" zu helfen. Nicht nur die Kenntnis des Glaubens und ein an dessen sittlichen Normen orientiertes Leben in der Diaspora ist das Ziel der Arbeit in der Diaspora, sondern auch "die Bewahrung des Brauchtums"[93] und damit zwangsläufig die Konservierung einer spezifisch nationalen Färbung des Islams.

Heute scheint der Staat in der Religionsbehörde nicht nur eine Waffe gegen die sich muslimisch artikulierende Opposition zu sehen, sondern sie auch dazu zu benutzen, die Auslandstürken auf eine distinguierte national-religiöse Identität zu verpflichten, sie in der Diaspora als eigene Gruppe zu erhalten und damit in den verschiedenen europäischen Ländern eine ihm treu ergebene Lobby zu etablieren. Die Leitung der Diyanet befürwortet heute den Verbleib der türkischen Muslime in Westeuropa und ihre Naturalisierung im jeweiligen Aufnahmeland (nach Möglichkeit in der Form der Doppelten Staatsbürgerschaft). Man sieht die Lage der türkischen Muslime in der Diaspora jedoch analog zu der der jüdischen und armenischen Auslandsgemeinden. Juden und Armenier lebten seit Generationen außerhalb ihrer Heimat und ihrer Staaten und seien sich doch stets ihrer distinguierten nationalen und religiösen Identität bewußt. Nur eine sich ihrer eigenen Identität[94] und ihrer Wurzeln bewußte und gleichzeitig über politische Partizipationsmöglichkeiten im Aufnahmeland verfügende Gemeinde könne im Ausland als Lobbygruppe für die Heimat tätig werden.

Der Blick aus Ankara auf die europäischen Gesellschaften und ihre Institutionen ist noch immer von tiefem Mißtrauen geprägt. Im Unterschied zu den anderen türkisch-islamischen Organisationen in der

93 Uslu 29.3.96.

94 Soytürk 29.3.96. Der verwendete türkische Begriff *özbenlik* legt eine primordiale, unveränderliche Vorstellung von Identität nahe.

Diaspora ist bei der Diyanet davon auszugehen, daß ihr behördlicher Charakter sowohl die Etablierung einer in Europa groß gewordenen Führungsschicht verhindert als auch die Bildung von Kanälen, über die Wissen über die sittlichen und moralischen Selbstverständlichkeiten der christlich-säkularen Gesellschaften nach Ankara gelangen und die dortige Wahrnehmung korrigieren könnte.

Trotz allem betont man in der Behörde die Bereitschaft zur Zusammenarbeit in der Diaspora. Man will in den jeweiligen nationalen Islamgremien, die sich in den verschiedenen europäischen Ländern gebildet haben, mitarbeiten und sieht durch deren Entstehung die eigene Existenzberechtigung dort auch langfristig nicht in Frage gestellt. Der aktuellen Kooperationsbereitschaft der Auslandsgliederungen der Diyanet sind jedoch enge Grenzen gesteckt. In der BRD beteiligte sich die DİTİB mehrere Jahre am Gedankenaustausch unter den Organisationen des *Islamischen Arbeitskreises Deutschland*. Nach der Umbenennung des Arbeitskreises in *Zentralrat der Muslime in Deutschland*, ein Name der bewußt in Anlehnung an den *Zentralrat der Juden in Deutschland* gewählt worden war, und den Bemühungen um eine Institutionalisierung des Islams in der BRD Ausdruck verlieh, stellte die DİTİB ihre Mitarbeit ein. Als Modell für eine islamische Organisation in einem westeuropäischen Staat wird von der DİTİB auf die österreichische Lösung verwiesen.[95]

Die Religionsbehörde in der Türkei

Im Gegensatz zu den 60er Jahren, der Phase der Arbeitskräfteanwerbung, als die islamische Religion als explizite Legitimation des Staates keine Rolle spielte,[96] präsentiert sich der türkische Staat heute sowohl innen- als auch außenpolitisch allgemein stärker mit Hilfe der Religion. Als Folge der neuen geostrategischen Situation im Balkan und im Nahen und Mittleren Osten wird die ideologische Einflußnahme im Ausland immer wichtiger. Die Religion bietet dafür zu einem guten Teil die Legitimation, und die Diyanet ist eines ihrer wichtigsten Werkzeuge. Die Aufgaben der Behörde sind gewachsen und ihr Stel-

95 Uslu 29.3.96.

96 Was sicher zu einem Teil den damaligen Verzicht auf die Betreuung türkischer Arbeiter im Ausland erklärt.

lenwert in der türkischen Politik gestiegen.
Dementsprechend unterscheidet man in der Zentrale der Diyanet heute folgende Zielgruppen, je nach dem Grad, in dem sich die Behörde dem Anliegen dieser Gruppen verpflichtet fühlt (oder sie auf den türkischen Staat zu verpflichten sucht): 1. Vatandaşlar = *Staatsangehörige* = Bürger der Republik Türkei; 2. Soydaşlar = *Artgenossen*, = Angehörige der Turk-Völker und Bewohner der ehemaligen Besitzungen des Osmanischen Reiches auf dem Balkan, wie Bosniaken, Albaner, Pomaken und 3. Müslümanlar = *Muslime* = Die Gläubigen allgemein, die Muslime der Welt.[97]

Dieser Unterteilung wohnt eine eigentümliche Spannung inne. Zwar bedient sie sich Kriterien wie Sprache, "Rasse", "gemeinsame Geschichte" und Staatsbürgerschaft, doch verwendet sie diese nach eigenem Gutdünken und konstruiert die genannten Zielgruppen eher neu, als daß sie solche tatsächlich in der Realität vorfände. So spielt das Kriterium *Sprache* bei der Konstruktion der ersten Gruppe keine Rolle und die *Staatsbürgerschaft* ist allein entscheidend. Die Konstruktion der zweiten Gruppe erfolgt im Bezug auf die Muslime des Balkans über die Verwendung des Kriteriums "gemeinsame Geschichte" und im Bezug auf die turksprachigen Muslime Mittelasiens über die Kriterien "Rasse" und *Sprache*, die willkürlich kombiniert werden. Es steht in Übereinstimmung mit der festgestellten nationalistischen und pragmatischen Ausrichtung der Behörde, daß gerade religiöse Unterscheidungen, Konfessionen, überhaupt nicht zu existieren scheinen. Innerhalb der *Staatsangehörigen* wird nicht nach Sunniten und Alewiten[98] unterschieden und innerhalb der Sunniten nicht nach den Rechtsschulen der (meist türkischsprachigen) Hanefiten und der (meist kurmandschisprachigen) Schafiiten. Auch bei der Gruppe der *Artgenossen* erfolgt keine Differenzierung nach dem Bekenntnis, und Ankara beansprucht albanischen Bektaschi, aserbaidschanischen Schiiten und kasachischen Sunniten gegenüber die gleiche religiöse

---

[97] Uslu 29.3.96.

[98] Auch die türkischen Religionsbeamten in Europa sehen die Alewiten als Angehörige der gleichen Religion *und* Konfession (Hanefiten) wie die sunnitischen Türken, vgl. Ahmet Lale, Avrupa'da yaşayan insanlarımızın İslâm'ı Avrupalılara iyi anlatamamalarından dolayı, İslâm ters anlaşılıyor, in der in Deutschland erscheinenden pro-islamischen Monatsschrift *Genç Kalem* 2, (5-6-7/1995), S. 20-21, hier S. 21 (Interview, Ahmet Lale ist Religionsattaché des türkischen Generalkonsulats in Essen).

Autorität. Gerade diese Freiheit, die sich die Behörde bei der Auswahl und bei der Anlegung der genannten Kriterien nimmt, verweist darauf, daß sie eher ein Instrument des jungen Nationalstaates darstellt denn eine gewachsene religiöse Autorität.[99]

Für die relative Beliebigkeit der religiösen Orientierung und den Pragmatismus der Religionsbürokratie steht auch, daß um der Erreichung außenpolitischer Einflußnahme willen, die Berührungsängste der Religionsbürokratie mit inoffiziellen religösen Gruppen merklich zurückgegangen sind. So arbeitet das Erziehungsministerium heute mit religiösen Gruppen zusammen, die noch vor 1980 als größte Gefahr für die 'laizistische Ordnung' des Landes präsentiert wurden, und unterstützt in den neu entstandenen Turk-Republiken und in verschiedenen Ländern des Balkans Schulen und Bildungszentren von Untergruppen der Nuristen und Zweigen des Nakschibendi-Ordens.[100]

Die politische Orientierung der Religionsbehörde

Aussagen zur politischen Orientierung der Kader in der Religionsbürokratie lassen sich nur mit allem Vorbehalt machen.[101] Beobachter meinen, die Angehörigen der oberen Etagen seien tendenziell eher laizistisch und nationalistisch ausgerichtet, wohingegen die Beschäftigten in den niederen Rängen eher eine islamistische Orientierung hätten. Tatsächlich heben leitende Personen stets hervor, daß religiöse und nationale Identität untrennbar miteinander verbunden seien. Man

[99] Tatsächlich ist die inhaltliche Autorität der Behörde gering. So wandten sich in den zehn Jahren von 1986-1995 die Gläubigen insgesamt nur in 5964 Fällen schriftlich um Auskunft in religiösen Fragen an die Diyanet als ganze. Davon kamen insgesamt 963 Anfragen aus der türkisch-muslimischen Diaspora, die allerdings nicht nur Westeuropa, sondern beispielsweise auch Saudi Arabien miteinschließt, wo ebenfalls seit langem türkische Arbeiter tätig sind. Vgl. *Yeni Yüzyıl* 11.2.1996, S. 3.

[100] Insbesondere können sich Lehrer für den Dienst in jenen Einrichtungen beurlauben lassen, können Lehrmittel und Unterrichtshilfen bereitgestellt und finanzielle Zuschüsse gewährt werden. Diese Neuregelung vom Januar 96 löste vor allen Dingen deshalb Interesse aus, weil die 13 Schulen und drei Bildungszentren, die der türkische Staat in diesen Ländern selbst unterhält, unter Mittelknappheit leiden. Vgl. die in Europa erscheinende Wochenzeitung *Cumhuriyet-Hafta* 12.1.1996, S. 4.

[101] "Die *Diyanet* steht rechts." schreiben Binswanger & Sipahioğlu 1988, S. 78. Sie machten in der Behörde sowohl Anhänger der Wohlfahrstpartei als auch der extrem nationalistischen *Grauen Wölfe* und des religio-konservativen Aydınlar Ocağı-s aus, jenes *Intellektuellenclubs*, dem das Urheberrecht für die Türkisch-Islamische Synthese zusteht, vgl. Binnaz Toprak Religion als Staatsideologie in einem laizistischen Staat *Zeitschrift für Türkei-Studien* (1/1989), S. 55-62.

bezieht sich auf den Koran, in dem es heiße, daß die Vaterlandsliebe Ausfluß des Glaubens sei. Im Übereinstimmung mit dieser turkophilen Orientierung wird bei Gesprächen über die türkisch-muslimischen Gruppen in der Diaspora die *Türk Föderasyon*, ein Ableger der rechtsextremen Partei MHP lobend erwähnt. Ihre Mitglieder würden in aller Regel die Gebete in den der Diyanet angeschlossenen Moscheen verrichten.[102]

In einer gewissen Abhebung von dieser nationalistischen Orientierung in den oberen Rängen kursieren in den Amtsstuben der Diyanet heute eher die Zeitungen des stärker politisierten Islams, nämlich Beklenen Vakit und Yeni Şafak, in denen offen kritisiert wird, daß die Behörde die Religion unter Aufsicht eines im Grunde nichtislamischen Regimes stelle.[103]

Die Größe der Religionsbehörde

Im Frühjahr 1996 sollen etwa 1000 Beamte der Diyanet in Europa tätig gewesen sein. All ihre Imame und Vorbeter stehen vor großen Schwierigkeiten. Sie können in aller Regel weder die jeweilige Sprache noch besitzen sie nähere Kenntnis über das Land, in dem sie Dienst tun werden, geschweige denn, daß sie über Lebenserfahrung in einer modernen, säkularen und individualisierten Gesellschaft verfügten. Ein dreimonatiger Sprachkurs bereitet sie auf ihren Einsatz vor, nach dessen Absolvierung sie jedoch in der Regel "gerade einmal selbständig einkaufen gehen können."[104] Die Dienstzeit beträgt vier Jahre. Als Grund für diese relativ kurze Dienstzeit werden in Ankara zum einen die Visa-Vereinbarungen mit den Aufnahmeländern angegeben, zum anderen wird auf den niedrigen Lohn verwiesen, der es den Imamen unmöglich mache, sich dort wirklich für längere Zeit niederzulassen. Der Etat der Behörde habe im Jahre 1996 bei 22-23 Trillionen Türkische Lira (440 Million DM) gelegen[105], womit u.a. die Gehälter von ca. 80 000 Bediensteten im In- und Ausland bezahlt

---

102 Gespräch mit Arif Soytürk, Leiter der Westeuropa-Abteilung des Präsidiums für religiöse Angelegenheiten, Ankara 29.3.1996.

103 Vgl. etwa den Kommentar von Yaşar Kaplan, Diyanet ile hıyanet arasında nasıl bir ilgi vardır? *Beklenen Vakit* 5.3.1995, S. 2.

104 Uslu 29.3.1996.

105 Uslu 29.3.1996.

worden wären.[106]

106 *Yeni Yüzyıl* 16.6.1996, S. 3.

Die Millî-Görüş-Bewegung

Zwischen Integration und Isolation

Günter Seufert
Institut der Deutschen Morgenländischen Gesellschaft, Istanbul

Der politische Charakter der AMGT (IGMG)

In ihren Selbstdarstellungen legt die größte nicht-staatliche Organisation des türkischen Islams in der Diaspora, die *Vereinigung der religionsnationalen Sicht in Europa*, AMGT[1], zuallererst Wert auf die Feststellung, daß sie nicht die Auslandsorganisation der pro-islamischen Partei der Türkei sei.[2] Diese Betonung der organisatorischen Autonomie ist nachvollziehbar, denn das türkische Parteiengesetz verbietet die Gründung von Auslandsorganisationen. Bisweilen geht die AMGT noch einen Schritt weiter und weist auch zurück, daß es sich bei ihr überhaupt um eine politische Organisation handele.[3] Als Gründe dafür lassen sich der allgemeine Druck des laizistischen Regimes und eines großen Teils der türkischen Presse, aber auch die herrschende Rechtslage in der BRD anführen, die die Möglichkeit einer staatlichen Anerkennung ausschließlich für solche Religionsgemeinschaften vorsieht, welche sich am Modell der christlichen Kirchen orientieren.[4]

[1] Die Vereinigung nennt sich seit 1995 IGMG, *Islamische Gemeinschaft Millî Görüş*. Sie ist allerdings unter ihrem alten Namen bekannter, der auch ihre politische Haltung und ihr Selbstverständnis besser zum Ausdruck bringt.

[2] Diese Partei war bis zum Januar 1997 die *Wohlfahrtspartei*, (Refah Partisi, RP). Ihre Nachfolgerin nennt sich Fazilet Partisi, *Tugend-Partei*. Vgl. zu den Distanzierungsbemühungen beispielsweise eine Gegendarstellung des ehemaligen Vorsitzenden Osman Yumakoğulları an die Zeitung Hürriyet, dokumentiert in *AMGT Bülten* (3/1995), S. 9.

[3] Erklärung von Osman Yumakoğulları, der eine negative Bewertung der Organisation durch den türkischen Geheimdienst, MİT, zurückweist, dokumentiert in *AMGT Bülten* (4/1995), S. 14.

[4] Gefordert werden beispielsweise eine einheitliche Verwaltungsstruktur, einheitliche Dogmen, Glaubensaussagen und eine einheitliche Interpretation der konkreten Handlungsanleitungen, die aus ihnen abgeleitet sind, eine Hierarchie, innerhalb derer die letztendliche Autortät für die Festlegung der Lehre und des praktischen Handelns der Glaubensgemeinschaft zweifelsfrei erkennbar ist.

Ein Bekenntnis zur pro-islamischen Partei oder auch nur zu einem politischen Auftrag der AMGT würde deshalb nicht nur das negative Image der Organisation in weiten Teilen der Öffentlichkeit[5] verstärken — ja ihre Existenz gefährden, sondern auch den Bestand der Mutterorganisation bedrohen.

Unabhängig von dieser Selbstdarstellung kann kein Zweifel daran bestehen, daß die AMGT eng mit der Partei verflochten ist. Dafür seien nur einige Indizien angeführt. Der langjährige Vorsitzende der Organisation, Osman Yumakoğulları, fungierte bis zum Jahre 1995 als Verantwortlicher der Deutschlandausgabe der Millî Gazete (Nationalzeitung). Diese in Istanbul konzipierte Tageszeitung wird nach den Direktiven des Vorsitzenden der Partei gestaltet und gilt als ihre Hauspostille.

Desweiteren haben sich einflußreiche Angehörige der AMGT in der früheren Wohlfahrtspartei parteipolitisch betätigt. Yumakoğulları selbst ließ sich im Dezember 1995 zusammen mit Azım Genç (alias Abdullah Gencer), einem seiner Stellvertreter im Amte des Vorsitzenden, auf der Liste der Wohlfahrtspartei ins türkische Parlament wählen. Als dritter ehemaliger AMGTler gelangte in dieser Wahl auch Şevket Yılmaz in die Große Türkische Nationalversammlung. Yılmaz war vorher Bürgermeister der Schwarzmeeranrainer-Stadt Rize und davor wiederum Mitglied des Exekutiv-Komitees von AMGT.[6] Insgesamt kandidierten bei diesen Wahlen um die dreißig Angehörige von AMGT erfolglos für die Wohlfahrtspartei, der bekannteste von ihnen zweifellos Ali Yüksel, der über Jahre hinweg das Amt des Generalsekretärs von AMGT bekleidete, als erster *Scheich al-Islam*[7] der BRD von sich reden machte und heute eine der beiden Teilorganisationen vertritt, in die sich die AMGT seit ihrer Reorganisation 1996

---

[5] Vgl. als Beispiel dafür Reymer Klüver, Gesellschaft mit beschränkter Weltsicht, Süddeutsche Zeitung 28.4.95, S. 3.

[6] Vgl. *AMGT Bülten* (1/1995), S. 21 und 23.

[7] Der Begriff und das Amt, das er repräsentiert, nehmen Bezug auf den Şeyh ül-İslâm, die höchste islamische Autorität des Osmanischen Reiches. Mit Gründung der Republik wurde dieses Amt aufgehoben und durch das *Präsidium für religiöse Angelegenheiten* (Diyanet İşleri Başkanlığı) ersetzt, das heute direkt dem Ministerpräsidenten untersteht. Vgl. zum Wirken des Präsidiums in der europäischen Diaspora den entsprechenden Artikel in diesem Buche. Mit dem *Scheich al-Islam* versucht AMGT einerseitsin der muslimischen Diaspora eine 'zivile' Alternative zur Behörde zu etablieren und bringt damit andererseits ihre Favorisierung des Osmanischen Reichs zum Ausdruck.

aufgliedert hat.[8]

So wie sich Angehörige von AMGT in der Türkei in den Reihen der pro-islamischen Partei betätigen, so reisen die Prominenten dieser Partei regelmäßig zu Konferenzen, Vorträgen und der feierlichen Eröffnung neuer Institutionen des Verbandes nach Europa. Neben dem Vorsitzenden der Wohlfahrtspartei, Necmettin Erbakan, kamen 1995 und 1996 vor allen Dingen Parteimitglieder nach Europa, die offizielle Funktionen ausübten, Parlamentsabgeordnete oder Bürgermeister sind *und* die darüberhinaus ob ihres Wissens und ihrer Rhetorik in islamo-politischen Angelegenheiten bekannt sind. Dieser Definition genügten z.B. die Abgeordneten Halil Çelik (früherer Bürgermeister von Urfa, der durch 'radikale' Vorstöße von sich reden machte), Abdullah Gül (intellektueller Berater Erbakans für Außenpolitik und in seiner Regierung Minister für Auslandstürken), Şevket Yılmaz (früherer Bürgermeister von Rize und bekannt für seine Angriffe auf den Republikgründer Kemal Atatürk), Oğuzhan Asiltürk (Abgeordneter, Mitglied des Parteivorstandes und drittstärkster Mann in der Partei), Halil Ürün (Bürgermeister von Konya, dem Ausgangsort der Bewegung), Recep Tayyip Erdoğan (Bürgermeister von Istanbul und heute populärster Politiker der Türkei[9]), Nusret Bayraktar (Stadtteilbürgermeister des Istanbuler Kosmopolitenviertels Beyoğlu), sowie Arif Ersoy (Bürgermeister von Çorum). Wie Feigenblätter wirken gegen diese gesammelte Prominenz der Partei die Abgeordneten anderer rechter Parteien, die aufgrund des einen oder anderen Anlasses den Weg in die Kölner Zentrale der AMGT finden. Auch bei den türkischen Gästen der AMGT, die ihren Ruhm intellektueller Tätigkeit verdanken, fällt auf, daß sie nicht nur gute Muslime sind, sondern allesamt den Islam primär als Auftrag zu politischer Aktivität verstehen. Dies gilt u. a. für Dr. Süleyman Akdemir, der die Diskussion um das Gesellschaftsprojekt der Partei maßgeblich beeinflußt hat; für İhsan Süreya Sırma, einer der verbeamteten Theologen, die am offensten von der Notwendigkeit einer islamischen Ordnung reden; für Aytunç Altındal, ein 'zum religionsnationalen und politisierten Islam konvertierter ehemaliger

---

8 Weitere Kandidaten für Abgeordnetenmandate waren Recep Çınar, Hasan Damar, Harun Aytaç, Şerafettin Öztürk, Kemal Homan, Münip Özer, Eyub Fatsa, Sabahattin Gencer, Mehmet Türk, Yusuf Işık, Erdoğan Karadeniz, Ayhan Yılmaz, Şener Şentürk, Nail Dural, Abdurrahman Dizman, Hamza Çakır, Turan Aras, Ali Çoşkun, Eşref Yağcıoğlu, Hasan Ünal, Rüştü Kam, Ramazan Yıldız, İsmet Çataklı, Tevfik Taşpınar und Ali Toy, vgl. *AMGT Bülten* (12/1995), S. 7.

9 Vgl. die Jugendstudie *Türk Gençliği 98: Suskun kitle büyüteç altında*, İstanbul Mülkiyeliler Vakfı SAM, Konrad-Adenauer-Stiftung, Ankara 1999.

Sozialist', der heute vor der Verschwörung der christlichen Kirchen gegen die Muslime der Türkei warnt, und dies gilt in gleichem Maße für den Journalisten Hekimoğlu İsmail, ein ehemaliger Offizier, der unter diesem Pseudonym an die Öffentlichkeit tritt, und für Abdurrahman Dilipak, einem früheren Journalisten der Parteizeitung, der die Partei heute aus einer islamistischeren Ecke heraus kritisiert.

Der politische Charakter der AMGT tritt jedoch nicht nur in ihrer Verbindung mit der pro-islamischen Partei des Heimatlandes hervor, sondern er bestimmt auch Wort und Tat der Organisation. In der BRD bemüht sie sich um Kontakte mit den Vertretungen der muslimischen Länder und lädt zu diesem Zweck deren diplomatische Vertreter zum gemeinsamen Fastenbrechen.[10] In Gebeten für die bedrängten Muslime und für ihren Kampf in Bosnien und Tschetschenien fällt religiöses Bewußtsein und islamische Solidarität genauso zusammen wie in den Spendenkampagnen der Organisation , in deren Verlauf zum alljährlichen *Opferfest* (kurban bayramı) bisweilen die lebenden Schlachtopfer selbst, bisweilen nur ihr Fleisch, oder auch nur der Geldbetrag für ihren Erwerb in aller Herren muslimische Länder gesandt werden.[11] Nutznießer dieser zuerst von der AMGT praktizierten Opfertierkampagnen sind primär drei Gruppen: 1. Muslimische Minderheiten auf dem Gebiet des ehemaligen Osmanischen Reiches, vor allen Dingen des Balkans: Bosniaken, Türken in Westthrakien, Türken und Pomaken in Bulgarien, kleine Minderheiten in Rumänien und die Muslime Mazedoniens, des Sandschaks und Albaniens, aber auch die Turkmenen und die sich islamo-politisch betätigenden Kurden des Nordiraks, 2. turkstämmige Muslime in Zentralasien und 3. muslimische Gruppen, die sich in bewaffneter Auseinandersetzung mit Nichtmuslimen oder laizistischen Regimen befinden, wie in Tschetschenien, Dagestan, Abchasien, Tadschikistan, Kaschmir und Palästina. Führer der entsprechenden islamischen Bewegungen und diplomatische Vertreter sich islamisch verstehender Staaten sind immer wieder zu Gast bei der AMGT.

In ihren Medien, der bereits erwähnten Millî Gazete und dem allmonatlich erscheinenden Mitteilungsblatt AMGT Bülten (seit 7/95 unter dem Namen Millî Görüş & Perspektive), schildert die Bewegung politische Ereignisse in muslimischen Regionen vornehmlich als Wi-

---

[10] Vgl. *AMGT Bülten* (3/1995), S. 2.

[11] Die Form dieses *Fernopfers* hat sich meines Wissens aus dem Wunsch der türkischen Arbeiter in Europa entwickelt, ihren zurückgebliebenen Angehörigen ein würdevolles Opferfest zu ermöglichen. Erst anschließend wurde das *Fernopfer* Ausdruck internationaler muslimischer Solidarität.

derstand unterdrückter Muslime, die für ihr gutes Recht streiten, ihre eigenen Verhältnisse in islamischer Selbstbestimmung zu regeln. Beispiele für diese Sicht der Dinge finden sich in der Berichterstattung der genannten Periodika über Bosnien und Tschetschenien, ebenso wie in der über Aserbaidschan, Pakistan, Palästina, China, Kaschmir, den Sudan und Algerien. Zur Veranschaulichung der so konstruierten Blickrichtung dient folgendes Zitat aus der Monatsschrift des Verbandes:

"Für die Kreise, die den Islam als Feind wahrnehmen, existieren zwei gefährliche islamische Länder: der Iran und der Sudan. Sie sollen (angeblich, GS) den Islam exportieren und Terror säen. Aber in vielen muslimischen Ländern haben die Islamisten keinerlei Chance den Mund aufzutun, so in Marokko, Algerien, Tunesien, Libyen, Ägypten, Jordanien, Saudi Arabien, Syrien, im Irak, in Usbekistan, Tadschikistan, Indien und Indonesien. Doch werden diese Länder (gerade, GS) dafür gelobt. Und besonders Ägypten wird dafür belohnt, daß es in den letzten Jahren fünfhundert Islamisten zum Tode verurteilt und zwischen zehn- und dreißigtausend Islamisten ohne Gerichtsverfahren in den Kerker geworfen hat. ... Schaut man sich die neuesten NATO-Pläne an, wird deutlich, daß es der Westen ist, der hinter all dem steckt. Für den Westen ist nur ein toter Muslim ein guter Muslim. Prüfen Sie doch einmal, welches Land der westlichen Welt einen Bericht über Menschenrechtsverletzungen hat, der aufführt, wie in den muslimischen Ländern die Rechte der Muslime verletzt werden, wie die Muslime in den Gefängnissen gefoltert werden? Kein einziges!"[12]

Kaderpolitik in der Diaspora

Wie erscheint in der Wahrnehmung des Verbandes, der eine solch religionsideologisch gefärbte Interpretation der Weltlage verbreitet (die Tatsachenfeststellungen des Zitates müssen traurigerweise anerkannt werden), die Lage seiner eigenen Mitglieder, die als muslimische Minderheit zwar unter 'christlicher Herrschaft' und in einer säkularisierten und damit weitgehend gottlosen Gesellschaft, aber auch in relativ demokratischen Verhältnissen leben? Wird die stark politisch geprägte Interpretation des Muslimseins und des Islams, wie sie aus den undemokratischen Verhältnissen und oft gewalttätigen Auseinandersetzungen in den Ländern der muslimischen Welt erwächst, auch für die Be-

12 İlhan Bilgü, NATO neden İslam'ı düşman seçiyor?, *AMGT Bülten* (3/1995), S. 12-13.

schreibung der eigenen Stellung in einer differierenden Lebenswelt als treffend empfunden?

Damit ist die Beurteilung der Aufnahmegesellschaft durch die Mitglieder des Verbandes angesprochen, und es muß als erstes festgestellt werden, daß es, wie in jedem Verband, auch in der AMGT gerade zu diesem Punkt einen ganzen Chor unterschiedlicher Meinungen gibt. Auf allgemeine politische Stellungnahmen zur Politik in der Türkei oder zur Lage der Muslime in der Welt ist sich gerade deshalb relativ leicht zu einigen, weil hier die Übernahme zentral formulierter Überzeugung nur geringe Auswirkungen auf die eigene Lebensführung haben kann. Eine dezidierte Stellungnahme zur Gesellschaft, die einen umgibt, hat indes unvermeidlich Konsequenzen für die Organisierung des eigenen Alltags. Um jedoch auch für diesen Bereich den politischen Charakter der Vereinigung zu demonstrieren, sei eine keineswegs beliebige Stellungnahme angeführt: Auszüge aus der Rede des damaligen Generalsekretärs Ali Yüksel auf der 11. Jahresvollversammlung der europaweiten AMGT Jugendorganisation des Verbandes am 13. Mai 1995 im belgischen Genk.

"Die Jugend ist die Form, in die sich der Geist der islamischen Revolution ergießt. Geist und Idee dieser Revolution werden mit einer Kraft, die das Universum zum Erbeben bringt, in diese Gußform fahren. Wie glühendes Eisen werden diese Inhalte in die Form gegossen, und es entstehen Kaderpersönlichkeiten. Es kommt alles darauf an, daß die Jugend bis in die letzten Ritze mit diesem Geist erfüllt wird und den islamischen dava[13] zu ihrem innersten und ureigensten Anliegen macht. Diese Jugend wird ihre Mütter und Väter, ihre Großmütter und Großväter und all die Generationen, die ihr vorausgingen, allein deswegen achten, weil sie Muslime waren. Sie wird nicht in die Lage kommen, in der sich heute die Führungskader des Islams befinden, und sie wird weder in ihren Einstellungen noch in ihren Haltungen zu einer dieser toten Generationen werden, an denen die (islamische, GS) Geschichte so reich ist, die es nicht fertig brachten, wirkliche Muslime zu sein. ... Auf diesem Fleck der Erde (Belgien, im weiteren Sinne Europa, GS), wo die Sonne untergeht und wo das Licht zur Unterdrückung wird, sehe ich jeden einzelnen von euch als ein Leuchten in der Dunkelheit. Hier, wo alles im Morast versinkt, seid ihr, die Jugend, kraft eurer Durchdrungenheit mit Glaube und Ver-

[13] = allgemein *das Anliegen, die Bemühung, der Zweck eines Kampfes, der Sinn einer Sache*, konkret: die *Ausbreitung und Förderung des Islams.*

trauen, des Morgens leuchtende Blumen."[14]

In diesem kurzen Abschnitt finden sich viele der Strukturelemente und Topoi, ohne die moderne politische Ideologien nicht auskommen: Da ist der manichäische Gegensatz zwischen dem Prinzip des Guten und des Bösen, symbolisiert als der zwischen Licht und Finsternis, und da ist die Gewißheit einer besseren Zukunft.[15] Läßt sich der Gegensatz zwischen Licht und Finsternis noch als Erbe des religiösen Weltbildes deuten, stehen die Verurteilung der alten Generation, die die mehr oder weniger passive und unpolitische islamische Tradition verkörpert, und die zentrale Rolle, die der Jugend für die Erlösung zugewiesen wird, für den modernistischen Charakter des politischen Islams.[16] Neben der Verwendung von Begriffen wie *Kader* verweisen die Bilder aus Produktion und Technik, das *glühende Eisen*, die *Gußform*, die gewaltigen *Energien*, darauf, daß sich da die Bewegung einer sich industrialisierenden Gesellschaft zu Wort meldet.[17] Ziemlich verunglückt ist dagegen das einzige Bild, das dem Islam wirklich vertraute (Pflanzen-)Symbolik benutzt, die *leuchtenden Blumen.*

Die Fixpunkte der politischen Ideologie und die Ziele der gesellschaftspolitischen Betätigung.

So eindeutig sich der islamistische Charakter der AMGT aufzeigen läßt, so vielfältig und oft in sich widersprüchlich präsentiert sich ihre Politik als ganzes. Unzweifelhaft jedoch läßt sich trotz aller Kritik der proislamischen Parteien am Regime der Republik Türkei und trotz aller Distanz der AMGT zur DİTİB, die Vertreterin des türkischen Staatsislams in Europa, eine starke Fixierung der *Vereinigung der religionsnationalen Sicht* auf den türkischen Staat feststellen.

Die Organisation eröffnet ihre Generalversammlungen nicht allein mit einem feierlichen Koranvortrag, sondern diesem folgt unvermeidlich das gemeinsame Absingen der Nationalhymne. Dadurch daß die

---

14 AMGT Gençlik Kolları Genel Kurulu Belçika'da toplandı, *AMGT Bülten* (6/1995), S. 7-9, hier S. 8-9.

15 Vgl. zur Verwendung der Symbole in der Arbeiterbewegung die Hymne der deutschen Sozialdemokraten: *"Brüder zur Sonne zur Freiheit / Brüder zum Lichte empor / Hell aus dem dunklen Vergang'nen / Leuchtet die Zukunft hervor."*

16 Hier trifft sich der politische türkische Islam mit der Ideologie, die zu bekämpfen er angetreten ist, dem Kemalismus. Vgl.: *Rede an die Jugend* von Mustafa Kemal Atatürk (Gençlik hitabesi).

17 Vgl. dazu beispielsweise den Titel des Romans des kommunistischen Arbeiterschriftstellers der Weimarer Republik, *Willi Bredel,* Wo der Stahl gehärtet wird.

türkische Flagge an zentraler Stelle des Tagungsraumes ihren Platz findet, erfährt die Präsentation der Staatssymbole ihre Vervollständigung.[18]

Tatsächlich läßt sich die Organisation insbesondere türkischen Behörden und türkischen Medien gegenüber an Heimatliebe von niemandem übertreffen:

“Wo wir auch immer sind, unsere erste Sorge gilt unserem Heimatland. Wir tun alles dafür, daß unsere Menschen sich nicht von ihrer Tradition und ihrer Kultur lösen. In Europa sind wir eine ehrenamtliche und kostenlose Lobby der Türkei, und wir sind es gerne. Keiner kann uns von der Türkei trennen.”[19]

Es ist bekannt, daß die Republik Türkei[20] diese Liebe nur ansatzweise erwidert. Zwar behauptete der Vorsitzende der Organisation “Die Zuständigen unseres Staates meldeten sich jedenfalls primär bei Millî Görüş, wenn es darum ging, mit öffentlichen Aktionen unsere nationalen Interessen zu vertreten und unsere nationale Einheit zu sichern ... ”[21] doch sieht sich ihr Generalsekretär genötigt, in seinem Rechenschaftsbericht zu fordern “... daß die Botschaft und die Konsulate sich nicht einem Teil der Staatsbürger widmen und sich einem anderen Teil verschließen dürfen ...”.[22]

Trotz dieser Zurückweisung durch die Behörden ihre Staates unterstützte die Organisation den Aufruf der damaligen Ministerpräsidentin Tansu Çiller, die zur Linderung der chronischen Finanzkrise des türkischen Staates seine Bürger in den europäischen Ländern aufforderte,

---

18 Beide Symbole der Republik Türkei fehlen beispielsweise bei den Zusammenkünften der radikaleren Cemaat-i İslâmî, die von dem mittlerweile verstorbenen Cemalettin Kaplan ins Leben gerufen wurde. Vgl. zu dieser Gruppe den Beitrag von Fulya Atacan in diesem Bande.

19 Osman Yumakoğulları, Bizim metodumuz diyalogtur, çatışma değil, Interview des damaligen Vorsitzenden mit dem Wochenmagazin Nokta, dokumentiert in *Millî Görüş & Perspektive* (7/1995), S. 34.

20 Bis zu einem gewissen Grad bleiben die Grundlinien der türkischen Politik ungeachtet von Regierungswechseln die gleichen. Daran hat bis heute auch die Regierungsübernahme durch die Wohlfahrtspartei nichts geändert. Mit der Anführung der *Republik Türkei* als politisches Subjekt wird auf diese partei- und regierungsübergreifende Linie türkischer Politik verwiesen.

21 Osman Yumakoğulları, İslam Avrupa'da haklı yerini alacaktır. Interview mit der religiös-konservativen Tageszeitung *Zaman*, dokumentiert in *Millî Görüş & Perspektive* (9/1995), S. 6-8, hier S. 6.

22 Ali Yüksel, Hizmetlerimiz Hakk'ın rizası içindir, *Millî Görüş & Perspektive* (8/1995), S. 2-4 (Auszug aus dem Rechenschaftsbericht), hier S. 4.

ihre Ersparnisse auf türkischen Banken zu deponieren.[23] Mehr noch, trotz ihres gespannten Verhältnisses zur Religionsbehörde, die Vertreterin des türkischen Staatsislams im Ausland, ist der türkische Staat in den Augen der AMGT in den Aufnahmeländern noch zu wenig vertreten, und man fordert "die Einrichtung eines Ministeriums für Fragen der im Ausland lebenden Türken"[24], ein Begehren, das von der Koalition aus *Wohlfahrtspartei* und *Partei des rechten Weges* (Doğru Yol Partisi, DYP) unter Necmettin Erbakan, prompt erfüllt wurde.

Der Widerspruch zwischen der oppositionellen Grundhaltung zum Regime der Republik und der gleichzeitigen Staatsfixierung der Organisation löst sich auf, wenn man unterstellt, daß die AMGT eine zentralistische staatliche Religionspolitik, die sich nach den Vorgaben *ihrer* Organisation ausrichten würde, sehr wohl vorstellen könnte. Hinweise darauf sind zum einen die unermüdliche Unterstützung, die die Wohlfahrtspartei der in ihrer inhaltlichen Ausrichtung von ihr kritisierten Religionsbürokratie in der Türkei zukommen läßt, und zum anderen die süffisante Bemerkung des Sprechers der Organisation Hasan Özdoğan. In einem Gespräch mit dem Autor am 15. Januar 1996 in der Kölner Zentrale des Verbandes meinte dieser, daß sich die Ausrichtung der Religionsbehörde und ihr Verhältnis zur AMGT sehr schnell ändern könne, wenn in der Türkei erst einmal die Wohlfahrtspartei am Ruder wäre.

Ihren eigenen Worten nach also orientiert die "Migrantenorganisation AMGT" ihre Mitglieder auf das Herkunftsland und tut einiges dafür, daß die Verbindungen der Migranten zu ihrem Heimatland gewahrt bleiben. Sie veranstaltet Jugendfahrten, die den Jugendlichen die islamische Tradition des Landes und die ruhmvolle Geschichte des türkischen Großreiches der Osmanen nahebringen.[25] Sie organisiert Türkisch-Kurse für die Dritte Generation und setzt sich dafür ein, daß Türkisch als zweite Fremdsprache an den deutschen Gymnasien anerkannt werde. Darüberhinaus favorisiert er die Erteilung des Religions-

---

23 Osman Yumakoğulları, Asıl bölücülüğü MİT yapıyor, *AMGT Bülten* (4/1995), S. 14.

24 Osman Yumakoğulları, The first ten years (Auszüge aus der Rede des Vorsitzenden auf der 11. Ordentlichen Generalversammlung ins Deutsche übersetzt), *Millî Görüş & Perspektive* (8/1995), S. 39-41, hier S. 40.

25 "Auf unsere in Europa lebenden Jugendlichen machten die Moscheen mit all ihrer Pracht und ihrer tiefen religiösen Atmosphäre einen gewaltigen Eindruck; sind sie doch die Symbole unserer Vergangenheit und unserer Zukunft", heißt es etwa in einem Bericht über eine solche Jugendfahrt, die auch nach Ankara (zu den Zentralen der Wohlfahrtspartei und der Mutterlandspartei) sowie ins religiöse Konya führte. Siehe: Gençlerimiz Türkiye'deydi, *AMGT Bülten* (3/1995) S. 18-19.

unterrichts in türkischer Sprache und propagiert damit die Vermittlung einer spezifisch türkischen Version von Islam.[26] Ein ähnlicher Effekt ist von der alljährlichen Ausrichtung einer Messe für religiöse Literatur zu erwarten, für die 1995 sechs Sattelschlepper die Bücher 65 türkischer Verlage nach Europa brachten.[27]

Der Eindruck, daß in den Führungskadern der AMGT der türkische Nationalismus nahezu gleichberechtigt neben dem islamischen Glauben steht, verstärkt sich insbesondere dann, wenn Stellungnahmen über das Verhältnis der Türkei zur westlichen Welt und über innertürkische Konflikte ins Blickfeld geraten.

Was letzteres betrifft, distanziert sich der Verband ausdrücklich von "jeder Sympathie für politische Ansichten, die nicht mit unserer nationalen Struktur und unserer nationalen Einheit im Einklang stehen"[28] und übernimmt damit implizit die offizielle Position vom ethnisch und kulturell einheitlichen Staatsvolk der Republik Türkei.

In Fragen des Verhältnisses des Landes zu Europa unterscheiden sich die von den Medien des Verbandes veröffentlichten Positionen allein deswegen nicht von denen der pro-islamischen Partei weil in beiden nahezu dem gleichen Personenkreis Platz für die Verbreitung seiner Ansichten gegeben wird. Der Verband hat, mit anderen Worten, noch keine intellektuellen Kader hervorgebracht, die eigene außenpolitische Vorstellungen zu formulieren und zu publizieren in der Lage wären. So unterstellen die Medien des Verbandes in der Diaspora — wie die der Partei in der Türkei — Europa die verdeckte Unterstützung der PKK und das Ziel, die Türkei zu spalten.[29]

Wie sehr die Wahrnehmung Europas durch den Verband noch von der Perspektive der Partei in der Türkei und ihrer dortigen Intellektuellen bestimmt ist, trat anläßlich der Diskussion um die Zollunion

---

[26] Beachte die Nähe,der AMGT zur von der Wohlfahrtspartei *offiziell* kritisierten nationlistischen *Türkisch-Islamischen-Synthese.*: " ... weil der weitaus größte Teil unserer Mitglieder *aus der Türkei* kommt, ist es uns genauso unmöglich, auf die *türkische Sprache und Kultur* zu verzichten, wie auf religiöses Wissen". Yüksel 8/95, S. 2. Daß die meisten Mitglieder aus der Türkei kommen muß jedoch keineswegs heißen, daß sie nur über die türkische Sprache erreichbar wären, und es ist interessant, daß eine Verständigung der türkischen Muslime mit anderen in den jeweiligen Aufnahmeländern lebenden Muslimen über ihren *Glauben* keine Rolle zu spielen scheint.

[27] Yüksel (8/1995), S. 3.

[28] Yumakoğulları (4/1995), S. 14. Im gleichen Artikel weist der Autor darauf hin, daß sich der türkische Staat für die Mobilisierung der in Europa lebenden türkischen Staatsbürger gegen die dort zu beobachtenden politischen Aktivitäten der PKK an die AMGT gewandt habe.

[29] Vgl. Zeki Ceyhan, Hop oturduk, hop kalktık, *AMGT Bülten* (4/1995), S. 21 und ders., Sinirler gergin, asaplar bozuk, *AMGT Bülten* (5/1995), S. 21.

des Landes mit der Europäischen Gemeinschaft hervor. Die Zollunion wurde als Schritt zu einer Annäherung miteinander unvereinbarer Zivilisationsmodelle geschildert, als der Versuch, Feuer und Wasser zu verbinden, und Europa wird als das genaue Gegenteil des Islams vorgestellt:

"Zwei unterschiedliche Geschichtsverläufe, Kulturen, Glaubensüberzeugungen und Weltansichten, deren Blut sich in keiner Weise miteinander verträgt..." Daraus kann nichts Positives entstehen: "Sie versuchen, einem muslimischen Körper einen Priesterkopf aufzupflanzen und einen neuen Menschentyp zu erschaffen. Das kann nicht klappen. Wenn so etwas aus dem Labor entspringt, dann ist es ein neuer Frankenstein, der auch das Blut des Westens trinken wird."[30]

In dieser aus der Türkei auf die europäischen Gesellschaften gerichteten Perspektive kommen die Zwischentöne christlich-muslimischen Zusammenlebens ebensowenig vor wie die Ausdifferenzierungen, die sich in der Diaspora unter den Muslimen ergeben, als deren Folge ein großer Teil der Migranten jede Verbindung zu den Moscheen und Moscheegemeinden verliert. Folge dieser undifferenzierten Wahrnehmung ist es, daß von der Türkei das Bild eines Europa gegenüber ohnmächtigen Landes gezeichnet wird, ein Bild, das jedoch unvermittelt durch Großmachtträume und Allmachtsphantasien abgelöst wird. Allmachtsphantasien sind das, die ihre Verwirklichung zu einem guten Teil der Existenz von muslimischen Diasporagemeinden verdanken. So kann man in ein und demselben Artikel schreiben, daß der Westen zur Durchsetzung seiner aggressiven Ziele ein neues Feindbild produziere und sich gleichzeitig auf die eigene Schulter klopfend meinen, der Westen habe allen Grund, die Muslime zu fürchten. Nie werde der Westen deshalb einer Integration der Türkei in Europa zustimmen, denn:

"Sie wissen doch, wie sich die Arbeiter aus der Türkei in Europa um ihren Glauben scharen. Sie können sich vorstellen, was es für Auswirkungen hat, wenn der bereits jetzt 15-20 Millionen zählenden Gruppe der Muslime in Europa noch mal 60 Millionen (Muslime der Türkei, GS) hinzugefügt werden. Dann hat der Westen (=Europa, GS) zwar fast 400 Millionen Einwohner, aber die Muslime stellen dann davon fast 100 Millionen. Bis dahin braucht es nicht viel, dafür sorgen die Übertritte zum Islam, die Einwanderung und die Geburtenrate. 25 Prozent der Einwohner, jung und dynamisch, die sind wohl in

30 Abdurrahman Dilipak, Ne olacak bu memleketin hali? *AMGT Bülten* (3/1995), S. 14-15, hier S. 15. Auf den wahren Kern der Worte Dilipaks bezüglich der Folgen einer rein technischen Modernisierung kann hier nicht eingegangen werden.

der Lage, ganz neue Entwicklungen einzuleiten, das ist eine im soziologischen Sinne kritische Zahl."[31]

Nach dem bisher Gesagten erscheinen folgende Vorstellungen als die Fixpunkte der Weltanschauung, wie sie die AMGT vertritt. Der Westen und Europa verkörpern das genaue Gegenteil all dessen, wofür der Islam steht. Der Westen und der Islam stehen sich unversöhnlich gegenüber, und dieser Widerspruch läßt sich nur dadurch auflösen, daß das Licht (der Islam) früher oder später die Finsternis (der Westen) besiegt. Während der Westen und der Islam in dieser Perspektive nichts Gemeinsames haben, sind der Islam und die Türkei, genauer, der Islam und die türkische Sprache und Kultur eine Symbiose miteinander eingegangen, als deren Folge es Menschen aus der Türkei in Europa nur über die türkische Sprache und Kultur möglich ist, ihre Religion unverfälscht und ohne Verlust wesentlicher Bedeutungsdimensionen an ihre Nachkommen weiterzugeben. Daß das Türkische an sich so untrennbar mit dem Islam verbunden ist, ist der Grund für seine Ausgrenzung aus Europa und für die Aggressivität des Westens, die sich wie gegen alles Islamische auch gegen das Türkische richte.

Zwar kommt die AMGT zumindest nicht explizit zu dem Schluß, den die DİTİB zieht und der lautet: *Wer die türkischen Muslime vom Glauben abbringt, der tut das, um die Türkei zu schwächen*; doch die Anlage des Weltbildes ist gleich; und die Auseinandersetzung zwischen der AMGT und der DİTİB erscheint als Streit feindlicher Brüder.

Was bis jetzt von der AMGT mitgeteilt wurde, legt es nahe, auch als Ergebnis ihres Wirkens unter den Muslimen primär eine Verstärkung von Rückzugs- und Isolierungstendenzen anzunehmen. Darüberhinaus wäre nicht nur das weitere Schließen der muslimischen Reihen, sondern auch die Produktion von Feindbildern zu befürchten. Kann die politische Praxis einer Organisation, die eine solchen Diskurs führt, auf anderes gerichtet sein, als auf die Etablierung von Inseln muslimischen Lebens, die klar von der mehr oder weniger feindlichen Aufnahmegesellschaft getrennt bestehen?

Auf diese Tendenz scheinen die (bislang gescheiterten) Bemühungen der AMGT um die Gründung einer islamischen Gewerkschaft und einer Islamischen Partei (für die BRD) zu verweisen.[32] Damit im Ein-

31 Ebenda, S. 14-15.

32 Vgl. dazu Metin Gür, *Türkisch-islamische Vereinigungen in der Bundesrepublik Deutschland*, Brandes & Apsel, Frankfurt a.M. 1993, S. 44 ff.

klang stehen Initiativen zur Gründung eigener Schulen, besonders in Belgien und in den Niederlanden. Auf dem Programm stehen ferner (ganz ähnlich wie das auch von Angehörigen der Religionsbehörde formuliert wurde) die Gründung eigener Kindergärten und Kinderkrippen, und längst bestehen eigene Jugendclubs und Sportvereine, eigene Sport- und Kulturzentren sind in der Konzeption, und auch über eigene Krankenhäuser und Altersheime macht man sich Gedanken.

Doch so sehr diese Zielvorstellungen von der AMGT inhaltlich auch denen der Religionsbehörde parallel sind und so sehr auch die organisatorischen und intellektuellen Zentren beider Organisationen[33] von der Türkei aus nach Europa blicken - im konkreten *Handeln* der Angehörigen dieser Organisation ergeben sich nicht vernachlässigbare Unterschiede. Das unterschiedliche Handeln resultiert aus der gegensätzlichen *Stellung* der beiden Zentren im Machtgefüge der Türkei (Regierungsanbindung vs. oppositionelle Tradition) einerseits, und aus der unterschiedlichen *Struktur* beider Organisationen andererseits, nämlich politisierte religiöse Gemeinde hier und Religionsbürokratie dort.

Aktivierung und Mobilisierung

Bei der Analyse der verschiedenen Dimensionen des Diskurses innerhalb der europäischen Ableger der Religionsbehörde wurde festgehalten, daß diese Diskurse in ihrem Zusammenwirken unter den Migranten Tendenzen von Abschottung und Selbstisolierung verstärken müssen. Der religionsbürokratische Charakter der DİTİB begrenzt darüberhinaus die Möglichkeit von Außenstehenden, diesen Diskurs zu beeinflussen und überläßt seine Gestaltung damit den verbeamteten Religionsspezialisten in und aus der Türkei. Den in der Diaspora lebenden Muslimen verbleibt im großen und ganzen, Belehrung entge-

33 Daß sich die Zentren aller Organisationen türkischer Muslime in Europa noch in der Türkei befinden, ist ein Faktum, das zum großen Teil die Struktur der Diasporagemeinden und ihr Verhältnis untereinander erklärt. Vgl. die realistische Einschätzung eines Angehörigen der Religionsbehörde: "Was die Aufsplitterung nach verschiedenen Orden, Schulen und Gemeinden (cemaatçilik) der Muslime in der Türkei ist, das ist sie auch hier (in Europa, GS). Gäbe es diese Struktur und die einzelnen Gruppen in der Türkei nicht, würde sie auch nicht existieren. Mit mangelnder Zufriedenheit (an den religiösen Diensten des Staates im Ausland, GS) hat das nichts zu tun." *Ahmet* Lale, Avrupa'da yaşayan insanlarımızın İslâm'ı Avrupalılar'a iyi anlatamamalarından dolayı, İslâm ters anlaşılıyor, *Genç Kalem* (2, 5-7-8/1995), S. 20-21 (Interview), hier S. 21.

genzunehmen, Verhaltensvorschriften zu befolgen und sich im Übrigen zu der Diasporagesellschaft distanziert zu verhalten.

Der Charakter der AMGT als einer Parteigemeinde, deren Angehörige sich sowohl zu den bestimmenden Kräften innerhalb des türkischen Staatsapparats[34] als auch zur Aufnahmegesellschaft, ihren Normen und Werten, grundlegenden Überzeugungen und Prioritäten in Opposition sehen, legt ihnen dagegen nahe, für die schrittweise Veränderung dieser Situation aktiv zu werden. Unabhängig von der bisweilen frappierenden Ähnlichkeit zwischen den Diskursen der DİTİB und der AMGT kann deshalb ein sehr unterschiedlicher Grad an Aktivität und eine sehr verschiedenartige Haltung zur Aufnahmegesellschaft vermutet werden.

Obwohl die AMGT auch bei konkreten und sozialpädagogisch sinnvollen Aktionen, wie beispielsweise der Ausschreibung von Wettbewerben auf Feldern wie Photographie und Journalismus oder bei Kursen zum Erlernen so verschiedener Dinge wie klassischem türkischen Liedgut und Computerprogrammen, einen Vergleich mit den Gemeinden der Diyanet nicht zu scheuen braucht, kommt es in diesem Zusammenhang darauf genausowenig an wie auf die Organisierung von Hafız-[35] , Arabisch- oder Türkischkursen. Wichtiger ist, daß der oben genannte Aufbau von muslimischen Parallelstrukturen vom Kindergarten bis zum Altersheim, von der Sportanlage bis zum Krankenhaus in den Vorstellungen der AMGT zwar durch öffentliche Mittel des jeweiligen Aufnahmelandes zu unterstützen, aber unter tatkräftiger Beteiligung - und noch wichtiger - unter gestaltender Leitung der islamischen Gemeinde durchzuführen sei.[36] Eine solche Orientierung jedoch erfordert die Kooperation mit Stadtverwaltungen und Nachbarschaftsgemeinden, mit Kirchen und Trägern der Freien Wohlfahrtspflege, mit Parteien und Interessenverbänden sowie mit Landes- und Bundesministerien. Darüberhinaus muß sich jede Argumentation diesen Stellen gegenüber auf die grundlegenden Wertvorstellungen berufen, die in den europäischen Aufnahmeländern die alleingültigen sind:

34 Daran hat die Regierungskoalition aus RP und DYP nur sehr bedingt etwas geändert, vgl. oben.

35 Hafız = derjenige, der den Koran auswendig vortragen kann.

36 Der auch auf Seiten der AMGT immer wieder erschallende Ruf nach dem türkischen Staate hat eher rhetorischen Charakter. Denn einerseits versteht der türkische Staat die generelle Versorgung mit Sozialeinrichtungen auch im Lande selbst nicht als seine Aufgabe, so daß man dies mit gutem Gewissen auch gar nicht von ihm fordern kann, und andererseits opponiert die AMGT mal offen (DİTİB), mal versteckt (islamischer Religionsunterricht) gegen die Übertragung der inhaltlichen Ausgestaltung 'islamischer Dienstleistungen' in der Diaspora durch den türkischen Staat.

Schutz vor Benachteiligung und Diskriminierung, Recht auf Entfaltung der eigenen Persönlichkeit und Glaubensfreiheit, Demokratie und Chancengleichheit. In einem so angeordneten Felde der Argumentation sind die Glaubensaussagen und Anbetungsvorschriften der Religion, in deren Namen man aktiv wird, von der Mehrheit der Bevölkerung nicht geteilte Werthaltungen. Die Anhänger dieser Werthaltungen können sich nicht auf diese selbst, sondern nur auf jene allgemeinen, auf der Freiheit des Individuums fußenden, Prinzipien berufen, die im Namen individueller Rechte auch eine an Sonderorientierungen angelehnte Lebensführung schützen. Aktivität in europäischen Gesellschaften verlangt deshalb eine zumindest verbale Übernahme ihrer grundsätzlichen Werthaltungen, die damit - weil niemand in getrennten Welten leben kann - zur bestimmenden Werthaltung der Akteure selbst werden muß, je länger diese Aktivität andauert, desto mehr.

Die Selbstorganisation ihrer Mitglieder in einer gegensätzlich strukturierten Gesellschaft, die im Charakter der AMGT als ausländische Schwesterorganisation einer (zumindest im Bewußtsein ihrer Mitglieder) oppositionellen Partei der Türkei angelegt ist, verlangt die Heranzüchtung von Führungskadern, die sowohl über die Religion, in deren Auftrag man handelt, als auch über die Gegebenheiten in Europa Bescheid wissen müssen, wobei - weil die Alltagsbewältigung die entscheidende Größe darstellt - das säkulare Wissen für Führungsqualitäten zunehmend wichtiger wird. Was für die Aufgaben in der Verwaltung und für die Leitung der Gemeinde gilt, gilt auch für die religiöse Unterrichtung des Nachwuchses. Nicht ihre religions-ideologische Ausrichtung, wohl aber ihr Charakter als eine von mehreren Diaspora-Organisationen türkischer Muslime kann es der AMGT langfristig ermöglichen, solche Religionslehrer auszubilden, wie sie von Seiten der Aufnahmeländer immer wieder gefordert werden: solche, die neben theologischen auch über sprachliche und kulturelle Kompetenzen für die Aufnahmeländer verfügen.

Die Beispiele dafür, daß auch das Handeln im (vermeintlichen) Auftrag einer oppositionellen Ideologie, allein aus dem Grunde, daß es *innerhalb* der (im Grunde abgelehnten) gesellschaftlichen Wirklichkeit des Aufnahmelandes realisiert wird, Kompetenzen für das Bestehen in dieser Wirklichkeit schafft und damit integrationsfördernden Charakter hat, lassen sich nahezu beliebig vermehren. In folgendem Ausschnitt aus einem Artikel der Monatszeitschrift der AMGT wird dies am Modell der argumentativen Verteidigung des Islams deutlich, der von den Medien der Aufnahmeländer nur entstellt wiedergegeben werde. In dem Artikel werden den Mitgliedern der AMGT und ihrem Nachwuchs folgende Empfehlungen gegeben:

"Sie sollten im alltäglichen Leben aufhören, sich zu verteidigen und selbst aktiv werden. So sollten sie z.B. ihre Nachbarn zum Tee einladen und ihre Religion erklären. Die Kinder und Jugendlichen sollten in der Schule Arbeiten über den Islam schreiben oder zumindest in ihren Arbeiten den Islam erwähnen. ... Die Muslime sollten verstärkt Berufe im Mediensektor annehmen und sich für Tätigkeiten wie Journalist, Autor, Ingenieur bei Theater, Film und Fernsehen entscheiden, für Berufe wie Kameramann und Tonmeister."[37]

Eine neue Interpretation des Islams

Das Bild vom Islam, das es zurechtzurücken gilt, ist eines, dessen gewalttätige und terroristische Schattierungen sich der gestaltenden Kraft der Medien verdanken, andere Komponenten wie 'Frauenunterdrükkung', 'Ritualismus' und 'Hinterwäldlertum' sind wenigstens bis zu einem gewissen Grad Ergebnis der Konfrontation der Mehrheitsbevölkerung mit spezifischen Verhaltensnormen der muslimischen Einwanderer. Zurechtgerückt kann das Bild des Islams deshalb nur werden, wenn es neben der so modernen wie ihm nachträglich zugewiesenen Konnotation des Terrorismus auch von Dimensionen gereinigt wird, die als Verharren in der Tradition bzw. als Traditionalismus gefaßt werden können. Denn wer seine Religion einem Außenstehenden oder gar einer fremden Gesellschaft erklären soll, dem ist allein damit, daß er eine Vorstellung von ihr hat, daß er selbst sie kennt, nur ansatzweise geholfen. Er muß die Religion auch so darstellen können, daß sie bei 'den anderen' als in sich schlüssige, nachvollziehbare und sinnvolle Einheit von Lehre und Verhaltensvorschrift erscheint.

Die Kritik der Tradition

Im Grunde genommen geht der Prozeß jedoch tiefer und betrifft keineswegs nur die eher propagandistische Seite der Verteidigung der eigenen Religion und Kultur dem Fremden gegenüber. Vielmehr genügt ein Religionsverständnis, das sich in der bloßen Fortsetzung der Tradition erschöpft, bereits den Notwendigkeiten des gesellschaftli-

---

37 İbrahim Keleş, Alman medyası fundamentalist, *Millî Görüş & Perspektive* (8/1995), S. 21-22.

chen Wandels im Herkunftsland nicht mehr, worin der Grund für eine so moderne Erscheinung wie sie die islamistische Partei der Türkei darstellt, zu suchen ist. In sich modernisierenden und modernen Gesellschaften geraten früher selbstverständliche traditionelle Verhaltensmuster, Normen und Orientierungen durch die Konfrontation mit einer Vielzahl unterschiedlicher Lebensstile, die sich auf einem regelrechten Markt ideologischer Überzeugungen behaupten müssen, unter einen ihnen bis dahin vollkommen fremden Begründungszwang. Da traditionelles Verhalten in modernen Gesellschaften in weiten Bereichen seine Funktion verliert, ergießt sich der *mainstream* religiösen Lebens jetzt nicht in das Bett einer ohnehin aussichtslos erscheinenden Rechtfertigung traditioneller Formen von Religiosität, sondern führt die genannte Konfrontation in einer Kritik der Tradition, die ihre theologische Berechtigung in der sogenannten 'Rückkehr' zu den Quellen der Religion findet. Die Hinwendung der Gläubigen zum 'Text', die Verschriftlichung der Diskussion, die Intellektualisierung der Debatten, die Medialisierung der Kommunikation und die damit einhergehende Vereinheitlichung vormals unterschiedlicher regionaler Sonderformen religiösen Lebens können als die Charakteristika dieses Prozesses genannt werden.[38]

In der europäischen Diaspora scheinen die genannten Entwicklungen mit einer gewissen Verspätung eingesetzt zu haben, was direkt aus dem Fehlen intellektueller Trägerschichten[39] erklärbar ist. Diese Situation hat sich jedoch mit deren Erscheinen in der dritten bzw. vierten Einwanderergeneration so gründlich gewandelt, daß manche Wissenschaftler bereits von einem allgemeinen Reflexionsprozeß über den Glauben unter den Angehörigen der jungen Generation sprechen.[40] Tatsächlich richtet auch die AMGT für ihre Jugendlichen nicht nur Arabischkurse aus, die den direkten Zugang des Gläubigen zu Koran und *hadis*, den Heiligen Texten des Islam ermöglichen sollen, sondern sie organisiert darüberhinaus auch europaweite Wettbewerbe, in denen

---

38 Vgl. Günter Seufert, Politischer Islam in der Türkei: Islamismus als symbolische Repräsentation einer sich modernisierenden muslimischen Gesellschaft, Beiruter Texte und Studien 67, Stuttgart und Istanbul 1997.

39 Ihre "Plausibilitätsstruktur" nach Berger/Luckmann, vgl.: P.L. Berger & T. Luckmann, Die gesellschaftliche Konstruktion der Wirklichkeit: Eine Theorie der Wissenssoziologie, Fischer, 6. Auflage, Frankfurt am Main 1992.

40 Prof. Abdoljavad Falaturi, Köln, sah für diesen, seiner Meinung nach notwendigen Reflexionsprozeß der Muslime in der Diaspora die günstigsten Voraussetzungen,, vgl. seine Äußerungen in F.M. İlhan, Die Zukunft des Islam in Deutschland: 3. Islam-Tagung der Konrad-Adenauer-Stiftung, Tagungsbericht in *AMGT Bülten* (4/1995), S. 29-31 und (5/1995), S. 28-30, hier (4/1995), S. 30.

sich die Kenntnis der Schrift an ihrer Interpretation vor vollkommen neuen und modernen Problemlagen in der Form zu bewähren hat, daß für Fragen von Rassismus und Fremdenfeindlichkeit, von Assimilationsdruck und Multikulturalismus genauso Antworten im Koran und im Prophetenhandeln gefunden werden müssen wie für die Probleme von Umweltverschmutzung und Atomkraftnutzung. Ritualistische traditionelle Frömmigkeit und die Legitimierung überkommener hierarchischer Sozialstrukturen ist von dieser neuen religiösen Diskussion ebensowenig zu erwarten wie die Heiligung einer anachronistischen geschlechtsspezifischen Arbeitsteilung. Als Beispiel dafür, wie die Hinwendung zum Heiligen Text die Kritik der Tradition ermöglicht, wie mit anderen Worten theoretische Reflexion und 'religiöses Bewußtsein' die Befreiung aus engen traditionellen Normen erlaubt, sei eine Passage aus dem monatlichen Mitteilungsblatt der AMGT angeführt, in der sich eine deutsche Konvertitin mit ihrer Kenntnis der Schrift gegen in der Tradition verhaftete türkische Muslime wendet:

"Es fehlt uns an Wissen. An Wissen um die reine islamische Lehre und deren Umsetzung. Vor allem fehlt uns der Mut und die Fähigkeit, uns um die Lösung theologischer Fragen selbständig zu bemühen. Weil es erstens anstrengend ist und zweitens Angst macht, folgen wir lieber dem einfachen Weg getreu den Buchstaben und unterwerfen uns einer Lebensweise, die jemand aus Tradition genährt als islamisch definiert. Uns wurde das beste aller Bücher, die gerechteste aller Lebensweisen in die Hand gegeben. Doch warum schauen wir nicht hinein und bemühen uns um dessen Umsetzung? Befreite nicht der Islam die Frau aus ihrem unwürdigen Dasein? Ist die Frau durch den Islam dem Mann nicht gleichberechtigt?"[41]

Auch wenn sich Leitung und Anhängerschaft der AMGT nur schwerlich alle Schlüsse, welche die deutsche Konvertitin in dieser Frage zieht, zu eigen machen können, die Tendenz, die Religion weniger als Vollzug überlieferter Lebensformen, denn als Auftrag zur Neugestaltung der Lebensführung gemäß der Schrift zu verstehen, ist allgemein. Zum Beleg seien Worte des langjährigen Vorsitzenden der AMGT, Osman Yumakoğulları, aus seiner Rede auf der 11. (europaweiten) Generalversammlung der Organisation angeführt:

"Laßt uns daran gehen, im Sinne des Korans bewußt zu werden. Laßt uns den Koran aus dem Einband nehmen und den Einband zer-

[41] M. Reimann-Khairy, Unterdrücke niemanden und laß dich nicht unterdrücken: Kritisches und Selbstkritisches zur Situation muslimischer Mädchen und Frauen in Deutschland, *Millî Görüş & Perspektive* (8/1995), S. 47-48 und 9/95, S. 47, hier 8/95, S. 48.

reißen, damit er nicht zur Schnur wird, an der wir baumeln. Auf daß er nicht (eines Tages, GS) fragt, warum habt ihr mich darin eingesperrt?"[42]

Erst mit der Schwächung der religiösen Tradition und ihrer Autoritäten und mit der Hinwendung zum Heiligen Text, die sich in den Zitaten ausdrückt, wird eine islamistische Diskussion möglich. Damit meine ich eine Diskussion, an der prinzipiell jeder Muslim mit einer gewissen Allgemeinbildung teilnehmen kann, die sich über Medien im öffentlichen Raum und nicht im engen Kreis der Gelehrten abspielt, die sich nicht nur mit juristischen, sondern mit gesellschaftlichen Themen allgemein beschäftigt und daher originär politisch ist, und die, weil sie in modernen Gesellschaften entsteht, auf die intellektuellen Herausforderungen der Moderne und auf die Probleme der modernen Gesellschaften Bezug nimmt. Die prinzipielle Medialität und Öffentlichkeit der Diskussion und die prinzipielle Egalität der Beteiligten sind die Charakteristika, welche die Entwicklungsmöglichkeiten dieser Diskussion entscheidend bestimmen. Eine solche Diskussion hat sich bisher sowohl in der Türkei als auch in der Diaspora nur außerhalb der Religionsbehörde entfaltet. Auf einige ihrer möglichen Konsequenzen für die Zukunft des Islams in der Diaspora soll im Folgenden eingegangen werden.

Distanz zum Nationalismus

Bei der Beschreibung der Orientierung des Handelns der türkischen Religionsbehörde wurde auf die intellektuelle Unfruchtbarkeit einer stark religionsnationalen Ausrichtung hingewiesen. Tatsächlich kann an dieser Stelle folgendes festgestellt werden: So wie die Einbindung des theologischen Denkens in einen den Nationalstaat legitimierenden und nationalistischen Diskurs der Entfaltung dieses Denkens abträglich ist, so setzt mit der Intellektualisierung der religiösen Diskussion eine vorsichtige Distanz zur nationalistischen Ideologie ein. Einige Interviewäußerungen mögen dafür als Beispiel dienen. Die Interviews wurden mit jungen türkischen Studentinnen, Mitglieder des Verbands aus Köln, durchgeführt und in seiner Monatszeitschrift abgedruckt:

"Islam und türkische Nationalität haben fast nichts gemeinsam. Ich bin der Meinung, daß die türkische Sprache nicht unbedingt erhalten werden sollte, damit man Muslim bleibt. Der Koran ist auf Arabisch

---

42 Osman Yumakoğulları, Bizler barış erleriyiz, *Millî Görüş & Perspektive* (7/1995), S. 9-11, hier S. 11.

geschrieben. Unser Prophet konnte auch kein Türkisch." (Hülya, geb. 1973, Jurastudentin).

"Ich bin auch der Meinung, der Erhalt der türkischen Sprache ist nicht unbedingt notwendig. Es kommt darauf an, daß man Muslim ist und versucht, den Islam zu leben, egal in welcher Sprache. ... Wäre es nicht praktischer, Arabisch zu sprechen, den Koran zu verstehen und zu interpretieren?" (Gülay geb. 1976, will Medizin studieren).

"Die Türken waren vorher keine Muslime. Die religiösen Begriffe kommen alle aus dem Arabischen und Persischen. ... Daher wird es kein Problem sein, auch ohne die türkische Sprache weiterhin ein Muslim zu bleiben. Die Bosnier sprechen kein Türkisch, obwohl sie unter osmanischer Herrschaft standen, und sind noch heute muslimisch." (Gülsüm geb. 1974, studiert Geschichte).[43]

In den Zitaten tritt der dialektische Zusammenhang von einer Hinwendung zum Heiligen Text und der Relativierung der Gefühle nationaler Zugehörigkeit deutlich hervor. Über das Verstehen des Textes wird die Religion jetzt etwas, das sich von der konkreten Lebensführung der eigenen Gruppe löst. Die Religion wird von einem tradierten und unhinterfragbaren Modell der Lebensführung zur Lehre.

In einer anderen Nummer berichtet der Redakteur der Zeitschrift von einer türkisch-muslimischen Hochschulgruppe, die sich entschlossen hat, ihre Sitzungen künftig nicht mehr auf Türkisch, sondern auf Deutsch abzuhalten, weil es auf Türkisch Probleme mit der Verständigung gebe. Außerdem könne man, so man auf Deutsch diskutiere, auch interessierte Deutsche und Muslime anderer Nationalität zur Teilnahme gewinnen. Der junge Redakteur kommentiert diese Entwicklung folgendermaßen:

"Hinübergerettet werden kann auf Dauer nur der Glaube, erhalten werden kann nur die religiöse Identität, die in Deutschland eine neue islamische Kultur hervorbringen wird. ... die Gesellschaft (wird, GS) es am Ende dieses Prozesses mit 'deutschen Bürgern islamischen Glaubens und türkischer (oder anderer) Herkunft' zu tun haben. ... Es geht in diesem Prozeß nicht um die Verfestigung einer ethnischen oder nationalen Minderheit, sondern um den Schutz einer religiösen Minorität und des ihr eigenen kulturell-religiösen Brauchtums. ... Religionsbindung heißt nicht Blutsgemeinschaft, sondern Glaubensge-

43 Ich möchte keine Hausfrau mit Diplom sein: Interviews in Köln, *Millî Görüş & Perspektive* (12/1995, S. 43-46.

meinschaft."[44]

Es muß an dieser Stelle wiederum herausgestellt werden, daß innerhalb der AMGT vermutlich nur eine kleine Minderheit bereit ist, die Konsequenz in dieser Radikalität zu ziehen. Doch so wie bei dem oben angeführten Beispiel die *Konsequenz* einer Kritik der Tradition für das Verhältnis von Mann und Frau zwar von der Leitung der AMGT nicht gezogen wird, der entsprechende *Denk-Mechanismus* jedoch auch von ihnen Besitz ergriffen hat, so scheuen sich die Verantwortlichen der Organisation, auch in der Beurteilung des Nationalismus die Konsequenz eines *Denkens* zu ziehen, das sie sehr wohl teilen. Wiederum seien als Beleg Worte des langjährigen Vorsitzenden des Verbandes angeführt:

"Der Mensch ist der Stellvertreter Gottes auf Erden, sein Spiegel, sein Freund, ja Teil von ihm. Und diese Eigenschaften teilen alle Menschen per Geburt, ohne jeden Unterschied ihrer sonstigen Eigenheiten. Deshalb ist der Mensch zu achten und ist ihm zu dienen, unabhängig von der 'Marke' unter der er gerade auftritt. ... Der Gott des Korans ist kein Gott einer bestimmten Rasse, einer bestimmten Region, einer bestimmten Zeit, eines bestimmten Heiligtums oder einer bestimmten Klasse. Der Gott des Korans ist kein Jehova. Er ist allen Menschen Freund und ihnen 'näher als ihre Halsschlagader' (Kaf (18)/16, Bakara (2)/257)".[45]

Die Leitung der AMGT kritisiert den türkischen Nationalismus offen, wo er in aggressiver Form auftritt,[46] sie setzt sich jedoch auch tatkräftig für die Erhaltung der türkischen Identität ihrer Mitglieder in der Diaspora ein. Als Ausfluß des Glaubens aber präsentiert sie einen islamischen Internationalismus,[47] der dem politischen Islam Konnotationen einer Dritte-Welt-Bewegung hinzugewinnt. Noch sind für die tatsächlich entscheidenden Kader in der AMGT Islam und Türkentum untrennbar miteinander verwoben, und die Verbindung erhält bisweilen gerade über den Dritte-Welt-Aspekt neue Nahrung. Doch zumindest innerhalb der gebildeten Jugend des Verbandes besteht die Tendenz, religiöse und nationale Identität getrennt zu betrachten und sich im Zweifelsfalle für letztere zu entscheiden.

---

44 F.M. İlhan, Religiöse oder national-kulturelle Identität: Ein Beitrag zur Identitätsproblematik der muslimischen Jugendlichen in der europäischen Diaspora, *AMGT Bülten* (3/1995), S. 30-32.

45 Yumakoğulları (7/1995), S. 10.

46 Vgl. Millîyetçilik maske olarak kullanılıyor, *Millî Görüş & Perspektive* (1/1996), S. 14-15.

47 Vgl. dazu den ersten Teil dieser Ausführungen.

Islamismus in der Diaspora

Der politische Charakter der AMGT, der im ersten Teil dieser Ausführungen herausgearbeitet wurde, besteht primär im Verhältnis der Organisation zur Türkei. In Europa ist der Verband bisher nur in Ansätzen in politische Auseinandersetzungen verwickelt gewesen. In der Bundesrepublik hat er Gegendemonstrationen gegen die separatistische kurdische PKK organisiert und sich damit ein Stück weit vom türkischen Staat funktionalisieren lassen. In anderen europäischen Ländern, wie z.B. in Holland, hat der Verband diese Aufgabe den Auslandsgliederungen der staatlichen Religionsbehörde überlassen.[48] Dieses in verschiedenen Aufnahmeländern unterschiedliche Vorgehen des Verbandes weist einerseits darauf hin, daß Zentralität und Straffheit der Organisation nicht absolut sind,[49] und zum anderen darauf, daß sie in dieser Frage ihre endgültige Linie noch nicht gefunden hat. Anders als beispielsweise die Islamic Party of Britain, die als langfristiges Ziel die Gewinnung von Mehrheiten in der britischen Gesellschaft und deren schrittweise Umgestaltung anstrebt,[50] haben sich innerhalb der AMGT Stimmen, die für die Bemühung zur staatsrechtlichen Umgestaltung der BRD votieren, kein Gehör verschaffen können. Von der internationalen islamistischen Polit-Diskussion beeinflußte Auseinandersetzungen über die Aufgaben der Diasporamuslime werden — zumindest in der BRD — ausschließlich außerhalb der AMGT geführt. Auf entsprechenden Veranstaltungen wird die Frage nach dem Verhältnis der Diasporamuslime zum 'Islamischen Staat' zwar immer wieder angesprochen, doch haben sich bisher jene Position mit großer Mehrheit durchgesetzt, die der sunnitisch-hanefitischen Schule folgend, keinen Auftrag der Diasporamuslime zur Umgestaltung ihrer Aufnahmegesellschaften erkennen können.[51] Vielmehr wird eine Gültigkeit der Scheriat nicht nur auf die muslimischen Kernländer be-

48 Gespräch des Autors mit dem Generalsekretär der AMGT in Holland Üzeyir Kabaktepe, am 28.5.96 in in der Aya Sofya Camii, Barjesweg 199, Amsterdam.

49 Der ehemalige Generalsekretär der Organisation, Ali Yüksel, meint zu dieser Frage: "Zu behaupten, sie (die AMGT, GS) werde von der RP oder von Necmettin Erbakan gesteuert, ist reine Spinnerei. Ein jeder mit etwas Verstand müßte einsehen, daß eine Institution, die ihre Aktivitäten den politischen Entwicklungen in der Türkei gemäß ausrichtet, in Europa keine Überlebenschance hätte." Ali Yüksel, Cumhuriyet Gazetesi gerçek bir yalancı, *Millî Görüş & Perspektive* (12/1995), S. 8-9, hier S. 9.

50 Vgl. S.M. Bleher, Die Islamic Party of Britain, *Millî Görüş & Perspektive* (8/1995), S. 42-43 (Interview).

51 Vgl. dazu den Beitrag über die türkische Religionsbehörde in der Diaspora in diesem Band.

schränkt, sondern ihre Einführung wird auch von der Existenz einer gerechten islamischen Gesellschaft abhängig gemacht.[52]

In den Ländern der Diaspora sind die Muslime der AMGT also nicht — anders als, zumindest mancher Islaminterpretation gemäß, in den islamischen Kernländern — direkt durch ihre Religion verpflichtet, an der Errichtung eines Staatswesens unter islamischem Vorzeichen zu arbeiten. Doch aus zwei Gründen stellt ihnen die Religion auch in der Diaspora, wenn auch keine staatspolitischen, so doch zumindest gesellschaftspolitische Aufgaben. Zum einen sind sie Mitglieder eines religiösen Verbandes, den primär seine politische, und das heißt auch aktivistische Haltung, von anderen (türkisch-) muslimischen Verbänden in der Diaspora unterscheidet. So ist denn auch eine gewisse Geschäftigkeit Teil der im Verband herrschenden Atmosphäre, und *etwas zur Verbesserung der Lage zu tun,* ist eine wichtige Konnotation seines Diskurses. Wichtiger jedoch ist, daß mit dem Fragwürdigwerden der religiösen Tradition und damit auch der traditionellen Form von Religiosität, diese sich jetzt neue Tätigkeitsfelder suchen und sich durch neue Formen religiösen Lebens darstellen und beweisen muß. In einer stark säkularisierten Gesellschaft, die auf Bemühungen zur Missionierung und Ermahnungen ablehnend reagiert, verfällt man deshalb auf das weite Feld sozialen Engagements, darin der Entwicklung der christlichen Kirchen folgend. Ein Redakteur des Monatsblattes der AMGT verweise auf folgenden hadis des Propheten: *"Wer ruhig schlafen kann, während sein Nachbar hungert, ist kein guter Muslim"*, und stellt das soziale Engagement der Muslime in der mehrheitlich christlich geprägten Gesellschaft als religiöse Pflicht dar.[53] Eine türkische Studentin, Mitglied des Verbandes, nimmt in einem Interview auf gleiche Weise Stellung:

"Zunächst zur Idee einiger Muslime: wir Muslime in Deutschland müssen sofort den islamischen Staat errichten. Das ist eine Utopie, nicht realisierbar. Ich bin dafür, daß wir nicht unbedingt in erster Linie als Muslime, sondern als Menschen in der deutschen Gesellschaft alle zusammen zuerst die sozialen und kulturellen Probleme überbrükken. Z.B. das Rauschgiftproblem oder auseinanderfallende Familien und die Vereinsamung älterer Menschen."[54]

Auf einem der alljährlichen Treffen deutschsprachiger Muslime ar-

---

[52] So beispielweise Omaia Elwan nach İlhan (4/1995), S. 31, im gleichen Sinne Nadeem Elyas in İlhan (5/1995), S. 28.

[53] İlhan (3/1995), S. 13.

[54] Ich möchte keine ... (12/1995), S. 44.

gumentiert der Vorsitzende eines mit der AMGT konkurrierenden islamischen Verbandes jene Vorschrift des Korans, nach welcher die Muslime das Gute befehlen und das Schlechte verbieten sollten, in dem Sinne, daß sie auch im Bezug auf das nichtmuslimische Gemeinwesen gelte, in dem Muslime leben. Ihm gelte es "Nutzen zu bringen" und von ihm gelte es "Schaden abzuwenden".[55] Er offeriert den Propheten als Vorbild für ein verantwortungsvolles Handeln des Muslimen in einer nichtmuslimischen Umwelt. Der Prophet habe sich im heidnischen Mekka 13 Jahre lang für positive Veränderungen eingesetzt und in der *Allianz für das Gut*e (Hılf ul-Fudül = erdemliler ittifakı), für die Entrechteten gewirkt. "Weshalb sollten wir Muslime heute diesem Beispiel nicht folgen?"[56] lautet der daraus gezogene Schluß.

Multikulturalismus und Versittlichung

Nach Ansicht vieler Sprecher der türkischen Muslime brauchen die europäischen Aufnahmegesellschaften heute die Unterstützung der Muslime zur Lösung dringender gesellschaftlicher Probleme. Der langjährige Vorsitzende der AMGT kleidet diese Überzeugung in folgende Worte:

"Ich glaube, die muslimischen Minderheiten haben in Deutschland eine glänzende Zukunft vor sich. Ihr Anteil an der Gesamtbevölkerung steigt ständig. ... Sicher beschränkt sich ihr Beitrag zu dieser Gesellschaft nicht auf ihre Arbeitskraft, sondern sie liefern auch einen moralischen und kulturellen Beitrag. Ein Beitrag, den die deutsche Gesellschaft dringend nötig hat."[57]

Es sind immer wieder zwei Bereiche, in denen die türkischen Muslime die Notwendigkeit ihrer Mitarbeit bei der Lösung der sozialen Probleme der europäischen Aufnahmegesellschaften sehen: *die Sicherung eines multikulturellen Klimas* in den europäischen Gesellschaften, insbesondere in Deutschland, und ihre *Wiederversittlichung*.

Der Beitrag der Muslime zur Wiederversittlichung der europäischen Gesellschaften wird nicht nur in der Zeitschrift der AMGT hervorgehoben, sondern ist ein auch in den Äußerungen von Führern anderer türkisch-muslimischer Gemeinschaften wie der Nuristen oder der

55 Nadeem Elyas zit. nach F.M. İlhan, Gibt es einen Ausgang aus der politischen Unmündigkeit für Muslime?, *Millî Görüş & Perspektive* (7/1995), S. 39-41, hier S. 39.

56 Nadeem Elyas zit. nach İlhan (7/1995), S. 40.

57 Osman Yumakoğulları, Avrupa'da İslam'ın geleceği parlak, *AMGT Bülten* (4/1995), S. 16-17, hier S. 16. Nahezu gleichlautend in Yumakoğuları (9/1995), S. 8.

Süleymanisten ein immer wiederkehrender Topos. In einem Artikel der AMGT-Zeitschrift werden die Mitglieder des Verbandes dazu aufgerufen, mit ihrem persönlichen Verhalten Modell für die anderen zu sein:

"Du bist der Soldat einer Armee, die diese Gesellschaft in Ordnung hält. Du mußt immer danach trachten, dem Guten und Schönen, dem Richtigen und Rechten zu dienen und den Menschen nützlich zu sein. ... Wir leben die Sittlichkeit des Islams und machen sie für unsere Umgebung nachahmenswert. ... Wir verwirklichen die Losung: 'Der ist ein rechter Muslim, dessen Hand und dessen Mund niemandem schadet'. ... Wer den Geist von Millî Görüş in sich trägt, der beachtet die sittlichen und moralischen Normen. Der bringt erst sich und dann die Gesellschaft auf den rechten Weg. Der ist in seiner Schule und an seinem Arbeitsplatz ein musterhafter Muslim, der denkt immer daran, daß er erst für seinen Glauben und den Islam steht und dann erst für sich selbst."[58]

Bei ihrem Einsatz für Multikulturalität will es den türkischen Muslimen nicht nur um den Schutz ihres eigenen Rechts auf ihre spezifische kulturelle Identität gehen, sondern sie versprechen, sich auch für andere ausgegrenzte Gruppen einzusetzen. Der ehemalige Vorsitzende der AMGT sagt:

"Unsere Aufgabe ist es, auf rassistische Provokationen bestimmt aber kaltblütig zu reagieren. Wir müssen uns im Rahmen der geltenden Gesetze und in Zusammenarbeit mit der in ihrer Mehrheit Fremden gegenüber aufgeschlossenen einheimischen Bevölkerung bei den Angriffen, die nicht nur die Ausländer, sondern auch andere soziale Minderheiten betreffen, solidarisch sein und die Freundschaft mit der einheimischen Bevölkerung vertiefen."[59]

Das Votum für Multikulturalität, das in der Zeitschrift der AMGT immer wieder abgegeben wird,[60] wird sowohl unter Hinweis auf das Beispiel des Propheten, insbesondere auf die *Gemeindeordnung von*

58 Sefer Ahmedoğlu, Güneşin doğmak üzre olduğu ufka bakarken, *Millî Görüş & Perspektive* (7/1995), S. 35. Eine ähnliche Position vertritt auch Rüştü Kam, Bir başka açıdan Hicret, *Millî Görüş & Perspektive* (7/1995), S. 36-37.

59 Yumakoğulları (7/1995), S. 10.

60 Mehmet Şen, Klaus Kinkel'i nasıl bilirsiniz?, *AMGT Bülten* (6/1995), S. 18-19, hier S. 19 und Mehmet Şen, Kanlı, canlı vatandaşlık, *AMGT Bülten* (3/1995), S. 16-17, hier S. 16.

Medina[61], als auch historisch, unter Hinweis auf das *Millet-System* des Osmanischen Reiches begründet.[62]

Kein Zweifel, die immer wieder vorgebrachten, doch nur selten in konkretes Handeln umgesetzten muslimischen Voten für die Wiederversittlichung der europäischen Gesellschaften dienen genauso wie ihre Begeisterung für kulturelle Pluralität und Multikulturalität primär der Verteidigung ihrer Gemeinschaften und der Rechtfertigung der spezifischen Sittlichkeit sowie deren kulturellen Formen der Lebensführung, die in diesen Gemeinden herrscht. Daß man sich zur Legitimation von all dem auf durch und durch säkulare Begriffe und auf Werthaltungen beziehen muß, die ihre Unangreifbarkeit aus der in modernen Gesellschaften bestehenden Heiligung des Individuums[63] erhalten, zeigt, daß sich die islamistische Diskussion in einer säkularen Gesellschaft zur Erklärung der Sinnhaftigkeit ihrer Religion auf die Werthaltungen beziehen muß, die in dieser Gesellschaft gelten.

Der Punkt, um den es mir hier geht, ist, daß die Übernahme von Werthaltungen nur über die Erfahrung ihrer Funktionalität für die eigenen Interessen ermöglicht wird.[64] Die Erfahrung einer solchen Funktionalität jedoch ist an gesellschaftliche Aktivität gebunden, und daß sie gesellschaftliche Aktivität ermöglicht - in wie begrenzten Ansätzen auch immer — erscheint mir der bedeutendste Vorteil der Schwesterorganisation der pro-islamischen Partei gegenüber der Auslandsorganisation der Religionsbehörde.

Die Relativierung, die die Bedeutung der bisweilen antidemokratischen, auf Abschottung gerichteten und Feindbilder produzierenden Ideologie der AMGT durch diese rein auf die soziale Struktur bezugnehmende Bewertung erfährt, glaube ich vertreten zu können. Spre-

61 Vgl. W. Ahmed Aries in F.M. İlhan, Menschenrechtskatalog nicht abgeschlossen, *Millî Görüş & Perspektive* (1/1996), S. 42-44, hier S. 43 und Yumakoğulları (4/1995), S. 17. Vgl. zu Diaspradiskussion und Medina-Konzept den Beitrag von Kadir Canatan in diesem Band und zur innertürkischen Diskussion um eine auf der Gemeindeordnung von Medina aufbauende Gesellschaft: Günter Seufert: Crisis and memory in Turkey: issues of political islam, in *Crises and memory in the Muslim world*, A. Pflitsch & A. Neuwirth (Hrsg.) BTS, Stuttgart und Beirut 2000.

62 Vgl. R.T. Erdoğan, Tek kültürü dünya felakettir, *Millî Görüş & Perspektive* (1/1996), S. 9 (Redetext).

63 Von einem "subjektivistischen Personal-Mythus" moderner Gesellschaften spricht beispielsweise Leo Kofler, Soziologie des Ideologischen, Kohlhammer, Stuttgart u.a., 1975, S. 121.

64 "People do not adopt or reject belief systems simply on the rationalistic grounds that they are intellectually coherent. Beliefs are adopted or rejected because they are relevant or not relevant to everyday needs and concerns." B.S. Turner, Orientalism, postmodernism and globalism, Routledge, London u.a. 1994, S. 9.

chen doch selbst Angehörige der Bewegung offen aus, daß es ihr im Grunde um die Erlangung politischer Partizipation und die damit verbunden Ziele, insbesondere das Recht auf die Gestaltung der eigenen Lebensverhältnisse geht, auch wenn diese Anliegen in spezifischen kulturellen Mustern vorgetragen werden:

"Der Modernismus hat Gott auf eine nur in seinen eigenen Augen Bestand habende Weise begriffen, und es ist heute unbedingt nötig, neue Interpretationen und neue Ordnungen dagegenzustellen. Die Menschen haben es satt, sich mit dem zu begnügen, was ihnen die wirtschaftlich Mächtigen gewähren; statt die vorgegebenen absurden Trennungslinien (zwischen ihnen, GS) einfach zu akzeptieren, suchen sie aufs neue nach Dingen, die sich schon in den Prinzipien der französischen Revolution ausdrückten, nach Gleichheit, Freiheit und Gerechtigkeit. Feststeht, daß man daraus größtmöglichen Wohlstand und größte Möglichkeiten für die einen und Unrecht und Unterdrückung für die anderen gemacht hat." [65]

Hoffnungsvolle Ansätze für eine Beteiligung früher abseits stehender und sich einigelnder türkischer muslimischer Gemeinden am gesellschaftlichen Willensbildungsprozeß in den Aufnahmeländern sind die Veröffentlichung von islamischen Zeitschriften und Zeitungen in den Sprachen der Aufnahmeländer, die Bemühungen um eine Institutionalisierung und Verrechtlichung der eigenen Gemeinden und die erfolgreiche Teilnahme islamischer Listen an den Wahlen der Interessensvertretungen von Einwanderern.[66]

Ergebnis

Während in den europäischen Gliederungen der Religionsbehörde ein eher theologischer und ein eher staatspolitischer Diskurs nebeneinander bestehen, findet sich bei der AMGT ein eher auf Abgrenzung von den europäischen Gesellschaften gerichteter und eher parteipolitischer Argumentationsstrang und daneben eine eher auf die Schrift reflektierende und Möglichkeiten zur Integration offerierende religiöse Argu-

---

65 Şen (3/1995), S. 16.

66 Ein Beispiel dafür ist der Sieg islamischer Listen bei den Ausländerbeiratswahlen in Hessen. Die Wahlen wurden notwendig, nachdem die rot-grüne Regierung einen neuen Artikel in die Gemeindeordnung aufnahm, der festlegt, daß Gemeinden mit mehr als 5000 Ausländern einen Ausländerbeirat einrichten müssen. Vgl. Hisham Hammad, Parteien müssen sich dem Islam öffnen, *Millî Görüş & Perspektive* (10/1995), S. 43-46 (Interview), hier S. 45.

mentationskette.

Die stärker mit säkularen und politischen Parametern arbeitenden Diskurse beider Organisationen entstehen jeweils in ihren Zentren, und *Zentrum* meint für beide Institutionen die organisatorischen Zentren in der Türkei. Die stärker religiöse und die intellektuelleren Diskurse beider Institutionen dagegen entstehen eher an Orten, die als Peripherien der Institutionen bezeichnet werden können. Dabei fällt auf, daß die Peripherie, in der die eher religiösen und stärker intellektualisierenden Texte der DİTİB entstehen, ebenfalls in der Türkei liegt, und konkret von den theologischen Hochschulen gebildet wird. Die institutionelle Peripherie der AMGT hingegen bilden ihre in den europäischen Gesellschaften lebenden Mitglieder.

Der religiöse Diskurs der AMGT entsteht zu einem guten Teil in Europa. Er ist auf die Legitimierung aktiven Handelns in den jeweiligen Gesellschaften gerichtet und scheint daher langfristig die Übernahme säkularer Werthaltungen zu ermöglichen.

Vom Korankurs zur Akademie

Die Islamische Akademie Villa Hahnenburg des Verbandes islamischer Kulturzentren

Yasemin Karakaşoğlu-Aydın
Universität Essen

Einleitung

Der folgende Beitrag befaßt sich mit dem 'jüngsten Kind' eines türkisch-islamischen Verbandes in der Diaspora, mit der Islamischen Akademie Villa Hahnenburg (ISLAH), die vom Verband der Islamischen Kulturzentren (VIKZ) ins Leben gerufen wurde. Grund, sich mit der Akademie zu beschäftigen, ist die Einschätzung von Kennern des Islams in Deutschland, daß die ISLAH, die Anfang 1999 ihren Dienst aufgenommen hat, auf neue Tendenzen innerhalb der türkisch-islamischen Szene in Deutschland verweist. Auch diejenigen, die diese Initiative des VIKZ als Imagepflege bewerten, sehen in einer solchen Akademie einen möglichen Impuls für konstruktive Beiträge der Muslime im Bereich der Erwachsenenbildung. Fest steht: mit solchen Einrichtungen eröffnen sich neue Möglichkeiten für Muslime, sich im kulturellen, religiösen und politischen Diskurs der Bundesrepublik einzubringen. Mit der ISLAH etabliert sich zum ersten Mal ein islamischer Akteur in der deutschen Erwachsenenbildung, in der zahlreiche evangelische und katholische Akademien eine lange Tradition kirchlicher Beteiligung bezeugen. Die ISLAH will denn auch staatlich als Weiterbildungseinrichtung anerkannt werden.[1]

Neu an dieser islamischen Bildungsstätte ist, daß sie weder ein Prestigeobjekt islamischer Staaten in Deutschland ist, wie etwa die König-Fahd-Akademie in Bonn, noch von etablierten deutschen Muslimen

[1] Vgl. *Bildungsprogramm der Islamischen Akademie Villa Hahnenburg*, August - Dezember 1999, S. 4 (Im folgenden zitiert als 3. Bildungsprogramm ISLAH).

initiiert wurde, wie das 'Haus Lützelbach', sondern von ehemaligen türkischen Gastarbeitern und ihren Kindern. Freilich ist die ISLAH nicht die erste Aktivität türkischer Muslime im Bildungsbereich. Nicht unerwähnt bleiben sollen die in Form von Selbsthilfeprojekten gestarteten Bildungsinitiativen wie die unabhängige Bildungs- und Begegnungsstätte für muslimische Frauen und Mädchen in Köln, das ebenfalls in Köln ansässige Institut für Pädagogik und Didaktik oder das Institut für Islamische Erziehung in Stuttgart. Dennoch kann die ISLAH als die erste Erwachsenenbildungsinitiative nach Vorbild der evangelischen und katholischen Akademien Exklusivität für sich in Anspruch nehmen. Daß sich damit eine wesentliche Veränderung in der Qualität christlich-islamischer Begegnungen ankündigt, stellt auch Gerhard Jasper, langjähriger Leiter der Islamberatungsstelle der Evangelisch-Lutherischen Kirche fest, wenn er konstatiert: "Bisher waren Muslime stets Gäste in christlichen Akademien. Jetzt laden sie als Gastgeber zu Schritten im Dialog ein. Das ist mehr als nur ein psychologischer Unterschied."[2]

Finanzier der Akademie ist der VIKZ, drittgrößter muslimischer Dachverband und -- was die Dialog-Partner angeht -- bestakzeptierter Vertreter der Muslime in Deutschland. Der VIKZ mißt denn auch dem Dialog und der Integration der Muslime einen besonderen Wert bei.[3]

Es ist natürlich noch zu früh, ein Urteil über die Zukunftsaussichten der Akademie abzugeben.[4] Es handelt sich deshalb bei dem vorliegenden Beitrag um den Versuch, deutlich zu machen, daß sich der Islam türkischer Prägung insbesondere im Hinblick auf seine Bildungsaktivitäten sehr dynamisch entwickelt. Das hat Einfluß auf den Dialog mit Nichtmuslimen und auf die Form der öffentlichen Präsenz des Islams in Deutschland.

Grundlage des Beitrages sind Multiplikatoren-Interviews mit der akademischen und geschäftsführenden Leitung der Akademie, sowie

---

2 Gerd Jasper, Die islamische Akademie ISLAH in Köln will den Dialog, *Mitarbeiterbrief* Nr.7/Juli-August 1998, hrsgg. von: Vereinte Evangelische Mission, Wuppertal, S. 34-35.

3 3. *Bildungsprogramm ISLAH*, S. 2. Vgl. hierzu auch die web-Seiten des VIKZ unter: http://www.islam.de/D200_organisationen/230_Selbstdarstellung/235_VIKZ.html

4 Außer den Programmen, der Selbstdarstellung der ISLAH, einigen Zeitungsartikeln sowie einer Erwähnung unter der Rubrik "VIKZ" in der 1998 von der Arbeiterwohlfahrt Duisburg hrsgg. Broschüre *Islam in Duisburg* (S. 18) liegt bisher kein Material über die Islamische Akademie vor.

informelle Gespräche mit Beobachtern und Mitwirkenden der türkisch-islamischen Szene, sowie einige schriftliche Materialien, wie die Selbstdarstellung der ISLAH, Presseberichte über die Akademie, und die ersten drei Viertel- und Halbjahresprogramme der ISLAH.[5]

Entstehungsgeschichte und äußeres Erscheinungsbild der Akademie

Im November 1996 erwarb der VIKZ die 1870/72 von dem Kölner Brauereibesitzer Johann Herbert Hahn erbaute neoklassizistische Villa. Das Gebäude, das unter Denkmalschutz steht und damals in einem stark restaurationsbedürftigen Zustand war, wurde in Eigenregie gründlich renoviert. Gemeindemitglieder stellten ihre Arbeitskraft kostenlos zur Verfügung. Nach Abschluß der zweijährigen Restaurationsarbeiten öffnete die Akademie Ende 1998 ihre Pforten.

Nach Angaben des Geschäftsführers der Akademie İsmail Birol, hatte der Verband vor, das Gebäude als Moschee für Gemeindemitglieder in Köln-Mühlheim, einem Stadtteil mit hohem Anteil türkischer Bevölkerung, zu nutzen. Mühlheim ist der Bezirk, in dem die erste Moschee des VIKZ -- in einem ehemaligen Ladenlokal -- gegründet worden war. Später wurde die Zentrale nach Köln-Nippes verlegt. Als sich herausstellte, daß die für eine Moschee notwendigen baulichen Veränderungen vom Denkmalamt nicht erlaubt werden würden, wurde eine Anregung des damaligen Landtagsabgeordneten der Grünen, Dr. Hisham Hammad, aufgegriffen. Hammad, der heute als Vertreter der "Aktion Courage" im Beirat der ISLAH vertreten ist, schlug vor, in dem Gebäude eine islamische Akademie zu etablieren.

Da der Verband keine konkreten Vorstellungen von der Tätigkeit einer solchen Akademie hatte, wurde ein Entwurf ausgearbeitet, der an Behörden, Verbände, Wissenschaftler, Kirchen, Politiker und Journalisten mit der Bitte um Stellungnahme verschickt wurde. Die überwiegend positiven Stellungnahmen wurden anonymisiert, nach Vorschlägen geordnet und im Hinblick auf Umsetzungsmöglichkeiten ausgewertet. Ziel war es - so die Leitung heute - von Anfang an eine transparente Einrichtung zu schaffen.

[5] Ich danke Prof. Dr. Peter Heine, Islamwissenschaftler an der Humboldt-Universität zu Berlin, Regine Fröse, Religionspädagogin; Irmgard Pinn, Soziologin und Zehra Yılmaz, Redaktionsmitglied des *Pressespiegels Islam in Europa* der VHS-Duisburg, für ihre Eindrücke und Einschätzungen zur ISLAH.

Der VIKZ gewährte der Akademie von Anfang an größtmögliche Unabhängigkeit. Ihre Leitung wurde aus den Reihen der Mitarbeiter der VIKZ-Zentrale in Köln rekrutiert. Geschäftsführer wurde der ehemalige Verantwortliche für Öffentlichkeitsarbeit im Bezirk Hessen, İsmail Birol. Die pädagogisch-theologische Leitung erhielt die Theologin Nigar Yardım, die sich im christlich-islamischen Dialog über NRW hinaus Anerkennung erworben hat.[6] Um die Unabhängigkeit der Akademie zu dokumentieren, übernahm das drei Jahre zuvor gegründete Islamische Frauenbildungswerk, das nun unter dem Namen Islamisches Bildungswerk firmiert, die Trägerschaft.

Der Dialog, der über Jahrzehnte ehrenamtlich geführt wurde, soll nun in eigener Regie institutionalisiert und auf "höchstem Niveau" weitergetrieben werden. Die Investitionen in die Akademie bezeichnet Birol daher auch als "Investitionen in den Dialog". Als weiteres Ziel wird eine "Integration der Muslime" angegeben.[7] Birol betont, daß damit nicht etwa ein Verschmelzen mit der deutschen nicht-muslimischen Mehrheitsgesellschaft gemeint sei, sondern intendiert sei, die Muslime als sichtbaren Teil der Gesellschaft zu etablieren. Er benutzt folgendes Bild: "Wenn ich Milch in den Kaffee gieße, dann verändern sich Farbe und Geschmack des Kaffees, aber beides ist noch als solches zu erkennen. Der Kaffee ist zwar dominant aber die Milch hat sichtbaren Anteil an der Veränderung des Kaffees, der jetzt auch nicht mehr seine ursprüngliche Farbe hat. Gebe ich hingegen Zucker in den Kaffee, dann löst dieser sich bis zur Unkenntlichkeit darin auf. Man kann ihn nicht mehr sehen." Die Muslime sollen wie Milch, nicht aber wie Zucker sein. Indem, so Birol weiter "wir uns zwar verändern, aber nicht unsere Identität als Muslime", wird weder eine Abschottung von der Mehrheitsgesellschaft noch ein Aufgehen in ihr angestrebt, denn "die Gesellschaft in Europa hat viele Werte, die sehr fortschrittlich sind, vor allem im politischen Bereich, wo Muslime viel lernen können. Wichtig für uns Muslime ist eine Aussage des Propheten, der sag-

---

6 Yardım tritt häufig als Referentin in Erwachsenenbildungsstätten, auf Kirchentagen sowie auf Diskussionsforen auf und kann auf eine umfassende Erfahrung zurückblikken. Vgl. Wolfgang Koydl, *Süddeutsche Zeitung* vom 22. März 1999.

7 "Um den besonderen Wert des Dialogs und der Integration der Muslime in die deutsche Gesellschaft zu unterstreichen, hat der Verband die Villa in den Jahren 1996 bis 1998 mit großem Aufwand restauriert und sie dem Islamischen Bildungswerk zur Errichtung einer islamischen Akademie zur Verfügung gestellt", *Bildungsprogramm der Islamischen Akademie Villa Hahnenburg*, April - Juni 1999, S.4.

te: 'Geh' und hole das Wissen, auch wenn es in China ist'. Das heißt, es kommt nicht darauf an, von wem man lernt, sondern daß man lernt. Der Islam war der Innovation, dem Fortschritt nie abgeneigt".

Vor diesem Hintergrund ist auch der Name ISLAH zu verstehen, der auf den ersten Blick ein Kürzel für Islamische Akademie Villa Hahnenburg zu sein scheint. Die Selbstdarstellung verweist jedoch auf das arabische Wort "ıslah". Es bedeutet *Reform* oder *Verbesserung*. Die Selbstdarstellung betont die Bedeutung *in Ordnung bringen, versöhnen und verbessern* und leitet daraus das Ziel "die Verbesserung des gesellschaftlichen Zusammenlebens in Deutschland" ab.[8] Im Osmanischen Reiche pflegten Bedürftige und Waise im "ıslahhane", dem Besserungshaus, Betreuung und auch berufliche Ausbildung zu erhalten. Das stellt das Gemeinwohl in den Vordergrund. Doch die Betreiber weisen auch auf die theologische Komponente des Wortes hin: der göttliche "ıslah" ist das "Streben Gottes, seinen Dienern Gutes zu erweisen".[9]

Die räumliche Anlage und Ausstattung der Akademie gibt Hinweise auf die ihr zugedachte Funktion. Das repräsentative Äußere symbolisiert das Streben nach einer "Integration der Muslime in die deutsche Gesellschaft".[10] Die Fassade wurde nicht verändert, und die Innenausstattung führt den neoklassizistischen Stil fort. Vier Etagen sollen verschiedenen Funktionen gerecht werden.

Im Untergeschoß wurde ein aufwendig und in klassischer osmanischer Tradition ausgestatteter Gebetsraum mit getrennten Bereichen für Männer und Frauen eingerichtet. Er verfügt über separate Eingänge. Unter Einbeziehung der Nebenräume finden hier circa 500 Personen Platz zum Gebet. An Festtagen werden den Betenden auch die Akademie-Räumlichkeiten zur Verfügung gestellt. Dies erklärt, warum am Eingang die Schuhe abgelegt werden und warum man bildliche Darstellungen vermieden hat. Ebenfalls im Untergeschoß befinden sich eine Großküche und ein Speisesaal für 60 - 80 Personen. Im Erdgeschoß finden sich das Arbeitszimmer des Geschäftsführers, der Raum des Pförtners und Hausmeisters sowie ein großer Salon für Veranstaltungen, der mit Polstergarnituren, Teppichen und Kristallüstern

[8] 3. *Bildungsprogramm ISLAH*, S. 3.

[9] Anläßlich der Eröffnung hrsgg. *Selbstdarstellung*, 1998, S. 5.

[10] Ebenda, S.5.

im orientalischem Stile ausgestattet ist. Darüber hinaus verfügt das Erdgeschoß über zwei, an den Salon angrenzende, kleinere Seminarräume.

Das Büro der Leiterin der Akademie und ihrer Mitarbeiter sowie zwei weitere Seminarräume und ein großer Vortrags- und Konferenzsaal befinden sich im ersten Obergeschoß. Das Verhältnis von Seminar-, Konferenz- und sonstigen Funktionsräumen verstärkt den Eindruck, daß das Gebäude vor allem durch Repräsentationsräume dominiert wird, deren Seminarraumcharakter durch die prunkvolle Ausstattung eher in den Hintergrund tritt.

Das Dachgeschoß wurde als Gästewohnung gestaltet; mit repräsentativen Möbeln im neu-barocken Stil, einer kompletten Küche und luxuriösem Sanitärbereich. Eine VIKZ-Mitarbeiterin erwähnt, daß die Möblierung in Farbe, Ausstattung und Stil nach Vorgaben der Tochter des Gründers der Bewegung erfolgte, als deren Auslandsorganisation der VIKZ gilt: Süleyman Hilmi Tunahan, ein Scheich des Ordens des Nakşibendiyye, der gegen Ende des Osmanischen Reiches und in den Gründungsjahren der Republik lebte. Die Louis-XIV-Möbel und die hellrosanen Teppiche und Tapeten, verweisen auf das Bemühen, eine luxuriös-repräsentative und gleichzeitig freundlich-wohnliche Atmosphäre zu schaffen.

Der Stolz auf die aus eigenen Kräften geschaffene Stätte ist ein Hinweis auf den Wandel innerhalb der islamischen Organisationslandschaft in Deutschland. Die Akademie ist darauf ausgerichtet, gegenüber der nicht-muslimischen Mehrheit ein neues Selbstverständnis der Muslime zu demonstrieren. Ohne Kenntnis der Migrationsgeschichte ist dies nicht zu verstehen.[11]

Das Bild des türkischen Islams war bisher vorwiegend durch ländliche, volksreligiöse Ausdrucksformen geprägt. Seine Aktivitäten waren die Sicherung der religiösen Grundversorgung und der religiösen Praxis der Gemeindemitglieder, zentriert auf den engeren Kreis der türkisch-muslimischen Moscheebesucher und ihrer Familien.[12] Mit der Villa Hahnenburg haben die 'ungebildeten muslimischen Arbeits-

---

[11] Vgl. Y. Karakaşoğlu-Aydın, Zwischen Türkeiorientierung und migrationspolitischem Engagement, in: *Zeitschrift für Türkeistudien* 2/96, S. 267-282, sowie: dies., Vom Gastarbeiter zum Einwanderer, in: Forschungsinstitut der Friedrich-Ebert-Stiftung (Hrsg.), *Von der Ausländer- zur Einwanderungspolitik*, Bonn 1994, S. 87-96.

[12] Vgl. den VIKZ im Internet.

migranten' aus eigener Kraft eine noble Bildungsstätte geschaffen. Vor diesem Hintergrund ist die Pracht der Innenausstattung zu verstehen. Sie steht für 'Hochkultur' und 'Wohlstand', für 'Zivilisation' und 'Schönheit des Islams'. Sie ist darauf angelegt, großstädtische Kultur in Anlehnung an osmanische Palastkultur zu demonstrieren.[13] Nach dem ideologischen Bruch mit der islamisch-osmanischen Geschichte durch die kemalistische Revolution und durch die anschließende Verwestlichung der Türkei schaffte die Migration auch noch eine räumliche Distanz zu dieser Vergangenheit. Es scheint, als solle diese ‘prachtvolle Vergangenheit’ sowohl der muslimischen Minderheit als auch der deutschen/christlichen Mehrheit in Erinnerung gerufen und erneut in Besitz genommen werden.

Pädagogischer Ansatz

Das Bildungsangebot umfaßt Themenbereiche wie “Politik und Gesellschaft”, “Persönlichkeit und Glaube”, “Persönlichkeit und Gesundheit” sowie “Sprache”.

Die Akademie wendet sich mit ihrem Programm zunächst an die angestammte Klientel der islamischen Organisationen, die türkisch-islamische Gemeinde, deren Bildungsstand sie heben will. Viele Angebote wenden sich an die Frauen, vor allen Dingen berufliche Basisqualifizierung wie die nach Geschlechtern getrennten Deutschkurse. Die Geschlechtertrennung erfolgt nicht aus Prinzip, sondern wird jeweils im Programm genannt. Zum Angebot für die Migranten gehören auch Kurse zum Erwerb des Internet-Führerscheins und Kommunikationstraining. Veranstaltungen wie Hepatitis-B oder "Meine Sehkraft nimmt ab" werden in türkischer Sprache abgehalten. Sie finden in Zusammenarbeit mit der Deutsch-Türkischen Gesundheitsstiftung (Gießen) statt und werden durch türkischstämmige Ärzte des Klinikums der Justus-Liebig-Universität Gießen durchgeführt. Kompetenzen im Umgang mit islamischen Quellen in der muslimischen Lingua Franca Arabisch, aber auch zur Verwendung im Umgang mit arabischsprachigen Geschäftspartnern werden in Arabischkursen vermittelt.

13 "Die Möbel der Villa Hahnenburg sind Imitate aus den osmanischen Palästen der Neo-Renaissance, entsprechen so dem Stil des Hauses und bilden zusammen mit dem Haus und dem Garten eine Einheit", *3. Bildungsprogramm ISLAH*, S. 2.

Andere Veranstaltungen widmen sich der Qualifikation von haupt- und ehrenamtlichen Mitarbeitern der Moscheegemeinden. Auf einer Tagung zum "Tag der offenen Moschee" üben sie die Vorbereitung einer solchen Aktion, erhalten Tips zur Öffentlichkeitsarbeit, zur Erstellung von Informationsmaterial und zum Umgang mit nicht-muslimischen Besuchern. Fortbildungsangebote drehen sich um das deutsche Schulsystem, die Kinderpsychologie und das Christentum. Langfristig wird eine Reform der Ausbildung von Imamen und Religionslehrern angestrebt. Als besonders notwendig erachten es die Mitarbeiter, den Imamen Begrifflichkeiten für Predigten in Deutsch zu vermitteln. Eine der zukünftigen Aufgaben der Akademie könnte darin bestehen, eine angemessene deutsche Terminologie zu erarbeiten, sowie die Durchführung von Zeremonien auf Deutsch zu lehren. Es besteht ein großes Bedürfnis nach dem Erlernen von "dem Leben und der deutschen Sprache angemessenen religiösen Präsentationsformen", so der Geschäftsführer, İsmail Birol. Die sehr emotional und mit großer Wortgewalt vorgetragenen Predigten mancher Imame zur Verdeutlichung der Höllenqualen, die einen nicht recht handelnden Muslim im Jenseits erwarteten, orientierten sich nicht an den bildlichen Vorstellungen und der emotionalen Welt von in Deutschland aufgewachsenen Muslimen und sprächen diese nicht mehr an, meint auch Cevriye Güler, die Leiterin der Bildungsarbeit. Ein Anfang sei dadurch gemacht, daß in der Moschee der Akademie im diesjährigen Ramadan mehrfach Predigten in deutscher Sprache abgehalten wurden.

Die Akademie bietet auch der neuen türkisch-islamischen Bildungselite Weiterbildung. "Tätiges Lernen" ist das Motto: man hält Vorträge und lernt, sich zu präsentieren und rhetorisch weiterzuentwickeln. Die Mitarbeiterinnen sehen sich als Vorbilder für nachfolgende Generationen von bekennenden muslimischen Frauen, die in außerhäusige Berufe drängen.

Veranstaltungen wie "Scheriat und Demokratie", "Politische Systeme in islamisch geprägten Ländern", "Islam in Deutschland", "(K)ein Platz in Europa (?), Konzepte zu Fragen des Islams innerhalb Europas" oder die Vortragsreihe "Geschichte des Islams" wenden sich an ein interessiertes deutschsprachiges Publikum. Vor allem Veranstaltungsserien zur Geschichte des Islams erfreuen sich, so die Leiterin der Akademie Nigar Yardım, großer Beliebtheit.

Ein vierter Komplex von Veranstaltungen, die oft von christlichen und muslimischen Referenten gemeinsam gestaltet werden, fokussiert den christlich-islamischen Dialog und interreligiöse wie interkulturelle Themen: "Wenn ein Kümmeltürke einen Giaur trifft, dann... Eine Tagung zu interkulturellen Wörtern und Unwörtern des Jahres" oder "Darüber müssen wir reden! Resümee des christlich-islamischen Dialogs", "Verständnis und Formen des Gebets im Christentum und Islam" oder "Alles was kommt, kommt von Gott". Einige Veranstaltungen befassen sich auch mit anderen Religionen wie eine von einem Juden angebotene "Einführung in das Judentum". Auch die diesjährige Tagung der Christlich-Islamischen Gesellschaft (CIG) fand in der Villa Hahnenburg statt.

Der pädagogische Ansatz ist an traditionellen islamischen Bildungskonzepten orientiert, zeigt jedoch starke Einflüsse westlicher Ideen. Die Didaktik und Methodik der Seminare orientieren sich an Konzepten, wie sie in anderen Erwachsenenbildungsakademien angewandt werden.[14]

Richtungsweisend für die Arbeit mit der muslimischen Gemeinde ist, so die Leitung der Akademie, die Frage: "In welchem Umfeld sollen meine Kinder in 20 Jahren leben?" Hier gebe es nur die Alternativen: Parallelgesellschaft oder selbstverständliche Integration. Da das Ziel aus ihrer Sicht nur die selbstverständliche Integration sein könne, wolle man als Muslim Anteil an allen gesellschaftlichen Problemen und deren Lösung nehmen. Daher bietet die Akademie auch Seminare zu vordergründig 'unislamischen' Themen wie Umwelt, Müllabfuhr oder Gesundheitsvorsorge an.

Es stellt sich die Frage, inwiefern die Akademie einen eigenständigen islamischen pädagogischen Ansatz, etwa in Anlehnung an den 'tevhid'-Gedanken klassischer islamischer Bildung, verfolgt. Dieses Ideal hat seine Grundlage im Selbstverständnis des Islams als Weg zur allumfassenden göttlichen Ordnung. Es bedeutet, daß Erziehung und Bildung nicht losgelöst von religiöser Erziehung und Bildung sein können. Denn die Einheit von Glauben und Bildung (türk. tevhid) steht in Zusammenhang mit der Einheit von Glauben und rechtem

14 "... eine auf modernen pädagogischen Gesichtspunkten basierende Bildungsarbeit vor allem durch die Muslime selbst", *Selbstdarstellung ISLAH* 1998, S. 6.

Handeln, dem Ideal und Ziel der Lebensführung eines Gläubigen.[15]

Ein solcher Ansatz wurde zwar prinzipiell befürwortet, nicht jedoch konkreter ausgeführt. Einiges spricht dafür, daß man sich in der Akademie dem tevhid-Gedanken verbunden fühlt. So betont die pädagogische Leitung den Wunsch, auf der Basis von Elementen des klassischen islamischen Bildungssystems neue Einflüsse zu berücksichtigen. Dabei müsse stets hinterfragt werden, inwieweit es noch islamisch zulässig sei, religiöse Themenbereiche mit einem säkularisierten wissenschaftlichen Ansatz zu behandeln. Die Leitung sieht vor allem Beratungsbedarf für die Mitglieder islamischer Gemeinden, für die sich die Frage der religionsgerechten Erziehung und Ausbildung der Kinder stelle. Yardım möchte eine Verbindung zwischen säkularisierten und islamischen Ansätzen der Wissensvermittlung herstellen. Sie bezeichnet ihre pädagogische Orientierung als eine Verbindung des "Problemansatzes" mit dem "Ansatz der Wissensvermittlung", wobei das Ziel nicht darin bestehe, eine völlig neuartige islamische Pädagogik und Didaktik zu entwickeln, nur um dem Bestehenden etwas entgegensetzen. Die Mitarbeiter sehen sich nicht in der Rolle von 'Revolutionären'. Es wird keine grundsätzliche Kritik an der traditionellen Methode der Wissensvermittlung in Koran-Schulen geübt. Im Gegenteil, klassische Formen der Wissensvermittlung, wie das Auswendiglernen und Repetieren sollen beibehalten werden, da sie sich über die Jahrhunderte bewährt hätten. Auch die moderne westliche Pädagogik, so Yardım, kehre heute wieder zu manchen vorschnell als 'veraltet' verworfenen Methoden zurück, in ihren Augen ein Beweis für die Zeitlosigkeit klassischer islamischer Lehrmethoden. Falsch würden diese Methoden angewandt, wenn sie sich auf ein schematisches, 'stures' Auswendiglernen beschränken ohne diskursive Auseinandersetzung mit den Fragen der Zöglinge. Viele Gemeinden hätten eine an Äußerlichkeiten orientierte Korankurs-Erziehung verfolgt und dabei die Vermittlung des Spirituellen vernachlässigt. Eine Überbetonung kognitiver Zugänge zum Koran durch die Einführung diskursiver Elemente in den Koranunterricht berge andererseits die Gefahr in sich, daß der spirituelle Zugang der Gläubigen zum Text, der durch das Rezitieren erreicht werde, verlorengehe.

15 Zum 'tevhid'-Ideal: N. H. Barazangi, Education, in: John Esposito (Hrsg.), *The Oxford Encyclopedia of the Modern Islamic World* [OEMIW], Vol. 1, New York 1995, S. 406-411 und S. A. Akbar, The Islamization of knowledge, ebenda, S. 425-428.

Bewundernd blickt man auf die evangelischen Gemeinden. Dort existiere eine fundierte Lernkultur, die das Fernziel muslimischer Erwachsenenbildung sein müsse. Man dürfe jedoch eine von den Zöglingen akzeptierte "Autorität des Lehrers" nicht im Gegensatz zu der Entwicklung einer Diskussionskultur in Klasse oder Seminar sehen. Der Islam habe über Jahrhunderte hinweg große Erfolge im Bereich der Bildung erzielt, es sei nun an den islamischen Pädagogen, sich in konstruktiver Weise, unter Einbeziehung der Anregungen von außen, auf diese Tradition zu besinnen. Ihr selbst hätten die Erfahrungen mit westlichen pädagogischen Methoden einem neuen Blick auf ihre islamischen Wurzeln ermöglicht, so Yardım.

Der Finanzier: VIKZ (Verband der Islamischen Kulturzentren e.V. / İslam Kültür Merkezleri Birliği)[16]

Der VIKZ hat in seiner mittlerweile 27jährigen Existenz in Deutschland eine beachtliche Entwicklung durchlaufen. Obwohl nicht wie Milli Görüş im Fokus verfassungsschützerischen Interesses stehend, wurde er bis vor kurzem als extremistisch und fundamentalistisch eingestuft.[17] Derartige Einschätzungen sind freilich immer abhängig von der jeweiligen Definition von 'Fundamentalismus'. Oft wurde seine

16 Die folgenden Ausführungen beruhen auf einer durch Feldforschung in den Jahren 1996 bis 1999 aktualisierte Version des Kapitels 3.4.3 VIKZ der von mir erstellten Publikation *Türkische Muslime in Nordrhein-Westfalen*, hrsgg. vom Ministerium für Arbeit, Gesundheit und Soziales NRW, 3. völlig überarbeitete Auflage, Duisburg 1997, S. 131-137. Im folgenden zitiert als MAGS 1997.

17 Bleibt Gürs polemischer Vergleich der "Süleymancılar" mit "Wölfen im Schafspelz" (Metin Gür, *Türkisch-Islamische Vereinigungen in der Bundesrepublik Deutschland*, Frankfurt a.M. 1993, S.60) außer Acht, so finden sich einige Einordnungen neueren Datums als "fundamentalistische Gemeinde" (Werner Schiffauer, Der Weg zum Gottesstaat, in *Historische Anthropologie*, Sonderdruck, 1. Jhrg 1993, Heft 3, S. 468-484). "... sie vertreten in der Regel fundamentalistische Auffassungen ... und sind daher als radikal einzuschätzen." so Martin Hoch: *Türkische Politische Organisationen in der Bundesrepublik Deutschland*, Arbeitspapier, hrsgg. von der Konrad-Adenauer-Stiftung, Sankt Augustin, August 1993, S. 11. Andere betonen den mystischen Charakter der Organisation, die zwar in Opposition zum staatlichen türkischen Verständnis von Laizismus stehe, aber nicht als politische Kraft in Erscheinung träte: "... they primarily want to run their own affairs and perform their rituals without interference from outside." Jeroen Doomernik, "The institutionalization of Turkish Islam in Germany and The Netherlands: a comparison", in *Ethnic and Racial Studies*, Vol. 18, Nr. 1, January 1995, S. 46-61, hier S. 50.

mangelnde Gesprächs- und Dialogbereitschaft kritisiert.[18] Neuere Untersuchungen betonen jedoch seine Offenheit gegenüber dem Christlich-Islamischen Dialog, die Verläßlichkeit als Dialog-Partner sowie seine parteipolitische Neutralität.[19] Die jahrelange intensive Öffentlichkeitsarbeit des Verbandes macht sich positiv auf seine Wahrnehmung durch die deutsche (auch wissenschaftliche) Öffentlichkeit bemerkbar.

Seit 1973 ist der Verband der islamischen Kulturzentren unter diesem Namen in Deutschland aktiv und ist damit der älteste in Deutschland ansässige Dachverband muslimischer Migranten. In einer älteren Selbstdarstellung führt der Verband seine Wurzeln auf die "Türkische Union", die sich bereits 1969 in Köln gegründet habe, zurück. Dem Kölner Vereinsregister ist zu entnehmen, daß sich 1973 das erste "Islamische Kulturzentrum" in Köln eintragen ließ. Dieser Verein wurde 1980 in "Verband der islamischen Kulturzentren" umbenannt.[20] Der VIKZ war innerhalb der verschiedenen Moscheevereine, die es bereits seit den sechziger Jahren gab, der erste, der sich für die Schaffung einer gemeinsamen Bewegung auf Bundesebene einsetzte. Er stellte schon 1979 den Antrag zur Anerkennung als Körperschaft des Öffentlichen Rechts, der jedoch abschlägig beschieden wurde, da der Verband damals die Kriterien nicht erfüllte.[21]

Der Verband versteht sich als Religionsgemeinschaft im Sinne des Artikels 140 GG und geht vom Verbleib der Türken in Deutschland aus. Seine Hauptaufgabe bestehe darin, Kindern und Erwachsenen Korankurse zu erteilen, in denen er ihnen die richtige Art zu beten und die Inhalte des Korans vermitteln will. Die Orientierung auf einen Verbleib in Deutschland drückt sich auch im Immobilienerwerb des Verbandes aus. Er ist unter den türkischen Dachverbänden derjenige mit den meisten eigenen Moscheegebäuden (200 von 300 Gebäuden befinden sich im Besitz des Verbandes). Seine Gemeindegröße liegt

18 So meinen Lier & Piest: "Eine Offenheit gegenüber der deutschen Gesellschaft ist durch die begrenzte Gesprächsbereitschaft des VIKZ nur ansatzweise zu erkennen", in: T. Lier & U. Piest, *Muslimische Vereinigungen und Moscheen in Köln*, Köln 1994, S. 31.

19 Vgl. hierzu *MAGS* 1997, S. 137 sowie Philipp Anderson, *Muslime in München*, hrsgg. von der Ausländerbeauftragten, München 1996, S. 27.

20 Vgl. Amtsgericht Köln, *Vereinsregister* Nr. 6851.

21 Seit 1995 liegt dem Kultusministerium NRW erneut ein Antrag des VIKZ auf Anerkennung als Körperschaft Öffentlichen Rechts vor.

seit Beginn der 90er Jahre konstant bei ca. 20 000 Mitgliedern.[22]

In der Öffentlichkeit und auch unter den türkischen Muslimen selbst besser bekannt als "Süleymancılar" oder "Süleymanisten" haftete dem Verband lange ein Geruch von Konspiration an. Die einschlägige Fachliteratur weist auf deutliche Verbindungen zwischen der Süleymancı-Bewegung in der Türkei und dem VIKZ hin.[23] Verbandsvertreter jedoch wehren sich gegen diese Bezeichnung, die auf die sunnitisch-hanefitische Erneuerungsbewegung gleichen Namens in der Türkei zurückgeht. Schiffauer charakterisiert die "Süleymanlı", wie er die Mitglieder des VIKZ tituliert, zwar als "fundamentalistisch", macht jedoch dabei folgende Einschränkung: "Die Süleymanlı sind Verantwortungsethiker: Sie versuchen mit ihrer Politik die Grundlage für ein islamisches Bildungswerk (d.h. im wesentlichen von Korankursen) zu schaffen, indem sie strategisch vorgehen, d.h. sich mit den jeweils amtierenden Mächten arrangieren." (Schiffauer 1993, S.479). VIKZ-Vertreter beschränken diese Verbindungen auf die Ausbildung einiger ihrer Hodschas durch Süleyman Hilmi Tunahan und auf die Konzentration der Verbandsarbeit auf die Durchführung von Korankursen, wie das auch die Anhänger Tunahans in der Türkei tun.[24]

Die Süleymancıs stehen in der Ordens-Tradition und unterscheiden sich vom orthodoxen Islam durch eine Ordenshierarchie und durch die Einteilung ihrer Mitglieder in einen inneren (in die mystische Lehre Eingeweihte) und einen äußeren Kreis. Ihr Name geht auf Süleyman Hilmi Tunahan zurück. Er lebte von 1888 bis 1959 und war Lehrer im religiösen Schulsystem des ausgehenden Osmanischen Rei-

22 Als Mitglieder sind die Mitgliederbeiträge zahlenden Personen zu verstehen, zumeist Familienvorstände. Bei einer durchschnittlichen türkischen Familiengröße von 4,1 Personen ist diese Zahl mit dem entsprechenden Faktor zu multiplizieren, um auf die annähernde Gemeindegröße zu kommen.

23 VIKZ und Süleymancı-Bewegung werden gleichsetzt von: M.S. Abdullah, *Was will der Islam in Deutschland?*, Gütersloh 1993, S.50; Karl Binswanger, Die Türkei, in: U. Steinbach & W. Ende (Hrsg.): *Der Islam in der Gegenwart*, 3. Auflage, München 1991, S. 220 und Schiffauer 1993, S. 470.

24 Siehe Ali Ak, *Zaruri bir açıklama*, Istanbul 1997; sowie eine Selbstdarstellung des VIKZ in Türkisch, Köln 1996, S. 6. Mit dem Begriff Süleymancı, heißt es dort, werde suggeriert, es handle sich um eine eigene Konfession des Islams oder gar um eine eigene Religion, in deren Zentrum die Person Süleyman Hilmi Tunahans stehe. Ebenso sei es falsch, die Schüler Tunahans als neuen *Orden* (tarikat) zu bezeichnen, vielmehr sei Tunahan selbst Mitglied der Nakşibendiyye gewesen und nicht Gründer eines eigenen Ordens.

ches. Der Scheich der Nakşibendiyye[25] war entschiedener Gegner des türkischen Laizismus, der durch die Kontrolle der Religion durch den Staat gekennzeichnet ist. Tunahans Reaktion auf das schrittweise Verbot des Religionsunterrichts (an Gymnasien 1924) und auf das Verbot der Orden (1925) war die Initiierung einer landesweiten, privaten Korankursbewegung. In den 30er Jahren selbst staatlich angestellter Prediger, sprach sich Tunahan Anfang der 50er Jahre scharf gegen die Verstaatlichung der Imam- und Hatip-Ausbildung aus (Imam = Vorbeter, Hatip = Prediger), was ihm Gerichtsverfahren wegen des Verstoßes gegen das Laizismus-Prinzip einbrachte. Die Korankurse und Internate der Süleymancı-Bewegung bilden in der Türkei eine Art private Parallelausbildung zur staatlichen Religionserziehung. Seitens des Staates werden sie -- in Abhängigkeit von der jeweiligen Regierung -- bald stillschweigend geduldet, erlaubt oder auch gefördert. Unter Vertretern der Türkisch-Islamischen Synthese, die nicht Anhänger der Bewegung sind, haben die Süleymancıs einen guten Ruf als orthodoxe Muslime, da sie türkischen Nationalismus mit der strengen Lehre der Nakşibendiyye (Disziplin, Gehorsam, Betonung einer strikten Befolgung der Sunna) verbinden.

Die Süleymancıs wurden in Deutschland lange als Sekte betrachtet, deren Islam-Verständnis in ganz besonderem Maße integrationsfeindlich sei. Der VIKZ geriet Anfang der 80er Jahre durch Äußerungen seines Hauptimams Tüylüoğlu in die Schlagzeilen. Dieser postulierte eine Unvereinbarkeit muslimisch gerechten Lebens mit Kontakten zur deutschen Gesellschaft. Auf die heftigen Reaktionen der Öffentlichkeit hin entschuldigte sich das damalige Oberhaupt der Süleymancı-Bewegung in der Türkei, der Schwiegersohn Tunahans, Kemal Kacar, schriftlich bei dem Vorsitzenden der deutschen Bischofskonferenz, und den Imamen des VIKZ wurden politische Äußerungen untersagt.[26] Seitdem bietet der Verband ein unauffälliges Erscheinungsbild.

---

25 Zum Nakşibendi-Orden siehe Hamid Algar, Der Nakşibendi-Orden in der republikanischen Türkei, in: J. Blaschke & M. van Bruinessen (Hrsg.), *Islam und Politik in der Türkei*, Berlin 1989, S. 167-196; Xavier Jacob, Derwischorden in der heutigen Türkei, in *CIBEDO* 1990, Nr. 5/6, S.129-157; sowie Nilüfer Narlı, Moderate against radical Islamicism in Turkey, S. 35-61, in: *Zeitschrift für Türkeistudien* 1/96, hier S. 45.

26 Vgl. Jochen Blaschke, Islam und Politik unter türkischen Arbeitsmigranten, in: Blaschke & Bruinessen 1989, insbes. S. 312-317 und Lier & Priest 1994, S. 39.

Aufrechterhalten wird dies durch die straff zentralistische Organisation des VIKZ.[27] Neue Zweigstellen im Bundesgebiet werden von der Kölner Zentrale initiiert und eingerichtet, und ihre Vorsteher, Sekretäre, Schatzmeister und Stellvertreter von dort eingesetzt (siehe § 4 der Satzung). Die Zweigstellen sind nicht in den lokalen Vereinsregistern eingetragen, sondern werden als Außenstelle der Zentrale im Kölner Vereinsregister geführt. Die zentralistische Struktur verschafft dem Verband ein bedeutendes Budget, das hohe Sicherheiten bei der Kreditaufnahme für Moscheeneubauten bietet. Diese Organisationsstruktur ermöglicht dem Verband auch die zentrale Nutzung des gesammelten Erfahrungspotentials. Jede Angelegenheit einer Zweigstelle kann so ohne Zuhilfenahme Dritter von der Zentrale aus bearbeitet werden. Die Zentrale übernimmt auch die Ausbildung der Hodschas. Dort erwerben sie die Qualifikation, um in den Zweigstellen als Hodschas/Imame tätig zu werden. 1998 stellte der Verband unter Vorlage des Lehrplans Antrag an die Bezirksregierung Köln, seine Ausbildungsstätte offiziell als Ergänzungsschule für islamische Theologie anzuerkennen. Die Bezirksregierung sah jedoch mit dem Hinweis darauf, der Verband habe das Recht, als Religionsgemeinschaft religiöse Ämter ohne Mitwirkung des Staates zu verleihen, keine Veranlassung dafür.

Neben dem Bemühen um Bestandswahrung und -verfestigung der Gemeinden gilt das Interesse des VIKZ vor allem den Jugendlichen. Im Vordergrund steht die Wahrung ihrer türkisch-islamischen Identität. Besonders die Jugendlichen seien gefährdet, in die Kriminalität und in die Rolle einer sozialen Randgruppe abgedrängt zu werden. Die Zentrale bietet eine Vielzahl von Korankursen und Kursen in islamischem Recht, Ethik, Geistesgeschichte etc. an. Der Verband richtet ebenso wie die anderen Verbände auch Verlobungs-, Hochzeits- und Beschneidungszeremonien aus und unterhält einen Beerdigungsfonds. Anders als die meisten anderen türkisch-islamischen Dachverbände verfügt der VIKZ jedoch nicht über eine eigene Frauenabteilung unter

---

27 Zu Gesprächen finden sich Vereinsvorsitzende oder Imame von Moscheevereinen erst nach Rücksprache mit der Kölner Zentrale bereit. Vgl. Ursula Mıhçıyazgan, *Moscheen türkischer Muslime in Hamburg*, Hamburg 1990, S . 32; H.-L. Frese & T. Hannemann, *Religion im Gespräch*, Bremen 1995, S. 17; Ulrich Best, Moscheen und ihre Kontakte nach außen, in: G. Jonker & A.Kapphan (Hrsg.), *Moscheen und islamisches Leben in Berlin*, Berlin 1999, S. 46-51.

Vorsitz einer Frau. Auch sucht man vergeblich nach einem ansonsten üblichen Verbandsorgan, in dem sich etwa die Linie des Verbandes, wie er sich seinen Mitgliedern präsentiert, verfolgen ließe.

Trotzdem hat der Verband in der deutschen Öffentlichkeit sein Image als lediglich religiöse Organisation stärken können. In seiner Führung nehmen heute gut ausgebildete Vertreter der zweiten Migrantengeneration wichtige Positionen ein. Im Zentralrat der Muslime, der Spitzenorganisation muslimischer Dachverbände, die hinsichtlich einer halboffiziellen Anerkennung als Vertretungsgremium der Muslime in Deutschland in den letzten Jahren einige Erfolge aufzuweisen hat, spielt der Verband eine wichtige Rolle. Parlamentspräsidentin Rita Süßmuth und einige Abgeordnete haben 1993 anläßlich einer Feier zur Wiedervereinigung die Verbandszentrale besucht. Zur Eröffnung neuer Moscheen wird die interessierte Öffentlichkeit mit bebilderten Broschüren eingeladen, die über die räumlichen Verhältnisse, die Größe der Gemeinde und die Finanzierung Auskunft geben.[28] Am wichtigsten ist der "Tag der offenen Moschee", den der "Zentralrat der Muslime" seit 1997 jährlich am 3. Oktober ausrichtet.[29]

Auf diese Öffnungspolitik nimmt der VIKZ auch in seiner Selbstdarstellung Bezug: "Der Verband der Islamischen Kulturzentren e.V. sieht sich stets im Dienste der Öffentlichkeit. In aller Offenheit zeigt er seine offenen Türen den Mitmenschen, unabhängig von ihrer Sprache, Religion, Rasse und Nationalität". Doch im innermuslimischen Zusammenhang wird der VIKZ immer noch als exklusive Vereinigung wahrgenommen.[30] Denn auch wenn die Moscheen des VIKZ prinzipiell allen Muslimen offenstehen, so scheinen Eheschließungen von VIKZ-Mitgliedern nur dann akzeptiert zu werden, wenn beide Ehepartner sich als Schüler Süleyman Hilmi Tunahans im Sinne des

---

28 Vgl. die Einladung zur Einweihung der neuen Moschee in Duisburg-Rheinhausen am 19. Mai 1996.

29 Die Reden zur Eröffnungsveranstaltung am 2.10.1997 betonten das Selbstverständnis des ZDM als deutsche Institution, die auch den Tag der Deutschen Einheit als ihren Feiertag betrachtet. Neu war die Erwähnung von "Andersgläubigen" und "Nichtgläubigen" neben Christen in der Eröffnungsrede des Geschäftsführers des VIKZ, İbrahim Çavdar, zu denen der Verband ein einvernehmliches Verhältnis wünsche. 450 Moscheen und islamische Einrichtungen, die namentlich auf einer öffentlich zugänglichen Liste aufgeführt waren, nahmen 1997 erstmals an dieser Aktion teil. Inzwischen ist im ZMD ein Arbeitskreis "Tag der offenen Moschee" gegründet worden.

30 Vgl. Schiffauer 1991, S.150.

VIKZ sehen. Auch die Moscheegemeinden vor Ort verhalten sich gegenüber Muslimen, die nicht zum VIKZ gehören eher distanziert. Nicht das Muslim-Sein als solches, sondern das Muslim-Sein im Sinne Süleyman Hilmi Tunahans bzw. seines Zweigs der Nakşibendiyye scheint eine Voraussetzung für engere Kontakte zu sein.

Schlußbemerkung

Vergleicht man die ISLAH mit dem VIKZ, dann lassen sich einige Unterschiede feststellen, die darauf hinweisen, daß die Akademie in ihrem Bemühen, ein vom VIKZ weitestgehend unabhängiges Erscheinungsbild zu bieten, erfolgreich ist. Auffällig ist zunächst einmal der freie Zugang zum Gebäude. Ein offenes Tor verweist darauf, daß auch unangemeldeter Besuch erwünscht ist. Auch wenn das Gebäude im Untergeschoß über eine Moschee verfügt, steht seine Funktion als Stätte des Gemeinschaftsgebets nicht im Vordergrund. Anders die räumlichen Bedingungen in der Kölner Zentrale des VIKZ, die eine sehr viel geschlossenere Atmosphäre hat, und in der auch der angemeldete Besucher durch den Moscheebereich in den Verwaltungstrakt geführt wird.

Auch die Tatsache, daß sich die Einrichtung nicht nur an die eigene Gemeinschaft richtet, sondern allen Interessierten ohne Berücksichtigung ihrer Religion oder Nation offensteht, verweist auf den Wunsch nach einem vom VIKZ unabhängigen Profil. So gehörten zum Angebot der ISLAH im Ramadan 1999 auch deutsche Freitagspredigten. Über die geplanten Themen der Predigten und die Prediger informierte die ISLAH in deutscher Sprache bereits im Vorfeld in ihrer Broschüre und via Internet. Eingeladen waren "alle deutschsprachigen muslimischen Männer und Frauen, aber auch interessierte Nichtmuslime".

Auch die Zusammensetzung ihrer Besucher, Referenten und Gastreferenten durchbricht das Klischee einer Fragmentierung der Muslime nach verschiedenen politischen bzw. religiösen Strömungen, die nicht miteinander kooperieren sondern konkurrieren. Personen aus dem Umfeld der Milli Görüş, selbst Funktionäre dieser Organisation, treten dort neben Beamten nordrhein-westfälischer Ministerien, Vertretern der Kirchen und Persönlichkeiten wie Prof. Dr. Ernst von

Weizsäcker, als Referenten auf.[31] Voraussetzung dafür ist lediglich Expertenwissen und eine um Objektivität bemühte Präsentation. Vor allem der anwachsenden türkisch-muslimischen Bildungselite[32] könnte die Akademie zukünftig wichtige Impulse geben und eine Plattform für erste Erfahrungen in der akademischen Bildungsarbeit bieten.

Ein zeitgemäßes Image vermittelt auch der Umgangston der Mitarbeiter und Mitarbeiterinnen untereinander. Anders als in der Zentrale des VIKZ, wo das Verhalten und der Ton im Umgang miteinander die Hierarchien spüren läßt, herrscht in der ISLAH ein offener, kameradschaftlicher Ton zwischen weiblichen und männlichen Mitarbeitern. Die Tatsache, daß Männer und Frauen sich -- mit Ausnahme des nach Geschlechtern getrennten Moscheebereichs -- in allen Räumlichkeiten gemeinsam und frei bewegen, ist ein wesentlicher Unterschied zur Zentrale des VIKZ, wo der Frauen- und Männertrakt deutlich voneinander getrennt sind und nur bei größeren Ereignissen auch Frauen im Verwaltungs- und Repräsentationstrakt anwesend sind. Neu ist auch die unübersehbare Präsenz von Frauen in führenden Positionen. Es könnte eingewandt werden, daß nach traditioneller islamischer Auffassung die Erziehung das genuine Wirkungsfeld der Frauen sei. Dies bezog sich jedoch in der islamischen Geschichte mit wenigen Ausnahmen auf ihre erzieherische Wirkung in der Familie und im Kreis der Frauen sowie auf die Betätigung als Stifterinnen. In der ISLAH hingegen zeichnen zwei Frauen, Nigar Yardım und Ceviye Güler für das gesamte -- überwiegend koedukativ ausgerichtete Programm -- verantwortlich.

Innovativ ist ferner die Beteiligung deutscher bzw. nichtmuslimischer Institutionen und Personen an der Konzepterstellung und ihre Ernennung in den Wissenschaftlichen Beirat. Daß es sich beim Wissenschaftlichen Beirat nicht um eine pro-forma-Liste schmückender Namen handelt, sondern die Mitglieder konkret an der Arbeit der ISLAH beteiligt sind, zeigt sich daran, daß zahlreiche Veranstaltungen in Kooperation mit im Beirat vertretenen Institutionen durchgeführt werden. Diese Form der Kooperation mit Instituten, Behörden und religiösen Vertretern der (christlichen) Mehrheitsgesellschaft stellt ein ab-

[31] Vgl. *3. Bildungsprogramm ISLAH:*, S. 7.

[32] Vor allem die türkischen Studierenden, deren Zahl im Wintersemester 1996/1997 nach Angaben des statistischen Bundesamts bei 22.000 lag.

solutes Novum für die islamischen Organisationen dar. Zweifel darüber sind sicher angebracht, ob eine evangelische oder katholische Akademie, deren Grundidee der ISLAH als Vorbild gedient hat, einer derartige Beteiligung von nichtreligiösen Institutionen Raum geben würde. Die Muslime sehen offenbar eine 'Bringschuld' im Hinblick auf Kooperationswillen, Flexibilität und Transparenz.

Ist die ISLAH Ausdruck einer neue Linie in der vom VIKZ geprägten Bildungselite, die sich gegenüber der Mehrheitsgesellschaft und gegenüber nicht-VIKZ-Mitgliedern zusehends öffnet? Oder handelt es sich nicht doch nur um einen geschickten Schachzug des VIKZs, der sich damit im Kreis der muslimischen Minderheit gegenüber der nicht-muslimischen Mehrheit als Brückenbauer im chrislich-islamischen Dialog weiter etablieren möchte? Die Transparenz und Offenheit der Akademie könnte davon abzulenken versuchen, daß sich die VIKZ-Zentrale weiter in ihren traditionell-geschlossenen Bahnen bewegt. Der Wunsch, innerislamisch etwas im Hinblick auf die Förderung und Integration der Muslime bewirken zu wollen, beschränkt sich derzeit noch auf die Förderung von Eliten für den christlich-islamischen Dialog auf gehobener Ebene. Inwieweit sich zukünftig auch die nicht im VIKZ organisierten einfachen muslimischen Gemeindemitglieder von der Arbeit der ISLAH angesprochen fühlen, wird sich erst im Laufe der Zeit zeigen.

Diesen Einwänden gegenüber ist jedoch resümierend festzuhalten, daß die ISLAH deutlich innovative Elemente in sich birgt, die offenbar auch aus dem VIKZ heraus vertreten werden. Sie repräsentiert den fortschrittlichen, auf Öffnung nach außen und Kontakt zur Mehrheitsgellschaft ausgerichteten Zweig des Verbands. Mit der Arbeit der Akademie demonstriert ein Teil der islamischen Gemeinde in Deutschland, daß sie sich von der Rolle der durch deutsche Wohlfahrtsverbände zu Betreuenden emanzipiert und im Bereich der Bildung und Beratung zunehmend Selbstverantwortung übernimmt.

Index

CÇ

D

E

F

G

H

Iİ

L

M

N

UÜ

V

W

Y

Z